"Everything students c[...] [...]houldn't,"
says Dixon after lookir [...] Ne should
teach them how to take co[...] [...] government,
jobs, social life, money, everything — but instead we cling to models of schooling
and childhood that trivialize the lives of teens by keeping them powerless,
and then we wonder why they are rebellious or apathetic." In Future Schools,
Dixon describes intriguing new models of childhood and schooling, and walks
us through the fabulous new kind of school we should be developing now.

FUTURE SCHOOLS

"What a dream is here in Future Schools: every child literate . . . every
child fit . . . every child possessed of skills and self-esteem. A block-
buster with a brilliant vision of education" (June Callwood, author
and social activist).

"I would not be surprised if Mr. Dixon receives a lot of opposition to
the ideas in his book. His arguments are strong and representative of
what children themselves feel about school" (Carey West, President,
Toronto Association of High School Student Councils).

"The very best element of this book is that it deals with the 'whole
child.' I could relate to many of the experiences, conditions, and
frustrations that the author describes. I laughed a lot as I read;
the human touch helps to make the book believable and enjoyable"
(Delores Neil, President, The Canadian Home and School and
Parent-Teacher Federation).

"Dixon writes in the spirit of John Dewey's social reconstructionism.
Educators who find in this book an unsettling criticism will also find
in it a spirit of hope" (Professor Michael Connelly, Director, Joint
Centre for Teacher Development, OISE).

FUTURE
SCHOOLS

R.G. Des Dixon

ECW PRESS

CANADIAN CATALOGUING IN PUBLICATION DATA

Dixon, R.G. Des
Future schools

Includes index.
ISBN 1-55022-172-8

1. Education. 2. Schools. I. Title.

LB17.D59 1992   370   C92-095191-0

This book has been published with the assistance of grants
provided by the Ontario Arts Council and The Canada Council.

Design and imaging by ECW Type & Art, Oakville, Ontario.
Printed and bound by Webcom, Toronto, Ontario.

Distributed by General Publishing Co. Limited
30 Lesmill Road, Toronto, Ontario M3B 2T6.
Telephone (416) 445-3333 (800) 387-0172 FAX (416) 445-5967

Published by ECW PRESS,
1980 Queen Street East, Toronto, Ontario M4L 1J2.

Table of Contents

for
the incomparable
Suzanne Fernandes

PREFACE

To have a direct vision. That is the thing.

— Pablo Picasso

Albert Einstein said, "When we released energy from the atom, everything changed except our way of thinking. Because of that, we drift toward unparalleled disaster." This book invites you to change your way of thinking about children and their schooling. Einstein also said, "Imagination is more important than knowledge." This book invites you to imagine, to share a vision of schooling that reaches beyond the myriad bits of knowledge upon which it is based.

Charles Darwin wrote, "Imagination is one of the highest prerogatives of man. By this facility he unites former images, independently of will, creating brilliant and novel results." I am not so foolish as to think many will judge this work of imagination "brilliant." But even the most unimpressed should find a measure of "novel results."

Teaching is an art, not a science. I am a teacher. So I look at schooling as an artist not a scientist. This book tries to be a piece of art, not science. It does not report research, makes few references to other books and has no bibliography. It makes its own statement as does any piece of art.

True, schooling consists of more than teaching: learning is a related matter which may fit more comfortably in the scientific camp. Even certain aspects of teaching — such as evaluation of student progress —

lend themselves to scientific scrutiny. Data from research are important. I use them all the time and am grateful to scholars who provide them. But on the whole, **objective, rational and intellectual observation and manipulation of the schooling phenomenon by academics should be secondary to subjective, emotional, instinctive insights that come from the total immersion of teachers in their art.**

The job of artists is to understand their art and then generate insights. To explore. To look at the world in new ways. To challenge assumptions. It is for scholars and critics to digest artistic output and then criticize, dissect, categorize, hypothesize, test, quantify, apply, annotate, cross-reference and otherwise expound, elaborate or castigate the artist's work. In scholarly endeavour, weighing evidence is the goal. In artistic endeavour, weighing evidence is just part of a complex conceptualizing process that creates and illuminates new goals.

Artists in all fields have much to learn from academics who scrutinize their work. But artists must never be subservient to critics. Yet that has happened in education: **teachers have surrendered leadership to academics**. They sit waiting for visions from academics which seldom come. Visions come from artists.

When great artistic intuition and intense scientific predilection occur in one person, we get a Nobel Prize winner or an Alexander Graham Bell. But they are few and there has never been one in the study of schooling. The last person who might have been short-listed was John Dewey and even he didn't write well enough to be read by the uncommitted. He died in the mid-twentieth century. Since then, there have been several astute academics who have surpassed scholarly limitations and become interesting, creative writers on schooling.

But they have always dealt with selected aspects of schooling. No one has gone on to describe a whole new model that can be fully operational in a decade or two. Perhaps they have been too busy with their specialties, the fragments. Or perhaps there has never been enough funding to stimulate research on new models: research on schooling has always been under-funded. But an additional powerful reason may be that many academics lack first-hand experience teaching for a long time in elementary and high schools.

Most schooling scholars are not school teachers. They are usually psychologists or sociologists though a sprinkling of other specialists enrich the mix. Psychologists study how children learn (motivation, human relationships, learning styles, etc.); sociologists examine school structure (organization, management, grouping, etc.). Superstar academics tend to combine psychology and sociology and add some "enrich-the-mix" dimensions along with creativity.

Edgar Friedenberg is a case in point. He never even attended school as a child in Louisiana but entered college at thirteen and took an elective in education along with his degree in chemistry. A doctorate in education at Chicago followed in 1946. He was a professor till he established himself as a U.S. national treasure of ideas about children and schools with *The Vanishing Adolescent* (Boston: Beacon, 1959) and *Coming Of Age In America* (New York: Random House, 1963). He moved to Canada and continued to contribute dazzling insights. But no new model of schooling.

Most schooling scholars don't generate dazzling insights. In the absence of overriding artistic intuition, they keep on measuring and assessing what they see around them. Most education research is done on the false assumption that the present models of schooling and childhood are the only ones possible. Research reports, and hence the literature of education, reflect that mind set. If a similar situation existed in the telecommunications industry, researchers might still be trying to improve telegraph lines and Morse code.

There is no sense waiting till chance tosses up a spate of Deweys who can write and Friedenbergs who are richly experienced school teachers. Synergistic teaming could work just as well: artists who stimulate scientists who stimulate artists. When the visions of teachers are published, academics apply scientific method to them. When scholars publish their results, teachers apply more intuition to the findings and come up with improved visions. The wheel goes round. It may be a slow ride but in a forward direction.

This is not to disparage books on schooling written by academics and others. Some deal with fragments in a useful way: reading, testing, curriculum design, teacher training, etc. Every aspect of schooling except holistic redefinition of the model has an extensive literature. A big, public bookstore near my house has over a hundred titles in the education section. Libraries have thousands. Much of this ink is misleading because it assumes the present model of schooling will live indefinitely; but it is already moribund.

Though schooling is not the only route to education, I use the terms schooling and education interchangeably because schooling is the only practical way of organizing, integrating and optimising educational opportunities for most children. The creative and logical extension of that belief leads to a premise of this book: that **the purpose of twenty-first century schooling is to serve all needs of children not met elsewhere in society**. The extension is logical because it is impossible to organize, integrate and optimize educational opportunities if unmet needs of children stand in the way. It is as simple and radical as that.

I posit another simple and radical premise: **The present models of childhood and schooling developed concurrently and recently — in the last six hundred years — and influenced each other. They are intertwined. To change our model of schooling, we have also to change our model of childhood. And vice versa.** We cling sentimentally to the traditional model of childhood, but the reality of childhood has been changing for half a century and is already out of sync with the traditional model of schooling which has not been changing significantly. The popular perception is the reverse — that childhood has remained the same and schooling has changed significantly; but it is a false perception.

It makes sense to guide the inevitable in the best direction. **Changes in the model of schooling must reflect changes that have already taken place in the reality of childhood; in so doing, they will validate and guide redefinition of the model of childhood.** Synergy again. The wheel goes round. It may be a bumpy ride but in a forward direction. **The most inevitable and most profound changes will be in children's rights**.

I hope to stimulate scholars, but **this book is mainly for parents, politicians, thought leaders, journalists, teachers, students, and every other citizen of the world concerned about the education mess**. Reform does not come from the top down, so I am speaking to the real change agents, the people. This book is a primer for evolutionaries who want to change schools radically — by planned evolution, not revolution — so that, at long last, schooling really does meet the needs of children, really does organize, integrate and optimize educational opportunities for all.

I say "citizens of the world" because the changes I propose apply in all countries. All use the same outdated, factory model of schooling. It evolved in Europe and North America before and with the industrial revolution and by the 1960s was entrenched globally. It makes little difference whether a school has five thousand students and happens to be in New York City or twenty-five students and happens to be on the banks of the Mekong River. Local cultures have marginally modified the model but left it intact worldwide. Third world countries can't smoke-stack their way into the future with obsolete industry any more than developed countries can.

On a scale of one to ten, schools in developed countries rate between three and four. If a country leads in one aspect of schooling, it is weak in another. The space on the rating scale between four and ten is empty in all countries. The present model of schooling is to real schooling as a package tour to Las Vegas is to real travel. Both journeys offer lots of show but little substance. Most participants are losers. The consistent winners are the people in charge.

The schooling model is laden with sores, tumors, fat, transplants, grafts, prostheses, shackles, back burdens, adornments, cosmetics, bandages and patches. Its skeleton is warped, its vital organs diseased. It begs to be disconnected from the life-support system that prolongs its agony. But no country has desireable images of future schools, so they all try to prolong the past.

The only images of schooling widely available to citizens, besides their own misty memories, are images on television and movie screens, and producers have made nothing but sentimental or ugly caricatures of schooling. No movie or TV program has ever offered even a depiction of good teaching let alone a model of good schooling. *Good-bye Mr. Chips* (1939) and *Lean On Me* (1989) may have been strong on drama and sentiment, but they were weak on education. In the fifty years between them, the model of schooling taken for granted by producers and viewers alike changed hardly at all, but the world it is supposed to serve changed profoundly.

Much of this book was written in North America: in Mexico, the United States and Canada. But parts were written on all continents in dozens of countries, developed, underdeveloped and communist.

In Ecuador, at the window of an old colonial hotel in downtown Quito, I sat writing about literacy and listening to newsboys outside sing like orioles, "Il Diario . . . Il Diario." I ran down to see if they could read the newspaper they were selling so musically. They could not.

In Calcutta, I lingered on a teeming street corner in the squalid east side making notes about hordes of uneducated street children and checking a local newspaper to see if it contained anything about education. It did: a story about the need for further tinkering with the British-type, high school examinations because 120,455 had failed and only 84,642 had passed. No mention of the millions of unschooled children on the wretched streets and in the filthy bustees.

Even when I wrote in North America, my notes and recollections took me back: to a numbing Osaka high school, full of passive memorizers, and to a very different Osaka primary school where a couple of happy little girls who felt like doing so, took my hands and joined my tour of the school; to another primary school in China where a shy five-year-old, hard at work in the school's on-campus candy-wrapping factory, sacrificed his production quota and single-handedly bridged the culture and generation gaps by secretly slipping into my pocket one of the candies he was wrapping; to a conversation with an intelligent boy desperate for an education, moments before he was knocked unconscious and dragged from a busy Sunday afternoon park in Santiago by Chilean police; to a drink near Picadilly Circus on the occasion of the American moon landing as the guest of a fifteen-year-old entrepreneur dressed in the tailored look of Savile Row, who in the two years since running away from home had established his independence selling bric-à-brac on Portabello Road. . . I wrote with all of them in mind.

There is no chapter in this book on funding a new model. Schooling costs would increase temporarily if my proposal were implemented. Presently, children go to school asking teachers, "What do I have to do to-day?" The proposed model turns schools around so children say to teachers, "This is what I plan to do to-day, and this is what I'd like you to do for me." When a teacher speaks for fifteen minutes to thirty students all in a passive mode, it takes fifteen minutes. If the teacher responds to the same thirty students individually for fifteen minutes each, when they are self-propelled, it takes seven-and-a-half hours. That costs. But in practice things won't shake out so expensively. Small group activity, volunteer teacher aids, new technology and other factors in the proposed model will reduce costs.

If a model of schooling included only what is visible in classrooms, a minimal version of my proposal could be operated at high school level for little more than current schools cost. The addition of all children under present school age would increase costs of primary schooling, but even that increase would be substantially offset by savings in daycare. But **a new model of schooling must include more changes than are easily visible in classrooms**: longer teacher training; retraining of practicing teachers; student residences; improved curriculum development; democratic school administration; a longer school year, etc. **Everything about schooling is included in the model I propose**.

Once the new model is up and running, savings in other social services (health, unemployment, welfare, justice) will more than offset additional education costs. I predict a significant net saving. If improved quality of life and increased productivity are factored in, the new model will be seen as a bargain. But even if this were not the case, we could still afford a worldwide change to a new model of schooling. We afford what we want to afford. If we want to fire at missiles from outer space, we decide to afford it even if the cost is incomprehensible.

Nobody knows what a trillion dollars means, yet the world spends more than that each year on armament. More than two million dollars every minute. This in a world where even conservative economists agree that **money spent on education creates more than twice as many jobs as the same amount spent on the military**. On average in industrialized countries the ratio of soldiers to teachers is 105 to one. If a quarter of the money consumed by the military were diverted to pedagogic perestroika, the human race would take a giant step forward.

Schooling is not just a social program. It is an industrial program. Education is the seminal industry. It fertilizes all other industries, gives them whatever life they have, whether lame and weary or whole and vibrant. The country that first twigs to the potential of creative research and real development in education, particularly new models for schooling, will take a quantum leap ahead of all other nations. The first country to achieve a ten on the rating scale of schooling will be the Florence of a new age of renaissance, the France of a new age of enlightenment, the Britain of a new age of discovery, the America of a new age of freedom and the Japan of a new age of recovery.

We afford what we want to afford.

— Toronto, Summer 1992

CHAPTER 1

CHANGING SCHOOLS

If there is a spark of genius in the leadership function at all, it must lie in the transcending ability, a kind of magic, to assemble — out of all the variety of images, signals, forecasts and alternatives — a clearly articulated vision of the future that is at once single, easily understood, clearly desirable and energizing.

— W. Bennis & B. Nanus, *Leaders*
(New York: Harper & Row, 1985)

We sat on the tarmac at Entebbe airport in the hours before dawn, forbidden by President Amin's thugs to step off the plane. I whiled away the night working on this book. A sleepless Dutch business man asked what I was writing. I read aloud: "Nothing in society is more inadequate to its chore than the universal model of schooling, except, perhaps, one-ply toilet paper; both concepts prevail though they have failed consistently, leaving us with dirty laundry and soiled hands. In the former case, if not in both, we should wash our dirty laundry in public and then wash our hands of the failed format."

He laughed, stopped fidgeting, and began asking questions that lasted the rest of the night, right through first-light take-off over the silver shimmer of Victoria Falls, past the snows of Kilimanjero resplendent in the sun, and right to Mombasa. He spurned the thrill of scenery and the balm of sleep to talk about schools. A Nairobi physician joined our conversation. One of us from Europe, one from Africa and one from

North America, and we understood each other because we had shared a common, powerful heritage: school.

School is one of the four ingrained icons for great mother. Worldwide, our brains have evolved in the last six centuries to embrace school (along with earth, home and church) in the sacred centre. But the school mother has a barren womb, and no injection of greenback semen will bear educational fruit.

We need a new icon, a new model of school, to imbed in the twenty-first century brain as great mother. That is our agonizing obligation: to bury the old mother and gestate a new one. Education is not alone in the mind-wrenching chore of exorcising the old and embracing the new. The universal imperative of our time is to adapt all tradition-bound institutions to the twenty-first century. Adaptation demands fundamental change, but instead of exorcising the obsolete school model, we keep trying to patch it up. Strange. Nobody thinks the nineteenth-century model of a steel mill or bank or intercontinental travel vehicle can be patched up to serve in the twenty-first century.

The mythology of a society and consequent rituals must be renovated regularly or become irrelevant. It is usually artists, not scholars, who create and renovate myths and rituals that go with them. Assumptions must be challenged, visions created, concepts replaced. Substituting open education for the usual rows in a few elementary classrooms won't do. We have to change our concepts and our visions of schooling and childhood.

What I am proposing for education may seem equivalent in religion to exorcising the cathedral and replacing it with the particle generator. Religious myths articulate the dream life of a people. But dreams change to reflect current realities. So myths that stick with the old dreams instead of changing to match the new become bad dreams, nightmares. Such nightmares have been articulated recently in Lebanon, Northern Ireland, Yugoslavia, etc. I can't say what the changes in mythology and ritual will be if religions evolve to match the twenty-first century.

But I would like to propose what the changes should be in schooling and childhood. I am suggesting the educational renovation can be done in an evolutionary rather than a revolutionary way, provided evolution begins immediately, takes no more than thirty years and is planned from the start. It may still be a wrenching experience because **our model of childhood must change in tandem with our model of schooling**. But even that difficult adjustment is preferable to the chaos if we fail to act.

The first step is to display the bare bones of a new model of schooling (along with concomitant essentials of a new model of childhood) so interested people can say, "Ah yes, I see what you mean." Then, if they think it a viable model, they can take it abroad in the land to flesh out through discussion and, inevitably, confrontation. The latter may entail taking peacefully to the streets and certainly to the media. It should happen in the last decade of the twentieth century. By the year 2000, a new model of schooling and of childhood should be in the public mind worldwide.

A deadly fault in all schooling innovations has been the false notion that instant implementation is possible, desirable and necessary and will yield immediate, positive results. Even when instant innovations show promise, they fail to generalize in education because the public has not been readied. A long period of discussion and consensus-building, focused upon a proposed model, should precede implementation. Other industries call it creating market readiness.

Once a new model of schooling takes shape in the public mind, **every aspect of the present model and every small or large proposed change can be tested against the new model**. Only if a present practice or a proposed change is compatible with the new model, should it be endorsed. Thousands of big and little actions taken over the years will become pieces of a new model developing, rather than patches on an old model disintegrating. If we do nothing more, that alone could lead to a new model of schooling. But too slowly and with the ever-present danger that entrenched defenders of the old model may successfully sabotage emerging elements of the new.

So **governments should set specifications and require local school authorities to develop and follow phase-in plans**. The change-over should begin before the year 2000 and spread over ten to twenty years. Governments should fund pilot projects of new-model schools and all school boards should be eager to host experiments. If not, private industry would be pleased to test models that meet government standards. The latter alternative has the advantage of circumventing foot-dragging education bureaucrats.

Getting the corporate sector involved in pilot projects could have a later payoff. It could keep multi-nationals from running off on their own, independent of state schooling, to create large-scale, telecommunications-based schooling/training for children and adults.[1] Instead, being already involved in the state school system in a controlled way, they would participate in the regeneration factor which must be built into any new model. Without research and development to constantly renew itself, any industry withers. Schooling has withered, partly due to lack of funding for research and development, but also because of hired hands at all levels protecting their turf. The present schooling industry is dying proof that the universal model of schooling lacks a regeneration factor.

Pilot projects must include most elements of the new model, not just selected classroom aspects. **A critical mass of elements must be changed in order to change the model**. A major reason why schooling innovations of the twentieth century have not substantially changed the traditional model is that each concept in turn has not included enough elements of schooling. Open education modified teaching methods, mainly in primary classrooms, but left unchanged such decisive elements of schooling as teacher education, retraining for all practicing teachers, age of entry to schooling, literacy and other mastery requirements, school administration, punishment, student housing, student government, high school curriculum, etc.

Anyone who thinks open education changed even elementary

---

1 This sentence exactly as it stands was written in 1987. On May 25, 1992, as the book was going to press, Whittle Communications announced the Edison Project which will build 1000 big, high-tech, daycare-through-high school private schools across America by 2010, with 200 daycare-through-elementary schools to be open by 1996.

schools, and even in the single dimension of teaching method, should hop around any continent and walk through school corridors. Look and listen. Don't be fooled by superficial changes in placement of furniture or children. Who is talking? Is it usually children teaching themselves and each other or is it teachers doing the same old act from a different part of the stage?

Only a concerned public can generate enough political clout to save school from wasting away, ravaged into irrelevance by linear, sequential nineteenth-century methods, like other defunct factories that litter the Western world. There are cheaper ways to warehouse children. When nothing much remains except the custodial function — because higher technology has done an end run around schools with better ways to educate and socialize — the revolution will have taken place, powered by the imperatives of high-tech business barons, not educators. Better a rapid, twenty to thirty-year evolution now than such a revolution a few decades hence if not sooner.

People are already doing something about the schooling mess, but the wrong things. A friend told me about his treasure hunt for the best school, public or private, in all of greater Los Angeles. Money no object. He even sat through classes in session. Shopping. He settled for an expensive private school in Santa Monica, and his children had to commute on the freeway in a car pool. All of this for a school marginally better than the neighborhood school at doing a few right things and a lot of wrong things. All schools in all countries are doing wrong things, some a little better than others.

Elite private schools generally conform most rigidly to musty norms of the present model and in that sense are among the most backward schools. They are more guilty than state schools of recreating the past through ritual maintenance learning. They are museums, totems of former times. Non-elite private schools are sometimes even worse. They usually exist to make money, indoctrinate captive children into a religion, promote parental philosophies, exploit artistic or athletic talent — any number of powerful, non-educational, primary motives that often manipulate and hence demean schooling.

The main contribution of private schools has been to pioneer, along with orphanages, domicile for children unable to live with parents. Now that orphanages and group homes for other than clinical or detention purposes are rare, private schools have almost to themselves the opportunity to develop alternate living arrangements that enhance childhood. They will fail because their notions of residence are as fossilized as their notions of schooling.

In other industries, the private sector is more innovative and productive than the government-controlled sector. New ideas emerge that generalize to transform the industries that spawned them. But in education, both private and public sectors cling to antique models.[2]

Both sectors on occasion throw up innovative showpieces. Summerhill, A.S. Neill's school in England, probably the most famous of the twentieth century, was private. But it had little lasting effect even in the next county let alone the next continent. The literature of American public education overflows like a corn popper bursting with little experiments energized by John Dewey's progressive education philosophy. But they have not made much difference even in Tennessee let alone Tasmania.

Decades after Neill and Dewey had their say, teachers still confront mega-millions of students every Monday morning in a way that has changed little since the nineteenth century. School remains a pufferbelly locomotive chugging incongruously through a high-tech landscape, spewing human soot.

Almost everything good in education has been done someplace. The Neills and Deweys and thousands of lesser lights come and go. They get their little moment to shine like lighthouse flashes but are soon enshrouded by clouds of tradition. Reformers may be tolerated, even indulged for public relations value, but when the experiment is over, nothing has changed except everybody has learned a few catch-words.

---

2 The Edison Project may be big enough and different enough and shocking enough that its high-tech and other changes to the model of private schooling will generalize throughout all public school systems.

Both public and private sectors discard real innovation or relegate it to some safe corner if it shows signs of multiplying and threatening the status quo. In both sectors, senior administrators are often luddite. Senior politicians on school boards, and governors on boards of private schools normally go dowsing for educational wellsprings using opinions of pressure groups as divining rods.

Among innovations never allowed to generalize are "alternative" schools within both private and public sectors. Most are not much of an alternative; still, parents or students shopping around can sometimes find an alternative school with one or two differences that appeal: a curriculum somewhat focused on a traditional academic or arts subject as in magnet schools or on a more exotic eye-catcher such as space technology; or emphasis on informality or formality; or provision for a particular learning style or teaching style or philosophy; or accent on therapy for children with a particular learning problem; or regression to prizes for jumping through academic hoops.

At best, the special quality of an alternative school is usually skin deep: scratch it and it bleeds the tired blood of the twentieth-century model. At worst, an alternative school is apt to be the old model tarted up in Summerhill drag.

Perhaps the greatest contribution of alternative-schools partisans was the lucid writing of A.S. Neill. From the twenties to seventies he wrote more significant information about children and schooling than any other person, though he also wrote and practiced some nonsense.[3] Even the best writers from the alternative school camp have not succeeded in altering the universal model of schooling, and alternative schools are so few as to be inconsequential.

Where government and school board regulations allow, some shop-

---

3 Most notably that children must be free to take or leave what the school offers, that they might freely opt to sit around at school doing nothing for months and years. On the contrary, while school attendance should be voluntary, all members of society have the responsibility to become educated, and if they elect to do that by attending school, they have the responsibility of working diligently at the required and elective programs.

pers move from school to school within the public system. In Britain it is a way of life for activist parents. In America, where enabling legislation lags, anxious parents think life will be better when they too can play "all change." In Toronto, twenty percent of parents and students take advantage of the option to choose other than the nearest elementary or high school. They may find some special program that pleases, or an ethos more compatible in one school than another. If so, they have found a better place for children to have wrong experiences.

Because there is no public image of right experiences, the publishing industry has rushed in with guide books on how to pick the best place for wrong experiences. Such shopping guides would be laughed off the market in any but the schooling industry. Imagine a guide to intercontinental travel that details the amenities and schedules of clipper ships.

Shoppers sometimes opt for the local school supplemented by private, after-school tutoring as a booster shot to blast children into the best universities. Tutoring has become a major spinoff of the mainstream education industry. In Japan it is a national passion. By the end of grade nine, half of Japanese children go to expensive, after-hours pressure cookers called juku and by the end of high school eighty percent attend even more formidable juku called yobiko. Most after-school schools feature more of the wrong things: excessive facts to be memorized for short-term retention and regurgitation on exams. But some, especially in North America, provide a real service: they teach children to read, write and cipher when the school system has failed to.

A few disillusioned shoppers opt for home schooling. They teach their own children, with or without correspondence courses supplied by the state. Do-it-yourself schooling probably satisfies needs of parents more than needs of children. Sometimes to the point of being an affront to children's rights. Parents bent upon molding children in their own image can do it better if they remove outside influences such as schooling, which inhibit the cloning attempt.

Still, a talented parent with plenty of time might do a better job of teaching basic skills (particularly reading, writing and ciphering) than most schools do. But there are few talented parents with free time. What parents usually can't do is provide social interaction and the myriad process opportunities that schools offer. But the real weakness of home schooling is that it is often just an eccentric offspring of mother school and shares her genetic weaknesses.

Most shoppers opt for schools within the state system where choice is allowed. But private schools are on the increase. In sixty-five countries, governments aid that growth with funding. They are encouraging the best-educated parents to abandon the state system. About three percent of Japanese children, six percent of British, eight percent of Canadian, twelve percent of American and twenty-five percent of Australian children attend private schools. Many more parents and students are shoppers in fantasy only; they talk about finding the perfect school but never do much searching because they lack money to indulge the fiction they cherish that state schools are better in some other jurisdiction and private schools are better than state schools.

Back-To-Basics

The usual premise of back-to-basics is that schools were once better than now. But in the thirty-five years I have been looking at schooling in over a hundred countries, I have seen steady improvement. Most schools do more right things and nearly all do wrong things better than ever.

By back-to-basics, some people mean back to teaching traditional subjects like history, chemistry and literature in which students memorize mountains of inconsequential facts declared temporarily sacred till regurgitated on exams. Others mean back to teaching skills of reading, writing and ciphering so everybody masters them. Sacrosanct subjects taught and tested for short-term retention of unnecessary facts certainly did exist, so we could go **back** to it (if one is so naive as to believe we ever left it). But we could not go **back** to teaching skills of reading, writing and ciphering to mastery level for everybody because that never existed.

Though schools successfully teach basic skills to more children than ever before, throughout the history of universal schooling the only students who have mastered basic skills have been those with enough natural bent to learn in spite of the school system, not because of it. Schools have never been good at teaching language literacy, cultural literacy (essential information that lasts), participation in democratic self-government, creativity, cooperation, tolerance or most of the other good things they pretend to uphold.

But they have been good at teaching other skills and values: violence (corporal punishment) is a good way to control people; censorship is safe but freedom of information and speech are dangerous; sex is dirty; competition is primary, cooperation secondary; the strong (adults) oppress the weak (children); uniformity and conformity are good, diversity and non-conformity bad; some superstitions are sacred, others sinful; children are chattel, etc.

The good old days never existed. Schools ten, thirty or fifty years ago were even more mindless, boring and irrelevant than now. I remember the agony of a six-foot boy trapped with me in a grade three and four classroom. He was twelve or thirteen and I eight. We sat glassy-eyed, daydreaming for escape, beside each other at the back of the room, both troublemakers and outcasts, he because the work was too difficult, I because it was too easy. Twenty years later I taught in schools full of the same glazed expression. Twenty years later still, I saw it in classrooms all over the world.

The only thing schools did better in the old days was provide for teenage social life, and they did that more by chance than intention. Schools never accepted responsibility for social interaction, but they allowed a certain amount at dances, and actually helped it along, provided it was clearly understood that clubs were extras, not the real stuff of education. Now, part-time workplaces, shopping malls, games arcades and junk-food eateries are centres for teenage social life. School dances and clubs serve the few who don't have part-time jobs.

The real danger in back-to-basics is the delusion that we can back up into a friendly old fortress. As soon as the movement emerged in the seventies, sensible people said forward-to-fundamentals would be a better slogan, and it would not be achieved in the present model of schooling. But mediocre educators, anxious parents, purveyors of test instruments, and especially the press and conservative politicians, found back-to-basics a handle suited to their grasps and purposes. In Britain, Margaret Thatcher hoisted the banner and led the long march backwards.

On June 8, 1988, more than a decade after most weary educators had given up trying to explain flaws in back-to-basics, the *New York Times* put it on the front page right under the venerable slogan, "All the News That's Fit to Print." The headline of an article boxed for emphasis read, "Schools' Back-To-Basics Drive Found to Be Working in Math." The article reported that a modest three or four percent of children, mainly black and hispanic and mainly in the south-east, did a bit better on very simple arithmetic. On everyday calculations such as interest on loans, there was no improvement. And there never will be until we stop fooling ourselves with back-to-basics and change the models of schooling and childhood so that numeracy and other essential skills, along with other aspects of self-propulsion, become the right and responsibility of every child.

Discipline

Discipline is usually included in back-to-basics rhetoric. Proponents are generally from the law-and-order school and mean by discipline, law enforcement from above rather than self-discipline from within. Perhaps they imagine that strictures which keep them personally from running wild need constant reinforcement throughout society, especially with the young. Years ago, the law enforcement approach kept classrooms polite and corridors quiet. Most high school students were middle-class and brought with them internalized norms of genteel behaviour. Debilitating emotional and physical deprivation were minimal, drug addiction and consequent need for money rare. Rewards of middle-class affluence made years of teenage powerlessness bearable, even enjoyable.

Now, all classes and kinds attend high school and bring disparate values. Some have been raised outside the laws of polite, middle-class behaviour. In that sense, they are lawless. The law enforcement approach no longer works because overt resistance to law enforcement is characteristic of the lawless. Enforcement and resistance escalate until the confrontation resembles a full-scale military operation. School becomes an armed camp or a concentration camp.

There are schools like that, mostly in big cities. New York City schools have over 2000 security guards, and the city spends over $50,000,000 a year on defence, a belligerence budget that must be the envy of tiny countries. Still, 1000 people a year are assaulted in New York City schools, a third of them teachers. For them, metal detectors were the educational innovation of choice in the eighties.

But most schools are coping with lesser levels of bad behaviour, much of it attributable to general diminution of manners and self-control. Most causes of bad behaviour lie outside schools, mainly in homes. But schools have to tackle all causes because **schools must meet needs of children not met elsewhere**. Schools will have to consciously teach manners and self-control starting in infancy and continuing throughout school years. When behaviour problems are rooted in emotional or physical deprivation, schools will have to intervene as early as infancy and provide missing nurture. Where behaviour problems derive from the frustrating powerlessness of the young, schools will have to give children real decision-making participation in determining their own destinies. One aspect of that will be student government with real involvement in discipline matters. Where homes are hopelessly unsatisfactory, schools will have to provide domicile from infancy.

None of these remedies existed in the good old days. And they were not included in progressive education, open education, continuous progress, mastery learning, cooperative learning or any other schooling ideas of the twentieth century. So it is futile to talk of achieving discipline by going back to the past.

Examinations

Most back-to-basics zealots include heavy-duty examination writing among the sacraments. Some fix upon re-examining teachers. They believe that identifying and keeping only teachers who have memorized what children are supposed to memorize will render a school system that works. That venerable view of school as memory factory/data warehouse is about as relevant to contemporary education as the homing pigeon is to current communications. The proper business of the education industry is dealing with data — locating, questioning, evaluating, organizing, analyzing, synthesizing, interpolating, projecting, speculating, creating, etc. Warehousing data is the proper business of the publishing, electronics, telecommunications and library industries.

Another manifestation of memorizing madness is the veneration of state-wide tests and examinations for students. Examinations usually measure two things: memorization for short-term retention and the knack of writing examinations. The world has little use for a mishmash of data accumulated in human memory for a few months and then lost. And the world has no need for skilled examination writers.

Proponents see standardized tests as weapons to bludgeon schools into excellence by comparing test results for teachers, whole schools, school boards and countries. "Shame them and they will shape up" is the belief. That kind of punitive thinking is anti-educational. So is its other half — "toss them a tidbit if they perform test-writing tricks well." "Payment by results" was tried in Britain in the nineteenth century and failed. It will fail again even if it is heads of state and of national teachers' unions who offer teachers and schools bribes for slightly higher test results. Standardized tests are important, but the most they can do is help individual students and their teachers monitor progress and identify problems. Tests cannot measure the quality of a school system because most criteria for quality are not readily quantifiable and not presently testable.

This is not to say that memorization of data has no place in schooling. All vital skills (reading, writing, ciphering, etc.) involve memorization of data. So do all the vital literacies (cultural, media, science, etc.). Cultural literacy involves memorizing essential facts and retaining them for life. But that is different from the overload of factual trivia for short-term retention that is characteristic of examinations.

Piling On More Courses

Firebrands storm institutional ramparts shouting, "Eureka!" What each has found is a way out of the education mess that requires an additional obligatory course for children or teachers-in-training, usually both. The pressure is so strong in France that school reformers think there should be a law which removes something from the curriculum every time anything is added.

What is wrong is the piling-on approach, not the topics being proposed: racial harmony, multiculturalism, values, ethics, world religions, sex, peace, conservation, drugs, social skills, nutrition, fitness, reading skills, problem solving, seminar and discussion group management, evaluation, labour, business and industry, money management, ageing, child development, computer literacy, children's rights, child abuse, human relations, media literacy, writing skills, school-to-work transition, consumer skills, law and the individual, international understanding, home maintenance, job-search skills, community service, trade, poverty, rock music, film making, political systems, parenting, time management, research skills, personal counselling, behaviour management, early identification and assessment, therapy skills, learning disabilities, native rights, children of divorce, heritage language, bilingualism, speaking skills, politics of food, leisure management, entrepreneurial skills, etc.

I have closed the list at fifty odd but there are lobby groups for as many more. Who could dispute the value of any or all? But who could find time? Assuming teacher trainees could master any fifty by studying each an average of two months, it would take a hundred additional months to graduate from teacher training. At eight months per university year, that totals twelve-and-a-half years. Neophyte teachers would start careers at thirty-five. If children spent three weeks on average studying fifty topics not currently obligatory, four additional years would be required. Parents would be nagging twenty-one-year-olds about home-work.

If we had a model of schooling that worked all fifty topics into a continuous **exploration process** instead of into courses for testing, then teachers would not have to be expert in dozens of subjects and students would not have to spend months memorizing unessential facts. The measure of rigour would be in the **process** of exploration. But we don't have such a model of schooling. Instead we have a model that packages facts to be memorized, tested and forgotten. And that has to be done in a too-short school day and year.

Pupil-Teacher Ratio (PTR)

Most teachers and many citizens think fewer pupils per teacher will clean up the education mess. Say, twenty children per teacher instead of thirty, forty, or fifty. The fact that Japanese and Korean teachers rou-tinely deal with huge classes that outperform much smaller North American classes in mathematics and science is an embarrassment to proponents of lower PTR. So is the fact that New Hampshire has more students per teacher than any other state but also has the highest average Scholastic Aptitude Test scores. But other and more powerful factors than class size account for the discrepancy in test scores between East Asia and North America and between New Hampshire and other states. Cultural conditioning to achieve in Asia and near absence of poor families in New Hampshire are the major factors. In any case, it is largely rote learning that is reflected in many test scores.

Rote learning served Japan well enough when the graduates' job was to copy Western technology. Now that the Japanese have caught up and have nobody to copy, they need creative non-conformists to lead them. But their education system yields too many uncreative conformists who follow. Japan, like the West, will have to change a lot more than PTR to unleash human creativity. As Jerome Bruner put it in *The Process Of Education* (New York: Vintage, 1960) "effective intuitive thinking is fostered by the development of self-confidence and courage in the student." Both qualities are inimical to present models of schooling and childhood which encourage instead, dependency and docility.

Improved pupil-teacher ratio is well-meant but short-sighted and simplistic, like pouring more social workers into existing welfare systems or more prison guards into judicial systems. The education mess will remain until fundamental changes in the model are made. Only then will fewer pupils per teacher contribute to the clean-up.

Parental Involvement

Democracy has traditionally been kept at arm's length at the school board level, and elected school boards are not even universal. At the school level, when parents get involved, they are usually kept on the periphery baking cookies. Even when sincere attempts are made to bring them right inside, the immune mechanism usually rejects intruders. Some places, notably Chicago, have partially democratized schools. Most successes have been fleeting and pseudo-democratic because: students are excluded; parental involvement has too little or no legal status so is dependent upon the whims of state, municipal and, especially, local school-system bureaucracies; the present model of schooling is intrinsically authoritarian.

Attempts to democratize that envision parents rather than society as the constituency are doomed. Schools nurture children on behalf of society, not just parents. Society pays the cost, not just parents. At most, a third of North Americans live in the classic family with two parents and minor children at school. Another third live in a variety of groupings, often transitory; about a third live alone. We are becoming societies of independent persons. By the year 2000, the number of married couples without children will rise by ten percent; the number of households without children will increase by twenty-five percent. Direct involvement of community people in school decision-making will have to include all these taxpayers.

Experience suggests that parents who get involved in decision-making at the school level do not represent even most parents, much less non-parents. They are not usually elected by all parents or by the total community. Activist parents jump in to promote ambitions for their own children and jump out again after the skirmish. If several scrappers band together, they become a partisan lobby. If they stay on after their own children graduate (which is rare), it is usually because they have political or religious ideologies to promote rather than open-minded interest in school programs.

Since such people have usually achieved their positions without due process, there being none worthy of the name, their presence and power cannot be explained away as the bitter that goes with the sweet of democracy. Rather, it indicates the inadequacy of the present model of schooling in accommodating democratic participation. All major innovations in schooling have failed to specify, formalize and legalize an administrative change that would involve parents and other citizens directly in school management.

Even when a parental-involvement program is no more ambitious than to improve contact between teachers and parents, it has limited value. The same few parents, mostly middle-class, respond again and again. When the reluctant are wooed into some semblance of participation, a comfort factor may be achieved and a lot of coffee drunk. But that does nothing to transform social inequities or the creaking model of schooling. Dull middle-class children continue to enjoy educational opportunities denied bright lower-class children because the latter continue to lack early intellectual nurture at home. Teachers and principals are in the position of airline pilots trying to justify their use of covered wagons to transport children. Culturally and functionally illiterate parents, who will remain culturally and functionally illiterate (and hence an educational detriment to their children), are convinced by the smooth-talking pilots that parents are contributing immensely when they occasionally board the covered wagons and help circle them around the campfire.

No New Models — Nothing in the Wind Tunnel

I go around the world asking people what is wrong with their schools and what should be done. They always suggest patches that range from job training to reinstating classical curriculum. Nobody envisions a new-model school and support system to match. Even people who have read the like of John Dewey, A.S. Neill, John Goodlad, J. Krishnamurti, Neil Postman, Silvia Ashton Warner and Ted Sizer have no new models in mind. Unless we develop one, schools in 2003 will be like schools in 1993. What passes for significant change will be palliative care. Mother school accepts a bit of transplanted skin now and then for cosmetic purposes but rejects transplants of life-saving organs.

School is school wherever you look. I have been looking since the mid-fifties in over a hundred countries and could set up shop as a teacher anywhere in the world on five minutes' notice. Schools are that similar. They all derive from the same European roots and, beyond the West, all late-comers have been influenced by the same proponents, mainly European colonialists and Americans. Teachers College at Columbia University is proud of its hundred years helping governments through-out the world to establish state school systems. In 1989 there were over six hundred foreign students from eighty-three countries studying schooling at Columbia, and thousands more at other American and Canadian universities, all intent upon taking the same message home.

In the fifties, people believed American schools differed from Cana-dian. So I matched Cleveland and Toronto and wrote a 233 page thesis comparing junior high schools in both cities. No substantial difference could be found, so I counted everything. In education, counting what already exists often constitutes research. The development half of the research and development continuum is virtually non-existent and limited to bits and pieces for patching. There are no schooling designers, no visionaries dreaming up new models. Nothing is on the drawing boards, nothing in the wind tunnel, nothing being tested and tuned.

In other industries, a significant part of budget, often six percent or more, goes into research and development (R&D). In education it is usually a fraction of one percent. **The main reason research, and particularly development, in education is limited to patches for the old model is the disgracefully low budget for educational R&D in all countries.** In 1989, the U.S. Federal Department of Education spent about 1.25 percent of budget ($287 million) on research. America's principal Federal education research agency, the National Institute of Education, spent less than fifty million. Meanwhile, International Business Machines spent almost seven billion on R&D! There were, in addition to the federal government, other funders of education research, but there were also other funders in the same field as IBM, and the latter poured thousands of times more money into research than all of the funders of educational research put together. By comparison, research in other industries is at least Easy Street if not Park Lane, while research in education is always Skid Row.

Because industries other than education have the money, their new models are forever being tested and touted. The public is constantly being readied through a mating dance in which industry struts its new feathers to the media long before mating season. So the public is in heat in time for the consummation. That is why we are driving computerized cars instead of flivvers and why we are aquiver about new stereo models before they appear in stores. But the schooling industry has no new feathers to flaunt, so it can't dance.

If the education industry spent as much on research, and especially on development, as other industries, the world would be dotted with prototype schools, holistic demonstration centers, and think tanks of creative educators. There would be design centres bringing together expertise and creativity from various fields to design the next generation of schools just as other design centres create the next generation of everything from cars to computers to genetic wonders. There would be a highly-developed profession of industrial designers in education. Star designers of schooling models would be celebrated. Instead, we have none. By now we would have sophisticated marketing strategies that mold and ready the public for changes. Instead, we just ask people what they want. Conditioned by what they experienced at school, they respond within the bounds of conventional wisdom. Stalemate. Stagnation.

Politicians respond the same way. George Bush anointed himself America's education President, but for "innovations" he rediscovered a few familiar patches: designation of certain schools as quilts on which to try selected patches; merit pay for teachers; year-round use of schools; parental choice of schools; prizes for schools with high test results. . . . There is such a chronic shortage of original thought about schooling that nobody expects it from potentates. We hope instead that each in turn will look into the hope chest of patches and platitudes and pull out some of the more benign relics for temporary exhibition whenever education is a hot issue.

We have the right to expect more from writers of both academic and popular press books about education, but they also respond to the education mess within the bounds of conventional wisdom. Even the most critical are so conditioned by traditional models of schooling and childhood that they can't conceive of anything else. They suggest we can stick one or two new parts into the old model of schooling and somehow make a difference in how the remaining scores of worn out parts perform. Such writers may do more harm than good because, in leaving most of the present model untouched, they reinforce the reader's mistaken belief that it is a viable model and is the only one possible.

Co-operative learning features the important idea of children working together, teaching themselves and each other. The Co-operative Learning Centre, at the University of Minnesota has provided much of the leadership. Meanwhile, Ted Sizer at Brown University helps turn the top-down nature of school decision-making into bottom-up control for teachers and some community participants. That and other aspects of Sizer's work are admirable. But neither the Minnesota nor the Brown project includes a critical mass of changes. So both will fade away leaving only residual reminders of brief glory, as did all their predecessors, including open education.

Because no new models have been in the wind tunnel, the opportunity of the nineties will be lost. Even before the 1991 plan of the Bush administration to designate a school in each congressional district as experimental, the school board of Dade County, Florida challenged corporations, academics, foundations, teachers' organizations, individuals — anybody — to design and run a new model of schooling in one or more of nearly fifty new schools around Miami. It is unlikely Dade county or any congressional district will opt to be a wind tunnel for a really new model. That might be construed by an unprepared public as equivalent to putting a new model airplane into use by an airline as an alternative to putting it through exhaustive testing in labs.

Besides, nobody has the specs for a really new model. But everybody has specs for favorite bits and pieces. So Dade County and Bush experimental schools are using the same old model of schooling modified to spotlight a few features. They are still without any vision of a completely new model to test those features against. That is also the problem in the Boston suburb of Chelsea where the University of Boston has contracted to run schools for ten years.

A few voices have eschewed piecemeal changes but instead of creating new models have proposed deschooling society. In the late sixties, Ivan Illich, with his disciples Everett Reimer and Dennis Sullivan, began such a movement and attracted luminaries including Jerome Bruner, John Holt, Jonathan Kozol, Eric Fromm and Paul Goodman as seminar leaders at their think tank, Centro Intercultural De Documentation (CIDOC) in Cuernivaca, Mexico. They proposed doing away with schooling and school systems in favour of informal learning.

Then as now there were no industrial designers of schooling to invite as seminar leaders so new models were never available for discussion. The failure of post-Dewey progressive education (which never got past being a modest variation of traditional schooling) was taken as proof that schooling, per se, was wrong. By the time I attended CIDOC, the momentum of deschooling was so strong that suggestions for saving the school system were few and came mainly from participants, not leaders.

I was there in March 1970 when Paul Goodman was guest star. When he occasionally made comments that even hinted the school system might be saved, he failed to show how. He said parents should run schools but should keep hands off curriculum, the latter being the business of children of all ages, with assistance as needed from teachers. A useful thought, but one that went no place because Goodman lacked a model for schooling that could incorporate the idea.[4]

It is not only radical infidels of academia who ignore new models. A leader among mainstream academics is Michael Fullan. His book, *The Meaning Of Educational Change* (Toronto: Ontario Institute for Studies in Education Press and New York: Teachers College Press, 1982) is a text of choice internationally. When Fullan diagrams the change process, he begins with Initiation (followed by Implementation, Continuation and Outcome). In front of all those should be a stage called Creation or Invention concerned primarily with whole new models of schooling.

When Fullan uses the words invention and innovation he refers to bits, never holistic models, and dismisses even inventive fragments: "It is well beyond the scope of my study to investigate the world of invention . . ." He should reconsider because there is no meaningful change, just death rattles, until invention is seen as seminal in the change process. Fullan dispatches holistic change in less than a page under the title Grandeur versus Incrementalism; however, elsewhere (page 102) he acknowledges the possibility of major change:

> The issue is not to eschew large-scale change but to decide whether the problem is important enough, and the resources adequate, to warrant the attempt. In such an attempt, concreteness and incrementalism of implementation are important ingredients. Large scale plans and vague ideas make a lethal combination.

---

4 Much of what transpired at CIDOC is available in Goodman's book, *Compulsory Mis-education* (New York: Vintage Books, 1964), Illich's *Deschooling Society* (New York: Harrow Books, 1971), and Reimer's *School Is Dead* (New York: Anchor Books, 1972).

Agreed. But no more lethal than piecemeal puttering with a school system already in the last stages of terminal irrelevancy.

In his second edition (1991) Fullan writes, "The challenge of the 1990s will be . . . changes that affect the culture and structure of schools, restructuring roles and reorganizing responsibilities, including those of students and parents." But such changes are impossible in present models of schooling and childhood, and Fullan envisions no new models. He says, "The greatest problem faced by school systems is . . . taking on too many changes indiscriminately." I say, the greatest problem is not having a new model against which to measure proposed changes.

Reports on education that pour forth in most countries always gather frightening statistics, recommend piecemeal puttering and provide sentimental solace. One called *Crossroads in American Education*, done by the Educational Testing Service, was released on Valentine's day, 1989. An appropriate day, because, except for useful statistics on nearly 1.5 million children over nearly twenty years, the report had nothing to offer but bromides: more rigorous course work, greater parental involvement, additional homework. . . . It was no more innovative than *A Nation at Risk*, the 1983 report of the National Commission on Excellence in Education.

Most reports offer one or two progressive suggestions, but more that are regressive. Their fatal flaw is that they always accept the present models of schooling and childhood. Hundreds of reports from governments, public agencies, foundations, academics, and teachers' organizations worldwide for fifty years have failed to reconceive either model. The best reports have glimpsed a better future that could not possibly be achieved with the present model of schooling. But even visionary reporters have offered a vision too vague, too fragmented.

The doyen of all reports, the 1967 *Plowden Report* in Britain, for all its half million pages of readable elegance, was incomplete. One sure sign that the authors and sponsors were enmeshed in the traditional model was the false assumption that schooling can be ripped into pieces. No report on schooling can be taken seriously unless it addresses schooling for at least the first eighteen years. The Plowden Report covered only primary schooling.

A later example of fragmentation was *Turning Points: Preparing American Youth for the 21st Century*, issued in 1989 by the Task Force on Education of Young Adults of the Carnegie Council on Adolescent Development. It rediscovered a few useful modifications in schooling that have been around for years and made a case for applying them to ten through fifteen-year-olds: house divisions to lend intimacy in big schools; co-operative learning; peer tutoring; more and better adult advisers; more life sciences; a health coordinator in every school. . . .

Those sensible ideas are just as applicable to older and younger children as to adolescents. And all are unlikely to thrive in the present model of schooling even if some reorganizing is done in a few schools to accommodate the flurry of pilot projects that sometimes follows reports. The changes are too few and applicable only to the middle part of schooling, leaving both ends unchanged. Turning Points argues that tinkering with schooling is not enough, but it tinkers with a few elements of one fragment of the present model!

Living and Learning (the Hall/Dennis Report), issued by the government of Ontario in 1968, offered an emotional and beautiful glimpse of a future that could not be achieved with the present model of schooling, but it was vague about how to realize its vision. The report was forward-looking, well-written and splendidly published, so it could have been the springboard for redefinition of the model of schooling.

But the Hall/Dennis Report was never implemented.

Reports gather statistics and then dust. They are published with a flurry of headlines. Everyone feels purged, having spoken out in preparation of, or reaction to, the report. There may be a few pilot projects that die soon or slowly. One or two recommendations may be patched into the school system. But if you take a seat and a window from a 747 and put them in a horse-drawn cart, you still have a horse-drawn cart. In 1989, the British Columbia government began implementation over ten years of a tiny forward step recommended by a report: removal of grade designations for five to eight-year-olds. That was equivalent to putting half an airplane seat on a horse-drawn cart and taking ten years to do it.

Academics, bureaucrats and a few thought leaders read reports. Most are not read by teachers, politicians or the public. The conscientious and literate read recommendations and press commentary. Most people read nothing. To disseminate the Hall/Dennis Report, the teachers' federation asked me to organize provincial and local conferences for teachers. Pre-selected participants usually arrived without having read even summaries sent in advance. I felt fortunate if most had read the recommendations.

The bit they read or heard made most teachers beyond the primary level feel uncomfortable about Hall/Dennis. It was in the open education vein. The unknown. It didn't fit the twentieth-century model of schooling and didn't spell out a new one. It seemed to suggest the present model could be wondrously transformed by good will, a magic wand of rhetoric, and letting children be freer. How could such a report be implemented? It wasn't. But the public believed the report was implemented. After fifteen years, folks blamed the transplanted seat and window for spoiling their horse-drawn wagon and threw them out.

Most who report, rail and write about dysfunctional schools are motivated by immediate problems: graduates can't read; children drop out of school and can't get jobs; teenagers take drugs, vandalize, steal, and get pregnant. But there are bigger problems too. If schools had been working properly, a century of universal schooling should have rendered a world population agreed upon enhancing the planet. Instead, till lately, we seemed bent upon destroying it. Now, selected aspects of willful destruction influence curriculum, but we stop short of dealing in-depth with root causes.

Biologist David Suzuki said, "overpopulation is putting the remaining species in danger of extinction. The future aim of the human species must be negative (population) growth, and we shouldn't accept anything less." No school is dealing seriously with overpopulation. Nor have we accomplished anything in schools to reverse other destructive forces such as economic disparity between north and south, mania for military holocaust hardware, and repression of free speech. Had freedom of speech and information been built, as they should have been, into the twentieth-century models of schooling and childhood, the Salman Rushdie affair of 1989 would never have happened, nor would the plague of political correctness that attacks freedom of expression at North American universities. Any graduate of an adequate model of schooling would know that it is the artist's responsibility to challenge assumptions and that without such challenges the world would be forever in the Dark Ages.

Major societal problems can be confronted and significantly amelio-rated by education. Krishnamurti spoke of "the right education" as the only hope "of uprooting the old ways of thought, freeing the mind from traditions and habits." Pessimists such as Ivan Illich say society must change before schools can change themselves or anything else. They are wrong. **Schools can lead society. It happened before when the present model of schooling was developing, between the fourteenth and twentieth centuries: the concurrently emerging models of school and childhood influenced each other but the school model was leader.** In *Nations And Nationalism*, Ernest Gellner shows that schools more than homes created modern national cultures.

Most people who talk of changing schools have no concept of the changes that will be necessary in the companion model of childhood to make a twenty-first century model of schooling work. Nor are they aware that the reality (though not the sentimental model) of childhood has already changed so much that it is out of sync with the model of schooling. For the moment, the redefinition of childhood is in advance of the redefinition of schooling. But the real model of childhood will have to change far more before either it or the model of schooling is equal to the challenges ahead. **By making intentional changes in the model of schooling, we can influence the new model of childhood that is developing.**

Education mandarins are unlikely to conceive or even endorse the necessary changes: most of them perpetuate a schooling model based on information accumulation even though the amount of information available doubles every ten years (some say five) and cannot possibly be stored in the human brain. When today's children are middle-aged, ninety-seven percent of the world's information will have been discovered in their lifetime, most of it after they finish school.

A permanent plethora of **information becomes useful knowledge only when people know how to process it** (find, check, question, sort, organize, compare, evaluate, coordinate, discuss, synthesize, project, interpolate, conclude. . .) not when they memorize isolated, random, temporarily-consecrated smidgens of it for short-term retention. There has to be a shift in emphasis: from content to process; from memorization to generic skills, pattern recognition and problem solving; from traditionally fragmented information packages to holistic integration, where borders between subjects are blurred or gone; from teaching to self-directed and self-propelled learning; from rote learning to exploration and creativity; from competition to co-operation; from mass to individualized education; from destroyer of self-esteem to builder; from pen and paper technology to electronic technology. . . .

The present model of schooling can't cope with changes, so the bureaucracy ignores the information explosion even though it shakes the foundations and the structure is falling apart.

CHAPTER 2

EXAMINATIONS AND EXCELLENCE

No educational system is possible unless every question directly asked of a pupil at an examination is either framed or modified by the actual teacher of that pupil in that subject.

— Alfred North Whitehead, *The Aims of Education* (New York: Mentor, 1949)

It is the first business of schools to get every student self-propelled, and the second business to get every student to want to do everything well, to pursue excellence.

At best a quarter of students get self-propelled in school. Or more accurately, in spite of it. It is more by chance than plan if they get hooked on excellence in the typical progression from somewhat child-centred (but still too child-passive) early primary school, through decidedly subject-centred (and predominantly child-passive) academic high school. Even students who get high marks on examinations are usually passive automatons who have no passion for excellence and no experience of mining their own creative depths.

Why should they? How could they? The system values examination marks, not self-propulsion or constant reaching for new insights. The false notion persists that excellence and rigorous examinations are synonymous, that the zenith of excellence must be an examination-centred, academic high school. Japan is famous for such schools, but all high schools are that way or minimally mutated: addition of courses and choice of programs has not altered the fact that most courses are delivered up to the god of rote. Schools are temples for the worship of high marks. Examinations are the sacred rite of passage. Teachers are priests. A third of the young are anointed. The other two-thirds are sacrificed as part of the ritual. For them there is no golden gate because they have failed to get high grades in the academic program required for university admission, or have graduated from a watered-down version, or have dropped out along the way.

Zealots would have us believe that examinations preserve standards. They are wrong. Standards are whatever we want to make them, and they can be maintained with or without examinations. Better without than with if examinations are misused as is now the case. The same zealots claim we need examination marks to determine eligibility for admission to higher education and employment. Another fiction. A detailed **process profile** for each student would tell parents, employers and universities more.

It is an unacceptable insult to human dignity to judge a person's high school achievement by a few number or letter grades. It is well within technological and administrative feasibility to base transition from secondary to tertiary education (or to employment) upon a full comprehension of each individual and his or her needs as they relate to the needs and resources of society.

Here is the acid test: have people who passed a high school examination in any academic subject write the same examination twenty, ten or even five years later. All will fail except the few who continue to use the content in their work or who have a particular aptitude or interest — the ones who didn't need an examination in the first place. Not only will most have forgotten the facts and concepts that constituted the course, they will also have forgotten any creative thinking evoked by the examination in the unlikely event that it evoked any.

In the 1989 film, *Stand and Deliver*, the dedicated teacher of calculus automatically understood, as did the movie audience, that most of his force-fed students would forget the facts as soon as the examination was over. When his high-scoring students were thought to have cheated and had to rewrite the examination, the teacher assembled the class to review the course because they would already have forgotten the information that earned them high marks a few weeks earlier!

I cleaned the attic and found posters on which I had summarized an entire university course in Religious Knowledge. The examination questions were attached. When I wrote the paper, I got an A. In the attic, I couldn't answer a single question. So what did the examination prove except that I could memorize for short retention and that I was good at writing examinations? The value in the course came from the process — listening in lectures, discussing, reading, working on projects — not from a product, my examination paper. Researching an essay, I attended churches of various faiths. That changed my religious belief and my life. It was the process of preparing an essay, not the product (the essay), that was of value.

Who cares if children memorize for short-term retention masses of details about characters in some novel? Or of five causes for this or that ancient conflict? Or three hundred and nineteen scientific code names? Nobody should care.

Some argue that a beneficial effect remains for life even though one forgets facts required to pass an examination. That is a specious argument. The residual effect comes from the **process** a student lives day by day in the classroom as he participates in a program of study. A British government report assessing elementary schools in 1931 put it this way: "The curriculum is to be thought of in terms of activity and experience rather than of knowledge to be acquired and facts to be stored." Fifty years later, in his paper, *Changing Curriculum In The Eighties* (Toronto: Ontario Teachers' Federation, 1982) Michael Connelly wrote: "Education . . . takes place in experiential situations."

Since examinations disrupt process and steal scarce hours available to teachers for creating a rich process, their contribution is more negative than positive. One day, a good teacher is tenuously guiding thirty children with different learning styles and capabilities through multiple interwoven activities. The next day, all that elegance is knocked out of the classroom with that bluntest of instruments — examinations. High schools are shut down for weeks with nothing going on except examinations. Students spend days at home between exams. This happens two or three times a year even if examination marks are only a small portion of the final mark. That portion is the decisive battleground that separates winners from losers in competitions for university places and prizes. Such is the power of the mystique.

Add to all that wasted time days lost preceding examinations when teachers suspend curriculum to coach for examinations. Then add days and weeks following examinations when teachers are too exhausted from marking to prepare or teach classes properly. After that, there are interminable department and full-faculty meetings to deal with examination marks.

Many teachers favour short-answer questions that are easier to mark than essay-type questions. Some have persuaded school systems to close schools even longer while they mark examinations. Some mark examinations so fast that any hope of valid and reliable results diminishes. Few teachers analyze each paper and make it the basis of the writer's remedial and developmental work following the examination.

Schools like short-answer questions but long examinations. The reverse should be true. An argument used to defend long examinations is that high school students must learn to write them in order to write long examinations at university — the purpose of high school examinations is ritual indoctrination! Because examinations are too long for class periods, the regular schedule has to be shut down.

Every high school should have examinations that fit class periods, spaced out and scheduled a year in advance into the regular timetable. If an examination must ask two or three essay-type questions instead of one, then it should be spread over two or three regular periods on different days by asking one question at a time. Every student should know from the start of term which regular periods will be used for examinations the same length as periods. Months before problems arise, computers can identify and correct conflicts in scheduling. **No school should be shut down for examinations.** To do so is unnecessary, anti-educational and costly.

As presently used, examinations are weapons to keep teens from term-end truancy. They are not a valuable form of mass assessment. Nothing follows from them except a mark. That kind of summative assessment may be appropriate where mastery of content is the desired output and later practice will assure that content is not forgotten. Such examinations seem compatible with one of the functions of universities — preparing people to be practicing experts in various disciplines. Universities are job trainers. If people want to be professional historians, philosophers or physicians, they should be required to retain and use the data involved, just as airline pilots and plumbers are required to do.

But it is neither fair nor sensible to apply that tradition to assessment of achievement at high school. Schools don't train experts for jobs; rather, they provide general education. Examinations should be used more to assess how well students **use** data than how much data they have memorized. This is not to say that courses are without a certain minimum of information that must be memorized. If it can be demonstrated that certain information is indispensible to individuals and society as part of cultural literacy, or to the further pursuit of the same subject where further pursuit by the individual student is either intended or mandatory, then retention of that data should be required. And retention of certain skills should be required.

But **most data in most academic programs is just input, and we must not confuse it with desired output. The desired output, the thing we need to recognize on report cards and diplomas, is the competent processing of information**, not the mental storage of it for short periods. Information that is merely stored is not knowledge; rather, it becomes knowledge when it is processed (checked, sorted, organized, questioned, supplemented, juxtaposed, interpolated, synthesized, reconceptualized . . .) into an insight or conclusion, or a step toward a new plateau of understanding. Toward truth. Einstein said, "Striving after truth is the only thing that gives meaning to life." And it is the only thing that gives meaning to examinations.

Whether a school examination is used for the major purpose of assessing use of data, or the minor purpose of assessing memorization of data, results should be used as a teaching tool by teacher and student to guide future work. But this is rarely done. A few examinations are "taken up" quickly in class but almost never is one used as the basis for the next work of each individual student. Usually, nothing but the mark goes forward or stays behind with the student. Examinations are used in a summative way when they should be used in a formative way. Properly conceived, an examination or a test is like a medical examination; it tells the professional practitioner what treatment, if any, is required. It is a private matter between doctor and patient, teacher and student.

Examinations have little value as summation because they don't measure the most important learning achievements: co-operation, leadership, tolerance, adaptability, humanness, courage, integrity, reliability, initiative, creativity, etc. And yet the skimpy information represented by examination marks is used in a decisive and punitive way by school systems to fail students. Universities use the same flimsy evidence to decide the future of individuals by accepting or refusing them.

If examinations are to be used in schools, then students should be taught how to write them. Much of what they need to know about examinations has to do with preparation: study skills (memorizing techniques, summarizing, reviewing, time-scheduling, weighing the importance of course contents, peer coaching, etc.); health issues (stress control, caffeine tolerance, nutrition); understanding ethics (cheating). Another whole set of skills applies to the actual writing of examinations. But such skills are seldom taught.

Instead most schools pretend that everybody knows by divine grace all the skills and tricks of study and examination writing or that children will learn to swim by being thrown into the examination ocean two or three times a year. Or it is assumed that occasional writing of a paragraph or story in English class or for homework will magically transfer into the ability to write sentence, paragraph and essay-type answers on cue at top speed in the tension of the examination hall.

Since much of the mark on history exams is determined by study skills and examination-writing skills, not by history, history teachers should spend perhaps an eighth of class time teaching study and examination-writing techniques. But history courses are too long. Besides, most history teachers have never sorted out the dozens of skills involved in studying and examination writing and have no experience in teaching them. So they hope some other teacher is doing it. But nobody is.

Students should be up to age/grade expectancy in study and examination-writing skills before being allowed to write any examination; only then will it be reasonable to rule out the probability that a low mark reflects lack of study and examination-writing skills rather than lack of accomplishment in a subject.

Teaching **study** skills is educationally defensible because the skills have value for a lifetime. But most **examination-writing** skills have little or no carry-over value. They are survival skills made necessary by the misuse of examinations in the present model of schooling. Much of the time in a training program for examination writing in the present model of schooling must be spent practicing high-speed sorting of questions and data and high-speed writing of answers. But where is it carved in stone that excellence is measured in two-hour dollops instead of three or five? There is not a discipline in the gamut from archaeology to zoology that is remotely related to written-response speed. And yet foot-race mentality has control, and excellence is measured with bells, whistles and stopwatches. How many millions are there who would have better jobs and lives if they had been given just one thing — enough time to finish exams? For the marginally learning disabled (who number millions though they are seldom identified), extra time is crucial.

The ability to think fast in writing may be of some slight value but is not nearly as important in the lives of most people as the ability to think quickly orally, or to think and rethink in writing at a slower and more careful pace. Even professional writers often work slowly. Mark Twain and S.J. Perelman, two of the most articulate, spoke of working hours over a single sentence or phrase. Both would have failed Advanced Placement English.

In any model of schooling, students will have to cope with standardized and other tests of skills and essential knowledge and with psychological tests. Pseudo-examinations, made up of multiple choice and other short-answer questions for easy scoring, require similar coping skills. So students must be taught how to write such tests. Teachers of skills such as reading, writing and ciphering sometimes fail to do that and get invalid test results.

Because most schools did not, a private industry grew up to teach children how to write the Scholastic Aptitude Tests used for admission by 1600 American colleges. Now, about half of U.S. high schools offer preparation courses for the s.a.t. But many high schools and all private companies and tutors have gone beyond the necessary service of teaching children how to cope with the format of the test and are further demeaning education by coaching content of the test as a catechism.

Examinations should be set and marked by the teacher of a class because the range of data and concepts that could be used to uncover a course is wide and the range of processes that could be experienced is infinite. Only the teacher knows the mix his students experienced. Standard examinations (state, board, city or school-wide) dictate what goes on in classrooms and diminish activity to the least common denominator. The opposite should be true: what goes on in each classroom should determine the examination, and it should reflect the greatest common denominator in classroom activity.

Even if set within a school, common examinations to be written by several classes become master instead of servant. Teachers cover courses instead of uncovering them. Teachers who refuse to teach examination content and instead go about the real stuff of education, penalize their students who must write examinations for which they have not been specifically coached, while students in other classes have had that coaching.

When I was teaching English, geography and history, I met with other teachers of those subjects to compose common examinations. We included choices so that students could opt for topics best covered in their particular classrooms. And yet, examinations always included items that were taught in my classroom in ways that didn't match the questions. I stopped whatever should have been continuing and retaught content specifically for examinations. So did other teachers. That is like forcing airlines to halt flights and fly all planes around in circles doing compulsory figures for several days. I have asked teachers all over the world if they teach specifically for common examinations. Most answer yes. I suspect the rest are lying.

As a young high school teacher in Le Havre, Jean-Paul Sartre refused to coach his students for state examinations, but they did as well as the rest. Sartre also discouraged rote memorization, note taking and competition. He imposed no punishments, gave no grades and set no examinations of his own. Instead he emphasized discussions. I presume Sartre had select students, because at that time in France, only advantaged students were likely to reach the senior level of high school. They probably did rote memorization on their own. But the more salient fact is that Sartre met with his students frequently, for long hours, at cafes and picnics. It was a floating seminar. With that much additional time, it was possible for him to weave into the fabric of discussion, the codes of state examinations. His colleagues using usual classroom hours had to teach examination content.

Everybody should know that common or **standard** examinations and **standardized** tests are two different things; and yet the media, the public and quite a few educators use the terms interchangeably. A typical example of press confusion appeared in the lead editorial of a national Canadian newspaper, *The Sunday Star* on April 26, 1987:

> a survey taken for the Star by Goldfarb Consultants found that parents, employers, university professors, and even teachers and high school students want a return to some form of standardized provincial examinations, abandoned in the late 1960s. As one businessman put it, "Standardized test results show you something."

There is no such thing as standardized examinations. If newspaper confusion had made planes identical with missiles, Muslims with Hindus, there would have been public outrage. But the muddled editor could and did, with impunity, confuse standard provincial examinations and standardized tests.

A page-two article in *The Japan Times* of August 12, 1976, began:

> Most junior high schools in Japan give their students intelligence tests prepared by businesses specializing in such tests to prepare the students for highly competitive senior high school entrance examinations.

The implication that tests of intelligence prepare students for examinations is ludicrous. They are psychological, not academic tests. The main thing they reveal is how much an individual deviates from the average on whatever it is the tests measure. (And that may be different from what they purport to measure; they may measure compliance, docility, conformity, passivity and, especially, advantaged background as much as they measure intelligence or academic aptitude.) Such tests are in no way preparation for examinations unless one assumes that: a high deviation value makes a student feel good and that will enhance examination performance; and a low deviation value scares a student into better examination performance. The newspaper reporter may actually have made that cruel assumption, but more likely he and his editors were just as confused as their colleagues in other countries about all aspects of assessment.

Any new model of schooling must include nomenclature for tests and examinations that everyone understands. What follows is based on existing names. Academics may fault my simplifications, but everybody will get used to them if the media will do us the favour of using them exclusively.

STANDARD always refers to an assessment common to a whole school, school district, state, province or nation. The key word is common; everybody from every class in grade ten English Literature, writes the same examination. Standard examinations are never standardized.

STANDARDIZED always means a test has been prepared and tuned by trying it out in advance on large numbers of

students to discover and correct ambiguities and especially to find out the usual range of scores for people of some similar circumstance, usually the same age or grade. When the test is finally used, we already know what to expect of respondents. Every student who writes the test can be compared to the total population of the same age or grade.

EXAMINATIONS attempt to measure achievement in subject disciplines such as history, geography and economics where handling of data is paramount rather than memorization of course content. Examinations are never used primarily to measure memorization of selected information for short-term retention. Instead, they are used to assess the creative application of selected information in combination with much other information and original ideas, to defend a thesis or explore new ground.

Examinations usually ask questions that can only be answered in sentences, paragraphs and essays, or, less often, in long, creative excursions into mathematical or scientific realms using appropriate symbols instead of, or in combination with, sentences. Such answers are impossible to standardize. Consequently, examinations may be standard but not standardized. Short answers, multiple choice, true or false and fill-in-the-blanks belong on tests, not examinations.

TESTS attempt to assess skills or recall of data or understanding of concepts. There are three types all of which use short-answer questions.

A-TESTS measure **ACADEMIC** skills or knowledge in subject disciplines such as calculus or **ADVANCED** skills or knowledge necessary for various literacies such as cultural literacy. The emphasis is on knowledge though skill is involved. The A in A-test stands for "academic" and "advanced" so is easy to remember.

B-TESTS measure **BASIC** skills such as reading, writing, and numeracy. The emphasis is on skill though knowledge is involved. The B in B-test stands for "basic" so is easy to remember.

One could bicker about which skills are basic and which advanced, but it is usually possible to tell which is foundation (basic) and which builds on the foundation (advanced). Keyboarding is basic (and more dependent on skill than knowledge) while computer literacy is advanced (and more dependent on knowledge than skill).

C-TESTS are PSYCHOLOGICAL tests administered and interpreted primarily by, or under the supervision of, psychologists. They are usually used to assess intelligence, aptitude, disabilities or talents. The C in C-test sounds like the beginning of the word "psychology" so is easy to remember.

I.Q. (Intelligence Quotient) tests are the most talked about but least understood C-tests. Everyone should know that an eight-year-old who scores like an eight-year-old has an ordinary I.Q. of 100. But an eight-year-old who scores like a twelve-year-old has an extremely high I.Q. of 150. An eight-year-old who scores like a four-year-old has an extremely low I.Q. of 50. Children with learning disabilities or from cultural minorities often get artificially low I.Q. scores because they have language deficits, not intelligence deficits. They may have normal or superior intelligence but are hampered by reading and other language disabilities that need special attention.

An I.Q. score is not a measure like height or weight. It is inferred rather than real. And inferences can be drawn about only a few characteristics: language skills, factual knowledge, mathematical and spatial abilities, fine motor skills, very short-term memory. . . . An I.Q. score tells nothing of social skills, athletic ability, self-knowledge, musical ability, creativity, motivation, etc. But it is the best single predictor of scholastic achievement (in the present model of schooling) and of occupational success. Even so, it predicts with only about fifty percent accuracy. And I.Q. has no predictive value at all about success in relationships, marriage, self-fulfillment, etc. Like all tests, it is just one tool to be used skillfully along with many others.

Another thing the press doesn't know is the difference between sample surveys and examinations. In *The Toronto Star* of June 23, 1988 there was a headline five columns wide, "Watch for results from these new exams." The story beneath had nothing to do with exams. It was about sample surveys. The reporter, who was described as specializing in education, never mentioned the term sample survey nor did she differentiate between examinations and tests.

SAMPLE SURVEYS use specialized A-tests and/or B-tests to assess how well children achieve particular curriculum goals. A pool of standardized questions is approved, and a random sample of students throughout the nation, state or school system is surveyed. The term is easy to remember because press and public are used to pollster sampling and surveying, and because everybody understands that sampling a bit of soup gives you an idea how good the whole potful is.

Sample survey scores (or scores from complete surveys of all schools) tell nothing about the differing backgrounds or aptitudes of students, so they never measure one of the most important goals of all curricula — to meet the individual needs of every student. A class or school with a lot of recent immigrants would have a different reading program and different test results than many other schools. A sample survey never tells the other good things that might have been going on in a classroom concurrent with the few particulars covered by any survey.

If results indicate that goals are not being achieved, maybe they are not achievable, or not valued locally, or not understood. Maybe the curriculum guideline was never implemented properly. It is a complex matter. The sample survey is just one step in the cyclic review of curriculum.

Sample surveys and other standardized test results are misused, especially in America and Britain and especially for improper comparison of schools. New Jersey sends reports to parents on the reading scores of various schools. The California Assessment Test is used to determine each school's ranking among other schools in California. One might have expected intelligent parents and teachers to object, but it was students who showed the most gumption. In 1989, seniors at West High School in Torrance sabotaged their own test papers in disgust when administrators and teachers stopped the process of education to harangue and coach them for the California Assessment Test.

Much of America is marching mindlessly into the past by using test results as the basis for financial rewards to school districts, schools and teachers. In the nineteenth century it was called "payment by results" and was made the norm in Britain in 1862. The poet and critic Matthew Arnold, for thirty-five years a full-time, government school inspector, wrote this in 1869: "As long as the whole grant-earning examination turns on results precisely and literally specified by the Department beforehand, so long the inspection will be mechanical and unintelligent, and it will inevitably draw the teaching after it."

Even if tests results are used responsibly, we need a different kind of review to supplement the usual survey. I call it **process tracking**. The idea is to pick students at random and then track all people in the sample every minute of every day for a month to see what process they experience.

While standardized tests should be used occasionally by jurisdictions as sample surveys, they should be used frequently by individual teachers as teaching tools.

Unlike examinations, which must be set or modified by the teacher of students being examined, A-tests and B-tests may properly be set at school board, state, or even national or international levels, because components of many skills and literacies are the same in Saskatoon as in San Francisco or Sydney. The main thing that makes international standardizing of tests difficult is cultural bias. The language and assumptions that underlie test items may be meaningless or mean different things to any cultural group other than the one for which the test was devised.

The national level seems to be the cost-effective and educationally viable level for standardizing tests. Even then tests must allow for cultural bias that derives from sex, socio-economic class or ethnicity. With that caveat, national tests of skills and essential information make sense and are educationally sound provided the results are used formatively as teaching tools and never used as the basis for rewards or penalties, or to compare students, schools, teachers, or countries.

Not all existing standardized tests are good. Most test instruments should be periodically reviewed and modified. Where no satisfactory standardized test instrument exists, a school system or even a school may invent its own school-wide or board-wide test. A school board or school might have to develop its own language tests for local children who are not yet fluent in the language of schooling and whose first language is an unusual one.

No test is perfect and the result of any one test is suspect. That is why a variety of test instruments should be used and one reason why skill testing and essential-knowledge testing should happen routinely and often. Another reason is so **deficiencies can be identified early and further testing used to diagnose the specifics of each individual's difficulties. Remedial and developmental work tailored to the diagnosed problems must then be mandatory, immediate and top priority**. Open education failed partly because the concept was unfriendly to testing and specific remediation based on diagnostic testing.

Few teachers know how to select, administer, score or interpret standardized tests. A paper called "Knowledge of Elementary Educators to Interpret and Use Standardized Test Results" reported to the 1988 conference of the Ontario Educational Research Council that teachers surveyed had a mean score of only 5.8 out of 16 on a test of their ability to interpret standardized test results! A test result poorly interpreted is worse than useless: it is a dangerous weapon. Hardly any teachers know how to author tests of skills that get at all aspects of the skill being tested. Few know how to do in-depth diagnostic assessment to uncover details of weaknesses revealed in standardized tests. Nor do they know how to prepare and use individualized remedial work based on test results.

Tests aside, teachers often set examinations that are ambiguous, unbalanced, too long, too short, invalid, unreliable or unfair on some other ground. Wherever I go, I ask students to show me recent examination papers. The commonest problem is poorly worded questions. I wonder how many millions of lives have been harmed because people misinterpreted vague or misleading examination questions.

In 1990, only three of eleven Ontario universities required teacher trainees to take a course in measurement and evaluation! **All teachers in training must master measurement and evaluation, and all practicing teachers must undergo on-the-job training to**

mastery level. For ninety-five percent of teachers, a period of weeks or months of carefully structured practice must be built into any retraining program to change a major teaching behaviour such as measuring and evaluating student progress and using the results as the basis for remediation and further development.

Another concept that press and public must learn is **STANDARD EVALUATION CONDITIONS AND STRATEGIES (SECS).** It is easy to remember because the acronym sounds like sex. Instead of setting standard examinations, or using standardized tests in the wrong way, **states should require schools to use standard evaluation conditions and strategies**. Every curriculum guideline and course of study should specify examination and test requirements as well as evaluation requirements (including weighting of marks) for all aspects of daily work: essays, projects, research, homework, speeches, examinations, classroom participation, etc.

In all subject disciplines, individual teachers should then set their own examinations following rigorous evaluation specifications in the guideline. Individual teachers should also be required to use and report tests specified by secs. All specified tests of essential skills and knowledge must be developed and provided to schools by jurisdictions (nations, states, provinces, school boards . . .). All such standard tests should be standardized or at least undergo rigorous scrutiny to make sure they are valid and reliable.

Secs results alone would give universities all the information they need for admission by marks. Contrary to public and press opinion, the predictive validity of high school grades is higher (about .48) than scores on Scholastic Aptitude Tests (about .42). With secs, high school grades would have greater predictive validity than present high school grades and s.a.t. scores combined (about .55).

When secs is implemented, we will have a school system adequate in **objective** evaluation of student progress. The present model of schooling and of teacher training makes it virtually impossible for teachers to learn and practice the other kind of evaluation, the kind that really promotes excellence — **subjective**, oral evaluation.

Excellence

I can walk corridors looking and listening, glancing into classrooms without entering, and get a fairly accurate excellence rating of a school. Everything should exude taste, style, panache, know-how, energy, organization, and humaneness. An aura of excellence comes from total commitment to excellence on the part of people paid to run schools. There is no room for: sloppy-looking teachers; teachers who reek of tobacco, alcohol, body odour or foul breath; teachers lacking interpersonal skills; cafeterias stocked with junk food; assembly programs lacking pace, interest or production values; weak school-to-community communications; dirty toilets, corridors or classrooms; careless keeping of attendance records; poor teacher attendance; frequent interruptions of classes; rote learning of irrelevant data; teacher-active student-passive classrooms; empty ritual; authoritarian violations of democratic rights. . . .

The daily work of each student must be treated as an exercise in excellence. Every essay, speech, project, group presentation, exercise, answer — every activity, every day — must be jointly evaluated orally by students and teacher. It requires good interpersonal skills and subjective evaluation skills on the part of teachers, and increasingly as they age, on the part of students.

By age ten or so, properly-trained students can evaluate themselves and each other in most activities. Teachers should join in group evaluations to add points missed by students and to escalate the level of oral evaluation. My truest exposure to excellence in education and my best years of teaching were in a junior high classroom where all students had been deliberately and thoroughly taught to evaluate everything, everyone, everyday — in large groups, small groups, one-to-one and individually. The pursuit of excellence was a way of life.

Given that students and teachers know how to evaluate everything orally and that an aura of excellence prevails, the next thing a school must do is involve every student in a never-ending series of excellence-oriented activities. Most of these will be student presentations of curriculum content. **Students must organize, assign, prepare and present to the group much of required curriculum; and they must continually evaluate the whole process** with teachers acting as consultants, managers, mentors, impresarios. . . .

This is more than mere open education where children work in groups pursuing their own interests. It is the logical and necessary next step wherein students rather than teachers become the active agents in pursuing required curriculum. Without the student-active factor taken to the heights of students teaching themselves and each other most of the curriculum, there is no excellence, no gold.

Beyond usual classroom programs, there are other important activities that are seldom mined by schools for the pure gold they contain because they are not compatible with schools driven by teachers standing in front of thirty students and peddling data. Plays, field trips, community service programs, science fairs, sports days, etc. — every school has them, but much of their potential is lost because they are too narrowly conceived and especially because **teachers do too much of the organization and management**. They don't know how to identify the skills needed to organize and manage such enterprises and then methodically teach those management skills to students. All teachers-in-training and all practicing teachers must be taught those skills.

Most games, particularly intra-mural and inter-school team sports, fail as exercises in excellence because they remain forever teacher-driven. **All recreation activities including all team sports during and after school hours should be largely run by children**; and training children to do the management should be as much the purpose of teachers as teaching sports skills.

Another essential element of any model of schooling that achieves excellence will be a full-time mentor for every child. His/her job is not to teach in any traditional sense but rather to know and nurture a few students (see chapter 22). Up to now, neither the ubiquitous model of schooling nor any innovation in schooling has included such a mentor, so excellence has never been achieved.

CHAPTER 3

LANGUAGE, MATHEMATICS AND SCIENCE LITERACY

People who don't read or write themselves with any frequency or joy have a hard time getting others to read and write. If students have trouble fixing their eyes on the printed page help them with that. If they have a hard time coordinating their hands and eyes and therefore find it difficult to write, give them methods to help themselves. Be specific about people's problems.

— Herbert Kohl, *Reading, How To*
(New York: Dutton, 1973)

Literacy requires: reading, writing, speaking and listening skills; a memory well stocked with common cultural knowledge; a sense of duty and determination to understand and be understood. **We need a new definition of literacy which includes "the obligation, the ability and the will to understand and be understood."** Shakespeare used only 34,000 words, some of which he invented, some of which are now obsolete. The 1989 Oxford English dictionary lists 447,500 words and phrases. With so much language growth and change, **the challenge is to be understood and not be misunderstood by one's contemporaries in the local, national and global village**.

So far all we have is the primitive concept of literacy as the ability to read and write. Those who do both but badly are said to be functionally illiterate. Nine years of schooling is the bench mark of literacy. But in Western countries, anybody who keeps on breathing can complete nine years of schooling. If there were good, comparable, standardized tests of all language skills and of knowledge (cultural literacy) for the ninth grade level, and if those tests were used in all countries, and if all students had to achieve grade expectancy on the tests before being granted grade nine standing, then nine years of schooling might be regarded as the threshold of functional literacy. But none of the ifs are true.

Eighteen, twenty or twenty-five percent figures usually used to estimate the functionally illiterate population in North America are misleading. More likely, **the bottom third of adults are almost illiterate, the middle third are functionally illiterate and the top third are adequately literate.** If that estimate seems harsh, consider the vast gray area that lies above the nine-year bench mark and even beyond high school graduation.

Some people can read but don't like to, feel no obligation to or refuse to. Some read at levels above any definition of functional illiteracy but can't cope with a quality newspaper. Some read so slowly they never have time. Some mouth words but understand and retain almost nothing. Some read but draw no inferences or wrong ones. Some read but can't interpolate or distinguish main ideas from trivia. Some read but can't scan.

Some read but have such a small vocabulary that no authors write for them. Some read but not critically. Some read provided an accompanying picture tells most of the story. Some read but are imprisoned forever within sports pages, horoscopes and TV listings. Some read but are so culturally ignorant that most content is beyond them. Some read provided the content doesn't include numbers that need processing or scientific or technological concepts. All these people are **functional** illiterates since they don't function as literates.

The gray area in writing is just as vast. It is generous to estimate that even the top third can write well enough to be understood, to avoid being misunderstood, to convey subtleties of thought and emotion. In the job-scarce early eighties, I designed an employment registry that helped move jobless teachers into business and industry or to teaching jobs abroad. Only a few applicants wrote good letters and resumes. If they had the skill to be understood, they lacked the will. Rarely did I see a well-filled-out, open-ended application form. Often I had to use a red pencil and "mark" applications submitted by teachers wanting to teach English overseas!

Employers complain that high school and college graduates can't write. An article in the May 1989 issue of the Canadian magazine, *Report on Business* began, "Spar Aerospace Ltd. needs engineers who can write a convincing proposal. The current crop boast impressive degrees, but you'd never know it from some of their attempts at written communication." Many colleges test the writing abilities of first-year students and find that a quarter or a third fail a simple writing test. In 1987, a predictable 28.6 percent at McMaster University failed; 48.3 percent of failures also failed their second attempt, and 58.1 percent failed their third. Most failures declined help, and those who completed a remedial course showed little improvement: eight out of twelve again failed.

Many of the top one-third get by with routine memos or letters but can't write a good report, proposal or brief. They avoid writing if possible and never enhance their careers or personal lives with writing. Notes at the "gone shopping" level of sophistication aside, probably ninety percent of the world's writing is done by ten percent of the population. Of those, perhaps one or two percent are professional writers or practicing amateurs: journalists, novelists, essayists, poets, playwrights, editors, advertising and public relations writers, etc. The other eight or nine percent are the few exceptional business and professional people who keep the wheels of business, government, courts, and education oiled with the well-written word.

And that is the top third. Many of the middle third have permanent writer's block. They go into digital paralysis at the thought of having to write anything more than a post card. Even the post card is likely to be devoid of interest. When forced to attempt anything substantial, they give premature birth to an unformed lump or else gestate long past term and then produce a monster with misplaced vital organs and multiple dangling appendages.

In the history of humankind, reading and writing are relatively new, so they get all the attention. Speaking and listening have been around since a couple of grunts and a shriek meant, "Let's run. I hear a landslide coming." They are taken for granted. At best, speech training in schools is largely informal — uninstructed and undiagnosed bits of oral reading, public speaking, and play acting, all too infrequent to be of much value except as fun for the talented few and torment for the rest. Even when some instruction is provided, it is more for appearances than from determination on the part of schools to teach speech. I was part of such a scam.

For years I taught a course called speech arts that was compulsory for grades seven and eight in a junior high school. Many parents were pleased to see traditional rhetoric reinstated. Administrators publicly praised their own acumen in carving off a piece of time from English and assigning a specialist teacher who would be sure to teach speech. But the carved-off chunk was only one period a week. Forty minutes. Thirty, after deducting arrival and departure routines, interruptions and announcements. About one minute per week for each student. Anything of value — from correcting ungrammatical speech to developing hidden talent — had to be done after hours.

In his book, *High School* (New York: Harper & Row, 1983), Ernest L. Boyer proposed a similar scam: a one-semester speech course to include "group discussion, formal debate, public speaking, and reading literature aloud." Trivial as it was, Boyer's proposal was considered bold at a time when math/science emphasis was favored over language by most critics.

In Britain, the 1989 report of the government's Cox Committee said, "There is little point in correcting the spoken language of pupils in any general way because it is unlikely to have a beneficial effect: against the pressures of home and peer group, teachers can have little hope of changing how pupils speak." That blunder did not go unnoticed in Fleet Street or Buckingham Palace, but nobody responded by insisting that speech be a distinct, obligatory school program.

Remedial and developmental speech training for all students in all grades remains virtually non-existent. Speech pathologists may deal with a few obviously speech-disabled children, but otherwise it is assumed (wrongly) that everyone automatically learns to speak current mainstream language pleasantly, clearly, audibly, grammatically, politely, convincingly, confidently; that everyone learns to ask questions, answer, discuss, converse, contribute, mediate, initiate, explain, direct, clarify, recapitulate, instruct, persuade, disagree, control body language, make eye contact, express emotion suitably, etc. Or else it is assumed that speech doesn't matter much.

As many people are sorted out, kept back, inhibited, diminished and degraded by speech limitations as by reading or writing limitations. Probably more. George Bernard Shaw gave us *Pygmalion* and we were amused but not informed. His message reached around the world as *My Fair Lady*, but Professor Higgins' lessons taught school systems nothing about speech training.

It is not just that a well-spoken person makes a better impression and thus has better job and social opportunities. Many years of tutoring individuals lacking language skills convinced me that improved thinking always goes hand in hand with improved ability to express thoughts orally when students are deliberately taught speech. That thoughts become words is obvious. But it works the other way around too: words become thoughts.

Listening gets even less attention than speaking. Hearing is usually considered only in terms of deafness but should be considered in terms of autism, hyperactivity, learning disabilities, behaviour problems, etc. Ear infections in infancy may impair learning by inhibiting muscles of the middle ear that are supposed to screen noise interference and focus relevant sound. A child so afflicted is unable to screen out the background noise of life that most of us "hear" but don't "listen" to. Instead of punishment or nagging or even tutoring, a child with that kind of hearing problem needs specific exercises to rehabilitate weak ear muscles.

But even if hearing is perfect, listening may not be. Hearing is physiological. Listening is emotional and intellectual. Important sound is selected, assimilated, organized, retained, responded to internally and finally, responded to verbally. I doubt that more than a third of the population can consistently perform the first four steps adequately even in casual conversation. Often in inter-personal relationships, and certainly in business and professional life, the sound being processed is far more intellectually challenging than casual conversation. Even relatively simple messages are often made complex by emotional content that must be read from audible clues such as pitch, tone, inflection and speed or from visual clues such as eye contact and body language. All these listening skills and more can be taught but seldom are.

We can also teach children to feel the obligation and possess the will to communicate well — just as surely as we can teach them the obligation and the will to be physically fit. In both cases, a change in our value system as well as our school system will be required. In both cases, the school system could take the lead and by doing so, change the value system. So far schools have dealt only with reading and writing, and less than a third of young people learn to do either adequately.

Back-to-basics supporters usually assume that schools used to do a better job of teaching reading and writing because, years ago, people who finished all or most of high school could read and write adequately and now they can't. In the good old days, few young people went all the way through school or even entered high school. In the 1915 revision of his essay, "School and Society," John Dewey said only five percent of the school population of America finished high school and that much more than half left "on or before the completion of the fifth year of the elementary grade." In Quebec, only fifty-seven percent of fourteen-year-olds were still in school as recently as 1964. But by 1992, virtually a hundred percent were enrolled.

Those who went through high school in the good old days were the few with aptitude and favored economic and environmental backgrounds. Among the large numbers who dropped out with five years or less of schooling were the counterparts of illiterates who nowadays hang on into high school. The two-thirds who could not read or write well in the past were not expected to because they had little schooling. The hard fact is that most would not have become good readers and writers even if they had stayed at school. Today, they do stay but never learn to read or write adequately because the school system is not constituted to provide for their needs, and it never was.

It is naive to look for salvation in phonics, word recognition games, basal readers, whole-book study, grammar exercises, state-wide testing, more literature classes, cultural literacy dictionaries, open education, co-operative learning or any other remedy. All have some value. What is lacking is an overall design for a school system that incorporates all the fragments into a functional whole. **It is possible to teach nearly all young people who pass through schools to read, write, speak and listen. But profound changes in strategy and priorities will have to be made. For the first time in history, the top priority of schooling will have to be literacy.**

The education establishment should admit that traditionally and at present, admission to school programs at all levels is based on short-term memorization of mostly inconsequential bits of content, on grade promotion and on age, rather than on mastery of prerequisite language skills and essential knowledge. **It is unprofessional, it is malpractice, but the norm universally is that students are not tested to see if they can read, write, speak and listen at the level of the course or grade they are about to enter!**

The tragic result is that the majority of students are attempting programs for which they do not have the necessary language skills and at the same time are denied mastery training in those skills. They drop out or scrape by or drop down to easier courses. They are failures because school is a failure, dunces because school is a dunce.

We must always ask, "Does he or she have the prerequisite language skills and cultural knowledge to proceed with the next chosen or obligatory program?" If not, remedial and developmental work must be successfully completed first. Anything less is cruelty to children and a violation of children's rights.

Presently, the biggest losers are immigrant and other minority-language children. Most of them experience English only at school, five hours a day, five days a week, 180 days a year. At home they spend ten times as long speaking another language with nothing but television to maintain their tenuous connection to English. And even television is increasingly available in minority languages. Under the best conditions, it takes six or seven years for most immigrant children to achieve fluency in a new language. The best conditions seldom exist, so they drop out of school or take dead-end programs. Even those who, because of high intelligence, motivation and rote memorization, get good grades, are often deficient in vocabulary, idioms, related cultural concepts, interpolation, conversation and other skills. Deficiencies forever inhibit their careers and lives.

Few teachers know how to teach reading because they have never been taught. With two degrees and two teacher's certificates endorsed to teach English (elementary and high school), I still had been taught almost nothing about how to teach reading or writing, nothing about teaching listening skills or speech, and nothing about how to diagnose language difficulties and design remedial programs. To learn those things, I sought out a course at the master's level and went back to university.

There lingers a false assumption that if teachers know how to read and write and know literature, they must know how to teach reading and writing. The few teachers I have seen teaching reading, writing, speaking or listening well have been mainly at the primary level. Much more often I have seen teachers doing a fair job of teaching reading and writing to the top one-third of students who have enough aptitude to learn easily, but even then mastery of language too often plays second fiddle to preparation for examinations on literary content. Teachers with a full program of literary appreciation have no time to teach reading and writing even if they know how.

There are five things to be taught and learned: **language literacy** (reading, writing, speaking, listening); **cultural literacy** (concepts that everyone needs to know as the basis for communication); **literary**

arts (contemporary and great literature); **literary performance arts** (writing plays, stories, novels, poetry, essays, film scrips, letters, journalism, etc.); **audio-visual performance arts** (acting, play and TV production, film making, debating, etc.).

It is time to end the confusion of literary arts with literacy. To become literate in all the terms I have described one does not and should not have to read Shakespeare, Milton, Carlyle, Joyce. . . nor write like them. To write like them would inhibit rather than enhance communication. While studying Carlyle, I wrote an essay in his style. It earned me an A. But none of my college friends could bear with it, let alone understand it. It was the worst essay I ever wrote from the point of view of communication.

For cultural literacy (as contrasted with literary arts), everyone needs to know a bit about literary giants and their masterpieces. But to know **about** *Romeo and Juliet* does not require analyzing and dissecting the play as if it were the corpse at a post mortem. A summary, an excerpt or two and a look at the Franco Zeffirelli film would fix the cultural literacy information for most people. Study of the whole play is for students who opt to do so.

Cultural literacy could be taught largely by computer programs and by generalist teachers. When it is English teachers who are charged with teaching that portion of cultural literacy which derives from great literature, they should be clear that their task is to teach compulsory cultural literacy information. That is not the same thing as teaching literary arts to students who have opted for credit courses in current literature, great literature or literary performance arts. Nor is it the same as teaching the reading, writing, listening and speaking skills that constitute language literacy. **Teachers and school systems will have to be restrained from teaching English literature when they should be teaching mandatory reading, writing, speaking, listening and cultural literacy programs.**

Virtually all high school English teachers and most elementary teachers need extensive further training to teach reading, writing, speaking and listening. And most English teachers will have to be retrained to teach cultural literacy: the beliefs and practices of traditional literary arts teaching will confound any attempt to teach cultural literacy. That kind of retraining takes months, not days (see chapter 18).

Unless retrained, most English teachers should be moved, along with English literature, to the optional arts section of schooling where several literary arts should be offered. Their reward will be that entire cohorts of students who enroll in optional English literature and other literary arts programs will be able to read, write, speak and listen, and will be culturally literate, and hence will actually be able, for the first time in history, to understand, appreciate and enjoy literature.

"Language across the curriculum" means teachers of all subjects should also consciously teach language while teaching lessons in their specialties. In a general way, they should, but they never have time and seldom have the skill to expressly teach reading, writing, speaking or listening. It is not surprising that teachers of mathematics don't know techniques for teaching language skills, but they often also lack another level of skill: they can't themselves read, write, speak or listen well. Writing seems to be the biggest problem. For years I have monitored materials written by teachers for student use. Even examination questions and assignment sheets are too often ambiguous, awkward, incomplete, disorganized, wordy, bombastic, etc.

Mandatory language literacy (reading, writing, speaking, listening) and mandatory cultural literacy programs must not be given credits toward graduation or college entrance. They are basic to life, like breathing; they are the birthright of every child and quite a separate thing from earning credits by passing courses in physics, history, English literature, creative writing, etc. All students must be required to study reading, writing, speaking, listening and cultural literacy in separate, non-credit, obligatory, often individualized programs every year and should be excused only by testing out each year at a high level of achievement. Testing out means that students can and should be tested before or during a program and excused if test results are good enough. There is no point in teaching people what they already know.

Mandatory language skills and mandatory cultural literacy are pre-requisites for all credit courses including high-level literary arts, literary performance arts, audio-visual performance arts (not to be confused with basic, mandatory, non-credit literary performance arts and audio-visual performance arts — see chapter 21). Children whose language skills and cultural literacy are up to standard must be free to opt for courses in which they study literature as literature and film as film: for appreciation, to develop critical judgement, to earn credits. They must also be free to take electives for credit in writing (poetry, fiction, non-fiction, plays, journalism. . .) as literary performance. Audio-visual performance options must also be available and will be popular: acting, stage & TV production, radio programming, film making, debating, etc.

Any child who meets necessary prerequisites for any optional credit program should be admitted regardless of age. But if a minimum age limit is ever used, it must be ten or less. After ten, so many well-taught children are ready for optional programs that it would be intellectual genocide to deny access.

For a transitional period, one or two credits in literary arts and literary performance arts could be mandatory rather than optional — only to comfort the establishment. If optional programs are properly conceived and taught, there will be no need to force participation. Nearly all students in a school system that makes them truly literate will voluntarily opt for literary arts (including history of literature and classical literature courses) and for literary performance arts.

The initial emphasis in literary arts courses should be on contemporary stories, essays, articles, humour, song lyrics, poems, plays, film scripts and novels of all types (including literary, science fiction, adventure, thrillers, mysteries, romances. . .). Unpublished works, and new works specially "published" inexpensively to be workshopped in schools, should be used. The joy of reading and critical judgement are best developed by exploring the real world of contemporary issues in uncensored, contemporary works.

The biggest roadblocks to such a necessary change are the publishing industry and pressure groups. The former lumbers along at nineteenth-century speed, seemingly unaware that electronic publishing makes it possible to get material from author to reader in days rather than years. Pressure groups are the modern manifestation of medieval book burners — people so committed to ignorance that they actually think ignorance, especially of sex, is of value to children.

With some exceptions (particularly children's classics), most of the sanitized showcase artifacts that currently constitute literature courses, especially in high schools, should be relegated unequivocally to history of literature or great literature courses where they belong and where they can, provided they are uncensored, be appreciated once students have found their way within literature of the present generation.

Since movies are the preeminent popular literature of our time, it is essential that schools give high priority to film study. That they still don't will be seen by future generations as testimony to the incompetence and intransigence of luddite leadership in education throughout the last half of the twentieth century.

The reading of whole books should not be abandoned in favour of excerpts, anthologies, readers, exercises, kits and tests; it is not either/or. In the teaching of language skills, all are useful if the reader can understand them. Infants and toddlers and all pre-reading children should be read to frequently from whole stories and whole books and should participate in the reading through questions, answers and games. But it is not true that all very young children will learn to read well from the whole-book approach (or the whole-word approach), even if skilled teachers try to weave in specific literacy skills such as spelling, once the children are comfortable with print and books.

If I were teaching very young children, I would centre much activity around whole books chosen from the best of classic and modern children's literature and around computer programs. But that doesn't mean I would never use sequential basal readers or graded anthologies. Most of the puny, fun-and-play readers in North America are of little value but the more substantial Swiss, Austrian and other European primers have what Bruno Bettelheim calls "visionary qualities and magic meaning." I would also use non-fiction chosen specifically for its cultural literacy content: history, science, biography, geography, arts, etc.

And because it is a great way to teach reading and writing and because I like to do it, I would spend a lot of time writing original stories, poems and plays for and with children using word processing and computer graphics. I would generate my own spin-off activities. But that is not to say I would never use attractive, pre-designed workbooks, computer games or teachers' guidebooks provided by publishers. Children enjoy a variety of follow-up activities and teachers can always use good ideas. And, yes, I would use phonics often. And I would teach grammar in the context of reading and writing activities and also by itself.

Throughout elementary school, I would keep checking and testing reading, writing, speaking and listening skills as separate entities. And I would regularly check retention of cultural literacy information. Long before high school age, I would have skills programs quite separate from and prerequisite for, arts programs such as literature, creative writing, and theatre. One of the reasons the open education movement of the late sixties had little effect beyond the primary level was because it did not include specific, separate, skills-development programs with rigorous testing and remedial requirements for all aspects of literacy.

Nobody at any age should be allowed to slip through the net into illiteracy. Constant checking is needed to prevent slippage. That means focus on the individual and it means frequent skills testing from pre-school right through high school. And it means immediate, mandatory, specific, individualized, remedial and developmental skill-building programs for those in need. To get a good mandatory skills program going, an important step is to establish performance and evaluation standards for all age and grade levels.

Mandatory curriculum guidelines must be developed, preferably at the national or state level, and then specific mandatory programs in detail, probably at the regional or local level. Learning materials including books, computer software, television programs, and kits have to be designed and field tested. Some good materials exist but not enough. The same is true of standardized tests for use in evaluating student progress and diagnosing specific problems.

Here is a worst-case scenario for the early years of a new model of schooling: a high school student with chronic deficiencies taking five non-credit requirements (reading, writing, speaking, listening and cultural literacy) will use half of the present school day leaving only half time to devote to other activities; so it will take twice as long to get through high school. But that is unlikely to happen. Each year, most students will successfully test out of one or more of the four mandatory language requirements and out of mandatory cultural literacy before or during term and be free to use the time for obligatory and credit courses. And with each passing year, more students will test out without additional training, as students better trained in early grades advance through the system.

At first, perhaps half of **the top one-third** of high school students will test out of reading without having to take any of the required reading program, but the other half will show a deficit in some aspect of reading and be required to do an individualized remedial and developmental program. Speed reading is a skill that most people can be taught, but few of today's college students can do it, which indicates that nearly everyone at high school should be required to study it.

Substantially fewer of **the top one-third** of high school students at every grade will successfully test out of writing without taking some components of the required program. Even those who have mastered grammar and sentence structure are likely to have problems with punctuation. Many will be weak in spelling, vocabulary, style, organization, clarity, etc. And still fewer will test out of speaking without remedial and developmental work. Even students in the top one-third may be generally inarticulate, inhibited, nervous or shy; some may speak ungrammatically even if they write grammatically or may lack oral vocabulary even if they have a larger reading vocabulary; others may lack modulation, volume, organization, clarity, etc. Many of them may be weak in ordinary conversation skills, and few will have had more than a token brush with public speaking.

As for listening, nobody knows how many of **the top one-third** will successfully test out each year without additional training, but it seems likely that somewhat less time will be required for upgrading listening skills than for upgrading writing and speaking skills.

A longer school day and longer school year will enable most of **the top one-third** of students to graduate within the usual time frame even with the addition of mandatory reading, writing, speaking, listening and cultural literacy. But many of **the remaining two-thirds** will take longer to graduate. That is the price we have to pay in the start-up period for universal native language mastery. The question is whether or not society wants to pay the price up front instead of paying four times as much later on for the carnage of adult illiteracy.

Some of **the lower two-thirds** will need an extra semester or two. This is the two-thirds of present high school graduates or drop-outs who can't write a good application letter, summarize the content of a meeting, make an effective public speech, read the best newspapers, understand a literary novel or poem, etc. Many can't write a simple paragraph, read food package instructions, fill out a job application form, or converse in an interview. Worse, many of **the bottom third** can't read or write anything. This is the one-third who presently sit in junior and senior high schools trying to cope with Shakespeare or American history or Australian geography when they can't even read it.

So far we have decided to pay the price of individualized programs for the learning disabled but not for the rest. A learning disability is a neurological problem that makes mental processing of information difficult. Fifteen percent or more may have learning disabilities. But a learning disability and a reading problem are two different things. **Vastly more children have reading, writing, speaking or listening problems than have clinically-defined learning disabilities.** The best school systems identify most of the learning disabled and provide special education. But all other children who are constantly below par in reading, writing, speaking and listening skills are left in regular classes to fall further behind each year. They don't qualify for special education.

It needs shouting from housetops that **all of the bottom third and most of the middle third of children need a one-to-one**

relationship with a teacher for prolonged periods in order to crack the barriers that keep them from language mastery. During the start-up years of a new model, and until good computer programs are in universal use, one language-skills teacher with one student or one teacher with a few students for hours on end should be as common in elementary and high schools as one teacher with thirty students.

It seems certain that computers offer a cost and time-efficient way of teaching language skills to mastery. They can't do the whole job, but when we have enough computers and software, and enough teacher retraining, computers will help us achieve real, system-wide language mastery for the first time. There is a computer program called LEEP which successfully teaches children with the most difficult of all reading problems, dyslexia. Another called PALS is for functionally illiterate adolescents. Most mandatory reading, many writing, and some speaking and listening courses should be done by computers and related technology today, but we have not developed enough software or trained enough teachers to teach with computers. We should do so immediately so that all skill-development and remedial programs can be individualized for each student with far less one-to-one teacher time.

Trained teacher aids, paid and voluntary, will also prove cost effective in improving literacy.

In all of this, schools will be pretty much on their own. Good homes that are presently preparing children for literacy will continue to do so. It is unusual to find literacy problems in children from homes where everybody frequently reads and genuinely enjoys books and where children are read to from infancy and stories are discussed. Inadequate homes will continue to prepare children for illiteracy. Low literacy is a family legacy passed from generation to generation. It is an inherited condition that schools could cure but have not.

Nothing done for adults is likely to change low literacy homes to high literacy homes in time to save any current generation of children. Adult education and retraining for the masses is forever bogged down at the level of basic literacy. The already advantaged literate are the only ones equipped to make use of high-level continuing education opportunities. Still, we must provide adult literacy programs as reparation for the sins of the school system. It is the humane thing to do and is cost-effective. Increasingly, those able to consume information, the literate, learn to avoid plagues such as smoking, drugs, clogged arteries and AIDS while the illiterate continue to die of them for lack of information that changes behaviour. The cost in lives and dollars is enormous.

Worldwide, illiteracy and the planet-threatening population explosion go hand in hand. Women bear the onus for limiting family size, but birth control campaigns are ineffective if women can't read labels and understand concepts. Costa Rica has the only high literacy rate for women in Central America. It also has the only low birth rate.

At least three-quarters of prisoners, two-thirds of the chronically unemployed and half of low-level and intermittent job holders are illiterate or functionally illiterate. In Canada, a country of twenty-seven million people, that kind of low literacy costs the economy over 10.5 billion dollars a year in lost productivity, retraining, industrial accidents and unemployment, according to a 1988 study by Woods Gordon for the Business Task Force on Literacy. A quarter as much spent up front would prevent illiteracy.

Adult literacy programs will always be too little too late. At best they yield a modicum of relief for blighted lives. They improve skills of some adults sufficiently to win them somewhat better jobs and increase productivity and safety. But they will never yield a literate adult population. And they won't break the cycle of low literacy. To do that, we must put most of our eggs in the future basket. We must decide that never again will we raise a generation of functional illiterates. It falls to schools to do the job.

Mathematics and Science Literacy

Schools must require that every child master number skills every year to age/grade expectancy. **With and without a calculator, every**

student must be quick and accurate doing addition, subtraction, multiplication, division, percent, weights and measures, graph reading, problem solving and all operations that are demonstrably necessary to a full life. Publishers Hill and Wang remarked correctly in advertising for John Allen Paulos' book, *Innumeracy*: "The widespread inability to grasp basic concepts about numbers leads to muddled personal decisions and misinformed government policies."

If number operations are essential to some academic subject such as calculus or physics but not to daily life, they have no place in the obligatory number skills program. And there is no reason why most people should be forced to study the various branches of mathematics. Few careers or lives would be enhanced by superior square rooting. **All mathematics courses beyond mandatory, non-credit, number skills programs must be optional programs for credit available to children of all ages.** When all students are number literate, far more will opt for mathematics from sheer interest and at younger ages. And more will choose careers involving high-level mathematics.

My observation is that **math essentials are missed while schools try to foist the trivial, exotic and specialized on everybody.** The same is true in science. Everybody has to be science literate, but not everybody has to study biophysics, astrophysics, organic chemistry, biotechnology, genetics, etc. Or even traditional physics, chemistry and biology. The only science program everybody should be required to take at elementary and high school is one I call "about science."

Mario Salvadori, an eminent trainer of science teachers, was quoted in the April 19, 1989, *New York Times* as complaining, "Teachers tell them (children) about science but they don't get the chance to experience it themselves." I agree with him. Teachers should not "tell" children. Children should learn to ask questions and search for answers. And they should "tell" each other. But what they should find out in mandatory science programs is **about** science rather than the intricacies of each branch of science. The latter is for students of all ages who opt to study science disciplines for credit.

Too often, making science notebooks becomes an end in itself. All over the world I see student notebooks full of meticulously drawn test tubes, labeled, underlined and colored. Or else children are busy memorizing for short-term retention, reams of periodic tables, formulae, codes and obscure scientific names that should be the domain of budding and full-blown scientists, not ordinary citizens whether adults or children. Everything the literate citizen needs to know about science can be learned without all that. Some words must be memorized because they are used in the media and hence are essential to cultural literacy: gene, clone, nucleus, fusion, chip, cholesterol, steroid, etc. All of them and all scientific concepts and principles that everybody needs to know can be explained in plain English — no complex equations, no formulae, no code names, no latin.

Included in science literacy is technological literacy. Only one small element of it should be taken away from science and given to language studies — computer literacy, defined as competent keyboarding and the effective and responsible use of any current generation of personal computers. Computer literacy is intensely language-related (alphabet, word processing, writing, print on monitors, hard copy, computer manuals, software instructions. . .).

Also included in math/science literacy is the essential history of mathematics and science and the relation of both to human development. Even such related matters as creationist objections to evolutionary principles should be included. Good designers of science and mathematics curriculum now link both disciplines with literary, social, political and economic developments. Science discussion in classrooms becomes moral values discussion. By emphasizing the meanings and uses of mathematics and science, curriculum makers give teachers new scope.

Most science and mathematics teaching, especially in elementary schools, is done by teachers who have studied no science or math since their own high school years. Unless they are competent generalists, they may feel shaky. For them, it is easy to teach simple mechanics with emphasis on memorized trivia and pretty notebooks. It is more difficult to teach meanings, uses, principles and relationships in plain English. **Students training as elementary school teachers must have specific training on content and teaching methods for mathematics and science as well as language.** The three together are so important that a year should be given to specific training in them over and above the usual training, unless a student-teacher tests out of one or more because of prior knowledge.

Practicing elementary school teachers must have extensive additional training during working hours. Most also need regular supplementation of their classroom efforts by resident or itinerant science specialists who work directly with children and also advise teachers. And they need better equipment such as microscopes, and teaching materials, particularly kits, audio-visuals and computer software. With good computer programs, even pre-school children can use and enjoy geometry and physics ideas.

Seymour Papert noted that math/science illiteracy appears to be similar to language illiteracy in that children fall into it at home long before they begin school. In *Mindstorms* (New York: Basic Books, 1980), he wrote, "Those children who prove recalcitrant to math and science education include many whose environments happened to be relatively poor in math-speaking adults. Such children come to school lacking elements necessary for the easy learning of school math." *Mindstorms* explains how Papert's computer language LOGO enables even small children to program computers, work with fundamental ideas of mathematics and science, make models and, in the process, overcome the cycle of math/science illiteracy that has been handed from one mathophobic generation to the next.

In the last decade of the twentieth century and the first few decades of the twenty-first, the focus of most science literacy activity must be enhancement of the environment. Our survival depends upon inserting an ecological imperative into all local, national and international political and economic activities. Only a scientifically literate populace can ask the questions and apply the pressures necessary to assure environmentally sound government and corporate decisions, and will accept an altered lifestyle which will reduce population growth, curtail consumption, restrict emission of toxic effluent, etc.

The necessary change in public attitude began in 1962 when Rachel Carson published *Silent Spring*. Before that, nearly everyone thought about pollution, if at all, as mere inconvenience — smelly smokestacks or dirty creeks. Carson rang the alarm on threats to the planet. Post-Carson consciousness-raising of the most elementary kind took twenty-five years. The hour is late and we must get on with a higher and more universal form of consciousness-raising if sustainable development is to become a reality.

CHAPTER 4

CULTURAL AND MEDIA LITERACY

— only a few hundred pages of information stand between literate and illiterate, between dependence and autonomy.

— E.D. Hirsch, Jr., *Cultural Literacy*
(New York: Houghton Mifflin, 1987)

People approve when **schools fail to differentiate between information necessary for essential skills or cultural literacy, and information that belongs in professional expertise or public domain reference warehouses**. Mindless worship of data derives from the unavailability of knowledge to the masses for eons — the acquisition of information became equated with privileged position.

Enough new facts are generated every month to keep students memorizing a lifetime. An essential core needs to be identified. Which facts are so significant that they transcend confines of discipline and become general knowledge critical to the well-being of person, community, nation, planet or universe? What knowledge should we take for granted when we communicate across tables or oceans?

All schools should have graded dictionaries of cultural literacy on videodiscs. And there should be fascinating computer programs, especially games, that teach the entire content of cultural literacy. Every classroom should have standardized tests of cultural literacy for all ages and grades. Mechanisms should be in place to keep computer data banks culled and updated.

The core of knowledge specific to community and nation needed by a Japanese child differs from the knowledge needed by an Italian child, but both need the same core of international and general knowledge. Among other things, both need the same science and geographical information: the causes and cures of the greenhouse effect, the location of all the countries in the world, etc.

Americans may be frankest in admitting the young don't know essential information. The indefatigable school critic Jonathan Kozol published *Illiterate America* (Garden City, N.Y.: Anchor, 1985) and sensitized the nation. The press often reports examples: forty-five percent of Maryland high school seniors were unable to pencil in their own country on a world map; a quarter of Dallas high school students could not identify Mexico as the country on the southern border of the United States; half the California college students examined in a 1987 project did not know the location of Japan.

Things are no better in Canada. When the Montreal newspaper, *La Presse*, sampled student knowledge, over sixty percent of Quebec sixth grade students didn't know that Canada's capital is Ottawa. And it is not just geographical knowledge that is lacking. It is every aspect of cultural literacy. The University of Saskatchewan Alumni Association found that half of 107 first year university students could not identify Lenin, Plato, Jacques Cartier, Pontius Pilate and Winston Churchill.

All over the world, I have asked my own questions and my impression is that cultural illiteracy is epidemic. Even countries that indoctrinate their own national glories fail on the critically important global dimensions of cultural literacy; political, religious and ethnocentric ideologies and paranoias stand in the way. All the more reason to make international cultural literacy a priority for schooling worldwide.

Much of the stuff of cultural literacy could be identified within traditional school subjects (geography, history, science, literature, art, music. . .) and could be learned by students (and tested) as they live the process of schooling — provided all students take all necessary subjects and provided subjects are well taught. If the provisos are not met, then cultural literacy must be taught and tested separately.

Some of the essential content of cultural literacy must come from realms that have been barely acknowledged by schools, such as religion. It plays such an enormous role in world affairs that it is impossible to understand what is going on without religious knowledge. Nobody should be indoctrinated into a religion at school, but everybody should know **about** major world religions including sects such as those of Islam, and the subdivisions of protestant christianity such as fundamentalist, evangelist and pentecostal. Yet when I interviewed Jewish high school students in Israel, they knew almost nothing about Islam and hardly anything about neighboring Arab countries!

Religion is a case in point where the amount of information necessary for cultural literacy is sufficiently large and so laden with considerations that need discussion, that schools will have to provide new mandatory study programs. The same is true of current international events.

For lucky children, outside activities contribute to cultural literacy: reading, hobbying, watching movies or television, travelling, talking with people at home and in the community. But a fail-safe mechanism at school must make sure that no child misses learning (or forgets) essentials.

It would be impossible and wrong to keep retesting all information from all programs children experience throughout schooling, but it is feasible to retest essentials. At regular intervals, all children should routinely complete computerized, standardized tests to determine whether or not they are up to age/grade expectancy in cultural literacy. Most will be, once schools give it priority. Those who are not must temporarily limit or suspend most regular programs in favour of remedial/developmental work using computerized lessonware and data banks especially designed for cultural literacy. The focus in regular class activity is on process while, in individualized remedial/developmental cultural literacy programs, the focus is on remembering facts and their meanings.

School systems worldwide are in disarray when it comes to identifying and monitoring essential information children need to remember. It is easy to identify a body of content to fill any course in any discipline.

It is far more difficult to select from each discipline items that transcend the confines of discipline and command a place in the common treasure trove of cultural literacy.

The United Nations should long since have contributed data banks for international cultural literacy, national governments for national cultural literacy. In 1980, I began a modest project in cultural literacy that died in 1984 for the same reason many innovations in schooling fizzle — lack of national government committment and funding. Canada, alone among nations, does not even have a national office of education! To deal with the Canadian government on any topic related to schooling is to be at the mercy of bureaucrats in various departments all hesitant to acknowledge that education exists below the university level.

I persuaded one government department to fund a booklet of important facts about Canada. Schools and individuals could accept the list as published or select from it the facts they considered essential and add their own choices. They could also add regional and local information. I wanted a computer data bank as well as a booklet, but government bureaucrats thought it best to do the booklet first. Protocol was followed and a committee formed under the aegis of a large teachers' organization. The booklet was to be called *About Us*. A government grant for the full cost was promised and partial payment advanced. Work began and continued for three years.

The project was on budget and on time, and the government had no complaints or suggestions for deletions or additions. Then, the ever-changing and ill-informed bureaucracy decided they would not pay for translation (to French) or printing till after publication. But there was no money for translation or printing! So now there lies moldering in a basement file the makings of a pursuit more important and challenging than any game and in no way trivial.

While *About Us* was being conceived, gestated and aborted, a more brilliant sibling was being successfully fathered by E.D. Hirsch Jr., professor of English at the University of Virginia. In 1983 he published a landmark paper called "Cultural Literacy," and followed it in 1987 with a best-selling book of the same name. The *Dictionary Of Cultural Literacy* came out the following year. Hirsch formed the Cultural Literacy Foundation to contribute a children's dictionary, cultural literacy tests and assistance to school curriculum makers.

The good news is that Hirsch stated a case for cultural literacy so well that it attracted worldwide attention and began a dialogue which should lead to a model of schooling that includes cultural literacy requirements. He is the king of cultural literacy. The bad news is that Hirsch is wrong about how children learn to read. He thinks cultural literacy information alone will make children good readers. He wrote, "Once the relevant knowledge has been acquired, the skill follows." If that were true, it would be easy enough to flood children with audio-visual information that includes every item of cultural literacy information on his or anybody else's list, and all would then automatically read well. But that is not so.

There are lots of well-informed children and adults who can't read or write well. I taught a youth who wowed teachers with his knowledge. But he couldn't read a newspaper, and it took four years of rigorous tutoring on specific skills to get him to that stage. Many children — I estimate about two-thirds — would still need long-term, specific instruction on reading skills (not to mention just as much instruction on closely related writing, speaking and listening skills) even if they were awash in cultural literacy information.

The reverse is also true — that drill and testing on reading skills will not make a reader of someone who lacks cultural literacy information. Both are needed. Until the king of cultural literacy gets that through his head, he will lead people down the garden path to one more short bandwagon ride. They have already had several bandwagon rides, most notably open education, that broke down for the same reason.

Hirsch has another hangup. In his zeal for national cultural literacy, he underestimates the importance of international cultural literacy. All major environmental and military threats to humankind and the planet and all opportunities to overcome them are international, not national. Matters that we still think of as national are really international —

finance, trade, travel, communications, security, technology, scholarship, ideas, fashion, music, sport, etc. Almost everything. Even beliefs and values, that used to be decided by each nation unilaterally, must henceforth be decided internationally if we are to survive as a life form.

Right now, nearly half of what an American child needs to know in English for cultural literacy is identical with what a Japanese child needs to know in Japanese. A couple of decades into the twenty-first century, more than two-thirds of cultural literacy information should be identical, though in different languages, whether a child lives in Beijing, Boston, Budapest, Baku, Brisbane. . . .

Hirsch also underestimates the importance of subcultures about which all citizens must be literate. He sees subcultures as under, instead of part of, the umbrella of national culture. Black and Hispanic are obvious examples in America of subcultures that are major components of the national culture, but there are many others: Native American Indian, Jewish, Polish, Italian, Chinese, Japanese, Vietnamese, etc. All of them have changed and will continue to influence the national culture in America so every citizen must know about them. Canada and many other countries have similar situations.

Hirsch is right that national culture is primary. The success of any unitary nation depends upon a rich national vocabulary of mutually understood words, facts and concepts. People romantically disposed to unrestrained multiculturalism within any nation would do well to study Hirsch on the critical need for common cultural coinage even in, especially in, countries that treasure subcultures. Countries that are proudly multiracial and polyethnic cannot be essentially and primarily multicultural. **There must be a robust, common national culture if there is to be a national identity.** There has to be a set of common information, concepts and values and a common language that supercedes every component subculture. Even if there are two or more "official" languages there has to be a common language everybody uses competently.

If there is a set of common information, concepts and values that everybody understands in more than one language, fine. But that rarely happens and only in small, isolated countries over a long period. In Paraguay, most people go to business in Spanish and to bed in the local language, Guarani. The information, concepts, values and two languages are common to everybody, every day.

In Canada, that has not happened and never will. The best Canadians can do is teach French and English to all children knowing many will never become fluent because there will never be enough opportunity to use the second language. That means heroic, long-term effort must be put into teaching both major language groups a common set of information, concepts and values that incorporates both founding cultures and a good deal from several subcultures including the aboriginal. All mainstream multiracial/polyethnic national cultures for the twenty-first century must incorporate subcultures that are part of them, whether large subcultures such as black culture in America and francophone culture in Canada, or the many smaller subcultures.

Encouraging people to view their subcultures as **alternatives** to the national culture (instead of parts of it) is a disservice to minorities. It is divisive and it blocks minorities from mainstream success. It is not race or colour which keeps minorities out of the mainstream. It is lack of shared culture — values, information, concepts, customs, mores, language, etc. Mainstream and minorities have no mutual footing, so there is nothing on which to build and sustain relationships.

Instead of thinking of immigration as an event, an airplane ride, we should understand it as a process that often takes two or three generations or until cultural literacy is acquired. Once that happens, most people define themselves more by economic class than by ethno-cultural origin. But that doesn't mean they give up their subculture unless by choice. An acquaintance who is a Canadian of Vietnamese origin made the journey in only ten years from boat person, to refugee camper, to non-English speaking immigrant, to university student, classical musician, writer in English, conversationalist. . . . But his successful conquest of mainstream culture did not in the least diminish his zeal for Vietnamese sub-culture.

Of the many minority-group students I have counselled and tutored, the ones who have overcome exclusion, prejudice, racism and separation are those who have first made themselves culturally literate in the national culture. And they have learned to speak and write the mainstream language competently. Once they have all the standard equipment for oral and written interaction, nobody equally literate much cares what colour they are or where their ancestors lived. Residual racial barriers between people tend to be worn away by a river of shared culture. Barriers may erode only slowly where they are deeply entrenched as in the permafrost of the Washington dinner party circuit, but in normal social climates, I have seen them break up like winter ice and silently melt away.

That its members are fluently culturally biliterate, or that they speak and write the mainstream language fluently, in no way diminishes a subculture. Quite the contrary. To realize a subculture is a **sub**culture component of the national whole, rather than a separate whole, is a liberating and empowering concept while multiculturalism is a ghettoizing, enfeebling, delusive and politically manipulative concept.

In the book, *Multicultural Literacy* (Saint Paul: Graywolf Press, 1988), editors Simonson and Walker include over 500 examples of items missing in Hirsch's list of facts and concepts that constitute cultural literacy. Suggested additions are mainly in categories the editors feel Hirsch undervalues: racial minorities and their subcultures, women, food and agriculture, environment, world geography, non-European history, plants and animals, etc. Simonson and Walker allow that omissions may be oversights but also insist, "Many result from a particular white, male, academic, eastern U.S., Eurocentric bias that severely limits Hirsch's . . . concept of American culture."

I have doubts about the validity of Hirsch's 7,500 essential items even within his too-narrow frame of reference. I find some exotic. With three university degrees and a lifetime in teaching, I am vague about some and blank about other items he thinks every high school graduate should know. Having agonized over entries in *About Us*, I sympathize with him and applaud his pioneering courage in daring to publish the starter kit that everyone else will improve upon.

At the expense of the laugh being on him, Hirsch has unintentionally shown how difficult it will be to develop and refine cultural literacy lists: he quotes with relish Benjamin J. Stein's favorite example of cultural illiteracy in geography. Stein and Hirsch ridicule a junior at the University of California who thought that Toronto must be in Italy, but it was Stein and Hirsch who were showing their cultural illiteracy. Both must have been unaware that, while Toronto is in Canada, Taranto is a major city, port and naval base in the south of Italy. In common pronunciation, Taranto and Toronto are almost identical. The student who confused them made a mistake about as significant as a typo. Hirsch made a howler.

The problem of what to exclude is just as difficult as what to include. Since the misuse of nuclear fission or genetic engineering by any country will destroy the world, we may be tempted into too much detail on those important topics but at the same time avoid the more dangerous matter of overpopulation because it encompasses cherished assumptions we don't want questioned. It is sobering that neither Hirsch nor Simonson and Walker included in their original lists either "overpopulation" or "population explosion!"

But both included more names from ancient mythology than I ever expect to encounter. To the best of my recollection, Nestor, Hydra, Isis, Janus and company have never surfaced in all my years of globetrotting, meetings, conferences, briefs, discussions, negotiations, writing, teaching, hosting television, living, relating and socializing — and only rarely in reading even though I read to the point of addiction.

Hirsch's greatest shortcoming is his naive assumption that an ardent program of cultural literacy is all that is needed to render a school system that works. His confidence in the redemptive, protective and generative value for schooling of classic fiction and non-fiction is as complete and as misplaced as that of Allan Bloom as expressed in his book *The Closing Of The American Mind* (New York: Simon & Schuster, 1987). Cultural literacy is just one ingredient in a new model of schooling. Neither Hirsch nor Bloom has any idea what the other ninety-five percent of the model looks like.

Media Literacy

Sooner or later, feature films will be studied in schools as routinely as novels and plays are to-day and for the same reasons: aesthetic appreciation and exploration of ideas, themes and the human condition. The same is true of pop music; the lyrics should be considered literature of our time.

Some, not all, rock music is junk both musically and poetically. Good or bad, it is the music and poetry of youth in the late twentieth century. Like junk food, junk movies, junk literature, and junk erotica (violent pornography), junk rock needs to be confronted, examined and understood by children (and adults) before they can recognize what is shoddy or shallow and reject it. The fact that opportunistic intellectuals have set themselves up as supportive connoisseurs and reviewers of junk music (and junk painting, sculpture, architecture, literature, movies, sports. . .) may be regrettable as a breach of taste and integrity, but it is their right. Their reviews should be studied along with the trash they promote so that all children learn to be crap detectors.

Crap detection is like swimming: it greatly increases one's chances of survival, is enjoyable, everybody can learn to do it, and an early-childhood start is advisable.

The famous motto in the upper left corner of *The New York Times* reads, "all the news that's fit to print." Who decides what is not fit to print? Every high school journalist knows the answer and resents censorship of school newspapers by administrators. There are equally important questions about photographs, magazines, pamphlets, advertising, radio, television, videos, computer-video interface, etc.

In the early sixties, I was head writer on a Canadian national television series for young teens called, *Time Of Your Life*. Concurrently, I was teaching the same age group in a junior high school. I was surprised and troubled that I had even less control over the content of my weekly television programs than I had over the content of my classroom curriculum. As edited and broadcast, my scripts seemed more appropriate to younger children, and even for them, patronizing.

Later, when I wrote a series for pre-schoolers, taboos and prescriptions, combined with the intrinsic characteristics of the medium, seemed also to guarantee programs that patronized children and kept them in their place within the stereotype of ignorant/innocent childhood. My search for answers led me to a series of seminars with Marshall McLuhan at the University of Toronto. By 1965, understanding media was on my list of essentials for teacher training and school curriculum.

In my travels, I occasionally met teachers with similar convictions. My impression was that teachers were more concerned than media professionals and that the British were ahead of other countries. By the early seventies, some elements of media literacy had gained footholds, if not status, in the schools of most developed countries. Australia now has some media literacy education in every state. In Canada throughout the seventies and eighties, Barry Duncan, Claudine Goller and a few other dedicated teachers flailed away at the establishment to get media literacy content into the curriculum. On March 1, 1985, I wrote a letter that was sent to the Ontario Ministry of Education as an official statement of the Ontario Teachers' Federation. It read in part:

> We feel that increased media literacy education is a more appropriate response than increased censorship to the growing concern about pornography. If freedom to exercise responsible judgment is the right and duty of every citizen, then it is the obligation of the school system to participate wholeheartedly and deliberately in the development of the knowledge, skills and attitudes that are the basis of responsible judgment.

Since 1987, the Ministry of Education in Ontario has required some media literacy training for teens but not for younger children. Too little too late. By the time they are teens, children are such veterans of television that they have internalized values and attitudes that are much more difficult to modify than they would be if media education began with pre-school children and continued throughout elementary and high school.

Even when governments or school systems specify a certain amount of media literacy training, there is no guarantee that anything significant will happen. Too few teachers are trained (or retrained) to teach media literacy. Many school systems are so tied to paper-book technology that electronic technology is at best an occasional visitor. A quarter century after most living rooms had television, most American classrooms were still without it. The 1989 figure for the U.S.A. was one classroom in ten with a television set!

That astonishing fact triggered the bold plan of one U.S. company to do what the government had failed to do. Whittle Communications offered free TV sets and satellite dishes in return for promises to use Whittle's programs and commercials in schools. Television sets and programs for schools should be provided by governments as essential equipment like books and computers. Foundations and industries that meet criteria set by government might then provide supplementary programming that meets content standards. The usual sponsorship recognition should be a credit such as, "This program was made possible through a grant from Mobil Corporation."

But television advertising in the usual form of spot commercials should not be kept out of schools. All manner of **television commercials must be studied in detail so that students learn how to analyze them.** Purveyors of junk food would not be anxious to sponsor news programs for schools if they knew every commercial would be criticized in detail along with the product advertised.

At home most children watch the same programs (and commercials) as adults. Not just afternoon soap operas and sitcom reruns — at 11.30 p.m. any night, at least three million American children age two to eleven are still watching television. Children's programming is whatever they choose to watch, whenever they choose to watch it. They have refused heroic efforts by television producers and well-meaning generation-gap makers to keep them in their own program ghetto. A 1988 study of fourteen and fifteen-year-old girls by Michigan State University reported that the average American girl sees annually on television, fifteen hundred sex acts or references to sex acts. The girls reported that parents hardly ever attempted to control their viewing habits.

Youth channels are beginning to improve the fare, but throughout the history of television, most programs made for teens have been squeaky clean, good-for-you, patronizing, simplistic, trivial or just plain silly and have been watched mainly by pre-teens. Teens have nothing against watching performers their own age in drama, comedy or information programming as long as the content and production values are comparable to adult programs. Both teens and adults liked the issue-centred Canadian program, *Degrassi High*, that played in several countries in the late eighties. It had almost nothing to do with formal education but used school intelligently as a metaphor for life.

Pre-teens (ages seven through twelve) watch adult soap operas, situation comedies, sports, and slickly-produced car chases and shoot-outs. In late afternoon, most opt for adult reruns even when "children's" programming is also available. Along with teens and young adults, they watch music videos full of sex, drug innuendo and violence. They are omnivors who gobble up nearly everything average and sub-average adults watch and much that intelligent and discerning adults enjoy.

That inclination was already evident in the era of radio. When I was an early pre-teen, I gave up Jack Armstrong, Superman and Orphan Annie. I sent in cereal box tops for my last decoder badge when I was eight. At ages ten to twelve, my favorite programs were *Lux Radio Theatre*, *I Love a Mystery*, *Mr. District Attorney*, *The Green Hornet*, Fred Allen and Jack Benny. I also liked Walter Winchell, Jimmy Fiddler and Lowel Thomas. And I liked comparing American news on WBEN or WSYR with Canadian news on CFRB. Nobody ever told me what to listen to, except my brothers.

Most pre-teens like nature documentaries and science-fiction made for adults. Being omnivorous, they also devour thrill-a-minute child/animal adventure and cartoons, but nothing except commercial revenue for advertisers would be lost by stopping production of such trivia. Pre-teens relate to child and animal performers just as well in quality drama and comedy productions that appeal also to adults. The best bet is to have as much high quality general programming as possible and teach children to be discriminating viewers.

The best children's programming has always been for children six and under. Unlike pre-teens and teens they are a unique audience with unique needs and interests. But programming is too often patronizing pap. I wrote TV for tots and was constrained by traditions of restricted vocabulary and concepts. When vacuous and condescending elements are excluded and reality on all levels is tastefully included, some programs for six and under can be tolerable, even relevant and interesting to all ages. And for the target audience, they can be as educational as they are fascinating.

Young children like to watch the same programs again and again, especially ones that are instructional as well as entertaining. They like to learn. Such programs should be on cassettes that children borrow from libraries or keep at home along with books. Instead, good and bad programs are broadcast again and again because so few children have parents or libraries that provide them with good recorded programs. Children can and do turn on the television. They are educating themselves as best they can.

In an important sense, we have come full circle in the treatment of children. Before the fourteenth century, children saw and heard what adults saw and heard. Then childhood was invented, and from the fifteenth to the twentieth century, children were increasingly segregated and prevented from seeing or hearing about sex, suffering, death, mental illness, marriage breakdown, most emotions, economics, finance, politics, etc. The wall of silence thrown up to keep truth from children was first breached by increasing literacy and proliferation of print late in the nineteenth century. Early in the twentieth century, cinema further eroded the wall. In the twenties, thirties and forties, radio joined the attack. After 1950, the wall crumbled. Television and other modern technology simply blew it away.

By the late eighties every child with a computer and modem could use the phone to bring any number of electronic bulletin boards to the home screen, including a wide choice of pornography. *The Sunday Times* of London reported on the phenomenon in Britain, on March 12, 1989, under the headline, "Children tune into computer porn by phone." An official of British Telecom was quoted as saying that BT was "not a guardian of the nation's morals." Nor is anybody, if guarding morals means stopping information flow to the young. Once again, no topic is secret from children.

That is cause for joy, not regret. A form of repression has been overcome. The right to information has been restored. We should rejoice that television and other media have come along to liberate children from enforced ignorance, but we must provide the training children need to be responsible consumers of vast amounts of information so they won't become victims of media. What children lack is what adult couch slouches lack — enough background knowledge (cultural literacy) to understand important topics broached in the media and the training and sense of obligation to be critical users of both information and media.

Repressers try to deny children enough education to understand information, or they try to censor the information. The former is an affront to children's right to information, and the latter an affront to freedom of expression and choice. And both are impossible: media are too powerful and too all-pervasive. Schools must deal honestly and openly with subjects like sex, disease, war, violence, poverty, politics, death, etc. And we must provide children with skills necessary to use media responsibly and with the will and sense of obligation to do so.

The very media that make it essential to bring taboo subjects out of the closet and into the classroom will deliver much of the necessary information and be integral to classroom process. It will be tempting to concentrate entirely upon topics — abortion, divorce, sex, violence, children's rights, nuclear accidents, war, political corruption, whatever — and ignore the role of media. We must simultaneously study messages and messengers.

There is no need to bemoan loss of innocence in all this. What children will lose is ignorance. They will still be the most playful, creative, imaginative and energetic of people. Just as loving, trusting, and respectful or just as unloving, untrusting, and unrespectful as before — unless they learn something that justifies some modification in their responses. They have that right and obligation in common with adults. Children can handle all topics they thoroughly research and truthfully discuss with other children under the direction of teachers who know and apply principles of good research and discussion. At every age, children take from full and honest discussion of any topic only what they are ready for. No more, no less.

A boon will come to us eventually as a result of media literacy. The quality of programming will improve because viewers will have better taste and will demand quality. Many trashy adult programs that now disturb us as children's fare will no longer be produced for lack of an audience. Nor will trashy children's programs be produced.

It is regrettable that so many media literacy supporters are stalled at the level of bewailing the dearth of good children's programming. Many have not yet realized that a long-overdue redefinition of the model of childhood is already under way, and child mastery of TV control buttons is evidence of it. Instead of joining forces of repression that espouse the hopeless cause of turning back the clock, **media-aware adults should rejoice that the beginning liberation of children expresses itself in their victorious, irrevocable, total access to media.** They have joined us. Instead of rejecting them, we should help them use media well. They are willing to learn.

Media literacy is about freedom of speech and information. Yet, in 1989 most media literacy supporters remained silent or even supported a misguided decision of the Supreme Court of Canada upholding a Quebec law banning commercials on television aimed at children up to age thirteen. Such an assault on a basic liberty (freedom of expression and information) should have caused a furor and would have if it had applied to any minority group except children.

Teachers of media literacy (along with teachers of English) bear responsibility for the well-being of democracy through awakening each generation to assaults on freedom of expression and to the consequent obligations of every citizen in the maintenance and enhancement of that pivotal freedom. Their responsibility is comparable to that of science teachers in awakening each generation to assaults on the environment and the consequent duties of every citizen in the maintenance and enhancement of planet earth. A better-preserved physical environment would be a hollow victory if the political environment deteriorated to repressive authoritarianism.

To be media literate, all children must learn to generate communications by actually operating tools of communication: newspapers, newsletters, microphones and radio transmitters, TV cameras and transmitters, computers, telephones, fax machines, etc. But a resolutely self-righteous and anti-child adult establishment has always resisted sharing access with children. In January 1988, North America was treated to yet another case in point: that ubiquitous sage, Ann Landers, agreed with a letter writer who objected to a mother teaching her three-year-old daughter to use the phone properly by creating for the child, a file card system with photos and phone numbers of friends, neighbors and relatives.

Instead of applauding the mother for early and creative training in the use of telecommunications, Ms. Landers wrote, "I think the mother who thought up that 'great idea' is temporarily disconnected." She went on to share with the millions her opinion that the child was being taught the telephone is a toy and how to make a nuisance of herself. In fact, the child was being taught that the phone is not a toy. If Landers had wished to add some advice, it should have been positive suggestions in telephone etiquette which would assure that the child not become a nuisance caller. But then, the obviously intelligent mother of that fortunate child was probably teaching telephone etiquette all along — while Ms. Landers was disconnected.

This one among many Landers gaffes would be merely amusing if it were not such dramatic evidence of approved repression of children and of utter failure to understand our obligations to help children become literate media users. **Until children are trained to actually generate as well as receive content in all media of communication, they will remain less than literate, less than masterful in managing the processes of freedom of information.** All children should produce and be responsible for the content of school/community radio, television and desk-top publications. If all schools were, as they should be, campus compounds for all ages, teenage students could help even very young students generate radio and television programs and newsletters.

A flea-powered radio station capable of broadcasting several miles or just a few blocks costs about five thousand dollars installed, including transmitter, sixty-foot tower and studio equipment. Desk-top publishing with laser printing costs even less. Community television broadcasting costs more but is not expensive and would pay for itself through grants from local business and advertising sold and controlled by children as part of media literacy education.

With satellites, children around the world can communicate directly with each other and share their television programming. It should be happening routinely by now, and universally within a few years, because it is essential to redefined childhood and to any new model of schooling. The dimension of international understanding alone should be enough to ensure that level of development. Instead, we have only occasional experiments that are applauded as cute by complacent adults who have not yet twigged to the redefinition of childhood and schooling or to the importance of media mastery.

CHAPTER 5

COMPUTER LITERACY

We are entering the new age of education that is programmed for discovery rather than instruction.

— Marshall McLuhan, *Understanding Media*
(New York: McGraw-Hill, 1964)

To me, **computer literate means able and willing to use effectively and responsibly whatever generation of computer technology is current**. Presently, that requires keyboarding (touch typing) and word processing skills.

Teachers whose students use word processing confirm that enhanced writing ability results. And any student who uses word processing competently will also be comfortable using most other computer programs. However, **in a revitalized school system where self-propelled, student-active learning is the norm, computer literacy training must always include competency testing on every aspect of using the current generation of computers and programs and must include specific remedial and developmental training for those whose test results indicate need**.

A certain amount of programming knowledge is currently essential to the creative use of computers and must be learned by all students, but that does not mean most students should take whole courses in programming at the high school level. The latter should be options for credit.

That most children are not computer literate long before the end of elementary school is a stunning indictment of the present model of schooling and the people who run it. In the last decade of the twentieth century most students still leave high school computer illiterate!

Computers are central in the military, banking, accounting, transportation, communication, manufacturing — in all major sectors of society except one; in the schooling industry, computers are incidental, an adjunct for occasional use in some classrooms and for administrative chores. In every other industry, computerization is preplanned: goals are reassessed; systems are analyzed; hardware and software are identified or specially designed; phasing in is scheduled; employees are trained; dislocations are anticipated and ameliorated. Only in schooling is there no such planning, so with every passing day, schooling falls farther behind other industries and the education mess is compounded.

The decision has not even been made by governments, school officials or the public that computers and related electronics will be the main technology of schooling. But that decision has long since been made by the power of computer technology. Meanwhile, schools run as they always have, on paper, pen and chalkboard technology. Educators may talk of integrating traditional and electronic technologies in schools, but it is only talk.

What most people mean by "integration" is a school system that continues much as it is now but is somehow magically enhanced by supplementary computers. They think computers can and will make **present** practices better: the familiar paper book will still be there in the familiar classroom with the familiar teacher doing the familiar lessons at the familiar chalkboard, but the wondrous computer will make things more efficient — like an electronic dishwasher in a charming country kitchen. That is illusion.

It is politically astute to use terms such as "integration of book and electronic technology" because of the comfort they provide; fear of the unfamiliar new is assuaged by retention of the familiar old. The fact is, computers don't need to integrate with print technology. They **are** print technology in its latest form. Everything on a computer screen is **print** or graphics, the very things books are made of. At the tap of a key, everything in a computer file can be printed on paper in typeset quality and format, at lightning speed, in every classroom. The reverse is also true: printed book pages can easily be "read" into the computer by optical scanner.

Entire books, even whole libraries, can be stored and easily accessed on various types of disks. All the art in the U.S. National Gallery is already available to schools on one videodisc. My dictionary and thesaurus are on one wafer-thin computer diskette 3.5 inches square with lots of room to spare. Soon all books will be published on disks or cards and viewed on computer monitors or portable electronic readers the size of books. **Paper books bound between covers won't go away but will become an art form; they will be the adjunct that computers are now and computers will be central.** Then, everything about schooling will change, just as every other industry has been intrinsically changed by electronic technology. Say goodbye to the old work place.

A few computers won't do. Imagine how ludicrous it would be if the steel industry just scattered a few computers around nineteenth century steel mills to see if they would take. That is what the education industry is doing. But it won't work. With computers, it must be all or nothing. "Nothing" will assure atrophy and museum status. A long time ago, by computer standards, on Feb. 8, 1982, the Canadian news magazine, *Maclean's*, quoted me correctly on page 29 as saying, "It's going to get to the point that, where computers aren't the norm, the public will simply say, the school is irrelevant — get it wired. We're moving toward a computer on every desk in every classroom." The writer concluded with her own words, "And soon it seems." Not so soon. But eventually, either by evolution or revolution.

Evolution led by educators must be planned and begun in this decade or else revolution led by computer corporations and the telecommunications industry will take place in the next. The corporate giants, led by Whittle Communications chairman Chris Whittle, began their move in earnest in 1992 with The Edison Project which will develop a chain of 1000 high-tech private schools across America by 2010. **If we want controlled evolution from present publicly-operated schools to computerized schools, every country must create and fund a comprehensive plan that will phase in all necessary changes.**

The main argument for dumping bits of hardware and software on schools is that computerizing universally would be too costly, so phasing-in is necessary. But dumping is not phasing-in. Phasing-in requires a master plan that includes all aspects of computerization, and no country in the world has such a plan for schools. They may have it for armies, airlines and automated auto assembly but not for education, the basic industry on which all other enterprises of society are built.

Commercial interests are only too willing to dump hardware and software for modest profits now and the certainty of handsome profits in the future when they are in control. Computer manufacturers are responsible for most computer happenings of any stature in U.S. schools. In the late eighties, Apple Computer Inc. did what governments and educators should have done: established an international computer network so elementary and high schools could share news, graphics, data, experiments, stories, music, video images, etc.

Schools wishing to join the network applied, not to any education authority at the state, national or international level, but to local Apple dealers! Apple headquarters decided which proposed projects were educationally worthy. Networked schools needed Apple's Macintosh computers, modems and software. The corporation let it be known that Apple dealers would donate equipment if various community agencies could not be persuaded to throw enough bake sales. But even the resourceful Apple must have run up against the harsh reality that most classrooms don't have the telephone lines necessary to access a network. And of the few who do, hardly any have budgets for phone calls.

Many teachers are afraid of computers. Not because they fear being displaced — that early notion died long ago — but because they sense, correctly, that familiar classroom waters they navigate comfortably will drain away and they will find themselves in uncharted seas for which they are untrained. Most teachers have declared themselves ready to retrain and change their roles accordingly. A few teachers' organizations, notably the Ontario Teachers' Federation, have been among world leaders in pointing the way.

It is governments of countries and senior education officials of governments and local education authorities who are compounding the education mess by refusing to commission and fund conversion of schools to electronic technology. All the politicians and mandarins have done so far is what neighborhood bake sales have done — dump token hardware and software into schools and smile for press coverage of the big event. Even if they dump a lot, it is still not significant. To be significant, there has to be enough hardware, software (courseware, lessonware, data bases, etc.), curriculum planning, teacher training and retraining and school system modification to constitute **a critical mass** of electronic thrust. Only then will computers kick in.

In schools, no technology since the paper book, pen and chalkboard has kicked in. The only one that has come close is duplicator/ photocopier technology and that has fallen short of full integration because its use by students has been largely denied and because copyright laws have interfered.

Film, television and newspapers, remain peripheral, partly because daily dynamics of the outside world are not yet welcomed in schools, much less integrated into classroom life, and partly because a curriculum-integrated film or television industry has never been funded. Some teachers make good use of film, television and press, but others rarely or never use them. In most classrooms, radio never happened, movies never happened, television never happened, computers never happened. Technologically, it is still 1900. No house, office or shop is without a phone. Cars, boats, planes, street corners and back yards have them. Pedestrians carry them. Phones are everywhere, except in classrooms. Telephones are the central nervous system of society and classrooms are paralysed by being severed.

Some people believe that dumping computer hardware and software on schools has computerized education. Instead it has polarized education. Some schools have computers, but others don't. A few teachers have been trained to teach with computers, but most have not. A few teachers use computers, but most don't — except, perhaps, as a toy. A few school systems do meaningful computer-related curriculum development, but most don't. Some children experience the real power of computers as learning tools, but millions don't. Some students get a fair crack at becoming computer literate, but most don't. The haves and the have nots.

It is naive to think one or two or half a dozen computers down the hall or at the back of classrooms somehow hurtles students into the twenty-first century. An occasional teacher gets real mileage out of those few computers. An occasional student becomes a devoted hacker. But the Victorian purity of most classrooms remains unscathed by two or ten computers.

Dumping is so mindless that most countries have not even bothered to establish and enforce rigorous, standardized functional specifications for educational hardware. Almost any kind of computer can be dumped, and we are already in a mess because of incompatibility and because many computers don't have functional capabilities school use requires. Not only do we need national standards, we also need international standards so software and teaching techniques can be shared worldwide and teachers and students can communicate with each other internationally without the barriers of incompatible hardware.

The cost of developing software is increased by at least fifty percent and usually a hundred percent or more because governments have not standardized operating systems of school computers. Instead of sharing, jurisdictions often do their own software development. When the hidden costs of replication in hundreds and thousands of jurisdictions is considered, the cost of software is increased astronomically.

The government of Ontario (Canada) has taken a stand and forced an educational standard on hardware manufacturers. Some other countries are adopting the Ontario standard. If that trend continues and if further educational leadership keeps control of the trend, we might actually achieve international compatibility of school hardware and software. But only if public and teacher pressure forces governments to conform. So far, pressure is lacking. Even within Ontario, there is far more non-conforming hardware and software in schools than hardware and software that meets Ontario standard.

Every child must have a featherweight computer for use at school, home and on-the-go to museums, libraries, meetings, research sites, school buses, vacations, etc. The separation of home and school, like the separation of subjects, will diminish, the borders will blur. That is inevitable as communities become computerized. Notebook-type computers for students must be compatible with the system used in classrooms and entire school districts and to network all schools nationally and internationally. The technology has existed for years and should long since have been designed into school-specific hardware. It would have been if the need had been military instead of educational.

The first microprocessor was developed by Intel in 1971. By 1975, the Altair 8800 was a red alert for any educator who cared to notice. The Commodore PET and Radio Shack TRS-80, first sold in 1977, were simple, reliable, inexpensive, powerful and capable of graphic displays, even animation. Government and school bureaucracies barely noticed, but a few individual teachers did. By 1979, the Atari 800, Apple 11 and other micros offered colour, music generation, and lots of peripherals.

A landmark publication, *Effect Of Computer/Communications Technology On Education*, was prepared by The Ontario Teachers' Federation and submitted to the Ontario government in the fall of 1981. Note that teachers, not government, took the initiative. The Premier of Ontario asked for a follow-up paper and I wrote one which was sent by the Federation, exactly as written, in December of 1981. Key points in the paper were:

> The goal . . . should be to achieve within the school system, basic integration of computer/communications technology . . . by June, 1986.

We are differentiating between basic integration and optimum integration. The latter would seem to require access to a computer at all times by all students. One can conceive of a time in the next decade (the nineties) when a computer is an integral part of every student desk. Or looking at it another way, every student will have his or her own computer.

Optimum integration will require 1,800,000 computers (for 1,800,000 Ontario students). The first stage, partial or basic integration can be achieved with a much smaller number of computers; however, there is a minimum number below which we dare not go. To be functional, to reach a point where the integration mode really kicks in, a certain number of computers will be required. To avoid being left behind as irrelevant, schools will require that certain number by a certain time. In our view, the certain number is about 180,000 (one computer for every ten students to achieve about half an hour a day per student at the keyboard) and the certain time is June 1986.

The planning will have to include much more than the acquisition of hardware. There are profound implications for the planning of courseware, curriculum documents, professional development, teacher education, public information, research and other matters.

The paper included a five-year schedule for phasing in hardware, software, curriculum reform documents, professional development, teacher education and public information that would have the school system up and running on computers by June 1986.

On the matter of research, the paper suggested "priority should be given to a major manpower planning study to examine the impact of computers on the teaching profession; it should be launched immediately with an interim report in June of 1982 and a final report by June 1983 at the latest." That research on the implications of computers for school personnel would have been nothing less than an attempt to envision a new model of schooling. It was not done. Nor has it been done any place.

The original publication and follow-up paper attracted international attention and became fodder for The Provincial Advisory Committee on Computers in Education which the Ontario Ministry of Education established and asked to report by June 1982. Instead, it reported in July, 1983. I was on the Committee (and two sub-committees, Training for Teachers and Long Range Planning). Seventeen members were from the Ministry, seven represented education agencies, and one book publishers. I thought it astonishing that there was no representation from the computer hardware or software industries.

The Committee submitted a substantial interim report after a year's work. Top-level government bureaucrats objected to a recommendation that all teachers be retrained. The Committee refused to change its stand and page 93 of the final report published in July 1983 said the Ministry of Education should by June 1986, "for all teachers, conduct in-service training, as required, that is at least equal to a thirty-hour course."

It was never done. And it has not been done in any country. Considering that thirty hours is only a beginning, the demand for that amount of computer training for all practicing teachers is modest. Thirty hours might be enough to show teachers how to use computers and simple programs, but it will take at least sixty more hours to show them how to teach with computers. And every teacher will have to be given a school-compatible computer to keep at home and will have to spend long hours practicing. Even then, most will emerge as shaky beginners. It will take at least a year of practice with coaching to make most teachers comfortable and competent teaching with computers.

After all that, they will need never-ending upgrading because computer hardware and software change rapidly and related technologies are forever coming on-stream to change and enrich the mix of classroom equipment. And nearly all teachers will need access to in-house technical experts to solve mechanical and operating problems.

Much retraining time must be devoted to changing teaching styles. Just check current TV and film portrayals for evidence that most teachers are stationed as always between chalkboards and rows of students. That is the only way most teachers know how to teach. It is teacher-active and student-passive. It is incompatible with computers as the main technology.

Until all teachers learn to teach in very different ways, ten computers at the back of the room, or even one on every desk, will be mere accessories, more decorative than functional. Teachers must leave the front of the room and start dealing with individuals, many of whom are doing different things, and with small groups of self-propelled students actively learning together. The promising though too narrowly-conceived idea of open classrooms that achieved brief attention in the early seventies foundered because most teachers were unable to abandon front-of-the-room teaching and because retraining for all teachers was never built into the open education concept.

Everything about the present model of schooling conspires to keep teachers talking in front of classes: tradition, school architecture, funding, parental expectations, teacher training, curriculum design, separation of subject disciplines, examinations, timetabling, hours of schooling, reward systems, supervisory practices, evaluation of teachers, evaluation of student progress, children trained to be passive, children untrained for self-propulsion. . . . All of these forces and more are still powerful and still sanctioned by governments and public opinion or public apathy.

It matters not a whit that governments and parent groups mouth the rhetoric of individualized schooling. Everybody knows that schooling is not individualized — except, perhaps, for a few students with marked exceptionalities at both ends of the spectrum of individual differences. But **schooling will have to be individualized before computer and related technologies can become the central technology of education**. That is one of the cardinal prerequisites of computerized schooling.

The other is that students must be active agents in their own schooling. **Before computers can be properly utilized, all children will have to be taught to be self-propelled learners**. The thought of large numbers of students responsibly taking learning into their own hands strikes terror into the hearts of authoritarian teachers, administrators, parents and politicians. They much prefer children who are seen but not heard, who do as they are told, who memorize and repeat, who follow instead of lead, who speak only when spoken to, who are passive rather than active.

In his book, *Mindstorms* (New York: Basic Books, 1980), Seymour Papert noted that the computer "offers children an opportunity to become like adults —. In doing so, it comes into head-on collision with the many aspects of school whose effect, if not whose intention, is to infantilize the child."

Even if all teachers were retrained to teach with computers and every student had a computer with the right capabilities and knew how to use it, we would still lack adequate software: courseware — equivalent to textbooks or courses; lessonware — equivalent to lessons; data bases — each of which stores and makes easily accessible huge amounts of organized information on a particular topic; and utilities, particularly word processing programs. We have good word processing programs, not nearly enough data bases, hardly any courseware and a burgeoning hodgepodge of good and bad lessonware. There are several reasons why software producers opt for bits and pieces of unrelated lessonware rather than holistic courseware or sequenced and related lessonware:

- a little lessonware program is far cheaper to produce and test than complete courseware;
- no curriculum planning is needed to justify and utilize occasional lessons, but real curriculum planning would be needed to justify and utilize any entire computerized course whether delivered by courseware or sequenced, integrated lessonware;
- a few computers in any classroom are enough when all they do is run occasional bits of lessonware, but every student would need a computer if entire courses were computerized;
- as long as most teachers are untrained in teaching with computers, it is impossible to computerize courses, but a few teachers are trained

and some will use whatever bits of lessonware are available;

- it is easy to use (or misuse) occasional software by forcing it into the old-fashioned mold of teacher-dominated, non-individualized schooling, but it is impossible to stuff entire computerized courses into the old mold.
- ardent amateur teams or even single aficionados can produce occasional lessonware in their spare time, but it takes teams of experts working full-time to produce courseware or sequenced, integrated lessonware.
- governments and school boards, unwilling to make long-term commitments, incapable of creative curriculum planning, and looking for fast flashy showpieces, have opted to fund bits of lessonware to wave before the public.

So far the public has behaved as governments hoped — like dazzled rubes at a medicine show. Many teachers are already aware that the lessonware scene is chaotic. There are countless thousands of lessonware items in the English language. Nobody has catalogued all of them. Such catalogues as exist are not standardized, often difficult to read, usually out of date and hard to find. Much existing software is poor quality or only marginally related to curriculum needs. Nobody has evaluated much of it. There is no standard evaluation system so even when evaluations exist, they mean little.

Nobody has devised a universal system to store and distribute software. Even within individual countries, chaos usually reigns, and more often than not, state and local situations are also chaotic. Typically, a teacher does not know whether lessonware exists to help teach a given lesson, how good or bad an item is or whether it really matches need, where to find a particular program or how to pay for it.

Only a few teachers use computers in any significant way — about ten percent in 1992 — and they use only a tiny percentage of existing lessonware. The same items are used repeatedly because they are familiar and available. Add to this the use of computers for occasional word processing, drawing, business training and computer science courses and you get the illusion of computer integration without the substance.

Any school system needs about fifteen thousand coordinated, sequenced pieces of lessonware to minimally computerize primary and secondary schooling. That number, large as it is, does not include a library of alternative programs for variety and to meet unique needs. Under present circumstances, putting all the parts together into a curriculum would be rather like assembling an automobile at home from unmatched bits acquired from hundreds of sources. Parts not found in the marketplace would have to be home-made. No teacher or school or school system has the time or money to put together a model that works.

To achieve computer integration, we need sequenced and related lessonware with multiple choices or else courseware with multiple choices. And it has to be available to all teachers and easily located by computer search. To achieve this, we need long-range curriculum planning by government that is as thorough and committed as military planning.

In the nineties, a long-range curriculum plan should be a computer integration plan and vice versa. But in the prevailing mode of school system management, neither governments nor school districts are required to have real strategic (long-range) curriculum plans or operational (short-range) plans that are faithful to long-range plans; instead, they need only reach into their first aid kits and pull out whatever band-aid seems about right to hide whatever wound is suppurating at the moment. Right now, the band-aid of choice is dumped hardware and software and a lot of razzle-dazzle rhetoric.

Only when we have a long-range, phase-in plan for a computerized curriculum will we know: which teachers have to be retrained by what date; which curriculum documents must be rewritten and implemented by what date; which classrooms must have computers by what date; what courseware, lessonware and data bases will have to be operational by what date; which students will have to be computer literate by what date. . . .

Suppose a long-range curriculum plan calls for computerization of the obligatory reading program for grade five (ten-year-olds) in year x, for grade six in year x+1, for grade seven in year x+2, etc. We can then retrain all grade five teachers in the classroom use of computers beginning, perhaps, in year x-2 or even x-3 if necessary, so that by year x all are retrained (and grade six teachers are already well into the retraining process).

Since we know how many students will be in grade five in year x, we can budget now to have exactly the right amount of hardware in grade five classrooms by year x, in grade six classrooms by year x+1, and so on. We can also make sure that while they are in earlier grades, all of the target group are given computer literacy training so they can operate computers when they reach grade five.

Far in advance, probably in year x-4 or earlier, we will plan in detail which parts of the mandatory grade five reading program will be done using computer lessonware and courseware and which parts using paper books and other methods. This information and all other requirements for the new program will be included in a new curriculum guideline which will be circulated in draft and polished in years x-3 and x-2.

By year x-4, contracts will be let for development of necessary lessonware, courseware and related learning materials. By year x-2, the new materials will be in the testing and fine-tuning phase. In year x-1, they will be mass produced and introduced to all the retrained grade five teachers at intensive workshops provided by the government to launch both the new curriculum guideline and the computer programs and other learning materials.

A comprehensive phase-in plan for any nation, state, province or school district should computerize every aspect of schooling within ten to fifteen years. The plan must include every child, grade, subject, teacher, and administrator in the system. It must be possible to look at the plan and know exactly when: grade eleven music will have a computerized composition component; LOGO will be standard in kindergarten; each administrator will undergo computer literacy training; bliss symbol and other specialized computers and programs must be ready for specified special education purposes; every child will be writing every day with word processing. . . .

The reality of nation states and the urgency of schooling problems suggest immediate action should be at the national level with each country making its own phase-in plan and commissioning its own software, all the while establishing international liaison to begin sharing materials and development costs. But if national governments fail, then states and provinces must act even though there will be costly duplication. If states fail, then each school district must make its own comprehensive phase-in plan.

This kind of thorough planning and phasing-in need not inhibit present ad hoc activities. Those who are dabbling in odds and ends of hardware and software can keep on doing it throughout the phasing-in period and thereafter if they want to. It is a relatively harmless (though costly and polarizing) diversion even if it is not of much value in computerizing schools.

Concurrent with planning and throughout the phase-in period, there must be a constant public information campaign to redefine the popular image of schooling. The ingrained notion of schoolmaster as front-of-the-room font of wisdom will die hard. So will scores of other obsolete images and some new ones. People imagine that computer literacy is an automatic passport to employment as a computer whiz. It is not. Learning to drive a car is not intended to make the learner a grand prix race driver. Learning to write well does not guarantee a career as a journalist. But everyone needs to write well, drive safely and work comfortably with computers.

Even people who should know better have bizarre notions about computers in schools: that they will dehumanize children; that they will put people out of work; that little children can't use them; that they are only good for drill and practice, etc. A Canadian scientist, so well known through his television broadcasts as to be a public figure, unburdened himself in the press of the egregious notion that computers don't teach children to think and have no place in grade school. This occurred more than eight years after grade schoolers by the thousands all over the world, many in kindergarten, had shown that by using computers and the computer language, LOGO, they learn to think like mathematicians and scientists creating mathematical concepts which lead them through geometry and into physics where matters such as velocity and acceleration become accessible to them.

Word processing, LOGO, simulations, data bases, tutorials, computer-managed instruction, drill and practice, assessment and testing, electronic blackboard, networking, electronic mail and bulletin board, virtual reality — each changes the nature of school. The computer exerts itself. Its capabilities demand to be used.

Consider the change from chalkboard to electronic blackboard. The chalkboard is by its nature a teacher tool. Only teachers can get at it. Remember how unusual it was for you as a student to be called forth and for a moment of glory share the chalkboard with the teacher? The electronic blackboard changes all that; every terminal can control displays on one big screen or simultaneously on dozens of small ones. It is the students' tool to manipulate information for demonstration as much as it is the teachers'. Teachers can use it from among the students. Previously, they had to stand in front. The change in position is profound in its implications.

All changes brought by computers have profound implications, but three of them will shake the foundations of schooling more than anything since Socrates laid them: unleashed creativity, unlimited access to information, and mastery learning — all of which are gigantic square pegs that won't fit the little round hole of traditional schooling.

The established model of schooling destroys creativity. Naturally-exploratory infants are systematically divested of creativity in favour of conformity through the medium of mass herding and the enforced passivity which makes herding possible. The computer is intrinsically individualistic and essentially creative. It demands active participation and rejects passivity. It is so attuned to different learning styles that it leads all users into intellectual exploration.

Word processing releases and promotes creativity. So does LOGO. So do simulations, and scores of applications that inspire drawing, design, music composition, mathematical and scientific exploration and every conceivable release of the imagination. Once schools are computerized, dazzling feats of creativity will be within the grasp of most students, and some very young people in many schools will enter the elite circle of acknowledged child prodigies long reserved for occasional musicians, athletes or mathematicians. **Once bright, computer-capable children in schools are demonstrably striking at the frontiers, even breaking new ground in arts and sciences and in computer programming and applications, and are communicating internationally by computer with each other and with professional adults in their fields of interest, it will be impossible to infantilize them, to cage them in traditional stereotypes of helplessness and subservience.**

Unlimited access to information will do even more to destroy those stereotypes. As Shoshana Zuboff points out in her book, *In The Age Of The Smart Machine* (New York: Basic Books, 1988), "the structure of access to information expresses the organization's underlying conception of authority." Since the invention of childhood in the fourteenth through nineteenth centuries, children have been systematically denied information and hence disempowered. As long as information was stored mainly in expensive books and the heads of adults, it could fairly easily be hidden from children.

By the time microcomputers were marketed, the popular press, radio and movies had already breached the wall thrown up between children and information. Television was blowing the wall away when computers came along to turn the slow blow into a gale. Soon it will be a hurricane in classrooms. As the old wall blows out, free-access information rushes in. And along with it, empowerment of children.

Self-righteous reactionaries, who presently storm about the land trying to impose on everybody else their own contempt for children's right to information, will find it impossible to censor computers as they have censored books. They will try but fail. With computers there are a thousand roads to town. Every child will become an expert navigator. If one road is closed, another or some combination never before tried will lead to the destination. Goodbye censorship. And good riddance. It was always demeaning and anti-educational. **By restructuring access to information, computers will modify ageist stereotypes and thus democratize our concept of authority. They will change the model of childhood while they change the model of schooling.**

Almost as elusive as access to information has been mastery of content. Traditional schools have never operated on the principle that all students must master all skills and information considered critical. Instead, schools have always been content with mastery of half or three-quarters of skills and information, and they have never bothered to separate critical from non-critical or to make sure that retention is for more than a few days or months. Because the technology did not exist to deal with students individually, schools took and still take the attitude that if a certain percent of the herd knows a certain percent of the skill or information, that is good enough.

But it isn't good enough. If it means anything, a mark of sixty-six percent on a test means a third of the skill or information has not been mastered. Imagine a pilot being allowed to move from flying a little one-seater to flying a passenger jet when he knows only two-thirds of the skills and information needed. **The computer makes it possible, and mandatory, that schools switch to mastery learning.** Virtually all essential skills and information at all levels of schooling can be taught, tested, monitored, documented, upgraded and otherwise fully individualized and managed by computer.

When the three changes — unleashed creativity, unlimited access to information, and mastery learning — are put together, they will melt away foundations and partition walls of the lockstep grade system, blur borders between subject disciplines, and transform relationships and responsibilities. **It becomes inevitable that students teach themselves and each other** more than they are directly taught by teachers.

School curriculum and everything that flows from it must be rewritten to make it congruent with imperatives of computers and related technologies. Curriculum developers (bureaucrats, academics, leading educators including teachers) must do brilliant new work that comprehends computers before curriculum deliverers (classroom teachers) can do brilliant new work that uses computers.

They might begin by imagining thirty computer-capable children in a meadow, each with a small computer. Give them one teacher who is computer-capable. Now add several more teachers and several more bands of children of different ages, all similarly equipped, until the meadow is full. How do we create a school and schooling for them? Watch what happens in the meadow. Children are already busy on computers, playing games, composing music, doing simulations, finding information, talking to far away people, exploring. . . . They work alone and in groups, often involving each other in new discoveries — a computer screen is a magnet for social and intellectual interaction. Children of different ages begin to mix.

Teachers move about to see what is going on. They get involved, confer with individuals and groups, make suggestions, team with other teachers. Commitments develop. Projects become defined. Student teams, sub-groups and committees are established. Schedules take shape. Criteria for quality emerge and become the basis for evaluation discussions.

But all of that is down the road. We should have been there a long time ago. We are about fifteen years behind other industries, and ten years behind projections urged upon politicians by people like me in the early eighties. In 1981, I came up with the recommended figure of one computer for every ten students by 1986. Half an hour a day for each student. In Ontario, the government now accepts the one-for-ten ratio, but for 1996! And they make it sound as though one-for-ten will mean real computerization. It won't.

One-for-ten is just the minimum amount of hardware needed to allow computers to kick-in as a significant component of the school system and only if all other factors are in place. We could have one computer for ten students and still be stalled at the 1992 level — of using computers as accessories and to teach children how to use computers — rather than using computers as the engines that drive the schooling industry. And once computers have kicked in, we will have to move on quickly to one notebook computer for each student and a different model of schooling or else computers will settle back into accessory status.

But to reach even the low and late figure of one-for-ten by 1996, the 1986 rate of acquisition of approved, school-specific hardware should have quadrupled by 1991. It didn't. In 1990 there was only one computer for every twenty students in American elementary and high schools. And there is no evidence that America or any other nation intends to run fast enough to be only ten years behind in 1996. Or 2006. More likely, schools will be fifteen to twenty years behind other industries — unless the public, parents, teachers and students wake up screaming from their rhetoric-induced reverie.

A beneficial side effect to computerization of schools is possible. It could rid us of text books. Publishers promote text books because they make more money from mass sales of one endorsed title than from the educationally superior alternative of many reference books in every classroom. Thirty different reference books on American history is a student-active concept that beats thirty copies of the same consecrated text. The latter is a student-passive concept. It is also bad pedagogy. Lazy teachers like text books because it is easier to have every child passively swallowing the same book than to have every child actively chewing on several books — tasting, comparing, rejecting, approving, blending, etc.

In most countries and particularly in North America, text book publishers are so careful not to offend any pressure group that texts are insipid. Books on the same topic from different publishers are almost indistinguishable. They are an insult to freedom of expression and information. There are too many important sources of information on any topic to pretend that any one can be anointed.

A very real danger is that text-book mentality will be transferred to computers by giving courseware text status and by merely publishing text books on videodiscs. Book publishers, sniffing winds of change, are already adding promotional poison for downwind consumption. And the same old lobby groups are gearing up to sanitize videodiscs and courseware.

In this sense, a wealth of lessonware for all age groups and all school programs that has been tested, sequenced and electronically catalogued, is superior to courseware. The censors will find it more difficult to keep up with a bounty of quality lessonware than with one sanctified item of courseware for each school program. But an array of lessonware alternatives will pose no problem for teachers because they and their students will be able to use electronic searching to locate lessonware that matches any need, and they will be able to integrate various selections of lessonware into a whole that meets curriculum demands. Even disparate sources of information other than lessonware can and should be catalogued for the same electronic search: paper books, magazines, pamphlets, clippings, pictures, maps, videos, films, records, etc.

None of this is difficult to do. The military routinely does planning and equipping that is thousands of times more costly. In schooling, it will allow teachers to win a battle more important than any military confrontation, the battle to preserve and extend freedom of expression and information.

Another effect of computerization is so obvious that it should not need saying but, incredibly, it has not yet registered with politicians or the public: **the way to make students sophisticated in technology is to make school a technological environment.** Let them live in high technology every day and they will be high-tech literate. Courses in technology will never do it. They affect too few and always deal with some fragment of technology that is soon obsolete.

CHAPTER 6

INTERNATIONAL LITERACY

The greatest problem in the world to-day remains the gap between the rich and poor countries, and we shall not begin to close this gap until we hear less about nationalism and more about interdependence.

— Queen Elizabeth II, Christmas broadcast to
the British Commonwealth of Nations, 1983

Schools have failed to make people citizens of the world. But in many countries they have succeeded in making people citizens of nation states. That is a significant step forward in loyalties — from tribal and sectarian, to regional, to provincial, to national. And it is an advance from the colonialist notion that people and their homelands can be owned by others. We should be moving on to internationalism. Instead, nationalism is rampant. In the mid-twentieth century, there were only about fifty nations on earth. At the end of the century there are over four times as many and counting. Each cripples its own economy in defence of a border that is non-existent on a photo from space.

There is nothing wrong with appreciating and preferring one's homeland, its political system, its culture, but it is easy to cross the line between appreciation and ethnocentric smugness or garrison mentality. With few exceptions, graduates and dropouts from school systems in all countries, including industrial countries, have crossed that line and we are left with populations too inward-looking, ignorant, isolated, self-satisfied, defensive and suspicious — a deadly combination when international economic interdependence and a shared deteriorating environment make it clear that the era of independent nation states is finished.

More than just trade and pollution are beyond the control of any one nation. So are communications, energy management, outer space, overpopulation, food distribution, terrorism, disease control, nuclear fission, genetic engineering, etc. One mistake by any nation could destroy all. If the danger were from belligerent space aliens, all countries would unite to save our planet, but when the danger is from within, we are slow to accept interdependence. From now on, **ultimate allegiance should not be to any nation state but rather to the planet and to a planetary moral code that must be synthesized from all cultures on earth.**

Schools must get on with the task by making international literacy obligatory for every child. A major weakness in schooling innovations of the twentieth century has been that they ignored international literacy.

There is confusion about names for the stuff of international literacy. In the seventies, when I sat on the founding board of the International Development Education Committee of Ontario, some people thought "development education" referred to child development and was a branch of psychology. In 1974, UNESCO made the following statement in their report on Development Education in Industrialized Countries:

> The objective of Development Education is to enable people to comprehend and participate in their own, their community's, their nation's and their world's development. Any process of Development Education must create a critical awareness of local, national and international situations starting from the perceived reality and perspective of the individual.

International understanding, international literacy and global studies are names that come closer to representing the scope. I use all three and also geevee (for global village); the latter is unique and may carry less unwanted baggage than the others.

An aspect of international literacy is shared language. President

Jimmy Carter's Commission on Foreign Languages and International Studies drew this conclusion in 1979: "Americans' scandalous incompetence in foreign languages also explains our dangerously inadequate understanding of international affairs." Ten years later, the National Governors' Association concluded that Americans' ignorance of foreign languages and cultures is a threat to America's future. What is true in the U.S. is true in Canada, Britain and Australia.

The minimum language requirement for every child in English-speaking countries should be fluency in English and near fluency in one other language. If there is an official or main second language, it should be required. Every Canadian should speak English and French, every American English and Spanish. The actual situation in the early nineties is that only a third of American high school students study a second language, less than a quarter for more than a token two years. Hardly any 1991 graduates were bilingual except some hispanics in America and francophones in Canada.

In any new model of schooling, mastery of a second language must be moved from high school to elementary school where it can be achieved naturally by nearly all children. Teachers have always known that high school is too late to begin. Yet only one American elementary school in six teaches a foreign language. North Carolina has got the message, and by 1993, all children in the state must begin a foreign language in kindergarten.

The gift of tongues reveals itself in young children, so electives in several languages should be available to elementary school children who are up to expectancy in required programs. It would be ideal for most children in the West to also speak Russian, Japanese and Chinese. They could be taught — schools in Holland, Switzerland and other European countries teach several languages to near fluency. Since the language of international business and travel is English, the minimum language requirement in non-English-speaking countries must include fluency in both the native language and English.

Even with shared language, international goodwill cannot be achieved in ignorance. It can only spring from shared knowledge of

world geography, characteristics of developing and developed countries, democratic/capitalist and other political and economic systems,
conservation and environmental concerns, food and wealth production
and distribution, cultural and religious differences, peace, armament
and war, human rights, value systems, etc.

Most high school graduates don't even know the political geography
they must transcend to save the world. Very few can locate on their
mental maps even the countries of the world, let alone main cities. They
don't know their way around the global village so they are shut-ins. They
find newscasts unreal because the places mentioned don't relate to their
space. Is Surinam beside Vietnam? The names sound alike. A reasonable
guess but wrong by half a world. **It is impossible to be world-
minded if the world is not in your mind**.

This is mother earth and we should know our mother's face. Not as
it is distorted by the Mercator Projection but honestly reflected as in the
Peters Projection. The bottom line below which we dare not go is this:
**every high school graduate must be able to locate on a map,
every country in the world.**

Everyone should also be able to locate major cities, rivers, oceans,
seas, mountain ranges and deserts. Average people should be able to
draw a simplified map of the world and mark most main political and
physical names. Many people should retain a thumbnail description of
nearly all countries, including bare-bones information on population,
language, religion, political system, economy and history. Grade and age
levels of achievements in this type of information should be established
and every student required to achieve those standards each year.

Arkansas requires a one-year high school course on global studies and
New York two years. Thirty-four states require or encourage some
international content. That is a beginning. Ontario tries to integrate
global village information into all subjects at all levels of elementary and
high school. In the early 90s, the Global Education Project of the
Ontario Teachers' Federation built networks, supported initiatives and
dispersed ideas and curriculum materials. Remarkable international
content has appeared at all levels and in all subjects in Ontario schools.

But only in some schools. The whole thing is optional! Most students still pass through Ontario schools without becoming internationally literate. Everything critical to survival of the individual and society must be compulsory, not optional.

An example of well-meaning but unsatisfactory curriculum is a unit packaged by the American Forum for Global Education. It is called World in a Chocolate Bar and is intended to show interdependence since ingredients come from many countries. But it inadvertently teaches a stronger lesson — that junk food must be great stuff since ingredients are brought long distances and schools make a big effort to teach about it. The junk food lobby must be ecstatic. Many items familiar to children have ingredients from several countries and should be used instead of candy: bicycles, houses, clothes, toys, sports equipment, etc.

A mandatory program of international studies, along with a mandatory second language, should be enhanced by four more universal programs all of which bring children of the world face to face: electronic telecommunications among the schools of all countries; student group travel to foreign countries; enrolment of foreign (visa) students in all high schools; and twinning of all Western elementary and high schools with counterparts in non-Western countries.

In a sky full of military and commercial satellites there are none for schooling. Just three or four dedicated satellites would allow schools everywhere on earth to share expertise, resources, ideas, concerns and projects. A little and late beginning is being made with the Olympus satellite to provide limited but continuing communication between a few European and Canadian schools. Concurrently in the U.S., a project called Star Schools uses satellites to improve science, mathematics and language skills.

At a time when all schools should have their own transmitting dishes, we have only such modest forays into current technology. We also have the ludicrous spectacle of technologically obsolete schools in all nations hitching occasional rides on commercial TV satellites to make senti-mental smiles-across-the-sea programs. Everyone applauds the cuteness of Russian and American children singing together. Then the plug is pulled and schools in both countries go back to primitive isolation. The right and obligation of children to communicate with each other, to intervene on behalf of their own future, to be active rather than passive, to have equal access with adults to communications technology — none of this matches the present models of childhood and schooling.

The public accepts group journeys away from school as educational provided they don't involve airplanes going to foreign countries. Air travel is equated with business or vacation, not education. But the big jet is an important education facilitator. The UNESCO definition of development education refers to the "perceived reality and perspective of the individual." Traditionally, the perceived reality and perspective of the individual student has been shaped almost entirely by local and possibly national experiences, with the acquisition of international awareness being dependent upon media-manipulated experiences from newspapers and television. Now, the perceived reality and perspective of the individual student can be modified by actual international travel.

Travel professionals don't have a vocabulary of educational travel as they do of pleasure and business travel. If they lack the vocabulary, they lack the concepts. I can't find any travel industry training facility using international understanding as the basis for courses in a department of educational travel, nor any that teaches an outline of elementary and high school curriculum, or child and adolescent psychology, or enough teaching methodology to make its graduates properly supportive of teachers who lead tours. They count plane seats filled but not educational objectives achieved. Even the new tourism academies within British and American high schools are without an educational travel focus!

Visiting teachers can't be expected to know street-level cultural information about foreign countries. Yet most local tour guides in all countries fail to explain it. Perhaps they are too close to put it in focus. Many guides in poor countries have never been abroad, so they have no basis for comparison. They reel off historical data about temples or sit silently while a different culture, life-style and economic order whiz past visiting students peering out bus windows. Golden learning moments are lost.

Even with good local guides at every stop, and the constant assistance of well-trained, paid or voluntary teacher aids, teaching on the road is an exhausting job requiring extraordinary organizational and interpersonal skills. An optional, intensive course should be available to teachers-in-training, and all school districts should provide in-depth training to a cadre of practicing teachers who will become travel specialists. All teachers need some training, but some should specialize. One specialist should be in charge of every student tour and should usually be accompanied by an appropriate teacher who is a classroom teacher of the students concerned.

There has been little opportunity for teachers to learn from experience because most teachers never lead foreign tours or lead only one or two. Even teachers who have been deeply involved seem often to be stalled at the historical walk-about level of thinking. Only a few have grasped the potential of student group travel as international literacy training.

Inward-looking nationalists claim children should learn about their own country first. They think every American student should travel to Washington, the Grand Canyon and Los Angeles instead of Haiti or Guatemala. The reverse is true. **Students should see a very different foreign country before their own.** Once they have a bit of travel experience within the home region, students should bypass the rest of their own country, including the national capital, and go on study visits to developing or politically/culturally very different countries.

Students from Denver who go on a school trip to Washington experience no real change of culture. Food, clothing, lifestyle, transportation — everything is the same. A mall supermarket is a mall supermarket. Children return home with new information and images which fit rather well with information and images previously experienced. There may be more national pride but not much really new understanding about being an American and none about being a citizen of the world.

But suppose students from Winnipeg take a study trip to Cuba or

Haiti. No malls. No supermarkets. Different food, clothing, lifestyle, sanitation, transportation, politics, etc. When those students arrive back in Winnipeg and step off the plane, they know for the first time what it means to be a Canadian. A rush of feeling for Canada, a sense of identity, a depth of appreciation comes sweeping in. It is a healthy kind of nationalism because it is outward-looking and based on personal experience of how it is with other people in the global village. After that kind of international travel is the time for national travel because students have a sharpened perspective that sheds light on regional nuances throughout their own country.

Every student in developed countries should experience at least one tour to a poor country. If a second tour is possible, it should be to a country as politically or culturally different as possible: Russia, China or Japan would be a better choice than Britain, France or Italy for American, Canadian or Australian students.

Unfortunately, given a choice of destinations for a first, second or third overseas tour, most students, parents, teachers and travel agents in developed countries will pick Paris, London and Rome. Those great cities stand behind Lagos, Jakarta, Mexico City, Moscow, Beijing and Hiroshima in terms of international understanding for students from North America. The only destinations that might take priority are Nazi death camps in Germany and Poland. Dachau has been whitewashed with paint and shame, but enough remains of it and other prisons to make a searing statement and pose the most profound questions of the century for children.

To date, student group travel has been optional and largely elitist — paid for by individual students who can afford it. Instead, **global studies tours should be compulsory and provided for every student without fee just as textbooks and school buses are provided now**. Once we have a commitment to curriculum for international understanding, governments will find funding. A tiny portion of present military budgets would suffice.

Student group travel burgeoned in the affluent sixties and early seventies, but it was ill-conceived tourism, not global studies travel.

Most groups went on barely-modified tourist packages during vacations and in a vacation frame of mind. It was a charade. One year, on the first day of the spring school break, over twenty-five thousand high school students left Toronto international airport, all in school groups, hardly any doing real educational travel.

To this day, many student group trips are thinly-disguised ski jaunts or fun-in-the-sun flings in Western-standard enclaves well protected from the reality onto which they are grafted. That kind of travel compares to educational travel as rape does to love-making. At best, most tours are historical walkabouts, ranging from mere shrine shopping in most cases, to occasional in-depth but narrowly focused studies. Walks through historical sites, no matter how brilliantly executed, do not constitute quality global studies. The history represented in those sites must be related to present-day life humming in their very shadows and that life must be related to life in other countries (developed, developing, democratic, non-democratic. . .) and to life back home.

A subject-related itinerary as a minor theme can be helpful in channelling the multiple inputs of a foreign environment. But history, geography, art, language, theatre — or whatever subject is used as a focus — must be related to the past and present life of the people and all of that to life in other countries. Only then does a subject-related itinerary move into the realm of international understanding, the major theme of all student group travel.

It is the duty of accompanying teachers to synthesize with students all information gathered and relate it to other countries and to their own reality. Some of this can be done back home in the classroom, but much is best done on location. Time must be scheduled at the end of most days for synthesis sessions. Students should discuss aspects of life they have recorded during the day as they go about cultural, historical, or scenic itineraries: transportation, industry, clothing, food shopping, housing, children, teenagers, women, men, old age, wealth, poverty, business buildings, crops, restaurants, stores, entertainment, friendliness, curiosity, facial expressions, street behaviour, health, social life, family life, books and newspapers, courting, cleanliness, music, vegetation, smoking, makeup, income, cost of living, pollution, policing, etc.

Every tour group should visit schools, yet it seldom happens. Given a choice, every overseas travel operator from Brussels to Bangkok will opt for another shrine instead of a school. It is easier to tread the beaten track to still another temple than to custom tailor a visit to the nearest high school. Actually, the latter is not very difficult. Schools the world over welcome foreign teachers and students as visitors. Arrangements should be made months in advance but may be made after arrival. Even impromptu visits are possible, profitable and easy. Either way, there must be talented teacher leadership to make sure visitors and hosts get to know each other, and all visiting students must have had advance training in how to: initiate interaction, interview, inform without bragging, respect cultural differences, etc.

Global studies should feature two-way visits, but since it is unlikely that students from poor countries will travel abroad in groups, it is essential that visitors bring something of their country with them. To do otherwise would be nouveau colonialism with the wealthy taking knowledge from the poor without reciprocating in kind. Visiting groups must bring a presentation about their hometown and country which may be as modest as family photographs carried by every student along with a few fold-out maps, charts and drawings, or may be as ambitious as a specially-made video, movie or slide-sound show. Visiting groups should also bring with them a simple, well-rehearsed stage show that can be presented anywhere, without lighting, microphones or elaborate props. Current dances and songs that invite audience participation should be included.

Some time should be arranged for every visiting student to be alone with a host student. English-speaking students are fortunate; nearly any place they visit they find students who are studying English. As long as visitors remain in their own group or even in twos, they have a protective cocoon of familiar company that inhibits their stepping into the reality about them. It is important for each visitor to be alone with a host student even if only for a walk or a meal. Students paired in this way have taken the first and most difficult step in knowing each other. To continue the relationship, each visiting student should leave a little gift with his/her new acquaintance: a close-up polaroid photo of the two and self-addressed, stamped envelopes with blank stationery and pen inside.

A good student educational tour can be done in one week, but two weeks is usually better and occasionally longer tours are justified. Briefing before a trip requires at least one full week since it must include study of the geography, history, culture and politics of the destination. Debriefing after the trip, if done well, takes another week. All of this is regular school work for both students and teachers. It is no more related to vacations than are school lessons in mathematics.

The proliferation of tourism is another reason for making educational travel a required school program. People must be taught to travel intelligently. Even in Western Europe, where political progress has reached the stage of a standard passport for all Europeans, educational progress is stalled at the level of travelling goons who terrorize soccer games and vulgarians who pollute watering holes.

In Britain, the number of citizens travelling abroad increased sixfold from 1968 to 1988. By the end of that period more than twenty-seven million Britons per year were visiting foreign countries. So many behaved badly that the image of the travelling Briton is no longer of the proper English gentleman but rather of the rowdy, the hooligan, the lout. Many who are not intentionally obnoxious, are so ill-informed about countries they visit and so ignorant of travel protocol that they are unintentionally offensive. The ugly American traveller who once had international boorishness almost to himself has been joined by the ugly Briton, Canadian, Australian, Italian, German. . . .

Even the Japanese must be included, though not for lack of decorum. They suffer from the universal failure of most modern tourists to prepare for travel by studying the history, politics, and customs of countries they visit; a list of monuments and shopping bargains taken from guide books is not good enough. Japanese tourists are also as guilty as any of camera addiction. Instead of coming to grips with a new culture by relating one-to-one with people, they hide behind cameras in the mistaken belief that they can confront the unknown back home, in the safety of their own living rooms, by enthusing over photos on a screen.

Nearly all of these people, had they experienced good global studies tours as students, would now be accomplished travellers, well able to enhance international understanding instead of international misunderstanding. It is stark evidence of the inability of the present model of schooling to rise to obvious necessity that it has stood by paralysed in the last half of the twentieth century when it has been obvious that the masses have taken to the skies. Not one school system has made so much as a middling effort to train people for international travel.

A case in point of our failure to behave either intelligently or honorably in matters of international education is our abusive treatment of children from less-favored countries who come to us for schooling. Children of the foreign rich and well-connected manage nicely, as they have for centuries, by buying their way into prestigious boarding schools. Their parents know the ropes and make all arrangements.

The rest, some as young as fifteen, are often from less affluent families who don't know the ropes. Children may have to make their own arrangements from a Malaysian village, or central Java or back-street Hong Kong. Through gossip or newspaper ads or travelling salesmen or paid local touts they find out about specialized overseas businesses representing themselves as colleges and offering quickie language and university-admission courses. Some such businesses are big enough to own or lease all or part of an industrial or office building. Some rent old schools. Others are store-front operations. All sound like the answer to prayers for a desperate family whose only way up is to buy an overseas education for one child.

Frequently, foreign (visa) students pay as much to attend store-front schools with nothing but a few makeshift classrooms as they would pay at a nearby public high school with all the amenities — libraries, gymnasia, science laboratories, optional programs, recreation facilities, nurses, guidance counsellors — and with a student body that includes local residents instead of being made up entirely of foreigners. But visa students don't know about the nearby high school because it doesn't advertise or send salesmen to Asia, Africa and South America.

Every embassy and consulate of English-speaking countries should publish and disseminate information on how to enrol in their high schools and should supply counselling and assistance. Most don't. I have seldom been so disgusted with my own country as when I have taken foreign students to Canadian embassies for information on Canadian high schools. External Affairs officials seem to think Canadian education begins at university, if at all.

In Singapore the Canadian diplomat in charge of such matters told me no good material on Canadian high schools was available for Malaysian students. He was a kindly fellow and regretted the dearth of information but explained that since education is a provincial matter, the federal government finds it difficult to provide assistance. At the time, there were thousands of Malaysian and other Asian high school students studying in Canada on federal visas and pouring millions into the Canadian economy. And at the time, the father of that diplomat was the former Director of Education for an urban school board back in Canada. Yet they couldn't come up with decent information on high schools!

Wealthy countries should welcome foreign high school students at low fees or no fees as a contribution to international understanding. We should recruit them as a precious resource. Instead, we discourage foreign students by setting high fees. Crass politicians pandering for redneck votes propagate the myth that modest fees would diminish opportunities for local children and enrich already rich foreigners.

In all the years I have helped visa students learn English, I have encountered few rich ones. Here are some realities I have encountered: a boy sleeping in the park because his parents were unable to get their government's permission to send more money; a student short of food because his sole-support mother, a street peddler of dishes, was short of money; several students who worked illegally at all-night restaurants to survive after they pooled resources to pay medical bills for one of them injured in an accident; six students living in one room to make ends meet; a sixteen-year-old who arrived with ten thousand dollars collected from the extended family but received nothing more from home in the six years it took to complete high school and university.

Even those with adequate funds have difficulties. Most have grown up in protected environments and have never been away from home or in charge of money before. They fall victim to predators, from car salesmen to pimps to vamps. Landlords are especially dangerous. I confronted one apartment owner who had taken a student's entire bank account by saying it was necessary and normal to pay a full year's rent in advance. When I demanded and got back ten months rent, the student was able to eat without working an illegal, all-night job for a pittance.

Loneliness is another problem. Most foreign students long to mix with students in the host country. (How ironic that we use the word "host" where hardly a shred of hospitality is evident.) Instead, they usually find themselves in cram schools that are ghettos set up solely to make money. Or if they find their way into a public high school, they are often ghettoized into segregated classes by the administration and ignored by local students. Since state-supported high schools don't have residences, visa students go at night to another ghetto, overcrowded flats they share with others from home. Lacking entrée into host country social life, they tolerate ghettoizing to avoid loneliness.

Because they are ghettoized, they speak their native language after school hours; so learning the language of instruction well enough to acquire university entrance is difficult. If they lived with native speakers of the local language, vocabulary, comprehension and pronunciation would develop naturally as an outcome of daily life. Instead, foreign students are endlessly enmeshed in language crash courses and tethered, in their loneliness, to electronic language labs.

In North America and Britain, overseas teens who rarely get to converse with native English speakers even when living in their midst, pour millions of dollars into the testing industry that has grown up to humiliate them with constant reminders that they are not yet proficient in English. Many never will be. In desperation, they keep paying to take tests of English as a foreign language that will open university doors to those with high enough scores. A more compassionate society would stop bleeding them for test money and start teaching them English in our homes and social life.

These displaced teens contribute millions to Western economies through purchase of transportation, schooling, books, school supplies, food, shelter, furniture, clothing, recreation, and essential services. Even if they paid no school fees, we would make money from them. And we will make vastly more when they go home to be political and business leaders and turn for trade ties to the Western country that once welcomed them as students. If it welcomed them.

If foreign students were routinely in our high schools and homes, we would learn enough about their cultures and countries to be welcome in the future as knowledgeable trading partners. Ironically, most of the visa students we are mistreating are from the Pacific rim, the very part of the world that is burgeoning as a trading giant and market for Western goods. But real and immense as it is, potential financial gain is not the main payoff to be had from providing properly for visa students. The priceless opportunity exists to mingle the young of many nations to the point that they actually get to understand each other. Such bonds are the greatest hope for survival as our world convulses into the twenty-first century.

We should provide the full range of support services we would like to see if the shoe were on the other foot and it were necessary to send our own sixteen-year-olds half way around the world, alone, to attend strange schools taught in a foreign language. If state-supported schools had residences, as they should, it would be desirable to have each foreign student room with a local. In the absence of school residences, school authorities, student governments and volunteer groups should arrange billets in neighborhood homes or, as a last resort, list and monitor rental accommodation.

A buddy system should be developed so that one or more trained and responsible local persons is paired with every visa student from the moment of arrival at the airport to departure months or years later, including long, lonely summers. Buddies teach when and how to look at people, how close to stand for conversation, how to chat, what questions one should and not ask, how to recognize and handle sexual advances, table etiquette, what to use and not use in a host's bathroom, banking and shopping information, public transit routes, medical and dental contacts and a hundred other things anyone within a culture takes for granted.

Usually, high school visa students come from disadvantaged countries lacking adequate high schools or universities. We should also welcome students from developed countries for long or short study at high school. I propose programs which can be initiated by schools, school boards and consortiums of boards willing to enlist support from government and other agencies. All can begin as pilot projects with one country, perhaps Japan, then expand to others.

The Japanese are hungry for English and they pay for it: on T-shirts, neon signs and records; in every high school; at commercial language schools throughout their country. They are purchasing entire American colleges, buying into others, and establishing their own colleges in America so they can send people to learn English. Still, the best way of making large numbers bilingual eludes the government, educators and parents of Japan.

Concurrent with all this is the growing conviction of the Japanese that their insularity must be ameliorated with sincere efforts to understand other cultures. They call it internationalizing. Their determination may be fueled in part by profit motives but there is nothing dishonorable about that. We should acknowledge the eagerness of Japanese to learn about our culture and language by creating new opportunities for their teens. In doing so, we will create new opportunities in international understanding for our own children. We will also make a lot of money, but there is nothing dishonorable about that.

We should offer Japanese teens summer English immersion wilderness camps that are packaged to include air charter, food, lodging, sight-seeing, cultural events, tuition, supervision, constant socializing with American or Canadian children — everything but shopping money: they will bring plenty. Formal English classes will be easy to plan since virtually all Japanese teens have some background on which to build. The real challenge will be to organize constant socializing with our children and to prevent visitors from cocooning and speaking Japanese. **Top priority of any program for foreign students should be at least one native speaker for every two visitors — day and night**. Only a few native speakers need to be teachers and other adult staff. Most should be teens. Some should be volunteer adults, including seniors.

Fees paid by overseas students could cover expenses of volunteer North American teens who live-in at camp as hosts and buddies. But many of our children would pay their own expenses and various agencies would subsidize such an experience in international living and hosting for our children. Major corporations in English-speaking countries and Japan should see the advantages of contributing. Another possibility would be to billet visitors in homes and operate in a day-camp mode near towns. Home billeting might or might not involve payment by visitors; it would eliminate virtually all costs for local students.

An attractive modification of the language-immersion camp is the summer school program. Many high schools already run summer schools for their own students; immersion English for overseas students could be added. A logical extension of summer language immersion is the immersion year. The emphasis should be on language, cultural studies and socializing, but many Japanese students staying for a school year could also take courses in other subjects where English is the language of instruction. Probably it would be possible to negotiate accreditation of such courses with the government of Japan. The important thing is that overseas visitors learn about us and we learn about them while they learn English.

Any of these proposals could also be conceived as two-way exchange programs if people in the West were as eager to internationalize as the Japanese are. Any astute Western country would hasten to subsidize such an opportunity to educate its future political and business leaders in the Japanese language and customs. At least there may be enough astute individuals in the West to establish pilot exchange projects on a user-pay basis. That would be acceptable as a start, but within a few years, we must find ways to exchange large numbers of our teens with other countries.

Exchanges at the university level are useful but involve such a minuscule percent of the population that universal world-mindedness will not result. Only fifty-five thousand North American university students study abroad each year, usually in countries most like us instead of most different. Less than a third of young people in even the most favored countries attend university, but **nearly everybody goes to high school so that should be the main level of student exchange.** Eventually, the West should have significant high school exchange programs, not only with Japan, but also with countries on every continent.

One model with built-in comfort factors would twin Western towns and cities with culturally different counterparts for student exchanges of a month or so. A load of sixteen-year-olds from Someville, U.S.A. is flown to Somegrad, Russia by U.S. military transport. On the return trip, the same plane carries Russian sixteen-year-olds from Somegrad to their waiting hosts in Someville. Meanwhile, a Russian military jet has done a comparable shuttle between Anothergrad, Russia and Anotherville, U.S.A. It is appropriate, even poetic, that military transport be used in the air and on the ground for this greatest of all peacekeeping operations. From the point of view of the military, it could be written off as practice for pilots, drivers and other personnel. From the point of view of humankind, it would be real value at long last for some of the trillions invested in the military.

Every group of twenty-five exchange students should attend the same or nearby high schools in the host country and live in the same or nearby neighborhoods. Students should exchange homes where feasible but could be billeted in other homes so long as a buddy system assures regular association with a host-country teenager. A hometown adult should accompany every twenty-five students. Retired teachers or other knowledgeable seniors in this role could be especially trained to be on-site counsellors and good-will ambassadors. A hometown teacher from each side should be the other accompanying adult and should become for the exchange period, a foreign-teacher-in-residence giving seminars in homeland language and culture.

Exchange students should study the culture of the host country, but language immersion, science, athletics and performing arts are also possibilities. Throughout the exchange period, phone calls and frequent satellite television transmissions should maintain communications among all parties and should be shared with the general public on both sides through broadcast or community cable television. Following the exchange period, every student should keep in touch with overseas buddies and their families by letter, phone and other information swaps. Partner schools should continue to be twinned by satellite television and computer.

Exchange twinning is more appropriate to high schools than primary schools. But there is another kind of twinning that suits both. All schools in Western countries should be twinned for long-term electronic information exchange with schools in developing or culturally/politically different countries. No school should be considered adequate until it is paired. Some North American schools have twinned for years, but most twinning has been superficial and limited to comfortable arrangements with equals, usually in Western Europe.

Costs should be borne by Western governments. It is not just a matter of establishing contacts, maintaining liaison, exchanging information packages, arranging satellite hookups, etc. There will be problems that require diplomatic handling. Real education quickly goes beyond exchange of folk songs. American students will ask questions about Colombia: Why is your murder rate six times higher than America's? Why has the government allowed over fifty judges, a justice minister and a presidential candidate to be murdered by drug dealers? Why have right-wing hit squads been allowed to kill over five hundred members of the left-wing Patriotic Union party? Why did the supreme court of Colombia annul the United States-Colombia extradition treaty and then reinstate it in 1989?

Or about Peru: Why did the government use tanks and tear gas to nationalize the banks? About Ecuador: Why did air force commandos kidnap the President and why did the government give in to their demand that an officer imprisoned for mutiny be released?

And these are questions asked of countries that are nominally democratic! The questions are even more disturbing when asked of the military dictatorships that rule much of the world. They don't welcome questions on human rights violations, nepotism, incompetence or corruption. But such questions must be asked. So must embarrassing questions coming in the other direction: Why does the FBI keep extensive files on American children who seek information on foreign countries? Why did Britain support the racist regime in South Africa by refusing to impose trade sanctions? Why do Canadian prisons hold a disproportionate number of native Indians? It is time children in rich and poor countries asked such questions.

Paulo Freire championed rights for powerless, uneducated adults when he said education must become "the practice of freedom — the means by which men and women deal critically and creatively with reality and discover how to participate in the transformation of their world." If we substitute "children" where Freire had "men and women," his formula is brilliant. Without the substitution, the formula is a well-meaning plea for too little too late.

The global village is in peril. Only our children can save it, only if they are world-minded, and only if **the main activity in global studies is the synthesis of a new, universal value system sifted from the present values of all cultures on earth**.

CHAPTER 7

HEALTH LITERACY

*A good education consists in giving to the body and the soul all the beauty
and all the perfection of which they are capable.*

— Plato

By Plato's standard, twentieth-century education fails. There can be no
beauty and perfection of the body — or intellect — without health. The
sick don't learn well.

Many children are in that gray area between clinical illness and
genuine wellness. Check any classroom for: pallid colour, sallow skin,
pimples, rashes, sores, bruises, dull hair, bloodshot eyes, flaccid muscles,
sunken chests, pot bellies, rolls of fat, sway backs, tantrums, listlessness,
apathy, drowsiness, hyperactivity, runny noses, coughs, breathlessness,
fatigue, headache, dizziness, cramps, constipation, foul breath, decayed
teeth. . . . And check attendance record and parents' notes for an
inventory of absentee illnesses.

Neither schools nor medical clinics do much about rampant, sub-clinical illness. They consider it normal. Yet literature widely available for
years says marginal health can be bettered with diet and exercise. When
more data are in, they may show that high-quality diet is about two-
thirds responsible for optimum health and high-quality exercise one-
third. There are other significant factors, most notably hygiene and
immunization. But in developed countries they tend to be well in hand,
and in all countries, steps to improvement are generally understood and

accepted (though so slow being implemented that, according to UNICEF, 3.5 million children died in 1987 for want of vaccine worth fifty cents per child).

Genetic diseases such as muscular dystrophy are still a scourge and much more research is needed. Other diseases may be caused by a mixture of genetic and environmental factors, the latter being partly or wholly discretionary. Children of parents with drug dependencies are at high risk. About one in six North American families with children in school has a problem-drinker parent. At least eighteen thousand Ontario school children live with an alcoholic. All may suffer alcohol-related birth defects and are more likely than other children to have learning problems, run away, go into foster care, become delinquent, and be victims of physical and/or sexual abuse.

About half the children of alcoholics will become alcoholics, often while still children. Young people become addicted faster than older people, and a lot of young people drink. A 1988 national survey by the U.S. Health and Human Services Department found that twenty-six percent of grade eight students and thirty-eight percent of grade tens had drunk five or more drinks on one occasion in the two preceding weeks. Beer is the drink of choice at teen parties, and hard liquor is often available.

Tobacco is the biggest drug threat to children. In May 1988, the U.S. Surgeon general reported to Congress that cigarette smoking is an addiction similar to cocaine or heroine addiction. The 1989 report said that smoking killed 390,000 Americans in 1985. We have known for years that women smokers often deliver underweight or premature babies more likely than children of non-smoking mothers to develop complications, die in the first month, be hospitalized for respiratory diseases, have learning difficulties, etc. Children with two smoking parents are likely to be ill and absent from school twice as often as children from non-smoking homes. They are also more likely to become smokers.

Hardly anybody becomes a smoker after eighteen. The Canadian Public Health Association reported in 1988 that the starting age for smokers had dropped from sixteen to twelve in just twenty years. Children are also attracted to snuff. In 1988, the British Columbia Cancer Research Centre found that twenty-seven percent of children ages five to eighteen used snuff by holding a lump in their mouths instead of chewing or sniffing it. Half of male students in the southern United States and ninety percent of teenage boys in Norway and Sweden use it.

Though tobacco and alcohol kill far more people than hard drugs and are more dangerous to more children, hard drugs hold more terror for adults who care about children. Tobacco and alcohol have a history of social acceptance whereas banned drugs are under criminal control, are highly and quickly addictive, often contain impurities, are easily over-dosed, and are so expensive that they encourage users to steal money.

Prohibition is to blame for the crime and violence aspect of the drug problem. To end drug-related crime, national governments may legalize and then control the sale of all drugs. That will leave only the social problems that go along with non-medical drugs whether legal or illegal. A sensible response to those problems has been to beef up drug, tobacco and alcohol information in schools, to make programs mandatory and to begin them in early primary school. All that is good and necessary but is not enough. Schools need chapters of Alcoholics Anonymous and similar groups for children already addicted to alcohol, hard drugs, soft drugs and tobacco. For prevention, all schools should have self-help groups with consultants and continuous counselling and support, for children of alcoholics, drug addicts and smokers, and for others at risk.

There are predictors of substance abuse in children: very young children who are aggressive are candidates for addiction. Instead of becoming wholesomely assertive, more and more children are becoming aggressive, even violent. Contributing factors may include television, war toys and sports, but most causes lie in home conditions: broken and dysfunctional families, violent parents, addicted parents, absent adults, rigidly authoritarian adult behaviour, poor diet and, especially, emotional unavailability of adults. All predictors of abuse will have to be monitored by schools and early intervention will have to be a school responsibility.

A characteristic of most children who turn to substance abuse is low self-esteem; it derives initially from home conditions, particularly the emotional unavailability of parents in infancy and later childhood. Genetic predisposition to addictive behaviour may be triggered in some by emotional hunger. Others may respond to emotional neglect with acts of defiance or despair. Society must restore self-esteem by filling the emotional vacuum with other adults who are emotionally available.

A significant reality shared by all children who smoke, drink or use drugs is the present model of childhood; it trivializes the lives of children, represses them, makes them powerless, denies their human and civil rights, impoverishes them. The result is often loss of self-esteem consistent with substance abuse, and in those children who keep some semblance of self-esteem, repressed resentment of lost self-determination is consistent with substance abuse.

In all of society, only the school system is big enough, and permanent enough, to respond boldly to these two real causes of substance abuse. Until both are confronted, all other efforts will be unsuccessful and abuse will continue. We will have to change the model of schooling to meet the challenge. An important first step is to admit that **most children who smoke, drink alcohol and use drugs do so to feel complete — like adults. Schools must lead the way in giving them a better way to feel complete: real emotional support and real power over their own lives.**

There will be resistance from the well-meaning lobby of people who still believe they can save the world by prohibition. They have a stake in the banning industry. People who still claim the family is universally self-correcting will resist. Guilt-ridden parents will resist. One such parent threatened me with a law suit when the press reported my mention at a public meeting of an alcoholic child I was counselling in junior high school; I had not revealed which child! The biggest obstacle may be the ever-present millions of parents who are themselves abusers of alcohol or hard drugs or both.

Children consume up to 2500 drugs and chemicals every day in food, liquid and air. The following were listed on the label of bread sold as hundred percent whole wheat: calcium propitionate, colour, calcium sulphate, ammonium chloride, potassium bromate, tricalcium phosphate, 1-cysteine hydrochloride and sodium stearoyl-2-lactylate. Pharmacology tells us which chemicals will kill us immediately. It sometimes tells us what amounts are safe in the short run but cannot identify many of the adverse reactions people will have nor which individuals will have them. Nor can it tell us who will die twenty years later from delayed reactions. And pharmacology tells us nothing about interacting effects of 2500 chemicals consumed daily.

Some effects may be on the brain. One in six Ontario children has an identifiable psychiatric disorder, but only twenty percent of them receive professional treatment. And treatment by mental health professionals rarely deals with individual reaction to chemicals. Lead may be implicated in behavioral disturbances. By the time they start school, half a million Canadian children have unsafe blood levels of lead according to standards of U.S. Centres for Disease Control. One reason is that before 1990 the Canadian government considered the cost to corporations of retrofitting refineries to produce unleaded gas more important than the health of poisoned children. In Mexico City, Bangkok and many third world cities poisoning has genocidal proportions.

Fire and traffic accidents take a huge toll. Large numbers of children are physically and sexually abused at home. Reports on contagious diseases continue to be shocking; 2.5 million American children have venereal diseases. A small news item in the *Toronto Star* of August 21, 1989 put the problem in a context previously reserved for measles and mumps; it reported that a fifteen year-old-girl had infected two neighborhood boys, eight and nine, with gonorrhea. AIDS is a growing threat to teens. Schools must teach honestly and fully about these matters from earliest childhood.

The effects of diet and exercise on health are so powerful that they demand our greatest efforts. They are critically important factors in alleviating or preventing health problems in childhood and later life. It is fair to say that home and school, through control of nutrition and exercise, hold not only the beauty and perfection of the bodies and souls of children in their hands but also their very lives. The trust has been betrayed. Not even the most innovative concepts for improvement of schooling, such as open education, have included high obligatory standards for exercise and nutrition.

Nutrition

Large numbers of children are unwell and absent so frequently that their skills cannot be developed by teachers. Students who are present are apt to lack energy or be hyperactive.

A school board survey in Ottawa reported in 1978 that over fourteen percent of children six to twelve were hyperactive. Many teachers estimate the figure at fifteen to twenty percent. The average classroom has three or more children, usually boys, who are explosive and chronically disruptive unless drugged, usually with Ritalin. The chronically inattentive are likely to be diagnosed as having attention deficit disorder and given that drug. Yet pioneers like the American pediatrician and allergist Dr. Benjamin Feingold have demonstrated since the sixties that a third to half of such children become normal with improved diets alone.

For nearly as long, Dr. Abram Hoffer, the Canadian psychiatrist world-renowned for his megavitamin treatment of schizophrenia, has been telling us that half of children with behavioral and learning disorders need more vitamin B3 and a quarter need more B6 than could be supplied by good diet. Their bodies have a biochemical need for additional vitamins, not for drugs like Ritalin. When vitamins are supplied, their behaviour and learning problems diminish and often disappear. It seems reasonable to conclude that behaviour and achievement of the entire school population would improve significantly just by switching all children to optimum nutrition. And at the same time, we would give children longer, healthier lives. But we have failed to act.

The best name one can put to it is negligence, but it is more than that. It is contempt for the young. Future commentators may be more explicit and call it genocide. The evidence will not be hard to find: many children are diagnosed with high cholesterol levels; autopsies on fifteen-year-old accident victims routinely disclose plaque in arteries and other degeneration associated with poor diet and lack of exercise; only five percent of youth get enough exercise for cardiovascular health. It is all on record.

So is the horrendous body count from cancer, heart attack, stroke, diabetes and half a dozen other scourges that follows years of neglecting diet and exercise. All victims are graduates of nutrition and exercise programs as provided, or rather, not provided, in twentieth-century homes and schools. A federal survey released by Statistics Canada in April 1988 said one in three persons will be struck by cancer, the number-one killer disease. At least a third to half of cancer cases and probably far more could be prevented. In November 1985 the American Cancer Society published ten steps to cancer prevention. Nine had to do with what people voluntarily put into their mouths.

The second greatest killer, cardio-vascular disease, has had so much publicity that even some illiterates know it is largely caused by poor diet, lack of exercise and smoking. The number three cause of death, diabetes, has had less publicity. In the mid-twentieth century, only ten percent of diabetes was caused by poor diet and lack of exercise. The other ninety percent derived from genetic predisposition. It took just forty years to reverse the figures. Now, ninety percent of diabetes is due to faulty life style and only ten percent to genes. More than half a million people become diabetic every year in North America. One child in five born late in the century will become diabetic.

National economies are devastated by escalating costs of illness. Hardly any of the money is spent on health, nearly all on sickness, most of it discretionary — caused by poor nutrition, lack of exercise, smoking, drinking alcohol and taking drugs. The sickness industry devours more money than education and will soon be second in misappropriation only to the military. The euphemistic label "health services" should be changed to "sickness services." Maintaining separate government budgets and departments for sickness and health might blast the public into realizing the stupidity of subsidizing discretionary sickness and lifestyles that cause it.

A turn-around would require that half of doctors focus on health instead of sickness. People taught in schools to do so, should take responsibility for their own health aided by doctors who know about nutrition, exercise and positive thinking. Every high school graduate should be sufficiently health literate not only to accurately describe symptoms but also to discuss with doctors all aspects of health.

Parents, politicians and educators, have virtually ignored the real causes of ill health and early death for millions, and rail instead about imagined threats to normal life span of children who safely share classrooms with AIDS victims. Or they fasten upon the remote possibility of attack by a stranger as the great threat and throw their energies into isolating children from adults by over-zealous streetproofing. Or they fantasize fabulous futures in a sedentary, back-to-basics curriculum.

We can't plead ignorance. I have hundreds of newspaper clippings that amount to a course in nutrition, and a library of paperback nutrition books available everywhere. Some of the information is conflicting, some complex. Still, the thoughtful and conscientious lay person can keep abreast of developments. But the majority of adults are illiterate, semi-literate or simply don't read substantial information in books or newspapers. Publishers have also printed specific warnings about poor nutrition. On April 14, 1973 the *Toronto Star* ran a typical front page story in the weekend edition that reached over 750,000 homes across Canada. The headline read, **"Bad eating habits of school children called epidemic**." The story quoted me correctly as saying:

— poor nutrition among school children is a serious problem that not only affects health but also the ability to learn; in a lot of schools it's reaching the stage where it's an epidemic; poor nutrition is not just a problem that affects the poor — you can see horrendous things among the well-to-do; people just don't know the importance of eating properly.

Warnings have gone unheeded. A National Cancer Institute study published in the *American Journal of Public Health* in spring 1988 reported: more than eighty percent of Americans eat no high fibre cereals or whole grain breads; daily consumption of quality fibre is only about a third of the desireable amount (three slices of whole wheat bread or three-and-a-half loaves of white bread supply the minimum requirement); most Americans eat no fruit on a typical day and twenty percent eat no vegetables.

Also in 1988, Health Management Resources of Boston and the Canadian Obesity Research Foundation warned that forty percent of Americans and thirty-three percent of Canadians would be obese by the turn of the century. The rate for those morbidly obese has increased ninety-eight percent since 1960. Adult obesity has gone up by fifteen percent, teenage obesity by thirty-nine percent and pre-teen obesity by an astonishing fifty-four percent. The usual North American diet is more than forty percent fat, mostly saturated, and sugar consumption averages a staggering 125 pounds per person per year. Many get half their calories from sugar.

A 1989 survey of member school boards by the Canadian Education Association, revealed that junk food lunches are the norm. A Nova Scotia board reported, "many children have a can of pop and a bag of chips for lunch." An Alberta board said, "Many children are poorly nourished not necessarily as a result of poverty. More often than not, it is a lack of parental training or caring."

In 1968, I walked most mornings past a tobacco shop as children were hurrying to school. Every day the same ones bought candy bars for breakfast. I asked the merchant why he didn't stock something more wholesome. I asked the school why they didn't serve breakfast. I asked the children why they didn't eat breakfast at home. In 1992, I walked past the same shop. A new generation was buying bigger candy bars for breakfast. I didn't ask anybody anything. I already knew the answers. Nobody cares. Only thirty percent of Canadian high schools even ban the sale of chocolate bars by their own students for fund raising. Plato is dead.

He would die all over again if he could see what nutritional neglect does to our children. A bus-load of boy scouts from Florida ate their way through a string of fast food outlets and candy counters in the United States and Canada. I encountered them between snacks in the shower room at the Y in Toronto. I thought they must be from some special camp for obese children. But the scoutmasters assured me they were just troop regulars. At least a quarter were swathed in blubber. Others were less larded but still pot bellied, and three or four were merely marshmallow soft. Some were skinny. Only one had some semblance of musculature. By the standard of ancient Greece they were rejects. The Spartans would have put them out to die of exposure on mountainsides. Instead, we kill them slowly with saturated fat, empty calories and inactivity.

Children have a right to proper nutrition that begins before conception. One can hardly expect healthy ova and sperm to develop on a junk diet of fried fat, sugar, white flour, caffeine, nicotine, alcohol and assorted chemicals. One evidence is decrease in the sperm count of young men. And sperm that do develop are increasingly apt to be clumped or lethargic. So determined is nature to reproduce the species, however, that some sickly sperm find their way to enervated eggs.

During gestation, maternal diet is critical to fetal health. Yet every pregnant woman is free to insult the fetus with trash food and violate it with chemicals. Whether through intention, ignorance, indifference or indigence, the ill-nourished mother condemns her unborn child to an inferior life. A widely publicized 1973 report of the U.S. National Academy of Sciences warned "brain growth may be directly affected if the fetus is malnourished due to improper nutrition for the mother."

More than a decade before that, at the Montreal Diet Dispensary, the renowned Agnes Higgins realized that malnourished mothers produced undersized babies who were more likely than other children to be sickly and have learning disorders. By 1973, she had shown that mothers given inexpensive food and vitamin supplements produced normal weight, healthy babies. The U.S. Centres for Disease Control studied three thousand babies born from 1968 through 1980 and found that women who took multivitamins for three months before and after becoming pregnant ran about half the risk of bearing a baby with spina bifida or other neural tube defects.

Newborn children are victimized by a powerful baby food industry that touts the glory of processed pap and disparages breast feeding. Yet UNICEF estimates that over four million infant deaths each year could be prevented by breast feeding. And many more millions of children would be healthier all their lives if breast fed by well-nourished mothers.

Poor children are the most victimized by inadequate nutrition, even in wealthy countries. At least seventeen percent of Canadian children and even more Americans, are poor. They tend to be born and grow up smaller and weaker. They have a greater risk of learning disorders, illnesses and absence from school. If their mothers smoke they are at even greater risk of being born prematurely and underweight, and more likely to be hospitalized and absent from school.

This at a time when health/fitness is touted as a craze. Perhaps it is. But mainly for an element of the middle class. And even in that limited group the notion prevails that exercise is paramount rather than diet. The exercise industry gets full marks for having generated the craze. If the food industry had done it, youngish, upwardly-aspiring urban professionals who are stalwarts of exercise fever, might be swarming to low-fat cooking courses and vitamin supplement seminars instead of aerobics classes and weight training workshops. Still, interest in nutrition is picking up and follows along somewhere behind exercise as an in-thing among trend setters. Surveys show as many as half of shoppers expressing some concern about good nutrition even if they don't yet practice it regularly.

Realization that we are destroying our bodies by internal pollution is seeping slowly into public consciousness as did the realization that we are destroying our planet by external pollution. Some farsighted teachers in a few schools are helping generate a nutrition movement. Their students conduct experiments and search the literature collecting data for essays and projects that illuminate nutrition problems and suggest solutions.

At the same time, schools are among the worst nutritional offenders. Try in any school cafeteria to buy a hamburger of low-fat meat seasoned with herbs instead of salt and garnished with fresh vegetables instead of sugar, salt and chemical concoctions; and try to get it on a whole-grain bun. No other kind should be available, but the acceptable one is the only kind not usually available. Or try to buy a glass of skim milk. Either it is not available or is laced with sugar and chocolate. Fried and other saturated fat foods abound even though the 1991 report of a U.S. government task force on health (the National Cholesterol Education Program) insisted that from age two children should restrict intake of all fats to thirty percent or less and saturated fats to ten percent or less of total calories.

The same school that sells saturated fat lunches may have classroom nutrition lessons with the right messages, but they are cancelled out by the cafeteria message. I have seen nutrition displays on bulletin boards above classroom tables where small children were being served sugary artificial drinks and chocolate cookies. The lesson was clear enough: talk about good nutrition but don't practice it. Be a hypocrite. Children learn that lesson early and well.

The rhetoric of health curriculum never translates into an individualized nutrition program for each child or even a generalized nutrition program practiced by each child and monitored by the school. And there is no guarantee that the classroom nutrition message even exists. By 1989, only nineteen states in the U.S. had made nutrition education a requirement.

Many teachers flaunt their disregard for nutrition. Some sponsor chocolate bar or cookie sales to raise funds. Coaches hand out fatty donuts and syrupy drinks. Role-model teachers eat junk and promote its use. In the *Toronto Star* of March 7, 1989, such a teacher was praised in a column: "He uses magic candy, pizza deliveries and a class field trip to McDonald's — all to make high school math easy and fun." The writer described that math teacher as "a role model who should inspire others to use imagination." Among his imaginative inspirations was a class trip for breakfast of forty percent fat at a junk food outlet and chocolate bars handed out to his students in the middle of exams as a "pick-me-up!"

In schools, we teach children to avoid running into traffic, but we don't turn around and shove them off the curb. We teach them to avoid drugs, but we don't turn around and ply them with crack. Why should we teach children to avoid destructive food and then supply them with it? Partly because most adults are themselves too irresponsible to manage their own diets and feel less guilty if they pull the next generation down with them. Partly because of indifferent physicians most of whom have never been closer to a study of nutrition than a token course in biochemistry and many of whom are hostile to orthomolecular concepts of medicine that consider nutrients critically important. Partly because the junk food industry is powerful and insidious in undermining important nutrition information that has become available to schools and to everyone who can read. Fast food moguls have invaded Children's Hospitals and are now peddling their wares from outlets lodged like tumors in the very insides of sickness centres that are themselves sick.

The nutrition crisis affects all countries. Eventually governments must act. To date, they have only issued warnings. The 1988 report of the U.S. Surgeon General summarized the certain causal relationship between poor diet and deadly disease but did nothing about it beyond reporting. Warnings are useful only to the favored few who are literate and accustomed to receiving and implementing print information.

The occasional fleeting involvement of local, state or national governments in school nutrition has usually been trivial and often misguided in that hunger and poor nutrition are treated as one. **All who are hungry suffer also from poor nutrition, but all who suffer from poor nutrition are not hungry; hunger affects a lot of lower-class children while poor nutrition affects vastly larger numbers of the lower, middle and upper classes.** Governments or volunteer groups sometimes scurry into action to fill empty stomachs, but most such programs serve poor children with inferior foods.

Ontario has at least 300,000 poor children. The best school-centred program I could identify in Toronto claimed to be teaching nutrition while it filled bellies with such junk as bacon, fried eggs, white-flour bread and pancakes, syrup, table fats, jam, cocoa and sugar. But even if a program for poor children did serve nutritious food, it would not be addressing the more important problem — poor nutrition among all children. Unfortunately, hunger programs disguise the need for universal nutrition programs.

Sometimes, here and there, an individual, group or jurisdiction takes thoughtful action on nutrition or exercise or both. In the mid-eighties, Rio de Janeiro switched students from their usual overburdened, three-shift schools to a new kind of neighborhood schools called "integrated centres for public education," with attendance hours from eight a.m. to five p.m. and three nutritious meals a day for all. Also included were free medical and dental care and a covered exercise area. The crowning achievement in a brilliant innovation was a student residence at each school for those most in need. This stunning revision in schooling didn't take the rest of the world or even the rest of Brazil by storm. Instead, it remained a curiosity, much commended but not emulated. One wonders what vestiges will remain after ten years even in Rio. Most innovations in schooling remain localized and eventually peter out because funding ceases or because the driving force, usually one person or a small group, moves on, gives up or dies, or because the innovation could not survive, grafted like a healthy alien organ, to the brain-dead body of mother school.

Serious efforts to improve the health of all students will continue to be frustrated by the existing model of schooling because it makes students passive recipients. Only when students are active agents in their own schooling can we expect every student to pursue a personal nutrition and exercise program. Nonetheless, **national governments should take a great leap toward universal health by supplying two nutritious meals and vitamin supplements daily to all children who wish to partake.**

Governments should also insist that all foods, from produce in markets to restaurant meals, be sold with complete nutrition information including details of all ingredients, additives and pesticides. The language of package information should be standardized so that all children can be taught to read and understand it. Call it nutrition literacy.

Exercise

Since the sixties there have been hundreds of articles in North American newspapers detailing deplorable fitness in children and urging rigorous exercise in schools as a remedy. On June 3, 1978, *The Canadian*, then Canada's largest circulation magazine, carried yet another article on the poor physical condition of school children titled "**Growing Up Old**." It characterized me as "a staunch advocate of increased physical education in schools" and quoted me correctly as saying:

> The school reflects the society and this society considers physical activity (in the school curriculum) as a frill.

Neither the public nor governments paid much attention except for ritual surveys and token projects in a few schools. There were voices raised and articles written by individual educators, but power structures never got the message.

In 1974–5, the Japan Teachers' Union objected to plans of the Education Ministry to conduct a nation-wide survey of physical fitness in primary and junior high schools. (The Health and Physical Education Council had expressed concern about the increased number of obese Japanese children and disquieting changes in patterns of childhood illness.) The teachers' union thought such a survey might promote rivalry among children or that results might be used in recruiting the fit for national defence forces! Individual teachers I spoke to seemed somewhat less obtuse. Most sounded merely indifferent or suggested survey funds be used instead to build playgrounds. A few favored the survey as a way to further alert the profession and the public to the problem.

If hype in the sixties and seventies had little success in improving fitness, follow-up in the eighties was no more effective. In Texas, a large scale 1983–84 study revealed that children were in much worse condition than in 1974. Concern was widely expressed. One might have expected radical intervention. Yet when I questioned teenagers in San Antonio for two days in 1987, I could not find one that had a personal exercise program. Many didn't even take physical education at school, and those who did described what seemed to be a sports and recreation rather than a fitness program. Few had anything close to satisfactory eating habits. None could tell me the approximate fat content of hamburgers and fries they were eating when I interviewed them.

Nationwide in 1987, according to the U.S. Department of Education, states required on average only 1.4 years of gym time in high school. Since then several states have considered reducing gym time to make more time for academic subjects. In Canada, in 1987, the University of Toronto surveyed fourteen-year-olds and found two-thirds of girls and half of boys could not do a single chin-up. Don't expect improvement. Only a quarter of Canadian teenagers take physical education classes at high school! Most fourteen-year-olds are in their first year of high school and, in Ontario, students are required to take only one credit in physical education (110 clock hours) in their entire four years.

Over three-quarters of those 110 hours are taken up with health classes, tests, examinations, announcements, getting to and from the gym, changing clothes, showering, watching demonstrations, hearing instructions, learning game rules, waiting turns, watching from sidelines, sitting on benches, being absent from school, skipping classes and being preempted by school closures for administrative convenience such as teachers' professional development days. Typically, students in a forty-five minute physical-activity period exert themselves less than five minutes. In New Jersey, the state department of education found that thirty percent of gym time was spent on trivia and of the remaining seventy percent, only a quarter was spent on fitness. The rest of the time went to team sports of marginal, if any, exercise value to most students.

Generally, physical education programs are concerned with health lessons in classrooms and with sports rather than exercise. School (and community) team sports are too intermittent to be more than accessories to a proper exercise program. Conditioning exercise before the season for a team sport is not usually well done and rarely sustained year round. Organized team sports require skill and constancy, so they usually serve the few who are skilled and interested over the many who are either or neither. The many usually become observers who sit in health classes learning game rules so they will know when to cheer.

Team sports are too expensive in time and money. Children waste hours packing gear, commuting to games, getting dressed and undressed, being instructed, sitting on benches and just standing around. The dollar cost for coaches, officials, transportation, facilities and equipment is huge. Football and hockey are the worst but not the only offenders. In 1991 dollars it cost parents, schools, sponsors or communities about $1200 dollars to outfit one boy for minor hockey (more for premium quality or goalie equipment): elbow, shin, and shoulder pads; shin pad straps; garter belt; girdle; gloves; helmet; face mask; protective jock support; regular pants; short and long shell pants; socks; skates; sticks; tape; suspenders; throat guard; bag. . . .

Add to that: arena admissions, registration fees, practice-time charges, repairs, tournament fees, gasoline, parking, snack food, etc. Parents of a child in top-level competition say it costs over $5000 a season. Injuries cost even more — sometimes, life in a wheelchair. It is sobering to check any paraplegic ward for hockey and football victims. According to a medical research team from the Canadian Sports Spine and Head Injuries Research Centre at Toronto Western Hospital, there were in Ontario alone seventy-nine cases of "catastrophic damage" from hockey in 1986.

The cost of moral injury is incalculable as students emulate the goons of professional football, hockey and baseball. By the late eighties, even basketball, as epitomized by Georgetown University and the Detroit Pistons, became an object lesson in fist, elbow and knee violence and in foul language, degrading gibes and ugly gestures.

Our obsession with adult-run team sports for children derives from four hundred years of boarding schools in Europe and America. Boys segregated and contained twenty-four hours a day, months at a time, on isolated eighteenth-and nineteenth-century campuses had to be kept busy and physically exhausted to keep them from lusty thoughts and practices. It worked, more or less, and the mystique grew that simulated battle rituals on the back campus under complex rules must at least tame the libido, assure conformity and act as spiritual tonic.

It was even proclaimed by headmasters, affirmed by chaplains and applauded by old boys, that aggression on the playing field dissipated aggressive tendencies rendering participants benignly peace-loving! Sober reflection and intelligent observation would have revealed the opposite to be true: aggression begets aggression, but then as now, true believers are not given to sober reflection and intelligent observation. That the Almighty was definitely on-side was assured and attested by assigning to games a sanctity status only marginally lower than chapel. To game was almost divine. Thus blessed, the school playing field was seen as a sure route for boys to corridors of power in government, industry and business. And in the twentieth century, to branches of show business known as college and professional sport.

The myth was cultivated that athletic activity somehow enhances academic achievement. Yet a study by the Women's Sports Foundation released in 1989 revealed no such relationship in a sample of thirty thousand American high school students tracked for six years.

The mystique lingers. Most of us recall reverently whipped-up emotions of long-gone high school football games because they were about the only approved outlets for pent-up emotions, actual sex being taboo. The blessed relief enjoyed is so warmly remembered that we assume the whole experience must have been at least character-building if not positively transcendental. Actually, it was neither. It was just organized aggression from which we learned aggression (and maybe how to get drunk from a hip flask).

It is ironic that team sports supposed to keep the young away from sex, carry sexual undertones, often aggressive. The hugs and bum-pats of victory are preceded by forceful body contact and that is preceded by team initiation rituals that often feature nakedness, shaving of pubic hair, domination and subservience, humiliation, flagellation. . . Locker and shower-room horseplay follows games. Between games lots of high school jocks inject each other in the butt with steroids.

Left to their own devices, children will organize, supervise and play rigorous games that have high-order social and exercise value. The best are often games children invent, but even traditional games take on real life when students run them. The less adults interfere, the more everybody runs, jumps and plays with zest. If adults help with facilities and consultancy, the games experience becomes as well, a high-order learning experience for children. **All team sports at schools should be organized, managed, coached, officiated and played entirely by students with teachers acting only as consultants.** Adult "teaching" should consist of teaching instead of performing the roles of instructor, coach, referee, manager, etc. The main measure of successful sports teachers or coaches should be their achievements in having students perform all management and instructional roles.

Community and little-league sports should follow the same model, but whether they do or not, schools should immediately opt out of adult-run team sports. And even student-run sports should be limited to relatively safe, non-violent and inexpensive choices and all should be played only as extra-curricular activities. Even though they have real exercise and learning value if student-run, they are not cost-effective in terms of time used regularly in a crowded curriculum. **Until team sports are banned from physical education programs and placed where they belong in student-run, after-hours recreation programs, lazy and glory-seeking teachers and coaches will continue to opt for them instead of real physical training.** And in the worst cases, many public and private high schools will continue to be athletic factories dedicated to churning out products for colleges dedicated to sports show biz.

Physical education must be compulsory and programs must guarantee a half hour daily of actual, sustained, rigorous exercise for every child starting in early childhood and continuing through all years of schooling. And every child should learn exercise skills that last a lifetime: swimming, calisthenics, racquet sports, weight training, power walking, cross-country skiing, etc. An array of stretching, muscle-toning, and cardio-vascular exercises should be second nature to everyone.

Even primary school students should know and be able to demonstrate and describe their own daily exercise programs, and older students should be able to explain the purpose of each component in their programs and modifications they expect to make as they age. Incredibly, most students have no such exercise programs. They may go through some motions sporadically at school, but there is no continuity, no daily workout, no cumulative record, no fitness profile, no remedial or developmental plan, no regular assessment, no individual goals, no sense of personal responsibility.

Instead we get excuses: not enough space, inadequate showers, shortage of trained staff, students unwilling to get sweaty, etc. All excuses would disappear if will and imagination prevailed. An exercise program that meets minimum requirements could be started in every school within days. Dancing is the exercise of choice for most children so it could be used. Not folk dancing or ballroom dancing or anything choreographed or slow or taught. Just currently-popular, non-stop, high-energy dancing every day for the last half-hour of an extended school day would satisfy both exercise and social needs. It could be done without significant cost — in classrooms, corridors, gyms, cafeterias and outdoors. All schools should add chinning bars across a corner of every classroom for upper body exercise.

Most schools could double the daily aerobic session by having every child run all the way home to shower after dancing. Those travelling by bus could load their gear and then run to a pick-up point.

Any new model of schooling must do all of the following to meet minimum health program standards:

1. Before each child enters school, and at least yearly thereafter, do a thorough physical examination, including a fitness and nutrition assessment, and then outline a developmental regimen in words children and parents can understand.

2. For every child, open a fitness (exercise) file and a nutrition file both of which are updated regularly throughout schooling and, thereafter, throughout life.

3. As soon as children are able to do computer or hand-written entries, have them maintain their own files, and even before that, help them verbalize the appropriate entries even though adults actually record them.

4. Make certain each child's file constantly indicates appropriate food and exercise clearly detailed in the child's own words and make sure a teacher or trained volunteer reviews the file with each child at least once a month to assess achievement and restate goals.

5. Get rid of all junk food in schools and mount unrelenting campaigns to remove it from school neighborhoods.

6. Serve a nutritious breakfast, lunch and snacks at school, free of charge.

7. Provide free vitamin and mineral supplements on a voluntary-use basis.

8. Schedule each child for at least a half-hour of formal, compulsory, vigorous, sustained exercise daily, exclusive of sports and games, using before-school, noon and after-school hours, with trained volunteers in charge where teachers are not available. When school hours are extended, compulsory exercise can be included during the school day or as vigorous, sustained dancing for everybody in the last scheduled half-hour.

9. Make health, particularly fitness exercise and nutrition, a compulsory school program at all levels, and require satisfactory participation and achievement before participation in optional programs for credit is allowed.

10. Establish a free, full-service, medical and dental health clinic at every school (or in the community and affiliated with nearby schools).

CHAPTER 8

SEX LITERACY

One must accept that the young human has always been biologically ready, in fact optimally equipped, to mate between the ages of thirteen and sixteen.

— Robert Ollendorff, *Children's Rights*
(London: Panther, 1972)

Irrelevance by omission is a major cause of the education mess, and the absence of comprehensive sex education is an example. You will search in vain in the writings of John Dewey and reformers who followed him for inclusion of compulsory and complete sex education as an essential in any new model of schooling. Open education was closed education in this respect.

Ignorance of sex is still widely regarded as an advantage for the young. More than fifty years after Alfred C. Kinsey brought sex out of the closet, most schools have not brought it into classrooms. Many have not even brought it into the school library. At least ten American states and three Canadian provinces do not specify any sex education, and most that do either make it optional or treat it superficially, infrequently or too late. We have to confront reasons for this untenable situation. It is not enough to dismiss sexuality as complex and contentious, nor to pussyfoot forever around problems by using incomplete sex education programs or none.

Sexuality is so important that the advantage of having control of it has not escaped notice by social, political and religious institutions since the dawn of civilization. As psychoanalyst Wilhelm Reich pointed out, repression of sex is the main method of inducing conformism. Repression starts in infancy and is firmly entrenched by age six. Adults, themselves repressed by institutional manipulation of sexuality, are only too willing to collaborate in sexual repression of children because they know conformism will make control at home and school easier. There is no thought, short of nuclear war, quite so terrifying to sexually repressed and dysfunctional adults as the power they imagine would be generated by liberated sexual energies of the young.

Unfortunately, controlling institutional forces have always based control codes more upon ignorance, myth, superstition and self-serving invention than upon knowledge, truth and respect for rights of individuals. In this aspect, Christianity is among the most blameworthy of institutions and shows little sign of making amends. Only Christianity, among world religions is inimical to the flesh. But that perverted hatred was added to Christianity long after Christ died. He would have been shocked at such a turn. His teaching did not attribute to sexual acts the dangers and sinister powers that are now part of Christianity. For the first two hundred years and more, Christian clergy married. Thereafter, as Europe faded into the black night of the Dark Ages, sexual sideshows such as consecrated virgins, castrated theologians and celibate priests became part of the act.

With much of civilization disintegrating into superstition, Augustine (354–430 A.D.) threw into the mix his invention of original sin, a doctrine which transformed sexual desire from a joyous gift of God to a perpetually frightening symbol of human sinfulness. The connection between sex and sin had been concocted. And it brewed throughout the Dark Ages. By the time enlightenment returned with the Renaissance, the brew had poisoned Christian thought, and to this day, nobody has found an antidote or a method of filtering accumulated poison out of Christian consciousness. Churches are prisons of sexual sublimation when they should be centres for celebration of all wonders including sexuality.

It is largely because we mistakenly think sex dirty and sinful that we refuse to accept and welcome the natural, developing sexuality of children — the better to save them from filth and sin. But there may be another reason — subconscious, repressed adult jealousy of the superior sexual charms and capabilities of teens. That they are more beautiful cannot be hidden. That teenage females are more alluring is sufficiently obvious that pious pillars of society must constantly lash out at elements of society that acknowledge the fact, particularly in advertising. It is equally true though not so obvious that teenage males would always out-shoot their fathers and uncles, if the sex game were played on a level field. And they would always recover first to shoot again and again. It is too ego-shattering to contemplate, so older generations pretend it isn't so. It is reminder enough of adult decay when teens exhibit superiority in tennis, swimming, skating, gymnastics, dancing, modelling, fashion, computer innovations, etc. We draw the line at sex.

Western Christianity's extreme neurotic obsession with genitalia and their uses may be unique but a major concomitant of that obsession, morbid prudishness, is also evident in one form or other, for one reason or other, in many non-Christian societies. Perverted prudishness thrives wherever illiteracy, functional illiteracy, ignorance, brainwashing, early indoctrination and blind faith exist along with entrenched religious or political power structures which benefit from control of sexuality. Prudishness fuels resistance to sex education in schools.

On three visits to China in the seventies, I was told by teachers that no sex information was in print except that there might be a few pre-Maoist biology texts from which the section on human reproduction had not been entirely removed. I was assured that birth control devices and information were given to everyone at marriage, not before, and that everyone thought that quite enough. In 1980, the post-Maoist government issued a sex manual that was superficial, inaccurate and silly. Masturbation was called "hand lewdness," and readers were assured it could be overcome by unswerving loyalty to socialism. That manual was considered too adult for school use. Somewhat better information issued for high schools in the late eighties met with widespread resistance from school and home. Many teachers and parents preferred no sex education at all. Parallels between Chinese and American situations are striking.

In India, there is virtually no sex education in schools, and even birth control information and devices are far from universal especially for the young and single. The population explosion is devastating. There is a birth each second. By the year 2000 the population will exceed that of China. I rode down from Chandigar to Delhi with an engineer who told at length how he wished schools would teach his children about sex since he could not, because of "cultural embarrassment," his term for debilitating prudishness. On the side of a building I saw the Indian alternative to sex education, this advertisement:

Abortion by Suction Process in Two Minutes, Family Planning Hospital, 34A Sashi Bhusan St.

One thing that will have to be accepted before we can have good sex education is that all teenage and some pre-teen children are sexual. When I completed a doctoral level course in psychology as a reading rather than a lecture program, one of the surprises was the number of direct and indirect references to pre-teen sexuality. In a sense, all children are sexual. In his book, *The Sex Researchers* (Boston: Little Brown, 1969), Edward M. Brecher says, "Human sexuality is not a phenomenon which makes its appearance in puberty and/or during adolescence, it is rather clearly visible during infancy and early childhood." Certainly, children are learning about their sexuality, learning to be sexual, all the time. **Sex education can never deal entirely with anticipated tomorrows; it must also acknowledge today.**

There is a clear public preference that teens not be sexually active which is in direct conflict with nature's (God's) clear preference that they be very active. Teenagers are caught in the middle. It is not their fault that God made them sexual or that opportunities for expressing that sexuality through coupling are now denied them. Till recently in human history, people coupled shortly after puberty. We behaved like other species.

Then physical maturation became earlier largely due to changes in lifestyle, particularly diet, and in disease control. Social maturation was hastened by communications and changed roles. Most late-twentieth-century fifteen-year-olds have been fully capable sexually for at least two years and many for three or four; and they are as generally sophisticated as twenty-year-olds were a few generations ago. Logic would have had society finding ways to move the age of coupling downward to match earlier maturation. Instead, society moved it several years in the opposite direction by keeping the young financially, legally and emotionally dependent further into adulthood. **In no other species are the sexually ready denied all sexual expression for five to ten years after maturation.**

With other innate drives, we permit or encourage expression as soon as capability exists: eating, smiling, walking, talking, exploring, thinking, creating, loving, etc. We even tolerate and provide suitable outlets for less appealing human traits such as aggression, envy and revenge. **Sex stands alone in the vehemence with which any expression of their drive is forbidden the young long after they are driven.**

Excuses for this extraordinary oppression are transparent. Some say teens are not emotionally ready for sex, but emotional trauma from consensual sex is rare and seldom if ever suicidal, whereas emotional trauma from academic and other approved competition is common and too often suicidal. And we routinely devastate children with traumas for which they are "not emotionally ready": parental fighting, divorce, custody battles, abandonment, poverty, hunger, malnutrition, physical battering, sexual abuse, corporal punishment, denial of rights, lovelessness, etc. Consensual sex seems, in comparison, benign. And research reports it to be so.

Others say health risks to mother and baby are greater in very young pregnant women. True — but largely because of improper care. Nearly all risks could be overcome with nutrition, lifestyle and medical supervision. There are also greatly increased risks for mother and baby when women over forty get pregnant and nobody would dream of forbidding them sex. Besides, birth control devices would be as effective for teens as for anyone if they were readily available and properly used. But they are not. And alternatives to intercourse could be just as effective if they were socially approved and known to all teens. But they are not.

The most satisfying, hundred-percent-effective form of birth control may be oral genital sex to climax. Other viable alternatives include mutual masturbation and sexual petting. Then there is the non-sexual alternative of just saying no. In a sexually neurotic society, the latter may require even more in-depth sex education than other alternatives. And it will require a change in our model of childhood and our concept of children's rights because many of the people to whom teens will have to say no (or yes) are adults.

Under the present model of childhood and the current concept of children's rights, children are not likely to say no to the very people most likely to abuse them sexually, their parents and other people around home. They are conditioned by reward and punishment to acquiesce. **Children will continue to be exploited and abused in every way, including sexually, until they share with adults the unequivocal right to say no to anybody in all situations except those involving accident prevention or observance of fair rules.**

Teens are subject to as many dangers from voluntary sex as older people: disease, dysfunction, unwanted pregnancy, abortion, disappointment, dissatisfaction, emotional lows, etc. They are also subject to as many sexual rewards as older people: relief, pleasure, joy, togetherness, satisfaction, emotional highs, etc. What teens are not subject to is any acceptable outlet for their sexuality.

Earlier civilizations, other parts of the modern world, and major Western scholars have recognized childhood sexuality, but it remains a taboo subject in the very Western countries where models for schooling have developed in modern times and spread worldwide; consequently, nothing on the topic is included in curriculum and childhood sexual practices continue in their primitive modes without benefit of enlightenment.

This at a time when earlier physical and social maturation has moved sex-related activity into the pre-teen group. Many females use cosmetics and glamorous clothing and hairstyles at age ten or earlier. The bump and grind gyrations of teens and young adults are also the norm in pre-teen dancing. Song lyrics are sexual. Dating begins before teen years. Sexual suggestion and flirtation permeate pre-teen phone chatter. All this is part of the redefinition of childhood that has already taken place in Western countries in spite of scorn heaped upon each aspect. But more than Western countries are affected.

UNESCO estimates there are forty million pre-teen street children in the world living a precarious existence on their own. I have seen thousands of them in Asia, Africa and South America — nearly everywhere except developed countries where there are lots of teens living on the street but not pre-teens. (That may be changing, especially in America. In 1989, when Houston opened a shelter for children living alone on the street, first to move in was a twelve-year-old girl.)

Pre-teen street children are usually sexually active, often regularly. Sex is one of their few joys and prostitution one of their few sources of income. And forty million street children entirely on their own are just the visible minority. Other millions live more or less "at home" but in economic or cultural conditions which make sexual expression for pleasure or profit part of their lives. While the numbers of such marginal children are far greater in poorer countries, they exist in all countries.

Because of the correlation with poverty, the facile response is to "blame" economic circumstance for childhood sexuality. That is wrong. Poverty is to blame for the degradation, exploitation and prostitution of children but not for their sexuality. Nature (God) gave them that. **For Western middle-class prudes to pretend child sexuality doesn't exist or to dismiss or revile it is bigotry and is contemptuous of children who are sexual.**

Meanwhile, without approval, teens the world over are sexually active, usually with each other but also with older or younger people. A national survey of 38,000 Canadian children in 1988 revealed that thirty-one percent of boys and twenty-one percent of girls had sex by grade nine, fifty percent by grade eleven. Probably, close to a hundred percent of post-puberty children masturbate, most of them regularly, but that is not approved either, much less valued as an authentic alternative, even though it is the most popular and preferred form of sexual activity among adults of all ages as well as children, and is a healthy option.

Society wants children to be healthy sexual beings but wants them to be non-sexual; the two aims are, if not in outright conflict, at least enormously difficult to reconcile. For a few teens (and adults) long abstinence is a viable option: those with little sex drive, those with another consuming passion, late maturers. . . . But what of the majority? Instead of demanding abstinence and pretending it exists, we should be approving moderation. Which is precisely what most teenagers practice. Fantasizing and masturbation are remarkably temperate expressions of sexuality. We should credit the teenage population for such moderation and discard once and for all the load of guilt we have been heaping upon them.

Instead, even educated people who should know better still manage to slip a stiletto of guilt into reluctant acknowledgement of masturbation as a legitimate pleasure. Ann Landers, after consulting an unnamed, "highly respected Catholic theologian" came up with this gem of grudging condescension and veiled invective in her April 25, 1989 column in major newspapers: "In most cases, individual acts of masturbation do not involve the moral quality of the person in such a way that it constitutes a serious offence." Most cases? Moral quality? In such a way? Serious offence?

Guilt and repression will in time turn many teens into adult sexual bigots who spend a lifetime hating their own sexuality and that of others. Guilt seems to be a central factor in frigidity and other sexual dysfunction. And during teen years, guilt feelings and consequent repressed sexuality contribute to aimless, idle, lonely frustration or, at the other extreme, to vandalism and violence in groups. **Much of the ritual**

mindlessness of teenagers is the public expression of private sexual frustration.

We have, at our peril, interfered with the demand of nature that a basic human need be met when the need arises. So far we have told the young to starve in silence, grin and bear it, take cold showers, play lots of hockey, etc. We will not even allow them to know about sex, much less practice it. We equate ignorance with innocence but ignorance equates with helplessness. Children who could, if informed, manage their own sexuality, are deliberately kept ignorant and helpless. Then we rage stupidly when the helpless are victimized.

None of this is to suggest that children (or adults) should be told to have sex. True self-regulation by children of their own sexuality precludes adult interference as either inhibitor or promoter. **Given full information about sex, as many children as adults will behave responsibly, probably far more, since every adult population is burdened with debilitating psycho-sexual baggage that the first generation of sexually enlightened children will not have to bear.**

Children who presently express sexuality in defiance of adult strictures are redefining the model of childhood. They are challenging assumptions about moral and social certainties that look old and shabby in the light of twentieth-century human and civil rights advances. It is happening so it must be discussed. How it will shake out in the end remains to be seen. Perhaps the order of change will be: the right to information, followed by the right to non-sexist child rearing, followed by the right to say no to people of all ages in all situations including sex, followed by the right to say yes to sex.

If some legal limitations related to judgement or ability to appreciate consequences or intellectual impairment are introduced, they should be applicable to everyone regardless of age. Persons of any age can be impaired or lack judgement. So the issue is not age. The issue is judgement. The only fair response is a test for everybody or nobody. A single standard of morals and behaviour for adults and children is at the heart of the child's right to self-determination. Equality for all, which is the very essence of human rights, suggests that consensual sex will eventually be fully decriminalized and the right to consent will apply to all people capable of exercising their rights.

Everybody in early childhood (birth through six) and most in middle childhood (seven through twelve), being temporarily incapable of exercising their rights, will be protected from all truly sexual advances. But they will have restored to them the right to be touched and stroked lovingly and the right to be exploratory and auto-erotic.

It will be most difficult to be fair to the minority of pre-teens who are in some degree actively sexual by choice. Successful sexual performance is learned, and such children are doing the natural thing when they begin to learn. Edgar Friedenberg pointed out that erotically precocious and talented children are not respected; instead, they are vilified.

Changes may take a century or come quickly. Cultural values are not absolute. Some change, if not monthly, at least yearly. Go to a decade, and change is noticeable in values and attitudes held more deeply. In twenty-five to fifty years, bed-rock values are sometimes transformed. After any century passes, the landscape of values is vastly changed. After two or three or half a dozen centuries, it is unrecognizable. A time frame for the changes in question is not our immediate concern. **Our imperative is to get issues out in the open and into discussion.**

It has not happened. Instead, public and professional meetings on sex education range from embarrassed silence, through shrill ignorance and bigotry to ritual waltzing around underlying issues. Frankness is considered a failing. Less accepted realities of the human condition are kept quiet in polite society because so many of those present at meetings are convinced sex is dirty. Their own upbringing has repressed, inhibited, even crippled them sexually; their guilt, frustration and anger may not be conscious but lie instead in the subconscious seeping poison. **Those who bear the heaviest burden of sexual guilt, repression and ignorance are the people who demand more sexual repression and the perpetuation of sexual ignorance.** They believe strictures that keep them from running wild need reinforcing. They think the epidemic of promiscuity that plagues adult society can be overcome by prohibition. But hard evidence and common sense tell us that teen years are the natural and proper time for experimentation. Repression of sexual experimentation in teens explodes into rampant promiscuity when the repressed reach adulthood. **It seems likely that approved, informed, responsible, self-regulated, natural sexual experimentation by teens would reduce if not preclude wanton adult promiscuity.**

Even the literate and relatively enlightened are likely to be entrapped in the bog of pious prudery that muddies the clean and beautiful. Millions of readers nod approvingly when Anne Landers rails against nudity at home. Lust used to mean something good: great sexual desire. But perverted popular thinking has twisted healthy lust and wrung from it a negative meaning; now, most adults think of lust as sinful and modern dictionaries are apt to add "obsolete" if they list pleasure as a meaning for lust. The highest primate still allowed to enter into God-given sexual ecstasy without guilt is the chimpanzee.

I represented 110,000 teachers on the sex education committee of a forward-looking association of physicians. Government officials from Health and Education were also members. Discussion was vigorous, articulate and productive but limited to practical matters, particularly prevention of teenage pregnancy and disease through improved sex courses at school, free birth control information and devices, and morning-after pills. Nobody else introduced deeper issues into the discussion and whenever I alluded to them, everyone else automatically stepped over them to more comfortable ground.

Perhaps a lighter touch is needed to launch discussion. I offer the following hypothesis: if the priests of antiquity had opted for the nose instead of the penis as the naughty appendage, there would now be noisy bands of zealots rising in righteous indignation about gents exposing their noses in public, anybody breathing openly, teenage boys blowing their own noses under bed sheets at night, and young couples rubbing noses without benefit of clergy. Or perhaps a common agenda of topics for research and debate at the community level throughout the world would help. The UN could publish agendas as part of an updated Convention of the Rights of Children: distinguish between sensual and sexual; distinguish between responsible and irresponsible use of his/her own sexuality by any child (or adult); distinguish between use by a child of his/her own sexuality and abuse of it by another. . . .

Whatever the approach, let public dialogue begin. Meanwhile, schools must occupy the minefield of sex education. They can't wait. **Full sex information is essential for children because they have the right and responsibility to understand the force that drives them and which they are expected to suppress.** And because ignorance can ruin or end their lives. Justice and human dignity demand the truth, the whole truth and nothing but the truth. The half-truth and enforced ignorance that is the norm in most jurisdictions is an affront to children's rights and to the professional integrity of teachers.

Given thorough information on all aspects of sex and continuous clinical support at school, a new generation could be the first in history raised in the concept of informed and responsible sex. Even if the total amount of teenage sexual activity of all kinds did not decrease, it would be more responsible and less agonized activity. Sexual inactivity would also be more responsible and less agonized. Actually, **the better informed young people are on sex, the more likely they are to delay sexual intercourse and the less likely they are to contract sex-related diseases or get pregnant.** Though future social and/or sexual dysfunction is probably the greatest sex-related danger facing today's teens, the public is more concerned about sexually transmitted disease and pregnancy. Both are far less likely to happen if sexual activity is planned and informed than if it is spontaneous and uninformed. Informed planning is done before arousal, in a state of thoughtful calm. Spontaneous sex is done after arousal in a state of euphoric abandon.

Two-and-a-half million American children have venereal diseases and teens are among significant spreaders. The accepted 1989 estimate was that a quarter of sexually active females from fifteen to nineteen were treated for venereal disease. In Nova Scotia, about thirty percent of all sexually transmitted diseases occur in teens. In Ontario, in 1989, a fifteen-year-old girl garnered press attention when she infected two male partners, ages eight and nine, with gonorrhea.

Throughout most of the eighties, AIDS remained largely a disease of adults, but as infection moved from a predominantly homosexual or intravenous-drug-using population to a general heterosexual population, it killed more and more teens. In the nineties, all sexually active teens are at risk. Even if they avoid injected drugs, those who use crack and other street drugs may be particularly vulnerable because drugs enhance desire, diminish inhibition and facilitate promiscuity. Because children have inadequate knowledge of transmission and prevention and especially because they have less access than adults to preventive strategies, AIDS could become a children's epidemic.

In the absence of a vaccine or cure, prevention through education and precaution is the only recourse. It must be early, complete education and the precautionary strategies must be specific and easily available. Television ads alone won't do; even when explicit, they are mere telegrams, good at raising consciousness in those who happen to see them, but too limited in reach and content and too intermittent to educate.

Even when schools have some sex education, they are apt to tiptoe around transmission and prevention in favour of virological and immunological specifics. Children must know in detail why anal intercourse, whether homosexual or heterosexual, is more dangerous than vaginal intercourse. There is a notion in sub-sectors of each generation of children that anal intercourse doesn't count, that it is just something people try behind the barn, like smoking filter-tipped cigarettes. Others see anal intercourse as a surefire way to prevent pregnancy. Some are innately attracted to it. All must be fully informed of dangers.

In New York City (where three-quarters of 200,000 intravenous drug users are infected) and in several other places, and in some subcultures, transmission of AIDS by shared drug needles far exceeds transmission by anal intercourse. In poor countries, particularly in Africa, vaginal sex is the main mode of transmission and the rate of infection is catastrophic. In all main modes of transmission, promiscuity is a factor and children must learn why and how.

On April 19, 1989, *The Toronto Star* quoted the president of the Canadian conference of Catholic Bishops as saying, "the use of condoms cannot be condoned or justified." In spite of the anti-prophylactic campaign of the Roman Catholic church, children have to understand that people who opt for intercourse in spite of risks must use quality latex condoms and spermicide and use them properly, and that even then, infection, like pregnancy, is possible if the condom slips off, leaks or breaks as may happen in five to ten percent of cases (more if cheap, old, or non-latex condoms are used or if they are used improperly). Children must also know that unprotected oral-genital sex is safer than intercourse though not entirely safe and that petting and mutual masturbation are considered safe.

The scourge of AIDS makes a sudden breakthrough in sex education and supporting prophylaxis necessary and possible. This may be the one good thing to come from a dreadful plague. **Long after AIDS is conquered, the legacy of sexual enlightenment will remain as a tribute to those who gave their lives.**

Another and older disease rages in the adult population and a new generation of victims is being infected at home and school. **Homophobia is either the cause or effect of pus pockets of malevolence that suppurate somewhere in the human soul; either way, it must be cleared up and good sex education is both prevention and cure.** People who understand and accept their own sexuality without guilt are unlikely to meddle in, much less hate the sexuality of others, whatever their orientation. And education will help homosexual children by boosting self-esteem and relieving their torment from homophobes.

Science has known for decades that homosexuality is in the usual range of sexual orientation in all societies. Whether it is determined entirely genetically or by some combination of inborn disposition and early environment is uncertain. In any case, the orientation is there, if not necessarily recognized or apparent, by the time a child enters school. A homosexual adult does not emerge magically from a heterosexual child at midnight on the eighteenth birthday. Since ten percent or so of adults are homosexual (and far more are bisexual), ten percent of children are also. Most know they are homosexual before eighteen, a few by age seven or eight, more by ten or twelve; the average age of recognition for males is fourteen (grade nine), for females, seventeen. Before and after recognition they are confused and struggling to understand their orientation.

But schools pretend not to know. So a school with a thousand students has an invisible minority of a hundred with no rights. They are subject to every slur and indignity of prejudice that ever plagued a visible minority, exacerbated by a level of irrational community ignorance and hatred unparalleled in the annals of racial bigotry. Among the perpetuators of prejudice are people in high places including school and church administrations. In December 1983, the Vatican released sex education guidelines that might fairly be described as hate literature; they called homosexuality (and masturbation) a moral disorder! Official Southern Baptists rhetoric in the eighties was just as strident and hateful.

School administrators usually content themselves with silence, censorship and occasional displays of breathtaking ignorance. In the spring of 1988, a newspaper run for young people by young people carried a small ad announcing a counselling service for homosexual students. At least two Toronto schools refused to distribute the paper. The principal of one was reported in the national press as saying, "I don't understand the necessity of counselling for them (homosexual youth) when there are so many other problems facing young people. Why centre out that? It doesn't seem like something I'd like to advertise."

That kind of homophobic mentality makes schools inhospitable to homosexuals. Even the ten percent of teachers who are themselves homosexual are kept almost silent. School boards that try to respond helpfully are not well-supported. In 1985, New York City opened a small high school for homosexuals driven out of regular schools. It was not surprising that a fundamentalist preacher appeared on the front steps to tell students they were going to hell and demand closure of the school. It was more disturbing that reporters with telephoto lenses staked out the premises and chased fleeing students into subways in search of quotes to feed the homophobic masses.

Most homosexual children remain in ordinary junior and senior high schools, hide their orientation or their agonies of uncertainty, and live a life of lonely pretense. They pass as heterosexual. Others are identified and then harassed, humiliated and usually ostracised. Lacking supportive counselling and health services, all are in danger of emotional, social and physical trauma. The U.S. rate of attempted suicide for homosexual teens is at least thirty percent for males and twenty percent for females, compared to ten percent in the total population of teens. There are no good data on homosexual children who succeed in suicide because their families don't know or won't tell their orientation, but knowledgeable people estimate that thirty percent of all teenage suicides are homosexual.

Official homophobia is so pervasive that most sex education programs avoid homosexuality, treat it negatively, or skirt around it with obscure references of no value. School libraries seldom have good information, especially for poor readers. Periodicals published in and for schools are routinely censored if they even mention homosexuality and are banned if they print anything moderate, informative or positive. Homosexual students are left without the support that good information brings, and heterosexual students are left in the ignorance that nourishes homophobia.

In 1985, five Toronto high school students, described in court as "ordinary," went at night to a park known as a meeting place for homosexuals and beat to death a man unknown to any of them who happened to be a respected, devoted and successful teacher-librarian in the Toronto school system. That tragedy resulted in a somewhat improved sex education program in Toronto that deals at least partially with homosexuality. But just a few miles away, and in much of the world, folks are waiting for their own local murder before putting homosexual information in the curriculum.

Teenage pregnancy gets only marginally better attention in many schools. About one in eleven Canadian teenage females becomes pregnant each year. In working-class or economically depressed communities, the rate is one in six. In The Netherlands, which has relatively good sex education throughout schooling, the teenage pregnancy rate in 1988 was 1.2 percent. In America, where sex education is rarely good and often non-existent, the rate was 9.8 percent! Alberta, with no mandatory sex education, has the highest teen pregnancy rate in Canada, while Quebec, with mandatory sex education in all schools, has the lowest.

Sweden has had sex education from kindergarten for decades and for about as long has provided free contraceptives through school nurses in all high schools. The teenage pregnancy rate is among the lowest in the world, and the average age at which females first have sex is among the world's highest and rising — 17.5 years compared to 14.5 in east end Montreal. The abortion rate for teens in Sweden is one-third of the U.S. rate. A 1986 study at Johns Hopkins University, and other studies, confirmed: **unwanted teenage pregnancies decrease when schools provide good sex education and birth control devices are readily available.**

Adolescent females who become pregnant and the males who impregnate them usually share one thing in common besides parenthood: they lack self-esteem — which leads to acts commensurate with feelings of weakness or worthlessness and to acts with an element of deliberateness (conscious or unconscious), or to acts of retributive defiance. Many feel all they have that anybody cares about is their sexuality so they might as well sleep around. Given an inadequate self-image, any of the following secondary causes may lead to pregnancy:

- lack of knowledge of human physiology and reproduction
- lack of contraceptives and related services
- desire to entrap a male
- fear of birth control
- societal or peer pressure to engage in sexual activity
- sex as a substitute when parental affection is lacking

- a baby seen as compensation for emotional deprivation
- desire to prove femininity or masculinity

There may be other secondary causes, but good sex education is not among them. Instead, it is the best bet for dealing with all secondary factors.

The school program must also include extensive counselling to help restore self-esteem. That is no easy matter because **a major cause of low self-esteem is the powerlessness that is the lot of all teenagers**. Their trivial role in society as defined in the present model of childhood is incompatible with their capabilities. In that sense, all teens are subject to diminished self-esteem and counsellors are forced to help victims accept humiliation gracefully. Still, good counsellors can deal helpfully with additional burdens that befall the least fortunate teens.

Every junior and senior high school should have a general health clinic that is also a sex clinic. A school clinic in St. Paul, Minnesota started out as a sex clinic providing VD testing and treatment, pap smears, pregnancy testing, contraceptive counselling and sex information. It attracted few students. Many were reluctant to be seen entering the clinic. Later, the sex clinic was changed to a health clinic by adding services such as physical examinations for athletics, immunization, and weight-control counselling. Use of the clinic's sex services rose rapidly because of anonymity.

Clinic staff should include both medical and counselling personnel specially trained in adolescent sexuality. They should furnish, confidentially, on request, free contraceptives and prophylactics along with instructions for use. Condom dispensers in school washrooms, including girls' washrooms, are better than nothing, but dispensing machines can't provide counselling which should go along with condoms. When school clinics in New York City supplied condoms in 1986, church leaders raised such a ruckus that school authorities discontinued the practice. Children were the losers.

Clinic staff should assist specially trained teachers with sex education in classrooms. A common mistake is to equate sex education with family life education and hand it over to teachers of that or a similar subject. **Family life education has a bias too narrow to accommodate sex education; family is just one context for and one aspect of sex.** More than half the children in most classrooms do not live in nuclear families and most will spend much of their sexually-active lives in other than nuclear families. All children are sexually single, and nearly all will spend substantial parts of their adult lives as singles living alone. Many will live as singles cohabiting serially with several sexual or non-sexual partners. Sex for single people, homosexuals, bisexuals, and old people cannot be stuffed into a container so small as family life, health, biology, parenting or any other school subject. **Sex education must be a separate program starting in infancy and running throughout all school years, and it must be mandatory.**

Until carefully chosen teachers-in-training are properly prepared to teach about sex, it will be necessary for local school authorities to train selected teachers as sex educators. Selection must be based on personal characteristics, not subjects taught. The best teacher of sexual literacy may also be a teacher of art, music, history, drafting, kindergarten. . . .

Schools must teach complete sex information because most parents can't, and it is the responsibility of schools to teach essentials that parents can't teach. Yet in 1988, the Ontario Minister of Education told a government committee on education the timeless tale so often repeated all over North America that it deserves to be inscribed for posterity on a large conical cap suitable for burial in a time capsule shaped like an ostrich head: "sex education is clearly an example of instruction that would be best dealt with at home along with ethics and values."

In his book, *Paideia Problems And Possibilities* (New York: Macmillan, 1983), Mortimer J. Adler lumped sex education with driver education and expressed the same durable dictum of dangerous wishful thinking this way: "It is our position that the school cannot and should not take over what has traditionally been the responsibility of families, churches, and other institutions charged with the well-being of youth."

Most adults can't and don't even talk to each other honestly and openly about sex. Inability to communicate about sex results from repression that most adults suffer. The whole point of sex education by capable teachers is to intervene in the endless cycle of non-communication so that at long last we achieve a human race that can communicate about sex, body parts and functions, feelings, pleasures, needs, yearnings, fantasies, fears, wants, values — girls with boys, girls with girls, boys with boys, children with adults, adults with each other, child with parent. But that achievement is a long way off.

Most parents are so ignorant of sociological, anatomical and physiological facts that they would fail a comprehensive, sex-information test. At least a third of parents are illiterate or semi-literate and hence unable to research the topic or keep up with the rapidly-growing literature of sex. Parents telegraph negative messages by skirting issues and by responses which children sense are vacuous, hypocritical, incomplete or just plain wrong. Or parents moralize and teens turn off. Many parents think they can get by with a romanticized, sanitized account limited to pregnancy and childbirth. Most give up and just hand over a book. Most wait too long. **Children must be told about sex long before they understand it; that way, they grow into understanding without a dangerous period of ignorance or the trauma of finding out too late.**

Few individual parents can anticipate the entire range of adolescent anxieties about sex and deal with them effectively. **Anxieties must be dealt with before young people can hear much of what is being taught about sex.** There are lots of anxieties, but penis problems will serve as one example. Size is an obsession with some boys, yet parents who deal with it at all are likely to serve up the old line that it isn't important because women don't care and even a tiny penis can do the job. Boys know intuitively and from experience that size does matter. Women know it too. The biggest audience response of universal recognition in the 1989 film, *Pink Cadillac*, came when a flasher asked the female lead what she thought of his exposed part and she replied with the ultimate put-down, "Looks like a penis, only smaller."

I was seated in a restaurant noting conversation at the next table. Four girls in the uniform of a private religious school discussed hair colour, clothes and homework. When a boy in stretch tights entered and stood at the order counter, one girl said, "See that guy. Is he ever hung. Wait till he turns around." They did, and he did, and all agreed. Visual effect is also important among males. Penis size can rival height, muscles, and handsomeness in establishing lockerroom status. Then there is the tactile aspect. A big penis is more fun because there is more to handle. Nearly everybody would rather play with a full-size car or gun or any macho symbol than a little toy working model.

It will not suffice to say anything between five and eight inches erect is normal. Or even to add for the sake of honesty that some penises are much bigger and some considerably smaller than average range. Girth is seldom mentioned, but a nine-inch penis is likely to be four times as massive as a four-inch penis. The range is so enormous and so obvious that boys dealt the low end of the scale can be ashamed, angry, resentful, jealous, withdrawn, afraid to undress in locker rooms. . . . And they can be the butt of cruel jokes. Some will fall for old folk remedies or new con games that promise growth.

Even the many who are average may envy the better-endowed, and the latter may share penis concerns other than size: it gets hard in public; when it stays hard a while my testicles hurt; it sticks straight out even when it's soft; it's crooked; it hurts when hard; it leaks at night; the foreskin won't retract; the foreskin is uneven; it's attached too high up (or too low down) on my belly. . . . Not many parents can adequately deal with such ordinary worries even if boys would mention them. As for somewhat thornier matters, how many parents can deal with minor afflictions that can agonize boys? A normal but unsightly condition with the irresistible name of pink pearly penile papules appears as a circle of bumps below the boss of the penis on fifteen percent of boys, many of whom are afraid girls will find out. Well-trained teachers and counsellors could and would routinely and thoroughly discuss all these concerns and many others.

Another problem is that parents who try to teach sex are often indoctrinating their own ideology more than teaching. In good sex education, as in all education, teachers are never trying to impose an ideology on students but rather to overcome sexual ignorance and help every student develop sexual values that are based on knowledge of all available anatomical, physiological and other scientific knowledge and on tolerance of various value systems, including the teacher's own, prevailing local value systems, and those of various sub-groups such as ethnic and religious groups.

One of the most insidious aspects of parental teaching is sex-role stereotyping. The rest of society, schools included, is guilty of the same sin; however, schools are more likely to acknowledge and redress the problem than are most parents. Parents allow boys more freedom of movement, more aggressive sports and more physical, outdoor chores around home. Clothes for boys are more utilitarian, less restrictive and less decorative. Boys' toys are action-oriented. Males are more often praised for what they do and females for how they look. Beginning with the pink blanket, parents teach female children to be soft, passive, supportive, cute, seductive, house-centred, artistic, emotional and dependent. Males are taught to be assertive, strong, competitive, independent, and unemotional.

These qualities are not significantly inborn according to sex. Inborn differences are physiological: height, weight, skeletal structure, life expectancy, etc. The only other substantiated differences are that girls have somewhat more verbal ability and boys slightly more mathematical and visual-spatial ability, and boys are rather more aggressive. But even those differences are average, not absolute.

Sexist parental practices inhibit early and full development of mutual respect and mutually supportive relationships between sexes, and this promotes sexual irresponsibility, exploitation and aggression in teen years and throughout life. By five or six, children have internalized so much sex-role stereotyping that it is difficult to free them. Every model of schooling should provide early childhood education for all children on a voluntary basis from infancy. Only with an early start can schools be expected to make boys more caring and girls more assertive and hence both more adequate in self-esteem.

When neither parents nor schools teach sex, children learn from each other, from the street and from media. Whether we like it or not, all children are being trained to be lovers. Much of what they learn informally is inaccurate, incomplete, confusing, contradictory, demeaning and shocking. Following is a partial list of misinformation found in surveys and interviews: sex eases menstrual cramps; acne is cleared up by sex; intercourse increases the size of breasts and penises; pregnancy is impossible if the male withdraws before ejaculation; forcing a partner to have sex is alright under some circumstances — girls sometimes say no when they mean yes; females don't enjoy sex or need it as much as males; masturbation causes pimples and insanity and exhausts a finite supply of semen. . . .

I used to pass a large book store where most browsers of sex magazines were boys twelve to seventeen. They were enjoying a bit of erotic stimulation, but many were also receiving the only explicit sex information readily available. The more literate could be expected to move on in the same store or in libraries to the vast literature of sex, but without guidance in separating trash from treasures.

The majority of teens read little but are the largest consumers of sexually explicit videos which they rent, buy, copy, borrow and trade. They are also good at using computer bulletin board pornography. The *London Sunday Times* of March 12, 1989, reported that hundreds of titles then available throughout Britain (by phone lines to home computers) appeared on home monitors as "vivid pictures . . . almost as realistic as television." Predictably, the reaction of adult society has been to hide and bemoan erotica and pornography rather than to satisfy the curiosity by teaching real sex education courses. Such courses should include evaluation of sex-related literature and film. **Sexual literacy requires early and continuing study of all facts about sex as well as all artistic expressions.**

Erotica cannot be hidden nor should it be. Even the sleazy, tasteless erotica that is commercial soft-core pornography cannot be hidden. It is everywhere and won't go away. Every neighborhood has collectors willing to share with each budding generation of enthusiasts. Violent and degrading sexual pornography is as easy to find. Anybody can produce it with a video camera, a polaroid or desk-top publishing. Children had better understand it, or exploiters will use it to convince them everybody should do what the nice people in the pictures are doing.

Sex material ranging from tasteful erotica through soft-core pornography to violent, hard-core pornography is the spectrum of a permanent form of pictorial and print art. Even the Vatican has a vast collection. It should be treated like any other art form. Children learn to discriminate and reject the shoddy only when they become literate in any art form (see media literacy, chapter 4). **We must stop confusing prohibition of pictorial or verbal representation with prevention of whatever is represented.**

Sex is a children's rights issue. In a new model of schooling, children's rights should be a separate and continuing program. Until then, appropriate existing programs should be responsible for related aspects of children's rights: English for the right to information, history or civics for the right to vote, sex education for the right to sexual equality, etc. **All sex education programs must tell children explicitly and early that it is normal and healthy for them to feel sexual desire (or not feel it) and that they have the fundamental right to be sexual (or not be) even though present laws and sanctions discriminate against them; and we must tell them how to recognize and rebuff real sexual abusers, especially around home, and the organized zealots who abuse them by convincing them they are victims and by denying their sexuality.**

It will take a long time to make all sex education programs champion children's rights. No matter. The journey must begin. An important first step will in itself take time: a change of focus from narrow to wide field. As presently taught in schools, sex is predominantly clinical, negative, religion-dogmatized and procreative. **The narrow focus on procreation as the only purpose for sex must be widened to include other common purposes: recreation, communication, compensation and domination.**

Compensation (profit of some sort) and domination (power in its many guises) are realities that every person is more likely to experience as victim or perpetrator if kept ignorant of the dynamics of sex. Recreation and communication are sexual purposes that should be understood and approved because most sexual activity is for one or both. Far less often, the purpose of sex is procreation or procreation in combination with recreation or communication or both. Perhaps the least understood purpose of sexual activity is communication. Self-expression through sex can be eloquent beyond words for both the verbally inarticulate and articulate and perhaps the only means of communicating the tender depths of longing and void that characterize life's journey. All of us are born alone and die alone and in between must strive as best we can to alleviate loneliness. Teens are journeyers too.

One further aspect of sex must have high priority and be dealt with in depth at school. The ecological concept of sustainable development when applied to the greatest of all environmental problems, over-population, becomes sustainable sex. **There will be real hope of saving the world only when sex education programs clarify sustainable sex as fully as all other aspects of sustainable development are presently being clarified by science, geography and other appropriate school programs.**

The Earth Summit of 1992 in Rio de Janeiro failed to come to grips with the population explosion, even though it is the mother and father of all ecological disasters, because world leaders and those who elect them are not yet prepared to face the truth. It is up to schools worldwide to prepare the next generation.

CHAPTER 9

STUDENT GOVERNMENT

The key to all child-centred education is self-government.

— A.S. Neill

When I was a high school student and president of the student council, I suggested poor classroom lighting as an issue. The principal told me to back off. I was a puppet and he pulled the strings. The only way I could pursue a legitimate concern was to write about lighting in my weekly column for the town paper. A quarter century later I wrote a film about schools and searched in vain for an exemplary student council. Many of the teen politicians I interviewed were disillusioned or angry. Most students were indifferent. Nobody felt meaningfully involved in school governance.

A few teachers thought more responsibility should be given to students, but most thought they had good student government if chocolate bar sales were well-organized. Administrators were defensive about the value of powerless student government and seemed uncomfortable, sometimes hostile, to my position that students have the right to more involvement. It was at the height of open education enthusiasm in the late sixties yet even elementary teachers who were proponents of open education were disinterested in student government and related children's rights. No schooling innovation of the twentieth century except A.S. Neill's has included student government as an essential component.

In the nineties, student governments still busy themselves with trivia

— what colour streamers to hang for the next dance or what kind of chocolate bars to sell for still another ritual fund raising. When a real issue arises, teacher advisers are supposed to defuse it, to subvert the democratic process. A few students play the game for fun, some for moments of glory it affords, some to build an impressive curriculum vitae, and some sincerely trying to be useful. But most high school and many elementary students realize the whole thing is trivial and ignore it.

Everybody knows that learning comes from doing, not from hearing about doing. It is a testament to professional incompetence and public indifference that students spend twelve or more years in school hearing about democratic decision-making but rarely practise it.

The result is a national tragedy in the U.S. and a problem everywhere. In the 1986 U.S. congressional elections, only seventeen percent of eligible people eighteen to twenty-four bothered to vote. The overall turnout was only thirty-seven percent. About half of Americans bother to vote in presidential elections. In 1988, George Bush was elected by the smallest voter turnout in sixty-four years. Japan, Britain, and Canada have better turnouts for national elections in the seventy-one to seventy-six percent range — but for local elections, voluntary turnout is usually less than fifty percent in all major democracies.

When pundits bemoan lack of participation, they identify some valid contributing factors: ignorance, illiteracy, sense of powerlessness, disillusionment, lack of good candidates, lackluster leadership, disinterest in issues, cumbersome registration, frequency of elections, etc. But they rarely mention lack of thorough training and practice throughout childhood in the democratic process. And that is the one factor which, if overcome, could eliminate most others. When teachers deplore lack of participation by adults in the electoral process, they usually mount mock elections for children in imitation of concurrent national elections. They believe such occasional charades will cause children to turn out and vote years later at real elections.

Mock democracy is fake democracy. There are, however, two good things to be said for it: it is one way (though not the best) to bring national issues into classrooms; and it proves that even young children can master issues as well as many adults. The latter should be emphasized by mock-election enthusiasts and should be publicized as the chief purpose. Proponents should stop deluding themselves and the public that mock democracy instills the habit of voting regularly years later. There is no evidence to support that assumption.

The fact that all students will become voters at age eighteen is reason enough to teach them how to participate in national, state and civic government through practice with real student government. But there is another reason, not yet as well understood but ultimately of equal importance: children's rights.

Schools share with the rest of society the residual, paternalistic, arrogant, even contemptuous belief that age is an acceptable reason for withholding rights of citizenship. In the wake of earlier liberation movements for blacks, women, old people and others, there is a growing realization among thought leaders that young people are citizens first, with all the rights of citizens, and children second. That realization, still only a one on the Richter scale of social earthquakes, will eventually shake foundations of the school system and bring them tumbling down unless they are newly shored up in the near future.

By developing strong and relevant student government, schools would fulfill their long-neglected obligation to teach the democratic process and at the same time would provide sane leadership to society in its inevitable move toward children's rights. A new model of childhood is implicit in the concept of children's rights, and schools will demonstrate important aspects of a new model when they have fully-functioning student governments.

Token improvements — getting rid of silliness that characterizes election campaigns — won't be enough. Anxious to do something, well-meaning people often deal with symptoms and leave real problems untouched: sending food handouts to Africa is easier than coming to grips with economic disparity. The real solution to starvation will require a fundamental change in the way we live; solving problems of student participation in governance of schools will require a fundamental change in the way we live in schools.

Well-meant experiments in participatory democracy won't suffice. One of the best is based on the late Lawrence Kohlberg's work when he was director of the Harvard Centre for Moral Education. He thought more democracy in schools would develop in children the concept of justice and thus enhance moral development. So he promoted class discussion periods run by high school students according to Robert's Rules of Order. But his idea of having students discuss issues that affect them never got much beyond some aspects of social life and behaviour. The experiments continue in some schools under the name "just community" programs.

Even where they are well run, "just community" programs are little islands of democracy in otherwise undemocratic, schools. Astute students could be forgiven for feeling manipulated, patronized and tokenized. If the programs were reconceived as beginnings of real student government instead of as isolated exercises in moral values education, they would hold promise and be an important step in the right direction. But it would be necessary to have and follow a timetable for phasing in substantial responsibilities for students. And it would be necessary to begin at the primary school level and involve children gradually and thoroughly.

A government manages its jurisdiction and looks after the welfare of its citizens. **The test of student government is this: is anything being managed by school or school district officials that could be managed by student government? If so, student government is not functioning properly.**

Student government must be involved, not patronizingly, and not merely in a token way, in decisions about the real stuff of education: budget, administration, school program, evaluation, faculty, public relations, discipline, recreation, etc. A.S. Neill missed the mark when he made Summerhill a student democracy but kept budget decisions from the children! Mrs. Neill controlled purse strings unilaterally from the back room.

Two responsibilities of governments are evaluating the present and planning the future. In the present model of schooling, teachers and administrators do all the evaluating in the board room, the classroom and the games room, and that is an important cause of the education mess. **If they were thoroughly trained, student governments could be valuable evaluators of all aspects of schooling including curriculum and teachers.**

Students can be creative planners. They often see better than adults seeds of the new in the old and the best of the old in the new. Their intense awareness of the real world of the young is without the sentimental hangups and blinkered perspective of adults. But they must be taught how to plan corporate change and they never are. Instead, student politicians are allowed or encouraged to stumble around in the same old rut. They may get a crash course in rules of order. More likely not.

All students should learn the basics of adversarial government: elected representatives, opposing factions, rules, motions, speeches, arguments, debate, majority vote, etc. And one aspect of student government (probably the main government) should be in that mode. But it is equally important that all students learn the basics of consensus decision making: direct participation by everyone, search for common ground, discussion, sharing, respect for differences, silent reflection, good will, mutual agreement, etc. And some aspects of student government (possibly class meetings, clubs and sports) should be run in that mode.

Student government should be particularly concerned with student welfare. Much activity will be in pursuit and protection of children's rights, not only in the abstract but also through: participation in all discipline matters; managing all social and recreational programs including team sports; making sure the needs of every individual are being met as well as the school can meet them. The latter includes involvement in counselling, guidance and health, in conjunction with teachers and clinicians.

The purpose of school discipline is to establish and maintain what some writers call social equilibrium and others call law and order. The most important factor is self-discipline by each individual; but the group has an important role. Writer and professor of psychiatry, Robert Ollendorff, spoke of the "bringing of order into one's experiences," and he insisted that age-group peers do a better disciplining job than adults. The best adults can do on their own is replace punitive with humane discipline. That is an important step forward. The next step is sharing responsibility with student government.

All school rules should issue from and be enforced by student government and its committees. Teachers and administrators should feed information and ideas into the process and may on rare occasions veto decisions of government using due process that includes an appeal procedure; but the main responsibility must shift to students if school discipline is ever to work in a society that increasingly acknowledges the rights of children and in which children themselves are already recasting the model of childhood.

That students can handle even difficult infractions has already been established in San Francisco and several other American and Canadian centres that teach conflict management to children. If they are thoroughly trained in mediation skills, students alone can deal with two-thirds of school blow-ups. With assistance from adults, they could also deal with most of the remaining one-third.

The school ombudsman — every school should have one — must see that individuals' rights are protected. While peer control is better than adult control at accommodating individual rights, it is possible for any government, including student government, to lose sight of individual rights. A case in point might be dress. Student government must take from administrators the arbitrary control they usually wield over the fundamental right to freedom of expression in clothing and hair style. But school government must then decide if the rights of the group are being infringed by individual choices and eccentricities in dress. If that can be established democratically, then student government must set a dress code that does as little violence as possible to individual rights and the ombudsman must support individuals who feel their rights are violated.

We are far from achieving such sanity. Most countries have some law that allows school administrators to dictate dress. In Japan girls are not allowed to wear make-up, jewelry, sheer hose, hair coloring or permanents. Boys have to keep their hair short and straight. Both sexes must wear uniforms. In 1988, the Supreme Court of Ontario ruled that school boards can set dress codes because the Education Act and its regulations give school boards responsibility for imposing school discipline in the widest sense and the power to do it. It remains for children and their advocates to shout that the law is an ass.

In 1969, the Seventh Circuit Court of Appeals in Wisconsin ruled: "The right to wear one's hair at any length or in any desired manner is an ingredient of personal freedom protected by the United States Constitution." But in Wisconsin and every other state where children's rights have been upheld in court, there are still official adult pressures to conform and tacit public support for traditional strictures that violate laws.

School dress is not a trivial matter. Contained within it are important aspects of deeper issues. Conspicuous and uniform dress for a group is historically an authoritarian method of arbitrary control: galley slaves, prisoners, soldiers, corseted women, etc. And regulated dress is also a form of status separation: peasants, monks, aristocrat, judges, nurses, etc. Modern societies have finally overcome regressively authoritarian restriction of individual autonomy to a point where individuals are largely free to opt in or out of dress conventions. Except children. School authorities are empowered to deny them freedom of choice.

There is also the issue of taste. Having it or not having it can affect careers and social life. A student of limited means whose budget for clothes is used up buying and cleaning someone else's truncated taste in uniforms has no opportunity to experiment and experience the feedback that leads slowly to taste and assurance. Teens know intuitively that they must go through this trial and error process. When forced into uniforms, many find ways to rebel.

I lived near a private school for girls. I saw girls change clothes, makeup and hair styles behind fences or in restaurant washrooms. A uniform skirt replaced a skin-tight leather mini in minutes leaving time for a quick smoke before class. After school, the process was reversed but at a more leisurely pace and there might be time to talk dirty and pass around a joint or two. One threesome told me they left home every morning in uniform, changed to civvies in the subway station, changed back to uniform near the school and reversed the whole process in the afternoon.

Most uniforms must be dry-cleaned and pressed regularly but aren't. All over the world I have seen unkempt boys in cheap-looking, ill-fitting, rumpled, stained blazers, flannels and ties. They never look as right as boys in clean jeans and T-shirts that fit. Nor do they look as comfortable or as ready for action. But then, restriction of action is part of the intention. There remains a fixed notion that blazers and flannels are sacred. Fundamentalists who defend or attack everything else with a Bible passage are unable to quote chapter and verse in favour of blue blazers and grey flannels nor anything condemning T-shirts and jeans. It seems unlikely that such distinguished masters as Moses, Jesus, Mohammed and Buddha had among their students a single individual who would pass muster as a proper preppie.

No matter what the uniform, it is an ugly concept. On a dusty roadside in Honduras, I visited a shabby country school. Outside, a skinny barefoot boy leaned on the wall in the hot sun and occasionally turned his head to look in an open window. He wore tattered gray shorts and an old, faded, blue shirt too big. Inside, the children wore cheap, worn-looking beige shorts and white shirts, mostly battered by time. That was a uniform; and the boy outside was excluded because he had no uniform. His father was too poor. So he stood outside, and when the children inside sang, he sang too. I raged.

Perhaps the most important issue that lies within the dress code dilemma is tolerance. As a species we don't yet value difference. We value sameness. Anything different is a trigger for suppression, bigotry, prejudice and hatred. Yet democracy is based on difference modified by mutual respect and co-operation. If democracy is to flourish, we must learn to respect each other not because we are the same but because we are different. **When we learn to tolerate individual differences in clothing and hairstyle we are practicing the democratic ideal in a real and practical way.**

Student governments can set dress codes that protect individual differences and still take care of other concerns: safety, hygiene, fitness without uniformity, possible theft of valuables, etc. Administrators and teachers can have a powerful impact by setting an example of tasteful dress, by providing a curriculum that teaches dress and related matters to everyone and by developing a model of schooling that gives every student a close, continuing relationship with a faculty member who has the time and talent to counsel on matters of taste and behaviour.

Another right of children that student councils should protect is freedom of information. Before they can protect it, they will have to achieve it. Censorship by school administrators is rampant. This is not mere editing of student publications to improve articles and make sure they are free of libelous or gratuitously-foul language. (Student journalists welcome that kind of help, and teachers have a responsibility to serve along with students on editorial committees that tend to such matters.) This is suppression of the free and open exchange of ideas that is the essence of education and of democracy.

Some censoring administrators are expressing their own repressive tendencies and others are bowing to repressive lobbies. Those who run schools with religious affiliations are frequent offenders, and secular schools are almost as bad. National governments allow this form of child abuse and courts uphold it. On January 14, 1988, the U.S. Supreme Court ruled five to three that public school officials have broad powers to censor school newspapers, plays and other school-sponsored activities. The court upheld the deletion by a school principal of two pages on divorce and student pregnancy from the school newspaper. It was a sad day for America and for democracy everywhere, but at least there was a sensible dissenting opinion from Justice William J. Brennan:

[the state educator's role] is not a general warrant to act as thought police stifling discussion of all but state-approved topics and advocacy of all but the official position. Otherwise educators could transform students into closed circuit recipients of only that which the state is willing to communicate and cast a perverse and impermissible orthodoxy over the classroom.

California in 1976, Massachusetts in 1988 and Iowa in 1989 legislated freedom of the press for students writing in school newspapers. A few other states have done the same or are considering legislation. The bills are authentic in every sense except one: they have residual authoritarian flaws that would never be tolerated if they applied to adults. The Iowa law forbids student journalism that might "incite students to break school rules." That caveat is bigger than the Grand Canyon. Practically every news story with real substance involves school rules in some way, so any miffed martinet principal could claim potential incitement and invoke censorship.

And what of unjust rules? Most reportage of the civil rights movement in the sixties and much consequent editorial comment could be construed as inciting citizens to break rules. Most reportage of the coming children's rights movement and much consequent editorial comment could be construed as inciting students to break rules. **Children cannot be denied the right to challenge rules.**

Massachusetts legislation ensures student editors' rights "provided that such rights shall not cause any disruption or disorder." Imagine the furor in the *Boston Globe* if major newspapers were suddenly restricted to printing only stories guaranteed not to "cause any disruption!" But that kind of throttle can be put formally in place to choke child freedom, and there is not a whisper of concern in any newspaper.

When the principal of a Roman Catholic high school in Ontario cancelled a fall 1986 issue of the school newspaper for being critical of church positions on sexuality and school funding, the student editor was quoted in the national press as saying, "Censoring ideas is reactionary and if the free press is going to triumph then I have to fight this." The principal was quoted as saying the views expressed in the student newspaper "were completely contrary to the views held by the church and I cannot allow them to be disseminated here. They can think all they want about that, but they can't write it." Wherever censorship erupts, students tend to emerge as voices of reason and school administrators as fools.

World and local issues and events should be reported to school and community from the students' point of view. In 1988, the Ontario town of Dresden enforced a midnight curfew on children under sixteen. It adversely affected students returning from baby-sitting, service-sector jobs, parties and movies in other towns. It was older people who were causing problems — driving while drunk, gathering at late night establishments and committing three-quarters of the petty crime — but it was convenient to lash out at children on the pretext of protecting them. In the nineties, night curfews proliferate to protect children from drug-related dangers just as rampant in daylight. Ironically, curfews add to the powerlessness and infantilization of teens which are the root reasons they get involved in drugs! The source, not just the symptoms of drug problems must be addressed. Freedom of movement and association are rights that should be protected not violated by police and politicians. Student journalists and editors should pounce on such violations of their rights.

The community as well as the student body would also be interested in stories inside the school that go unreported because of censorship. Student media and student government should scrutinize important discipline incidents and report them from event through disposition and aftermath. Some cases should be presented as infractions of civil and human rights. Locker searches and confiscation of personal messages should be reported for what they are — invasions of privacy.

Students should also use campus television and radio to inform the public. Electronic journalism is faster and offers more opportunities to do end runs around intransigent censors or simply wear them down with rapid-fire assaults of free speech. The ultimate end run is to bypass the school and broadcast on community cable and local commercial stations.

Parents, politicians, administrators and teachers should do an about face and encourage student media and student

governments to deal in depth with the very matters that are now being censored: sex, politics, social issues, values, trends, children's rights, redefinition of childhood, rules, etc. School government and school media should be the voice of children in these matters. And the adult world should listen and learn.

Where adults resist freedom of expression for students, the young should form school (or underground) chapters of Article 19, the international organization which fights censorship and takes its name from article 19 of the UN Universal Declaration of Human Rights: "Everyone has the right to freedom of opinion and expression." Students should also form affiliates of national civil liberties associations. Civil libertarians have been slow to reach out to school groups and individual children and even slower to defend their rights.

Student government must also fight censorship of books. Bands of book burners are forever intimidating school boards. They can't get it through their heads that teaching is not preaching, that literature is not dogma, that no book is taught to promote it but rather to criticize and evaluate it. Most book burners are determined to share their ignorance by banning books they have not read. Others may not be so ignorant but are just as prejudiced and just as determined to impose their prejudices on others. They are dangerous oppressors. They are child molesters in that they meddle with intent to harm children by denying information. **Freedom of information is so important to children and to society that students have a moral responsibility to challenge and defy school boards and administrators when they are the oppressors.**

It must never be assumed that real student government is an alternative to the franchise for children. Both are necessary and should co-exist. Student government could precede enfranchisement and be a powerful force in demonstrating that children individually and collectively are capable of self-determination. **Of the many children's rights student governments should pursue, the most important is the right to vote in all federal, state and municipal elections.**

In the wake of twentieth-century liberation movements, it is becoming increasingly difficult to justify depriving children of the right to vote. Why just children? Why not everyone who lacks whatever prerequisites children are assumed to lack: literacy, cultural literacy, knowledge of issues and candidates, understanding, rational decision-making ability, independence of thought, objectivity, etc. No matter what criteria one might impose on all prospective voters, children would fare as well as adults. Better. If a test, any kind of test, were required of all voters, children from present-model schools would do quite well. Children from new-model schools would outperform much of the adult population.

Most adults are ill-informed and don't study for elections. If they were enfranchised, all children would study in school for upcoming elections. **The study of election issues could be done informally but should be obligatory.** Even now, wherever children study for elections, as part of a mock election exercise, visiting candidates are amazed at their grasp of issues, knowledge of candidates, responsible approach and incisive questions. Candidates commonly report that a junior high school audience was among the best-informed and most participatory of the entire campaign. Teachers are impressed that children often disagree with political positions of parents and teachers; they may be conservative or liberal but tend to be moderate.

If there is no qualifying test for adults, there should be none for children; but a test just for children might be tolerable temporarily. It would comfort nervous adults and would establish the concept that responsibilities go along with every right. Such a test should apply to the middle group of children, ages seven through twelve. Infants up to six are unlikely to express an interest in exercising their right to vote; if an occasional exceptional child of five or six happens to be politically precocious, he or she should be tested on request.

Anyone thirteen or more should be enfranchised without a test. Brazil and Nicaragua have already lowered the voting age to sixteen without benefit of universal school study of election issues. The just and responsible thing for all democratic countries to do is to remove the age barrier and educate all present and future children to be informed voters.

The principle must be that every individual has complete rights from conception (or birth or some point in between if pro-abortion factions prevail). It is the responsibility of society to protect those rights until each individual chooses to exercise them. Each individual will begin to exercise various rights according to his or her own developmental timetable and needs; but generally, at puberty, every individual can be expected to exercise all rights personally, with or without benefit of counsel, whichever he/she chooses. Any individual may elect to exercise rights personally before puberty or may choose not to exercise rights after puberty.

Among complex issues on which children are likely to be better informed than half the adult population are the environment, energy and education. We can anticipate improvements at international, national and state levels in all three as a result of children's votes. The most important result of enfranchisement will be gradual demise of current expressions of teenagers' frustration at their powerlessness: vandalism, gang fights, petty crime, drug and alcohol abuse, dropping out, apathy, etc. As John Holt pointed out in his book, *Escape From Childhood* (New York: E.P. Dutton, 1974), "It is not just power, but impotence, that corrupts people."

All of this has been understood by some thoughtful individuals and groups since the early seventies. But they have made little progress toward reform. At the very mention of child liberation, ancient patriarchal juices surge like adrenalin and stimulate wrathful, righteous responses. Chattelite fervour rings like bells throughout the land calling the faithful to write indignant letters to newspapers. They marshall once again arguments their ancestors used to disparage proposed enfranchisement for workers, peasants, women, blacks, aboriginals, orientals, etc.

The Canadian Council on Children and Youth deliberately left enfranchisement out of its 1975 report on the status of children, *Admittance Restricted*. They knew it should be included but would attract so much authoritarian indignation that it would overshadow other issues. That kind of side-stepping in the name of discretion may be understandable but is no longer acceptable. The time has come for all individuals, groups and agencies who advocate on behalf of children to stand up as proponents of child enfranchisement.

Student governments should not have to sell junk food or go cap in hand to school or school district management for handouts. They should submit budgets and be funded like any other element of the school system. They must have the resources and clerical support staff to act on their own, subject only to non-intrusive, non-manipulative monitoring by senior levels of governance — school and school district management and ultimately, the state.

The student body should be represented in decision-making beyond the scope of student government. Edgar Friedenberg suggested students be given a desk in the principal's office so they could listen in. Students must be more than listeners; they must participate in principaling through representation on administrative committees which run schools (see chapter 19). Friedenberg suggested students learn firsthand by having school newspapers report hassles at school board meetings. Students must be more than reporters; they must be members of school boards participating in the hassles.

One way of doing it would be to make presidents of student councils members of school management teams and of school boards. Or else students could be elected specifically to serve at school and school board management levels. If a board has so many schools that it would not be feasible to have a student from each school on the school board, then student representatives could form an advisory council and elect two or three of their group as voting members of the board.

The chronological or developmental age at which students can handle various responsibilities has never been determined because real student government doesn't exist. It is clear from lighthouse trials that early teens can take on considerable decision-making responsibility, given a decent support system and adequate training. Children under seven will be represented by an advocate and those somewhat older by a student accompanied by an advocate.

For six years I was the teacher assigned to a Friday Night Club which regularly attracted over four hundred students at a school in a largely working-class neighborhood. The big draw was dancing but there were also games, sports, entertainment and refreshments. All of this was budgeted, planned, operated, patrolled and evaluated by student committees. Only two staff members attended, usually only one: me; one teacher and four hundred students. No policemen. The only other adult in the building was one janitor. I did nothing but circulate and chat. There were no incidents or injuries. The school was a junior high and the average age of the management team was 13.5 years. They were taught how to do a complex chore and how to evaluate details immediately after every event. Then responsibility was slowly handed over to them until they were running the show. The same must be done with every aspect of student government.

In school, as in the nation, not everyone will be or want to be a politician, but everyone must understand issues, vote intelligently, provide feedback to elected representatives, and participate in class activities related to student government. There must be one course every year for every student in which affairs of student government are discussed in detail — probably a required weekly program called student government. These classes must also discuss matters brought to their attention by student representatives on the school management team and school board. A possibility, especially after children have the franchise, would be to combine student government with the study of municipal, state and federal political issues. But there are advantages in keeping them distinct. Both internal and external politics will get their due if both are required programs timetabled separately.

Since student government is a top-priority learning activity, it must take place during the school day. All students elected to office must be given credits. Students holding high office, or on the school management team or school board, will put in long hours and must receive multiple credits. Universities should recognize credits in Student Government for admission and should particularly welcome students with credits earned for executive positions.

AFTER HOURS

—— the teenager, compelled to share the life of a city that cannot accept him as adult, collapses into "rebellion without a cause.". . . since TV, the drive to participation has ended adolescence, and every American home has its Berlin wall.

—— Marshall McLuhan, *Understanding Media*
(New York: McGraw-Hill, 1964)

If we really thought of young people as people, would we go on playing Bingo with their lives, demanding that they should be able to produce all the necessary pieces to match the standardized pre-ordained picture of what a satisfactory young person would be?

—— Charity James, *Young Lives At Stake: A Reappraisal of Secondary Schools* (London: Collins, 1968)

School is a part-time job for most children. Many spend more time watching television and listening to music than at school (or interacting with parents). Half of the fifteen-year-olds in a typical North American high school work at paid jobs fifteen hours a week or more; by eighteen, eighty percent work twenty hours or more. A conservative rule of thumb is that two-thirds of high school students work eighteen hours a week or more. And yet **the school system sputters along pretending the main activity of children is attending school.**

Parents endorse that pretense, but **the unspoken norm is that parents expect teens to be wage earners**.

Watching television, listening to music and working at paid jobs can overpower school. Add time for dancing, dating, private lessons, community sports, hobbies, social service, recreation, grouping, telephoning, household chores, worship, etc. No wonder so many children skip school — they have their main activities to get on with. Call them intermittent dropouts: here today, gone tomorrow, back the next day (except for period three which is a test). It beats the old method of dropping out. Permanent dropouts don't get diplomas; intermittent dropouts do.

A combination of late-twentieth-century circumstances affecting the young, taken together, constitute a major change in society that goes barely acknowledged as a whole, not acknowledged at all as a valid social movement. We focus on various parts as though they were unrelated: family breakdown, inadequate parenting, the beginnings of a children's rights movement, early physical and social maturation, communications and other technology, proliferation of teen culture, children as an economic force because of paid employment, functional illiteracy, irrelevant schooling, etc.

Meanwhile, negative outcomes of the present dysfunctional models of childhood and schooling are also mistakenly treated as unrelated abberations: teenage suicide, pregnancy, unemployment, academic failure, dropping out, absenteeism, alienation, drug addiction, gang swarming, delinquency, apathy, etc. The whole picture, which contains all of these, eludes us.

The school's immediate and deep involvement in the phenomena of children's devotion to television, music and part-time jobs should be as an aspect of society's integrated response to the larger phenomenon. But there is no integrated response, so schools must deal with fragments, putting them in context as best they can. **The mark of an authentic proposal for education reform is that it offers a vision of the whole reality of childhood and deals with a**

significant number of fragments. All innovations in schooling have failed to do that.

Working with television instead of ignoring it means: school must provide media literacy education throughout all school years; at least one teacher at all times must work with each child on his/her personal viewing activities to integrate them with school life; television programming must be incorporated into curriculum instead of being used as an occasional supplement; entire basic content as well as supplementary material for many school programs should be on videodiscs for direct use by students and teachers.

Teachers and other school system personnel should reach outward and intervene in all aspects of commercial television, film, radio and music. They should lobby for quality programming. School people will have to invade entertainment and communications industry board rooms and studios and demand a say, and the storm troops will have to be media-literate and production-wise as well as being astute educators. Too often, film and television producers avoid consultation with educators or consult establishment hacks. Much commercial programming fails to meet needs of children. It also misrepresents good teaching and learning practice, demeans children and teachers to fit old or hip stereotypes, and misses opportunities to be relevant.

Schools should be involved in the part-time job phenomenon, not in training for future full-time jobs. Many people think school is relevant when it trains for full-time jobs. Not so. Job training is relevant when it trains for full-time jobs. School is relevant when people emerge from it self-propelled, health-conscious, committed to excellence and the common good, computer-literate, able to read, write, speak, listen, think, solve problems, cipher, etc. Job training is an extra that requires additional funding and additional time. Not just occasional grants but big, sustained infusions of money. Not stolen moments here and there, but months and years of additional time for job trainees.

The education phase must come first. It may legitimately give way to job training as early as fourteen for a few people and as late as twenty-four or more for others. Presently, the school system provides some job training for young teens as typists, pressers, hairdressers, etc. (Universities provide job training for the twenties age group as physicians, engineers, teachers, etc.) It would clarify matters if schools offered only education and provision were made for job training in separate institutions or through apprenticeships and on-the-job training.

The false argument is made that specific job training is "educational" and hence can be done in place of other education activities. There is not time to do necessary education programs and also provide specific job training no matter how well and how "educationally" job training is done. **Students capable of more education should have it rather than job training; they and their country are being cheated if education time is stolen for job training.**

True, there is no point in forcing a bored but teachable fifteen-year-old who can't read, write or think to sit through history classes while he dreams of tuning motorcycles. He might better be learning to tune motorcycles. But it would be better still to teach him to read and write and to put him into learning situations that are truly within the education domain and which challenge and excite him. He can learn to tune motorcycles later and will be a better tuner and a better citizen for having been educated before being job-trained.

Generic skills applicable to a range of jobs provide a general background for later specific job training and lifelong retraining. **Schools should stop training students for specific jobs and instead should teach generic job skills and generic leisure skills.**

In the long run, hours of work will probably shrink. Many people will never have full-time jobs. Weeks of vacation and years of retirement will increase. People define themselves by their work, so life where work is a diminished factor requires a central fact to supplement or replace work. Humans have an inborn need to be constantly striving toward some goal, purpose, higher order, self-actualization, self-transcendence. . . . There must be a new emphasis on satisfying and constructive use of leisure time. Yet hardly anybody speaks seriously of schooling to deal with all that non-job time, not even union leaders for whom it is a time bomb.

If schooling were properly done, the problem would not arise. Self-propelled people use discretionary time in a satisfying and constructive way, so **the school system should teach self-propulsion as a basic in education**. It has failed to do so. The main, constantly-satisfying thing self-propelled people do is keep on learning. In view of the original meaning of the word school, it is an ironic testament to the failure of the present model that it has killed love of learning: the word derives from the Greek for leisure! Only the privileged jobless in ancient Greece had time for school.

Lip service is given to training in generic job skills and in the use of leisure time, but neither is taken seriously by most school systems. Every school should have a well-developed program in both areas, and every student should have a recorded, developmental profile of accomplishments in both. Each profile should be reviewed regularly by a teacher authorized to design appropriate remedial and developmental programs with and for each individual.

When schools refrain from specific job training and instead teach only generic skills, the few students who have clearly reached their limit educationally, should be excused from further schooling and trained for specific jobs in facilities separated from schools and called job-training centres; such centres might be run by school boards, but their separation from schools is essential in order to establish in the public mind that education is different from job training.

Among generic job skills for non-supervisory occupations are the following: attending physically, attending cognitively, reacting to others, task-focussed conversation, responding to information or directions, giving directions, etc. All of these can be taught and practiced at school, but they can be practiced with heightened reality at work. **Schools must develop working relationships with fast-food outlets, restaurants, supermarkets, chain stores, clothing stores, gas stations, hotels, hospitals and other businesses that employ**

students after school. Fast-food chains could teach the six generic skills above and dozens more. Imagine the possibilities for skills-development in marketing, costing, advertising, accounting, food distribution, public relations, etc. Instead, many fast-food operators regard student employees as a cheap, plentiful commodity to be used up and easily replaced. Such employers reduce skill levels to the lowest common denominator instead of elevating them to the highest possible plane.

Increased automation may modify but won't eliminate the appetite of fast-food chains for teenage employees. *The New York Times* of August 14, 1988, quoted the president of one chain as saying, "with the advent of more sophisticated equipment, there will be fewer people who will do more in a more hospitable environment." With the help of school systems, students could become as sophisticated as the new equipment and they would then demand that some aspects of the "more hospitable environment" be for their benefit.

In an ideal world, all students would become so self-propelled that evenings, weekends and vacations would be filled with voluntary, school-related learning. There would be no time for paid employment. It is that way now for the self-propelled few. They have no time to peddle pizza because they are busy creating computer programs or coal gasification inventions for science fairs or writing symphonies or whatever extensions of school they have dreamed up. But most students in today's schools are not self-propelled into intellectual and creative extensions of the program. Instead they get jobs. Others, who would like to pursue their own interests, can't, because they need the money jobs bring.

Both pizza peddling and symphony writing are realities in the learning environment of our times, and schools must give them status, guidance and accreditation as voluntary, after-hours contracts within the school system. They are optional extras for credit. Optional, in that they are not required for graduation and the choices are infinite. Extras, in that they are pursued outside the regulation school day and yield extra credits. A student who contracts for credit must write his symphony or peddle his pizza so as to get the most value from the experience. So all students must be monitored by specially-trained teachers. In some cases the teachers may remain largely within the school and function as mentors, but in many cases, teachers will have to visit employers and outside resource people to establish and maintain optimum learning situations.

School-to-work relationships have already been established by some high schools, often under the name co-op education (not to be confused with cooperative learning which refers to students working with each other in classrooms). But co-op education is a different and smaller concept than I am proposing. Typically, in co-op education, an insignificant percentage of the total school population (usually not more than three percent) get credit for paid or unpaid jobs in business, industry or social services. A few committed schools have involved twelve percent or more of students in at least one co-op placement for one semester. The co-op job situation is usually transitory and artificial, a set-up arranged by school administrators.

Programs take place during school hours, so participating students have to miss regular program and process. School is causing absenteeism. While there is nothing wrong with a student leaving the campus in pursuit of learning, it is not necessary or sensible to schedule jobs on a regular basis during school hours. Instead, **schools should make co-op programs of the real jobs that sixty-six per cent of students do after school, on weekends and during vacations.** Perversely, most jurisdictions expressly forbid or discourage schools from approving for co-op credit after-hours jobs that students find on their own!

Schools should not encourage students to spend big chunks of time at after-hours jobs even though most such jobs can be made to yield solid generic skills training. Four to twelve hours per week during term will suit most students. Four hours is ten percent of a forty-hour work week. Twelve hours is thirty percent. That is a lot on top of a full-time student load. Only on school breaks should students work longer; then, a forty-hour week is appropriate.

For non-academic students, typical jobs yield the satisfaction of accomplishment that school fails to provide, but they bore fast learners. If there is no generic skills component, most of what can be learned is learned in a few hours or days. Many jobs I had as a student were mindless: berry and apple picker, canning factory laborer, machine operator in an arms factory, hotel porter, waiter, truck driver's helper, warehouse laborer, spot welder, pipeline construction worker. All were a waste of time after the first day or week in the sense that I could have contributed more to my own growth and to society by spending the time developing my talents.

The paid jobs I had as a student which were valuable were as a swimming instructor and a newspaper reporter. Both jobs used and nourished my talents. Such jobs are difficult for individual students to find. Schools should fine-comb the corporate and public sectors to find intellectual and creative after-hours jobs for students. Many students could get similar nurture of their talents (though no paycheck) from creating their own free-time projects. That is why it is important to give as many credits to students who generate their own extra activities — whether entrepreneurial, creative, intellectual, humanitarian, or phys- ical — as to those who hold paid jobs.

Schools should (but don't) identify the talents of students in order to match them with job and project opportunities. In every school, in every country, sit students whose potential will never be realized because their particular talents have not been identified and nourished. Society gets unemployed or underemployed dropouts when it could have had writ- ers, inventors, humorists, dancers, designers, musicians, actors, figure skaters, scientists, composers, coaches, counsellors, mechanics, chefs, cabinet makers, politicians, organizers, etc.

Among the most prestigious after-hours jobs whether paid or unpaid should be those in social services or that enhance the environment. The local environment and the welfare of community residents are respon- sibilities of the student body. **It should be the business of student government to make sure every old or incapacitated person in the community is paired at all times with one or more student helpers**. Efforts must be made to bring the elderly into all schools and children into all homes and hospitals of the aged. Such activity builds social skills that bridge the generation gap.

In many high schools, after-hours sports, arts and hobby clubs are now minimal, maintained for the favored few who don't rush away to jobs. Once schools are in control of part-time jobs, extra-curricular activities will revive. The best ones should be offered for optional credit or should qualify as full or partial completion of a required program. A late afternoon sport should include a rigorous half-hour aerobic warm-up that would fill that day's exercise requirement. High-level chess might fulfil part of mathematics requirements and debating should be credited as part of English (speech) programs.

Student government, rather than school administrators, should organize extra activities, whether within the school or in the community. The school's corporate presence in formal, part-time-job co-op education should be largely a student corporate presence. Too often, the much-touted community committees and commissions established to connect schools with business and industry include everybody except students. Properly conceived and funded, student government could and should manage nearly all elements of the school/job interface. Teachers should act as consultants not puppet-masters.

Students should manage a semi-annual, weekend job fair at which local employers explain their companies and interview student applicants for part-time jobs. Another aspect of every job fair should be seminars for employers on child development, children's rights, generic skills, accreditation for paid work, etc. There should also be seminars for students, discussion groups of students and employers, and guest speakers. Major employers such as fast-food chains and business organizations such as the Chamber of Commerce could be expected to co-operate with student governments in mounting job fairs and would contribute funding as well as expertise. How could they refuse? **Children are critical to the economy; without them as cheap labour, several sectors would collapse: retailing, transportation, food services, entertainment, etc.**

Where no officially sponsored school/business community liaison committee exists, student governments should unilaterally establish and maintain communications with local industries and businesses to continuously generate projects and jobs, and they should encourage corporations to adopt schools or, more appropriately, to be adopted by schools.

Student governments should act as labour unions or should create student labour unions to protect the interests of student workers, and student governments and student labour unions, along with school systems and activists in education, will have to mount sustained campaigns to change labour laws that disadvantage children. Exclusion from jobs on the basis of age alone has to end because to withhold access to any advantage because of stereotyped assumptions is inherently wrong. Persons of all ages (races, religions, sexes...) have the right to be judged impartially on personal merit, not on suppositions.

Child labour laws of the nineteenth and early twentieth centuries served a useful purpose: they protected children from unfair and unhealthy conditions of work. Eventually, the same protection was extended to adults but in a much different way. Adults were protected from exploitation while retaining the right to work. Children were protected from exploitation by being denied the right to work. That injustice must be redressed.

Laws and practices vary widely in different developed countries and even from place to place within countries. In Leicestershire, England, fourteen-year-olds can work twenty hours a week during school breaks, but in Leicester city they can work only twelve. In Ontario, fourteen-year-olds on school breaks can work the same hours as adults but can be paid lower wages than adults for exactly the same work! The same unfair wage regulations apply to after-hours jobs during school terms.

This, at a time when pay equity for women is the righteous mission of political parties, labour unions and feminists. If the women happen to be under eighteen, wage discrimination is usually approved by everyone including feminists. The Ontario government even publishes a legal minimum wage for students which is almost twenty percent below the minimum wage for adults! Worse, government regulations exempt certain employers from paying even the disgracefully low student minimum. Among employers specifically allowed by law to doubly exploit children are churches, schools, communities and camps. The very pillars of society which claim to uphold interests of children are the most ardent abusers.

There can be no clearer evidence of residual children-as-chattel mentality than the Government of Ontario regulations which approve pittance wages, even lower than the already discriminatory student minimum, for "a student supervising or instructing children," or "a student employed at a camp for children." Children teaching children is the bottom of the heap! Imagine the uproar if minimum wage exemptions were announced for "a woman over forty supervising or instructing women over forty" or "a man over thirty employed at a Club Med or other camp for adults."

There are minor differences, but characteristics of child labour are similar in most Western countries:

- children work in spite of laws that say they can't
- children get only jobs adults don't want
- the best jobs are deliberately denied children
- children are ineligible for most promotions
- child workers below legal age are uninsured
- children are not protected from unfair firing
- children are paid less than adults for similar work
- children are denied pension and other benefits
- unions deny membership to children
- unions try to keep children out of the labour market

Children are exploited because of labour laws and attitudes originally intended to protect them from exploita-

tion. Thousands work thirty hours at school, ten at homework, twenty at outside jobs — sixty hours a week for slave wages. Student councils and rights activists should demand for children: job equality with adults; equal pay and fringe benefits for equal work; access to any job for which a person is qualified and equal access to qualification regardless of age; access to promotion and positions of authority; protection under the same safety and compensation programs as adults; the right to make contracts, etc. Affirmative action should be considered. In these and related matters fraught with self-righteous ageist bigotry, student activists, student councils and supportive adults will be advocating on behalf of the last of the niggers, children.

If the child-job dilemma is considered at all, it is usually from the point of view of hours worked, type of job, regulation of conditions and so on. **Rarely is the fundamental issue confronted: children's right to a piece of the economic pie.** Most children are personally poor even if their parents are not. For teenagers, poverty is particularly intolerable. Necessary expenses related to schooling include clothing, grooming, transportation, meals, books, activity fees, charitable collections, trips, supplies, etc. But teens are also obliged to reach beyond family and school into the larger society. They need money for dates and other social obligations, records, concerts, films, museums, galleries, tours, vacations, sports, fitness, and many more items and activities that are important to growing up whole. Increasingly, many aspects of young lives are inhibited by lack of a car or motor bike.

It is not the fault of teens that society has contrived to keep them dependent. If society wants it that way, then **society has to find a method of providing children, particularly teens, with a guaranteed and adequate income.** We must determine what income is adequate and who will provide it. There seem to be three possibilities: parents, government or children themselves.

Parents who can afford it could be required to meet the money needs of their children. Most parents don't. Five to ten percent of students in most North American high schools pay room and board and some are major family breadwinners. Even those teenagers who get an allowance of spending money rarely get a fair share of family income or an equal say in its use. Most don't get a regular allowance. They get an occasional handout or nothing. The allowance convention is observed by some in upper and upward-aspiring classes. Even there, it is usually a demeaning dole, an authoritarian, patronizing and arbitrary affront to civil rights and human dignity.

Children should have an equal voice in decisions about necessary household expenses for food, shelter and essential services such as dental care, and they are entitled to as much of remaining discretionary family income as are adults. With proper guidance by adults advocating the best interests of children, the young can learn to spend and budget well and to save for future exceptional needs. Children are good savers. With help they can be good investors. But not if they continue to be intentionally impoverished by residual authoritarianism.

Where parents fail or as an alternative, governments could pay each child at school a minimum wage. At the other end of the age spectrum, governments pay every citizen (or at least those in need) a living wage in the form of old-age pensions. But in the case of children, if there is any payment at all, it is too small to be a living wage. "Baby bonuses" as presently conceived are paid to parents, not children, and usually disappear into the general parental pool or go directly into month-end beer bashes.

Wages for children should be conceived as payment for the job of attending school and should be paid out through schools. Long ago Edgar Friedenberg suggested that perhaps school children should be paid by those who use them later on. Since schools are the sole source of future employees for all businesses, it seems reasonable to conclude that schools are working on their behalf and hence businesses should, through taxes, pay costs.

Or wages of students working after-hours could be at time-and-a-half of adult wages because it is overtime — they have already worked forty hours counting school-day and homework. Alternately, children can be allowed to enter the full-time labour market periodically with rights similar to adults, and education for them will have to be structured differently and spread over a longer period. **At this moment, millions of high school students are working fifty-five hours a week or more when school, home and paid-job hours are totalled, but nobody has bothered to create (let alone accept and control) a complete job description for students that matches the reality of their lives — school, extra-curricular activities, homework, after-hours jobs, household chores, etc. Children are the most exploited, overworked, and underpaid group in society.**

Homework

Of all after-hours activities, the sentimental favorite among adults is homework. Everywhere in the world, people tell me more (or, occasionally, less) homework will improve schools. Everyone has an opinion. Mine is that **homework is a literate middle-class concept and poses no problem for children of the few conscientious parents who actually practice traditional middle-class values.**

Children of parents with the best-paying occupations and social status do the most homework and hence get the most value from a model of schooling that features homework. The most academically-inclined students taking college-preparation courses do more homework and thus get more value from school than the majority of students who are taking less academic courses and are headed for low-level jobs. It is understandable, then, that middle- and upper-class parents support homework. But surprisingly, working-class parents often revere homework and call for more. They think of it as good medicine and feel guilty about not having taken enough when they were young. All classes of parents think schools that give large doses of homework must be serious places.

Committees of teachers and parents are forever in earnest discussion about homework. Their deliberations are about as relevant to most children as clerical discussions of how many angels could dance on the head of a pin were to peasants of old. The peasant masses were too busy trying to survive one more day by scraping subsistence from the land while enduring the exploitation of overlords. The child masses are too busy running households for absentee adults, working long hours at after-school jobs, leading some semblance of a social and personal life, and monitoring the pervasive realities of television and music that schools ignore — all this and more while enduring the exploitation, indifference, negligence or over-indulgence of adult overlords.

Committees always come up with neat lists of what teachers, parents and children must do to enhance medicinal effects of homework; they generate stopgaps that serve some people sometimes: guidelines for parents who want to supervise homework; how-to-do-it pamphlets for students; peer tutoring; parent volunteer tutoring; homework hotlines to call for help, etc. Stopgap devices and committee reports evoke visions of perfect little schools where every teacher knows exactly what every other teacher is doing and most of every peaceful day is taken up with careful planning of homework assignments.

Charming, healthy children (two to a family) take their carefully planned homework to a gracious home where mother (who is stylish and used to be a teacher before she got lucky and married a lawyer) is waiting at the front door surrounded by the aroma of fresh-baked whole-wheat bread. Father arrives home from the office to much excited hugging and kissing all around (dog included), and after a delicious meal of lean meat, baked potatoes, two fresh vegetables, green salad and apple pie made from scratch, and much joyous family chatter, all four settle down for an evening of quiet study disturbed only by the crackle of the fire and the contented sighs of the family dog curled up by the hearth. From time to time father looks up from his law book and smiles. Now and then, mother stops work on her next speech as president of the PTA and quietly helps the children — not too much, that would be cheating — just enough to show how much she loves them and what fun homework is.

Real children know it isn't fun. What rankles is being cheated of fun while other people in the house are having it. Frequently the "fun" is television, but it could be any activity more pleasurable and less lonely than slugging away at rote learning: puttering, talking, hobbying, telephoning, playing music, reading newspapers, drinking, working at a paid job, etc. The change needed is obvious: **if one person in the house has to do homework, everyone must do homework at the same time.** Ideally, each adult person should be taking a course, but there are other cerebral activities that qualify — research, household accounts, office work, preparations for community work, letter writing, reading to infants, etc.

At least a third of parents are functionally illiterate, and another third are sufficiently uncomfortable with literate pursuits that they seldom read or write and never study. They are constitutionally incapable of doing homework. Of the remaining third who are both literate and comfortable with reading and writing, more than half rarely do what could be classed as homework. That leaves about fifteen percent of all parents and guardians who actually maintain a "homework home" as defined on the basis of literacy.

But there are other factors as important as literacy. The order and organization required for a "homework home" is just a dream to most children. Their parents don't have the faintest idea how to organize the household through democratic discussion by all adults and children. They live in domestic chaos. The norms are some chance combination of constant television and stereo racket, yelling, fighting, instant gratification, inconsistency, absence of planning, lack of adult guidance for children or even interest in them, absence of parents, no communication between generations, alcoholism, poor nutrition, crowding, abuse, etc. Many homes don't even provide a minimally private space free from disturbance or even a decent work surface, chair and lighting.

The great homework imbroglio should focus upon adult behaviour because adults are causing the problem, but that will not happen, so assigned homework should be prohibited. The emphasis here is on the prefix **home**. It is assigned **home**work that should be prohibited, not individual study or assigned work.

Individual study is the essence of education and assigned work is necessary as long as we are stuck with the present model of student-passive schooling and during transition to a new model. Once students learn to be active agents in their own education, they will create most of their own "assignments."

Time must be provided so that nearly all individual study and all assignments can be completed at school; this can only be accomplished by lengthening the school day and year. Even that will not entirely resolve the homework dilemma. The present model of schooling is so disorganized that no high school teacher knows what assignments other teachers have loaded upon students. Sometimes the load is crushing. Sometimes there is no load at all. It is a matter of chance.

As a new teacher, I tried to avoid overloading students by coordinating assignments with other teachers. It never worked. Teachers are too rushed. They may not even know each other and can't possibly know every student. The irony is that the very students who are left to organize a load of assignments have never been taught how to organize! The school system just assumes that complex organizational skills, individual work habits and solo study skills develop spontaneously like pubic hair at the time of entry into high school. We need look no further for the reason many students drop out. School is the dunce.

Gangs

The urge to group remains from primitive times when it brought the young together as the strongest, bravest and most daring to fend and defend on behalf of the tribe. Now, the young have been denied such a noble purpose. Their lives have been trivialized, and they are kept powerless. Some are content to group and do trivial things. Others group in a spirit of smoldering frustration that their lives have been Mickey Moused. Some gangs are sub-groups within high schools. Others are street based. The latter have been an international phenomenon for half a century. *West Side Story* romanticized the post-Second World War New York version. The 1979 movie, *Quadrophenia*, spotlighted the British Mods and Rockers of the mid-sixties. No decade passes without a rash of press reports as each generation of journalists rediscovers gangs.

In the early nineties, while Israeli teens were getting together to play chicken dashing in front of cars, Palestinian teens were gathering to throw stones at Israeli soldiers. In North America, teens were "swarming" to hurt, humiliate or rob outsiders. On June 1, 1992, about 2000 Toronto teens skipped school and converged on the waterfront in gangs to attack each other and the police.

The J.G. Ballard novella *Running Wild* (Boston: Little Brown, 1989) told of children in an upscale English community who joined to rebel against trivialization of their lives by over-solicitous parents — thirteen fictional teens killed all their parents and disappeared into hiding to plan the assassination of a top political figure.

Most gangs in the West have lacked the leadership for sustained action. But competent leadership by adult criminals is a constant threat; and leadership could emerge from slightly older disaffected students, as happened in China in 1989. **As youth become more politicized, young teen leaders will emerge.** What is now an after-hours outlet for most teens who return daily like Cinderellas to their powerlessness at home and school will escalate into a full-time alternative for alienated children. A Chicago survey found that the lure of street gangs ranked along with pregnancy as the main reason for dropping out of school.

The usual adult response to any escalation in ganging is to beef up police forces, add more social workers and build another sports facility. No such moves will solve the problem. **We have to redefine child-hood to give children civil, human and economic rights equal to adults, and we have to redefine the model of school-ing so that it fully reflects those rights. When children can express their need to group while also expressing a sense of control over their own lives at home, at school and on the job, school, street and ethnic gangs will fizzle for want of fuel.**

CHAPTER 11

_____

ATTENDING SCHOOL

*We made a commitment to go to the moon. Can't we make a commitment
that no person will drop out of school?*

—Lauro F. Cavazos, U.S. Education Secretary, 1989

We no longer have compulsory school attendance; we have compulsory
enrolment. It is common for students to miss twenty days, over ten
percent of the school year. Some miss two or three times as much. Many
cut classes as well as whole days. A student I was tutoring showed me
his report card for one semester — eighty-four classes skipped, usually
by hiding out within the school or arriving an hour or two late. Because
students and parents think it quite alright to miss school, some teachers
prepare and schedule one or two extra versions of every classroom test;
they know some students won't show up for the original.

The breakdown of attendance began even before after-hours employment of teenagers proliferated in the seventies. One could almost say
children go to school when there is nothing else to do. Following is a
partial list of activities many parents and students think take precedence
over school: parents' vacations; travel; babysitting; household chores;
errands; medical, dental and hairdressing appointments; fatigue; sports;
visitors at home; late nights; shopping; lining up for show tickets; fake
illness; paid jobs. . . .

Parents are blamed for not setting a good example and not controlling
their children; students are blamed for being irresponsible; schools are

blamed for boring, irrelevant programs and poor enforcement of attendance requirements. It would be more sensible to take a fresh look at
the target group and their needs. Who are these people? Most don't
come from homes that resemble the classic middle-class family and yet
the organization, operation and spirit of the school system still assumes
they do. Schools have never adjusted to needs of children from lower
socio-economic or ethnic backgrounds or from broken or malfunction-
ing homes even though they are now the majority. And schools still have
not accepted that most students, including many from middle-class
homes, are personally poor and must earn money.

Though paid jobs held by students without benefit of school monitoring are a major factor, the problem of absenteeism reaches beyond
the job relationship and must be confronted by every community and
every school on a broad front. A crucial first step is to identify and track
every school absentee. Too often, absentees are only intermittently or
inaccurately noted. State authorities should develop and then require
rigorous computerized attendance checking. It is inexcusable in this
electronic age for teachers to count heads and shuffle reams of paper in
the slipshod methods of recording attendance still widely used.

Present definitions of habitual absence are so limp that nobody knows
what standard to enforce or how. A few habitual truants under school-
leaving age may be tracked down, but no real effort is made to melt the
dangerous ninety-nine percent of the absentee iceberg that lies obscured
by a flood of phony notes from parents, poor attendance checking, and
indifference. A report from London, Ontario in 1987 gave this profile
of "non-attending" (truant) students: three quarters were from grades
eight, nine and ten; half were boys and half girls; most had moved and
changed schools, a third of them more than five times; only a quarter
lived with two parents; dysfunctional families and lack of family support
were common. My conclusion is that **truants are mainly thirteen,
fourteen and fifteen-year-olds from homes incompatible
with schooling.**

Truants may be counselled, but attendance counsellors are too few
and overloaded. Most school boards have no social workers or too few.

Truants may be treated like criminals where their absence from school is illegal. Instead, schools should deal with chronic non-attenders as they should with the greater numbers who are also habitually absent, though intermittently, in smaller bits and pieces; all are part of the same problem. A firm stand must be taken because students who learn to be absentees while in school grow up to cost business and industry billions of dollars being absent from work. **The most valuable job-training school can provide is requiring every student to be present every day.**

One thing we must do is redefine unacceptable absence. Is it five days every term? ten? four periods a month? fourteen? one-third of classes in one subject but none in other subjects? every day in which a test is scheduled but no other days? the first two periods most mornings but no other times? every Friday afternoon? the week before and after all vacation periods? any period long enough to attract a school attendance officer? all of the above?

Unacceptable absence for students (and teachers) should be absence for more than two percent of the time. If a semester has one hundred days, each student is allowed two days of absence, four days in a school year. The same measure applies to individual classes missed. If there are a hundred periods a month, a student may miss two with impunity. Any amount of time missed beyond two percent leads to an attendance hearing before the student council (or an attendance committee made up of teachers, resource people, community representatives and students) with full support and participation by the school board.

The purpose of the hearing is not punitive but rather to identify and remedy causes and to arrange makeup of lost time required for graduation. School-based psychologists, counsellors, social workers, physicians, nutritionists and other professionals and volunteers should be available to help absentees; and school-based ombudsmen should protect their rights.

The choice of two percent is arbitrary but seems fair. A school is a living organism that bleeds and is weakened by absenteeism. In a school of 1 000 students operating on a 2 00-day year, the two percent allowance would mean four thousand student days or the equivalent of twenty student years lost annually. Surely enough blood wasted. We are presently so far off the mark that it will be necessary to start higher, perhaps five percent, and work down over several years to a two percent limit. Five percent totals over two weeks in a school year and is far too much. But it would be better than current attendance anarchy.

One mother told me she had no worries about her son's poor attendance because he was earning good money at a supermarket and could pass anyway. And he did. Mother, child and school all believed accumulating data for short-term retention and amassing lots of credits to be the greatest achievement. But living the process with optimum participation is the greatest achievement. Every student, every day, must contribute to the process for the good of the group as well as for personal sustenance. That twin responsibility, to give and receive, can only be fulfilled by being present and participating. **Ninety-eight percent of time participating in process must be seen as fundamental and hence required; even time missed for sickness should be made up.** Notes from personal physicians alone should not excuse absence because physicians endorse absenteeism rather than addressing fitness and nutrition problems that cause it.

If daily participation is not required and instead one has only to pass examinations, then schools are obsolete. It would be quicker, cheaper and more convenient to set up storefront operations to teach and test content using computers. Such approaches are useful for adults wishing to upgrade and for children pursuing a particular requirement, but they are no more than a fraction of what education of the young is all about.

It is up to governments to implement the two percent limit. If properly done, with a thorough public information campaign before the fact, there would be wide acceptance. The same is true of a change from compulsory to voluntary schooling.

The assumption that everyone between six and sixteen should be forced to attend school never existed in any society till recently. Compulsory attendance laws proliferated throughout the West in the nineteenth century. Still, by 1900 only five or six percent of Americans went through high school and most people would have thought it ridiculous to insist that everyone do so. Since then, compulsory schooling has spread around the world and is such a powerful concept that most countries think they should have more of it. Perhaps it served a purpose in establishing that everyone is educable and that childhood is a good time for schooling. But it is intrinsically unjust and must end.

Instead of compulsory schooling, we must provide universal availability of schooling and the right to it. A right is meaningless unless everyone has the means to exercise the right; **right to schooling must carry with it whatever support is needed to make attendance feasible: fees, supplies, food, clothing, housing, living wage, emotional nurture, etc.** No schooling innovation in the twentieth century has included this change, but it is essential for any new model of schooling.

A person who exercises the **right** to attend has the equally strong **responsibility** to be present, punctual and well-behaved, and to participate fully in obligatory and optional programs. **Regular attendance and good behaviour must be compulsory for all who voluntarily exercise their right to enrol.**

All citizens should have the legal responsibility to become literate and informed. Most people will choose to meet that requirement by attending school in childhood. If schools are properly conceived there will be no problem with low enrolment or poor attendance. Children will demand to enrol and will attend both physically and mentally. They will be there voluntarily knowing that a condition of participation is acceptable behaviour. Behaviour problems will diminish sharply, a change that will transfigure schools. Earlier rather than later enrolment will continue to be the norm, but individual circumstances may dictate that a few people attend intermittently or later in life.

A child whose right to attend school is not being exercised should be the concern of advocates whose responsibility is to see that children's rights are not being abrogated by parents or schools or others. Usually, a non-attender will be from a dysfunctional home, and it will be necessary either to make the home functional immediately or to remove the child to a school residence. Either the school ombudsman or the state ombudsman should be the advocate and should be assisted by advocacy committees of citizens to assess cases.

Where the choice of a child is not to enrol in school, and the ombudsman finds no abrogation of the child's rights and feels the child is competent to decide, the child should remain the responsibility of the ombudsman; he or she should help such a child use medical, recreational, counselling, housing and other services supplied by or through the school or elsewhere in the community. The ombudsman should also see to it that children who enter the job market have the same worker's rights as adults.

Professionals from all social services that support children should be moved permanently into schools. The few Florida schools that have done so have cut dropout rates to a third of the national average.

A step in the wrong direction is the punitive and abusive law in West Virginia which suspends a child's driver's licence for missing ten consecutive days or fifteen days in any semester, without acceptable explanation. No society would tolerate the cancellation of driving privileges for women or Jews or blacks who miss work. But there is more applause than derision when it is done to children. Such a flagrant violation of human and civil rights calls for marches on Charleston.

School Day and School Year

An absurdity of schooling in North America is the short work day and work year. Generally, the work day is less than 5.5 hours and the work year less than 200 days and too often the real figures fall as shockingly low as 4.5-hour days and 180-day years. Compare that with seven to eight-hour school days in South Korea and 240-day school years in Japan. Japanese children receive six weeks more schooling every year than North American children; over a twelve-year period, that adds up to two more years! Comparisons with Europe are also shocking; most grade six students go to school 27.5 hours a week or less in North America but thirty-two hours in Switzerland. The difference is so great that North American children can't be compared to others; they are apples and oranges.

The normal school day should be seven working hours and the normal school year at least 220 working days for both students and teachers. In addition, schools (or portions of them) should be open to students evenings and weekends for supervised, optional, individual study. There is no need to make Saturday morning attendance the rule as in Japan. Many children would show up voluntarily on Saturdays and Sundays to continue activities they regard as important.

School days could begin at 8 a.m., and in many countries they do. But I am suggesting the norm be 8:30 a.m. to 4:30 p.m. with an hour break for lunch and additional recess periods for young children. A seven-hour work day still leaves an ample seventeen hours each day for other purposes. And a 220-day work year still leaves a generous six weeks of vacation, eleven holidays and 104 weekend days. My preference is to close North American schools for one month of vacation in summer, one week at Christmas and one week in April. An alternative is to keep schools operating all year and allow individual students and teachers to choose their own vacation periods to a maximum of six weeks.

My concern about the year-round alternative is the violence it might do to education as a process. When the main goal is better accumulation of data by individuals for short-term retention and regurgitation on examinations (as it is presently), it matters little if some students and teachers are always gone for long periods while school remains in session. But when a major goal is better participation of individuals in group process, it is essential to have all members of the group present as often as possible. Short, scheduled absences of individuals on personal assignments could and should be accommodated, but multiple long absences for vacations scattered throughout the year would make scheduling within each classroom more difficult though not impossible. Even allowing that groups within the larger school population could always be made up of students and teachers who have opted for the same vacation period, the constant absence of a quarter or more of the total population would preclude cohesion.

If the option of keeping schools open all year is chosen, school systems will have to be restrained or they will merely stick the present, short work-day and short work-year into the new format and stagger student and teacher vacations as an administrative convenience; it is a way of stuffing more children into one building because a quarter are always on holiday. Los Angeles and sixty-five or more other school districts in the United States are already practicing such subterfuge. Several Ontario school boards may be following along. **The only valid reason for year-round schooling is to lengthen the school year for students and teachers to at least 220 classroom days.**

Open education and all other school innovations have failed to specify longer hours. Many teachers' organizations disgrace themselves by supporting the present short school day and school year. The Ontario Teachers' Federation has a policy statement that the maximum number of instructional days in one school year be 185. However, discerning individual teachers all over North America are apt to admit privately that longer school hours are needed. Students are more likely than teachers to favour longer hours. Wherever voluntary Saturday or summer programs are offered, they turn up in droves. Most parents also approve because supervision of children on excessively long vacations and short school days is a problem for them. And most parents want their children to have the additional education that longer school hours make possible.

Huge numbers of children spend two hours or more a day on buses. That totals 360 hours a year. More than fourteen weeks! Students and parents will be grateful when the time is used educationally. Daily bus trips of more than fifteen minutes should be school time. Seats on buses should be fitted with computer shelves, tv screens and audio equipment (for school-related programming). An adult other than the driver should be aboard to supervise (under the present model of schooling) and consult (under a new model of schooling where students are self-propelled learners). Even a basic sound system that allows each student to hear a talking book on earphones would be a big improvement over the travelling wasteland of restlessness that is the typical school bus.

Dropouts

Japan has a dropout rate under ten percent and possibly under five (depending on counting criteria). Comparisons with the West are startling. In 1989 about 3,600 American school children dropped out every day. A quarter to a third of Americans who start high school never finish. For black and Hispanic children the figure is close to half, but for Asian Americans, the figure reported by the New York City Board of Education in 1989 was thirteen percent. Chicago and several other American cities had fifty percent dropout rates in the eighties. In Australia the figure was even higher. Canada and most other developed countries had rates between twenty and thirty-five percent. Even allowing for local modifications in the ubiquitous model of schooling and for considerable differences in counting criteria and graduation requirements, the discrepancy in dropout rates confirms that factors beyond school doors and deep within the fabric of societies are involved.

Even more children **drop down** than drop out: they give up on difficult programs and take easier ones. Still more **hang around**: they linger physically having dropped out mentally, and eventually are given enough meaningless, borderline credits to push them out school doors. Those who drop down or hang around are as much a loss to society as those who drop out.

Among those who leave early are a few motivated mavericks who will make it on their own as entrepreneurs or artists. And there are a few level-headed workers who apply themselves to ordinary jobs, or training for such jobs, and get far more satisfaction than they ever got at school. For these people, dropping out is an instant passport to adult-hood and at least modest success. They should not be disparaged. They have the right to quit school just as adults have the right to quit jobs that are not right for them.

For these legitimate dropouts there should be fair labour laws and a far better support system to help them find housing, training and jobs. Long ago, Edgar Friedenberg observed correctly in his book *Coming Of Age In America* (New York: Vintage, 1963): "The present furor over school dropouts is not a result of any increase in the proportion of youngsters who do not finish school, but the fact there is no place for the dropout to go in our economy."

For most dropouts, the passport to adulthood is not a passport to success. The conventional wisdom that more education correlates with a better job and a richer life remains true. Dropouts tend to be losers after they leave school as they were during and before school. They are more likely to have low-paying jobs, be unemployed or be delinquent. Not all dropouts become delinquents, but the characteristics of a potential dropout are similar to those of a potential young offender. If we remedy the causes of dropping out we also remedy most causes of delinquency. It will be cost-effective. In 1987, researchers for the Intercultural Development Research Association in San Antonio reck-oned that $17.5 billion would be returned through higher incomes and lower social service costs for $1.9 billion spent keeping all grade nine students in Texas from dropping out.

Children of single-parent households are the most likely to quit school. Whether there are two parents or one, the lower the education level, occupational status and income of parents, the more likely chil-dren are to drop out; they arrive at school poorly prepared because they have not been read to at home and have not learned enough vocabulary or thinking skills or interests; they have low aspirations because the home does not demonstrate and convey high educational expectations.

At school, from early primary upward, potential dropouts have poor attendance, more than the usual number of learning disabilities, limited language and ciphering skills, lack of long-range goals, low self-esteem and self-confidence, underdeveloped life skills (manners, grooming, dress, conversation. . .), a feeling of alienation, the need for instant rewards, and a preference for concrete rather than the abstract thinking increasingly required in higher grades.

These and other **characteristics of likely dropouts can be identified in very young children, even in infants, and that is where intervention should concentrate.** Baltimore, Maryland, with a forty-five percent dropout rate, decided in 1988 to attack the problem at grade six. They should have reached down to pre-school years. In 1988, New York City looked at past records and concluded that an elementary school student absent eighteen days a year or more is likely to become a dropout. On the basis of that obvious criterion, they shifted a million or so of their forty million dollar dropout-prevention budget from high schools to elementary schools. A beginning. But why wasn't it done years ago, and why is most of the money still spent in high school years when it is too late? The answer is that crisis spending at the scene of the calamity has more visibility and more political appeal than early-prevention spending.

It is always politically fashionable to drag out the old dropout dilemma. Everybody has a band-aid solution: tinker with school or home in this or that way and the problem will disappear. A popular remedy at school is counselling. But it is always too little too late. A favored home cure is to have school people visit parents and make them more comfortable with schooling. Better links with parents improve schools, but parents of potential dropouts have proven and will continue to prove unreachable in any meaningful way. **Isolated, culturally distanced or dysfunctional families are not going to be changed significantly soon enough to save any current generation of potential dropouts.**

Major causes of dropping out that lie within the school system are seldom identified and never remedied. The main one is lack of skills in reading, writing, listening, speaking, organizing, studying, problem solving, etc. Most high schools don't teach such skills. They teach only subjects. They don't even bother testing every new arrival thoroughly to see if elementary schools have taught skills successfully.

Most dropouts (and delinquents) are illiterate, semi-literate or seriously deficient in one or more other skills necessary to survive the present high school system. They suffer frustration and boredom at school, so they leave (or drop down or hang around). The only solution is to **make skill-building the prime responsibility of high schools (as well as elementary schools)**. That would be a complete turn around. Not only would it require total rethinking of the school system, but also retraining of most teachers because they don't presently know how to teach literacy and other essential skills. Even then we would not have a fully viable school system for the twenty-first century because it would still be teacher-active and student-passive instead of the other way around, but at least, far more people should graduate, and all graduates should be able to read, write, speak, listen and cipher adequately.

Another cause of boredom is poor teaching. Some teachers are tiresome drones. Others are only marginally competent. Still others are disinterested or burnt out. Even among the majority of teachers who work hard and try to make courses interesting, there are few gifted performers. Yet they are caught in an ancient system that expects them to perform all day. Students are cast in the role of passive listeners, so they get bored. The problem will only be solved when the present model of schooling is replaced with one in which students, not teachers, are the engines that drive classrooms.

A further source of boredom is irrelevant courses — and irrelevant content within courses which could be relevant with better selection. Too many courses bog down in detail that lends itself nicely to examination questioning but does not matter to most people; **most courses, including mathematics, science, and history courses are burdened with fat in need of trimming.** High school students need a general education, not in-depth academic specialization. Those individuals who like a given subject will delve into it deeply and must be encouraged and helped to do so, but the same depth merely buries and suffocates others. Rigour comes through process and through handling information, not from memorization of endless details for short-term retention and regurgitation on examinations.

The other side of the irrelevance coin is that the outside world is too much excluded from school. Schools are like cooks who use canned food from the shelf and ignore fresh produce that grows all around. Valuable stuff in the educational pantry should not be ignored but should be mixed well with fresh fare that ripens daily in the community, country and world. Occasional admission of catastrophic events such as the Persian Gulf War of 1991 is tokenism.

Both yesterday and tomorrow should and will get their due, but relevance comes from seizing the world of this moment by the lapels and pulling it right into the classroom. Current events, popular culture, arts, international understanding, social service, student government, nutrition, fitness, sex, parenting, children's rights, environmental concerns — these should be central and obligatory in the curriculum, second in importance only to requirements in various literacies and essential skills of organization, research, problem solving, group learning, study methods, focused discussion, etc. Most present academic subjects should be offered as optional credits (but only when content and teaching methods are improved).

Dropouts are also alienated by the impersonal nature of schools. They feel nobody knows them, and they are right: they go through entire years without ever having a close relationship with a teacher. They feel they don't belong any place, and they are right. Students are like tourists on a whirlwind package deal — if it is eleven o'clock on Tuesday, this must be room 201. If something called a home room exists, it is a sham. The real home room of today's student is a minuscule locker in a crowded corridor only marginally homier than a prison, and even that home is likely to be out of bounds most of the day and subject to search without warrant.

Innovators who try to patch up the present school system often suggest solving the alienation problem and the organization of student work load by attaching every student to a mentor-teacher. In one form or other, that idea has been tried in every conscientious high school. The mentors of choice are often guidance counsellors who already have a full load and could not possibly take real mentoring responsibility for even one student, much less fifty or a hundred each; guidance counsellors don't have time even to locate that number of students frequently (let alone locating the constantly-changing data needed about each one), and they don't have time for necessarily long and continuing discussions with each student.

Or the miracle mentor envisioned by patch-up innovators might be the so-called home-room teacher. Most home-room teachers see their classes one or two periods a day, and the whole time is taken up with teaching the class, not talking to individuals. Worse, some teachers see their home rooms for only a few hectic minutes of attendance checking first thing in the morning. And virtually all home-room teachers have a full-day teaching load.

Many teachers lack the interpersonal skills needed to get close to individual students. All students confronted with such teachers know how to "talk adult" without ever revealing anything even though they long to talk to the right listener. And most home room teachers don't know how to teach either study or work-load management skills. Besides, the structure of the present model of schooling and the internal communication limits that are integral to it make it impossible to operate a mentor system with either guidance teachers or home room teachers as mentors.

What we need is a new model of schooling with a real home base that every student lives in or returns to at will all day, every day, every year, and in that home base, all day, every day, every year, must be a full-time, trained and skilled mentor, relieved of most traditional data-peddling chores, whose job is to know everything about his or her students and help them orchestrate their education and their lives (see chapter 22). All major schooling innovations of the twentieth century have failed, in part because they did not provide full-time mentors.

But mentors alone are not enough. **In any new model of schooling that works, students must have real power over their own**

lives. Lack of power is an important factor in alienation and apathy. Teens are physically, sexually and socially more mature than ever, yet are perceived and received by schools as eternally puerile. Schools anticipate and hence dictate that students behave immaturely. The low expectation of the school is telegraphed by an elaborate power structure from which students are excluded.

Students who make a hard-earned if marginal and precarious living, pay taxes, buy their own food and clothing, own cars, have lovers, and know their way around in the world are reduced to regimented, recidivist ring-around-a-rosiers the moment they enter a high school. Twentieth-century innovators have never taken seriously their responsibility for restructuring to include students in real decision-making power within the institution which so controls their lives. Even open education (among the most promising of attempts to patch up some aspects of the traditional model of schooling) failed, in part, because it made not the slightest provision for students in school management roles.

But many factors that cause dropping out are only partly school-related. A third of female dropouts are pregnant. Better sex education at school would help, but much of the solution lies beyond school. Nor can school do everything needed to allay fears of students who decide there is no use studying because a nuclear blast is coming. All of society has to help with that one — and with economic impoverishment of the young.

There are three levels of child poverty. The first two obscure the third. First is the grotesque poverty of children in developing countries. A shocking UNICEF report (The State of the World's Children 1989) says third-world debt is escalating the death rate of children. So much money is paid in interest to wealthy countries that surviving children share with parents the abject misery which results.

The second level of child poverty is that of the poor in developed countries. According to the U.S. Urban Institute, 9.6% of Canadian children and 17.1% of American children live below the poverty line. Forty-six percent of poor Canadian children and fifty-seven percent of poor American children are severely poor. In Metropolitan Toronto, about one child in seven is fed by charity food banks part of the time. That kind of poverty often correlates with more and longer illnesses, chaotic home life, neglect and low aspirations. And ultimately, it correlates with dropping out, dropping down or hanging around. By age fifteen, twice as many poor as non-poor children have fallen behind in school.

The third level of child poverty is less dramatic than the first two, so it gets no media coverage; nonetheless, its time as a social issue has come. **Children, in general, are poor. They, rather than old people or women or any racial group, are the poorest sector of society.** An important reason that many teenagers drop out of school is that they need the money a job brings. The job may be third-rate and only part-time, but it makes the difference between a modicum of economic power and the galling impotence of poverty.

Large numbers of students fall behind in school and drop down, if not out, from overload. Jobs crowd out school commitments. Fatigue is epidemic. The usual response of teachers and writers of reports is to urge that students be made even poorer by curtailing part-time work! Pundits rarely see the obvious need to provide children with a fair share of national wealth either through jobs or some form of guaranteed income.

A related cause of dropping out lies in part outside of school — health or, rather, the lack of it. Many teens are physically unfit and sub-clinically ill. They lack the stamina to be students. My guess is that when more precision is applied to compiling statistics, we will find that poor diet bears about two-thirds of the blame for both clinical and sub-clinical illness.

Another reason teens drop out of school is to escape an unhappy home. A few leave home, go on welfare, and remain at school. Far more give up school when they give up home. It is difficult to stay at school while finding and settling into a rented room that can be paid for with welfare or part-time employment. Such rooms are scarce, noisy, wretched and unsafe. Homeless teens usually live on the streets.

In 1989, the U.S. education department estimated that 220,000 children were homeless. The National Coalition for the Homeless estimated the number at between 500,000 and 750,000 counting those accompanied by homeless parents. Britain had at least 50,000 children living on their own. Minimum estimates for cities ranged from 5000 in Minneapolis to 12,000 in Los Angeles. New York, Chicago and Toronto all hovered around 10,000. Dropouts who continue to "live" at home for economic reasons have often left in every sense except the physical: necessity forces them to use the old places for clothes storage and sleep, but their lives are elsewhere.

To solve the dropout problem, we must first solve the housing problem. The answer is school residences or some other honorable, and desirable housing for teens who cannot live at home. Until we have residences at all schools, the only alternative is to persuade older people to open their empty rooms to teens. There is no shortage of rooms. Just a shortage of imagination and commitment. In the Middle Ages virtually all children of all classes were sent to live for long periods with other families. Some went to learn trades or be servants, but many went to learn manners and be "schooled" in some way. Even aristocrats sent their children to be pages or attendants in other noble households. A modern version of that ancient practice could solve the housing crisis and relieve the damaging tensions when parents and children don't get along.

School Residences

The December 3, 1964, edition of the Toronto *Globe and Mail* reported as follows:

What should the school of tomorrow look like?

R.G. Des Dixon, vice-principal of Cosburn Junior High School, yesterday pictured it as an institution that would cater extensively to the needs of problem children who he said are in danger of becoming delinquents unless they receive adequate attention.

Mr. Dixon suggested at a meeting of the East York Area Social Planning Council that East York build such a school, possibly as a Centennial project. The school, he said, would include a clinic staffed by nurses, doctors and psychiatrists and a building that would serve as a home for children whose parents are incapable of looking after them properly.

As a first-year teacher, I imagined how the lives of some of my students could be bettered if they lived all the time in an atmosphere of nurture instead of being sucked back into a sewer of ignorance and abuse every night. The school ran a model house across the street. Home economics classes went every day to cook and clean for conjured middle-class paragons. Nobody lived there! My suggestion that a few desperately needy students move in was met with scoffing and dismissed by management as radical boat-rocking.

I think it more radical to perpetuate the myth that all or even most children live in traditional familial bliss. Television producers of family series would have us believe that children live in charmingly decorated homes abounding in good food, good fellowship and good times, where life is one long series of hugs and laughs and all problems are solved amicably in thirty minutes. In this deception, television producers are apologists for the middle-class minority who cling to the blind belief that their household happiness, real or imagined, is universal and that therefore their values should be universal.

The upper classes have known for centuries that home is not all it's cracked up to be, so they pack their children off to orphanages of the rich, ivied boarding schools and posh summer camps. For those a bit older, there are college dorms and fraternity houses. And from them emerge captains of industry and state.

At the other end of the spectrum, the unparented poor used to have orphanages too. Unfortunately, they disappeared for want of proper funding under the pretext that better alternatives would be available. Instead, they should have evolved into residences with just as much style and prestige as any private school residence but belonging to the school down the street in every neighborhood. Prestige would not be as unlikely as some might imagine. Given the proper program and staff, a school residence could quickly become the home of choice for those living-in and the envy of many not so fortunate. Young people enjoy group living. Residence can satisfy the need to congregate with peers without the negative side effects of school and street gangs.

The latter day incarnation of orphanage that I propose will welcome all unparented children whether the condition of being unparented is caused by death, divorce, incompetence, indifference, ignorance, absence, inability, cruelty, contempt, incompatibility or other circumstance. Some students will be in residence only briefly, say, one school year, while others will live in year-round all their school lives.

Both long and short-term residents will be children who in their own view and/or the view of their advocates are better off living in residence than elsewhere. I am not proposing that we move prison schools for young criminals onto school campuses. In the short run we will continue to need secure, separate accommodation for delinquents. In the long run the need for prison housing will dwindle because school residences combined with a new model of schooling and of childhood will provide the kind of nurture that prevents most juvenile delinquency.

Nor will school residences, in the short run, accommodate all the children presently in foster homes. Some are too damaged, left so long in original inadequate homes that they are walking wounded; they are more in need of full-time crisis management by professional therapists in a clinical setting than the heroic holding-tank ministrations of over-whelmed, underpaid, volunteer parent substitutes. When society musters enough guts and good sense to rescue children from inadequate parenting at the earliest possible moment rather than after damage has been done, nearly all children who now live in foster homes will live in school residences, many from infancy. No decrease in the number of such children is likely in the immediate future; the trend has been to more children going into foster care each year even though fewer babies are born. At the same time, though the foster care system is dying, nothing has appeared to replace or even supplement it.

But former foster children will be only part of the total number who choose to live in residence. For many teens and their parents, life is a constant, debilitating clash of wills. Both sides will opt for the healthier alternative of residence life for part or all of teen years. Caring people unable to parent because of career demands, enforced absence, divorce, illness, or other reasons will opt for the boarding alternative at the neighborhood school. Other students will live in as a planned learning strategy. Residence life will provide them with order and organization to replace confusion and chaos at home that prevents them from becoming self-propelled learners. It will also provide affection and attention that builds self-esteem necessary for success in school and life.

Foreign high school students who come to affluent countries seeking educational opportunities unavailable in their homelands will live in residence at neighborhood schools. They will avoid exploitation by landlords and store-front cram-school operators and will learn about the host country by living and studying with local students instead of ghettoizing in barren flats. In return, local students will receive a priceless experience in international understanding.

Most resident students will spend some time with parents on week-ends and holidays. It is important to maintain the child/parent bond if possible. But some students will spend little or no time with biological begetters. **School residences will be a viable, rational, honorable, timely and welcome alternative to the functional family where no functional family exists for whatever reason or period of time**.

Not all children in residence will be attending school. Some will have opted to take jobs intermittently or permanently. Even young men and women in their late teens and early twenties should be welcomed in school residences. Where there are several past school age, a separate residence may be warranted. In either case, older residents must be part of the school community.

The emotional commitment, responsibilities, depth of discussion and range of activities in which every person participates in the democratic governance of a residence is a rich educational experience. It can't be achieved in typical authoritarian households where children are not even consulted let alone accorded full status as decision-makers in a consensus model of group management. The availability of evening and weekend learning activities and the ethos of a school residence will encourage further education.

Presently, there is no housing for people from thirteen through the early twenties who are on their own. In some jurisdictions, children past fifteen don't even qualify for the usual, inadequate children's financial aid because they are too old. Most have no fixed address. They are dismissed as street people, runaways or transients. All three names are pejorative. The impression is conveyed in the media and in conventional discourse that such children are aberrant, that they have no right to self-determination, that they should be captured and returned to parents. The reality is that most have been physically or sexually abused at home and virtually all are emotionally and mentally bruised.

In Toronto, at least seventy-five children under sixteen disappear from home each week, nearly all without the aid of adults. Disappearance rates are higher but harder to gauge for those sixteen or over because they are legally free to leave home and often are not reported to police for tabulation. Many congregate and perambulate a block from my house. I have interviewed scores, but never one from a healthy home. Even those who have taken to the streets for the summer and will return home reluctantly in the fall seem always to be escaping briefly from dysfunctional families. Most think the streets are physically or emotionally safer than home.

In spite of street-life hardships, most have no intention of returning home. Nor should they. They are refugees with legitimate claim to sanctuary. They would be endangered by extradition to their places of origin. Yet that is the usual response, sometimes with the well-meant but futile addition of token counselling for children and parents. Such reconciliations are rarely lasting; it is too late to undo damage of a dozen years, largely because parents cannot be sufficiently changed in time to make any difference.

Lacking an address or phone number for return calls, and often hunted, it is difficult for unparented children to find jobs or even get welfare. Yet some manage, against all odds, to continue at school. An amazing six percent of Halifax, Nova Scotia high school students live on their own. Every one of them should be considered for the Order of Canada. They are heroic. But most children on their own never get past making ends meet. They are universally malnourished and usually tired. Many become drug users and that means they have to find drug money. Some panhandle. Some survive on petty theft. Others learn to break and enter. Quite a few deal drugs, and the number is growing. But the main source of substantial income is still prostitution. Half of male and female prostitutes are eighteen or less. Most started at fifteen or sooner. Every child has the credentials, and on-the-job training is readily available at full pay. Whoring is the teen profession, not of choice, but necessity.

People under sixteen are usually forbidden by law to hold factory jobs and those under fourteen to hold even service jobs. It is useless to tell teens living on their own to live on air or take fifty dollars a day for full-time drudgery in restaurant kitchens when they can make three times as much selling their bodies or ten times as much selling crack part-time. The usual response of society is to pass more curfew laws denying teenagers freedom of movement, an affront to human and civil rights that no government would dare impose on adults. In March 1989, Washington D.C. curfewed people under eighteen off the streets after eleven p.m. Frustrated politicians couldn't get at the powerful adults behind murders and drug empires, so in an act of fury, they got the children instead. Such laws are as futile as they are unjust.

The sensible response to the phenomenon of part-time and full-time street children is to give them adequate, legitimate income and housing. We must provide dignified, desirable housing for those already living on their own and those still with incompetent parents. Most communities offer nothing, so many children head for big cities. The biggest cities may have hostels or shelters that offer temporary haven; a handful of people get a roof and food for a few days, usually because a few concerned adults have battled indifferent or hostile citizens to found and sustain a youth shelter. Noble as it is, such crisis intervention is a stopgap not to be confused with permanent residences available to all young people at all schools as a normal alternative to family living.

Residence staff should include teachers of all ages who choose to be part of the live-in community. There are always teachers who welcome the challenges and rewards of living their calling full-time. Other adult residents should include seniors and the kind of people who presently become foster parents. Some will be and should be paid, but many will be unpaid volunteers. All will be richly rewarded.

There is no other initiative any Western country could take to reduce the dropout rate and improve attendance that would be anywhere near as effective as adding residences to schools. For that result alone, it would be worth doing and cost-effective. When all spin-off social benefits are factored in, the move to residences becomes an improvement imperative unparalleled in the history of schooling and child-rearing.

CHAPTER 12

CHILDREN'S RIGHTS

As unsettling as the prospect of children's liberation may be, it is helpful to remember that demands for children's rights are not meant to destroy family life, but to improve it; not meant to end education, but to vitalize it; not meant to rupture the relationship of adult and child, but to enhance it; not meant to undermine parents, but to liberate them; not meant to threaten society's survival capability, but to strengthen it.

— Richard Farson, *Birthrights*
(New York: Macmillan, 1974)*

The present models of schooling and childhood incubated together and during the long gestation became Siamese twins sharing a nervous system; if one is wounded, the other also feels pain; if one is diseased, the other suffers similar symptoms; if one is dying, so is the other.

Children as chattel is the one powerful concept that the model of childhood contributed to the model of schooling. Otherwise, **the emerging model of schooling led and fed the emerging model of childhood.** Most people think it must have been the other way around, but it wasn't until the late nineteenth century. The hiving off of children for separate treatment in buildings called schools fostered

---

* Everyone interested in a new model of childhood should read this important book, also published in paperback by Penguin in 1978.

the previously non-existent notion that children are quite different from adults. Later, proliferation of boarding schools in post-Renaissance Europe encouraged the segregation of children from adults to replace the integration of the Middle Ages.

As schooling lengthened, childhood got longer to accommodate it until, by the mid-twentieth century, the United Nations was able to define childhood as everything up to age eighteen, a notion that would have been rejected as mad in the Middle Ages. The model of childhood that emerged willy-nilly to match the evolving model of schooling has been mythologized to such stature that it is even more unassailable than its twin. Yet both must be set upon.

Both concepts — universal, prolonged schooling and childhood — are only about 600 years old and must be considered new and tentative in the 6000-year history of civilization and the 100,000-year history of humankind. Think of them as pilot projects overdue for serious evaluation and reconsideration. Both evaluations have been more or less under way for a century, and both have gathered momentum in the last fifty years, but both are still far from comprehensive. Data from both evaluations may be invalid and unreliable and conclusions prejudiced because the work has come from scholars unconsciously biased by their pre-conditioned concepts of childhood and schooling.

Cultural historian of childhood and schooling, Philippe Aries, in his book, *Centuries Of Childhood* (New York: Random House, 1962) is as transparent as he is constant in his unsupported assumption that the models of childhood and schooling emerging during the Renaissance were superior to medieval models and that twentieth-century models are superior to developmental stages of preceding centuries. Aries assumes (wrongly) that the present practice of rigid separation by age is superior to the seventeenth-century practice of mixing ages. He writes, "Our modern sensibility is revolted by this mixing of . . . young boys [ages eleven and twelve] and adolescents in the same class." Not my sensibility; mine is revolted by arbitrarily separating them. **Arbitrary separation according to age in the current model of schooling institutionalizes the generation gap by conditioning**

children to relate only to their own age group.

In his book, *The Disappearance Of Childhood* (London: W.H. Allen, 1983), Neil Postman is equally conspicuous in his devotion to the existing concept of childhood. Though he documents aspects of an emergent new model of childhood, he sees no virtue in the changes, feels no excitement about new beginnings. He writes from the prejudiced position declared in his introduction, "To have to stand and wait as the charm, malleability, innocence and curiosity of children are degraded and then transmogrified into the lesser features of pseudo-adulthood is painful and embarrassing and, above all sad."

A third famous writer about children is psychiatrist Robert Coles. His five books in a series called *Children In Crisis* (Boston: Little Brown, 1967–77) and two more on the political and moral life of children are heavy on case studies intended to illuminate the tortuous path of childhood and light on ideas for a better path; but a graver weakness is that his interviews were done in children's homes, "enabled by willing, indeed wonderfully hospitable parents," and in schools with "the considerable cooperation of school authorities." Hardly circumstances conducive to critical reconsideration of the models of childhood and schooling, and indicative of Coles' acceptance of givens that should not be accepted.

Even Vance Packard's book, *Our Endangered Children* (Boston: Little Brown, 1983) is a dirge of regret rather than an anthem of affirmation. Most of Packard's suggestions are for life-support systems to sustain dead institutions.

Another problem is that investigative studies are limited mainly to fragments of present models rather than to holistic studies of those models or to new models of childhood and schooling. The schooling evaluation has bogged down because the evaluation of childhood has been cursory. There has been plenty of study, mainly by psychologists, psychiatrists and pediatricians, of the individual child but not nearly enough study of the present model of childhood by sociologists, historians, anthropologists, political scientists, economists, architects, urban planners, criminologists, theologians, jurists, etc.

A continuing problem is that the two evaluations are not connected in the public mind. Even educators who genuinely want to recalculate schooling usually fail to consider our notion of childhood part of the equation. One reason for the failure of open education was its failure to comprehend and accommodate a new model of childhood. **Until we get a workable concept of childhood, we can't achieve a workable concept of schooling. And vice versa.**

Activists who care most about children are on opposite sides in the appraisal of childhood: those who advocate protection of children want to fine-tune the present model of childhood; those who advocate protection of children's rights want to replace the present concept of childhood with a new one. **Protection of children and protection of children's rights are two different and often conflicting matters.**

Rights, in this context, means hard-core, small and large 'p' political rights that will liberate children and redefine childhood. It does not mean the general truths about quality of life that the United Nations declares to be rights of the child. The latter have value only insofar as they point up with aphoristic brevity some principles which are as deserving of reinforcement for all other age groups as for children: everybody **needs** love, food, medicine, education, a name, a nationality, special care if handicapped, relief from disaster, a chance to be useful and develop talents, protection from exploitation, an environment of peace and brotherhood that is free of discrimination on the basis of race, colour, sex, religion, national or social origin, etc.

What the UN calls the **rights** of the child are really the **needs** of the child and the adult. The **right** of the child is to have his **needs** met. **Meaningful talk of children's rights by the UN or anybody else must be in terms of full civil and human rights**, the kind of rights that give children and their advocates enough political power to see that children's needs are taken seriously. Such rights are outlined in the UN Declaration of Human Rights, and it is this rather than the misnamed UN Declaration of the Rights of the Child that should be the anthem of children's rights activists.

The UN notion of children's rights leaves the present, obsolete concept of childhood unchallenged — not surprising since the prototype version of the Declaration of the Rights of the Child adopted in 1924 by the League of Nations was conceived by organizations bent upon protecting children, not their political rights. Subsequent versions, adopted by the UN in 1959 and 1968, were more polished but still superficial and firmly based in the current conservative concept of childhood and family.

Nonetheless, a few points in the 1968 declaration unintentionally opened the door to deeper discussion of rights. Principle 9 explicitly forbad "exploitation" of children but, naively or hypocritically, assumed that exploitation is the exclusive domain of traffickers and employers — the child "shall not be the subject of traffic in any form; shall not be admitted to employment before an appropriate minimum age." In the real world, children are also exploited by schools that detain them against their will, religions that indoctrinate them before they are able to resist, national constitutions that fail to guarantee them equality regardless of age, righteous bigots who keep them ignorant by denying them information, parents who chisel them into clones of themselves, economic and legal systems that keep them poor, power structures that keep them powerless, etc.

The 1989 Convention of the Rights of the Child improves upon the 1968 Declaration but falls short of specifying full civil and human rights. Document #1 of the UNICEF Briefing Kit on the Convention exposes the UN's fatal flaw when it says, "the very status of a child means in principle that he or she has no political rights." It is not surprising that the UN is stalled at such an archaic notion of status and of political rights. All member nations are still more or less entangled in the jungle of patriarchal tradition. It is slowly being hacked away from women, but the machetes have barely begun to swing in liberation of children.

Children as chattel is a tradition that still disables children. The intent chattelites of old toted up children as inventory along with cattle, pigs, sheep, fields and measures of grain. They enjoyed and exercised life and death power over offspring. In a lot of countries and many sub-cultures within countries, including Western countries, little has changed: children are still brutalized and still considered property. The ancient chattelite notion that a child has no identity except in relation to some adult continues unabated. But in polite mainstreams of Western societies, most old expressions of chattelite tradition have given way to modern variations; like a virus, the tradition mutates when attacked and emerges alive and virulent in some new disguise.

Chattelites still claim sovereignty over children but are usually content to merely beat them privately. They still inventory offspring as assets (two children, two cars and a dog named Lassie). Children are still, in a sense, economic assets even though they were officially removed from the work force as part of their downgrading when childhood was defined. Now, their own children are assets to politicians and corporate employees at all levels as proof of their eligibility for any position of trust in a chattelite society. And parents save money because teens labour for incomes at slave wages.

But today's children are mainly emotional assets. The most advanced chattelites, who are enlightened enough to eschew beating their children, still insist upon the right to dominate them. The emotionally self-serving and thoroughly chattelite notion that parents have the right to mold offspring in their own image goes almost unchallenged in spite of pious protestations to the contrary, often in the form of rhetorical smokescreens. The most famous is from Kahlil Gibran's book, *The Prophet* (New York: Alfred A. Knopf, 1971), published in 1923 and reprinted eighty-seven times. Three million copies have been sold in America and it has been published in over twenty languages.

The most famous verses on the status of children have been reprinted countless times in newspapers and magazines and read on radio and from pulpits:

> Your children are not your children.
> They are the sons and daughters of life's longing for itself.
> They come through you but not from you.
> And though they are with you yet they belong not to you.

You may give them your love but not your thoughts,
For they have their own thoughts.
You may house their bodies but not their souls,
For their souls dwell in the house of tomorrow,
Which you cannot visit, not even in your dreams.
You may strive to be like them, but seek not to make them like you.
For Life goes not backward nor tarries with yesterday.

Everyone applauds the message but nobody heeds it. For sheer hypocrisy, the Gibran-quoting scenario challenges such other favorites as a chapel full of military officers and defence contractors amening turn-the-other-cheek gospels, or fat parishioners motoring contentedly home from church to resume their gluttonous pursuits after still another uplifting reminder from the pulpit that half the world is starving; or, for that matter, authoritarian elementary and high school teachers endorsing Gibran's description of the consummate teacher: "If he is indeed wise, he does not bid you enter the house of his wisdom, but rather leads you to the threshold of your own mind."

Until the message registers, children will remain chattel, candied ornaments or precious darlings perhaps but, nonetheless, chattel. The message is this: **Children don't belong to parents; they belong to life, to life's yearning for itself**. Parents get the privilege and responsibility of serving that yearning by providing nurture. Nothing in the contract with life gives parents the right to exploit, indoctrinate, intimidate or dominate children. Nothing gives them the right to mold children into copies of themselves. Nothing gives parents the right to use children for their own aggrandizement, emotional ends, power trips. . . .

People who can't have their own way anywhere else can feed their damaged egos by bossing children. That is the parent power trip — the only chance to be the complete master of a complete victim. Nearly every failed adult in the world can play God once in his life by exercising absolute authority over a child. The only qualification needed is the same one dogs have — to be in heat for five minutes. And even when that basic qualification is supplemented by a modicum or even a lot of applied intelligence, the main motivation for procreation (beyond being in heat) is likely to be the desire to leave something behind as evidence of having lived. The second most likely non-sexual motive is equally self-serving — to produce a hedge against present or anticipated loneliness or poverty.

The parent power trip is enjoyed even by chairmen of boards and presidents of countries because no job, no matter how exalted, offers such complete and sustained mastery over another human being. Since slavery went out of favour, parenting alone has provided ensured ownership of helpless human flesh for at least eighteen years.

In most people, none of this is deliberate or even conscious. These parents are not modern monsters. They are for the most part, pillars of society, the present bearers of the leadership load that has for thousands of years kept families, tribes, villages, provinces, nations and empires together. But like their predecessors, they will not readily perceive the evil inherent in cherished practices. Instead, at the first hint of revelation, they will man (and woman) the barricades to protect their turf. That is what child protectionists and sanctity-of-the-family apologists are doing. They are polishing the benevolent, authoritarian skin of an apple that is wormy with injustice. They are busy keeping children helpless, powerless and possessed. They oppose the liberation of children. They are chattelites.

The basic principle of children's rights is that all persons of either sex, whether 2, 52 or 102 have the same human and civil rights. There can be no double standard. Chattelites don't accept the principle. How could they? It denies their right to exploit children for adult purposes. Slave owners did not accept a similar principle for a similar reason. Nor did the upper classes. Nor anti-semites. Nor white supremacists. Nor chauvinist males.

Children share with old people the battle against ageism. Both age extremes are victims of myths generated by the powerful middle. So pervasive are the myths that they become self-fulfilling expectations: the old stay in rocking chairs of one sort or another because they are supposed to; the young stay in playpens of one sort or another because they are supposed to. But the old will be freed before the young because forces of resistance to liberation of the young are stronger and munitions for resistance more amply stowed in the dumps of chattelite tradition.

Chattelite thinking is everywhere. It aggrandizes adults, especially parents, to sanction their domination of children, and it demeans children to justify their subservience. Parent puffery precepts have been cultivated so long by self-serving adults that they have achieved a status beyond mere sentiment and are by now virtually sacred. Some **are** sacred in one religion or another.

"Honour thy father and thy mother" was written by a chattelite father or mother. If an equally self-serving child had written it, it would read, "honour thy children." If an enlightened person had written it, it would read, "honour each other." Even if we assume that the original wording was made exclusive to parents in order to focus for the moment on the parenting role (rather than to condition children to abject obedience), it still needs rewording to: "honour motherhood and fatherhood as important roles and honour everyone who fulfills either role well." The **role** of parent (or judge or teacher or whatever) is to be respected but the individual filling that role at any moment must earn respect by performance. One respects the presidency of a nation, the office, but not an incumbent whose performance is shameful.

Yet chattelites insist "father knows best" in the face of devastating evidence to the contrary: more children are brutalized sexually, physically and emotionally by their fathers than by all other people put together. All three kinds of abuse are likely to be power trips. Forceful incest probably has more to do with power than with love or libido. Corporal punishment and emotional aloofness are perverted power plays.

Motherhood has been elevated from the merely honorable image of bearer and nurturer to an image approaching sainthood. Saints must at least live an exemplary life, be thoroughly investigated and endure a long probationary beatification before being canonized. Mothers, including the many who will never perform the role credibly, get there automatically just by giving birth, thanks to a sustained chattelite image-making campaign consolidated by their invention of Mother's Day.

If Mother's Day and Father's Day were used for honest evaluation of every incumbent rather than knee-jerk veneration, the two festivals would disappear, withered away by adult chagrin. But that could never happen because honest evaluation, when nearly every child has been conditioned from birth to feel guilty and beholden, would require the services of a psychiatrist for nearly every household, and there aren't nearly enough shrinks to go around.

If parents were evaluated by children released through therapy from conditioned inferiority feelings, among the first things likely to happen would be the use by many children of their parents' first names. As long as parents are called by role/relationship names (father, mother, mom, dad), they garner unearned status that enhances authority. The vehement enforcement of mommy and daddy nomenclature by each generation of parents is in defence of power.

That chattelitism in its present mutation is sugar-coated with benevolence matters not a whit; the core is as virulent as ever. It causes a chronic secondary infection that is almost universal: repetition compulsion. Many parents feel driven to reenact unresolved conflicts from their own chattelized childhoods; the war zone is the home, and losers in the endless battle are the children of each new generation. Even when battles are bloodless, they are emotionally devastating to victims. Perhaps widest spread of all is velvet-fisted violence done to the human potential of young people denied autonomy by parents who try to satisfy their own unfulfilled neurotic needs by keeping children dependent.

In spite of this, and volumes of evidence notwithstanding, sanctity-of-the-family apologists have mounted a mighty crusade fuelled by nostalgia and desperation, a crusade so mindless in conception and reception that an American president was able to sail into office in 1988 on waves of absurd rhetoric that made capital punishment and a gun in every house into "values of the American family" sure to yield "a kinder and a gentler nation." Any astute politician in the Western world has only to shout "family values" and the chattelite masses snap to attention, salute enthusiastically and pack for the crusades, no matter what sentimental or cynical nonsense is draped like a flag on the icon of family.

While adults, parents in particular (and their power structure, the family) are being exalted by adults for adult purposes, children are being demeaned by the same people for the same purpose. History confirms there is no more effective defence of privilege by those in power than to promulgate into conventional wisdom the invented inferiority of any minority: native peoples under colonial administrations, Eastern European immigrants to America, blacks in Western countries, Koreans resident in Japan, women, children. . . . Even when children are indulged and adored as pets, they are belittled since that aspect of their acceptance is self-serving on the part of adults who need an obedient love object and find a child more responsive and malleable than an animal.

We have built into the very language we speak many subtle and not-so-subtle put-downs of children that relegate them to inferiority and servitude. In nearly every country where English language newspapers and books are published, I have seen children referred to as "it." Adults, never. No writer would say, "an adult and its dog passed by" but nearly every writer would say, "a child and its dog passed by." A child is a thing, an "it," a piece of property. Yet philosopher Martin Buber warned that every healthy interpersonal relationship demands an I-Thou and never an I-It relationship.

Language is laced with sayings that imply the inferiority of children: "spare the rod and spoil the child;" "children should be seen and not heard;" "children should speak only when spoken to;" "children should know their place;" "don't send a boy to do a man's job;" "sort the men from the boys." Even "women and children first" is a put-down created as a clever diversion by the very men who unequivocally put themselves first. Children and their advocates must be on guard against patrons bearing gifts of special status. The price of being special is too high. Being equal is infinitely better.

I use the word "adultish" to mean (from the child's point of view) overbearing, smug, dictatorial. But there is no word "adultish" in a dictionary made by adults. If there were, it would resound with positive meaning: mature, full-blown, responsible. There is, however, in every dictionary, the word "childish" which means (from the adult's point of view): puerile, asinine, fatuous, foolish, simple-minded, arrested, irresponsible. All demeaning connotations. Even the most exact meanings of the word childish have a negative ring about them: babyish, unsophisticated, immature, infantile, infantine, juvenile. "You are so childish," is always an insult, never a compliment.

Minor, as applied to children, is negative in its precise meaning: a person not permitted by law to enjoy full civil rights. And the word carries a burden of other loaded uses: inferior, piddling, junior, trifling, lower in standing. Major, the closest thing to an adult opposite of minor, is loaded with positive connotations: better, higher, superior, main, chief.

Smug adult condescension is built into hollow accolades: out of the mouths of babes; not bad for a twelve-year-old; she's a regular little mother. . . .

We ask children, "What do you want to be when you grow up?" The implication is that they will be nothing till age eighteen or more. Nobody asks adults, "What do you want to be when you grow old." Nor do we ask children, "What are you now?"

Kid, the alternative word for child, is demeaning; it means a young goat. Teenage love is called puppy love — dog love. It is impossible to conceive of an adult who is not a legitimate adult, but millions of children have been told they are not legitimate children. Can there be a more vicious epithet than illegitimate child?

The word "custody" derives from the latin word for watchman and means imprisonment or guarding. It is applied only to criminals and children.

Precocious is a word hardly ever used except in reference to children who defy gratuitous adult prohibitions and do something early and well, in spite of the odds. It means "developed or matured earlier than usual." But in applying it to capable children, we manage to imply there is something unnatural going on. It is a derogatory term. "She's a precocious child" means she is a smart-ass and must be kept in her place. Adult wisdom has an understood, if unspoken, proper place for every type of smart-ass.

The word prodigy is also derogatory; it is probably significant that one dictionary meaning of the word is "something monstrous." Along with autistic savants, child prodigies are put down by adults as not quite proper or, at best, as cute curiosities. And they are allowed to practice only in selected cerebral, artistic or athletic spheres: a child prodigy is never allowed to practice in politics or sex, seldom in research, finance, management, etc.

When Mozart was wowing the concert circuit with keyboard artistry at age six and his own compositions at seven, the freak show response was already creeping in, and it was barely possible or okay to be a child and be considered capable of doing whatever you were capable of. Not just in music — in anything that older people did. The years were 1762 and 63. The curtain was falling. In England at the same time, the remarkable Thomas Chatterton felt it expedient to hide pre-teen genius by attributing his Rowley Poems to a long-dead, imaginary adult.

Four hundred years earlier, it would have been totally okay for either boy, or any child, to be himself, to perform like adults in any activity, regardless of age. Two hundred years later, it was a virtual taboo. What happened between the fourteenth and twentieth centuries, and particularly after the seventeenth century, was the invention of childhood. Before that, from time immemorial, children a bit past infancy, say seven or eight, were accepted as people with pretty much the same rights, obligations, opportunities or lack of them as older people of the same sex, race and class.

Children were chattel but no more so than wives. They ate, lived, loved, slept, partied, worshiped and worked along side adults. Adult stories, songs and dances were children's stories, songs and dances. Dress was identical.

Children were not considered innocent, so there was no need to keep them ignorant. Nothing was hidden from them. They were rarely, if ever, excluded because of age from doing what they were able to do. All pre-fourteenth century children were precocious by modern meanings and measures.

Then, a radical new notion, that children were in need of reforming, was promoted by religious interests who also provided schools in which to do the reforming. Slowly schools proliferated in the fifteenth through eighteenth centuries. Thus began both the separation of children from the rest of society and the related notion that children should be "protected" from the mainstream, the better to effect their purification. The innocence/ignorance of children as a goal had been invented.

Religion also contributed to the emerging concepts of schooling and childhood such staple components as hierarchy, dogma, ritual, belief, paternalism, catechism, memorization, etc. High schools are direct descendants of cathedral choir schools begun in the Middle Ages to train a select few as choirboys and clergy by having them memorize and repeat chapter and verse. There were almost no elementary schools in the Middle Ages. They arose slowly and separately, mainly with and after the Renaissance, and never had any connection with secondary schools. Thus, the church inadvertently created the separation of secondary and elementary schools which plagues the present model of schooling.

Another ancient tradition that contributed to the new concepts of schooling and childhood was the military: authoritarianism, platooning, unquestioning obedience, discipline, drill, punishment, uniform dress, etc. Seventeenth-century academies in France were run like armies and were devoted to training officers at a time when thirteen was considered old enough to command troops in battle.

Groups targeted for subjugation are easier to isolate if they dress differently. Special dress for children first appeared in the seventeenth century. Dress, along with schooling and most other aspects of the invention of childhood, spread slowly downward from upper to lower classes.

Like other innovations that accompanied and followed the Renaissance and Reformation, the concept of childhood became more refined, and sophisticated with time. Only in the nineteenth century did the concept subdivide into rigid strata of childhood. A century or two before that, differing capabilities of different ages of children was not much of a concern. That a child was not an adult had been accepted, but beyond that, a child was a child was a child. Not any more. There is now a strict stratification of childhood based on age that both fuels and is fuelled by the lockstep system of grades in schools.

The assembly-line concept of both schooling and childhood matches the factory model that emerged concurrently during the industrial revolution. Goods are processed in fixed steps along a conveyor belt, and so are children. In schools they fall off the assembly line midway as dropouts or roll off the end as graduates. In the community, they roll off the assembly line as finished goods called adults. Instead of being a full-blown part of life, childhood is mere preparation for life to come.

As a social convention, late twentieth-century childhood is the universal parallel of nineteenth-century bound feet in China; both conventions require constant restriction, retard growth, subjugate a large minority, deform for life, and are thought by the perpetrators to be beautiful. All apologists for the present model of childhood are unshakable in their conviction that protracted helplessness is beautiful, and they want more of it for everybody young. Six years of infancy is not enough; they want the sentence tripled, even quadrupled. Closet chattelites, in their role as child advocates, recoil from self-confidence and independence in children. They call it loss of childhood, loss of being free of responsibility.

Being free of responsibility translates into being powerless, and chattelites want to keep children helpless by denying them responsibility. Their cry is "a childhood for every child." None of them detects the overtones of self-serving sanctimony echoed along with their cry. None of them sees that childhood is a defined and confined space into which people are stuffed. "A peoplehood for every child" would proclaim a nobler cause.

A particularly cruel aspect of the childhood fabrication is the extension of it beyond puberty and ever further into the teens and twenties. The discerning Edgar Friedenberg said, "adolescence is a political condition, not a biological one or a psychological one." Economic, job-qualification and housing policies are indeed political policies, and they are forcing young people to remain with parents far too long, sometimes a preposterous quarter century or more.

The extension is rarely defended except in terms of mythical differences between youth and adult as artificial as contrived differences that made niggers of blacks in America. Once concocted differences are removed, blacks are just people. In the same way, teens become just people when contrived differences are removed. Being young (or black) ceases to be an invented social station and becomes just another among dozens of human variables: tall, articulate, intelligent, reliable, energetic, shy, black, white, old, female, young, etc.

Myths of social station are difficult to dispel because they become self-fulfilling prophecies in two ways. The victim group as a whole is seen to behave as expected even when many sub-groups and individuals do not; society is largely blind to actual behaviour which doesn't fit the stereotype, especially if subtly expressed and not criminal or if geographically distant. On the other hand, the target group often does behave as expected, there being little choice open; they have been robotized from birth and besides, retribution for the aberrant is too certain, too severe, and too unjust.

Children of the present model of childhood, by and large, behave as the model dictates even though they are capable of better and few would naturally choose the role they are forced to play. They are conditioned from infancy to be as helpless, incompetent, unreadied and unproductive at fourteen as their counterparts six hundred years earlier were helpful, competent, readied and productive. We predestine them to be retarded, so they are. The vacuous, fun-and-games school readers of the twentieth century have been the catechism.

We expect children to be irresponsible, irrational, disorganized, unreliable, immoderate, thoughtless, ignorant/innocent, superficial, silly. . . . So they are. We train them to be subservient, obsequious, unquestioning, unassertive, acquiescent, passive, conformist. . . . So they are. We force them to be regimented, indentured, oppressed, repressed, suppressed, disenfranchised, manipulated, exploited, dependent. . . . So they are. We insist they be directed rather than self-directed. So they are.

The natural need to be self-directed is subverted and either shrivels or festers. Of late, there seems to be more and more festering and at earlier ages. Imposed and prolonged powerlessness is being tolerated by fewer and fewer children. Most of those afflicted are not aware what is disturbing them. They feel malaise but, like so many allergy victims, cannot identify causes. It is interesting and disturbing that in 1989, in Los Angeles, the teenage verb of choice meaning "to party" was "to rage."

The primary symptom of malaise is diminished self-esteem. It may not be easy to see because an underlying sense of powerlessness (the largest though not the only cause of low self-esteem) may be cloaked in bravado, cheek, devil-may-care merriment, approval-seeking behaviour or other disguises. The more obvious secondary symptoms include smoking, drinking, drug-taking, ganging, vandalism, promiscuity, pregnancy, lethargy, recklessness, aggressiveness, hyperactivity, alienation, failure, dropping out, suicide. . . . Less obvious but also serious are other kinds of secondary symptoms: acquiescence, conformity, hypocrisy, dependency, boot-licking, deviousness, duplicity, etc. Those darlings of chattelites, the neo-traditionalist teens of the nineties — perhaps a quarter of the total teen population — tend to be contentedly over-conformist, dependent, obedient, self-centred and self-satisfied.

Society is forever alarmed about certain of these symptoms. Study groups are formed and reports written. Solutions recommended usually favour more of something: prohibitions, police, social workers, recreation facilities, clinics, hot lines, etc. Nowadays, more education often heads the list. News media reverberate with decisions to attack drug problems by making drug education compulsory from kindergarten. There is nothing wrong with telling kindergarten children the truth about drugs. They should be told the truth about everything. Early drug information will help most children make better decisions whichever camp they are in, users or non-users. And it will keep some children in the non-user category because complete information is a building block of self-esteem: it relieves the helpless feeling of ignorance. But teaching them all about drugs won't stop most children from taking drugs because their self-esteem needs a much bigger boost than drug information alone can provide.

If we want children to have such strong self-esteem that they shun drugs (even when many of their parents are users), we must return to them what current concepts of childhood and schooling take from their lives: meaning. When we usurp their authority, many children assert themselves with drugs, liquor, tobacco, tatoos, noise, fads, fast cars, promiscuity, etc.

Adolescents are naturally risk-takers. They are programmed by nature to be as courageous as they are strong, resilient and adaptable, the better to defend the rest of the tribe whether the enemy is aggression or stagnation. But when we deny them significant say in the management of society, or even of their own lives, we deny them meaningful outlets for their bravery. Their response to powerlessness is to express their moxie defiantly because they are not allowed to do it responsibly. They drive recklessly, play chicken, take dangerous drugs, form warring gangs, vandalize, steal, have unsafe sex, lead double lives, etc. Among those who lead double lives, are many who play the neo-conservative role at home and school but cut loose when they think it safe.

An astonishing number of teens make the absolute assertion, register the ultimate defiance, take the supreme risk — they attempt suicide. More succeed than in any other age group: one every ninety minutes in the United States. Suicide is the second largest cause of death in American teens. Only accidents take more young lives and many accidents result from intentional recklessness or drunkenness only marginally less assertive, defiant and risky than attempted suicide. In Canada, a federal government task force reported a 400 percent increase over a period of fifteen years in the rate of fifteen to nineteen-year-old suicide. Japan, Finland, Hungary and many other countries have equally shocking statistics.

Far more teenage boys than girls self-destruct. Eighty percent of all suicides in Ontario are males between sixteen and twenty. Nature intended males to burst into physical, sexual, mental and every other kind of adult action at puberty. They are genetically programmed that way. But we have stopped them from being men and have ordered them to remain children. We have trivialized their lives.

The consequent untenable status of boys is exacerbated by the way we raise them. They are denied touching, hugging and tenderness and trained to be unemotional, competitive, tough, aggressive, possessive, dominant and silent. We condition them in this sexist way because of ancient paternalistic beliefs; they are chattelized so they too will grow into aggressive, authoritarian chattelites. But then we expect them at puberty to put all that dynamite on hold for many years. If, instead, they were raised with affection and gentleness to be affectionate, gentle, cooperative, patient, communicative and empathic, they would be better able to tolerate the frustrations of teen and adult years.

There are some apparent reasons why the need to be self-directed, when subverted in children, now festers more often than it shrivels. All children are so exposed to materialism and consumerism that they crave incomes to respond and soon become acutely aware of their economic powerlessness. Another reason is that the reality of broken families and working parents cries out for more autonomy and more recognition for children who shift for themselves. But chattelite tradition condones their continued powerlessness at home and scorns their achievements in shifting for themselves. Parental autocrats who parachute in to boss them now and then, usually on weekends, are more resented than full-time autocrats of yesteryear because the paratroopers interrupt burgeoning freedom.

A third reason is that chattelite tradition still condones the powerlessness of children in schools which remain patronizing, paternalistic and authoritarian at a time when democratization is spreading in institutions except those serving the young. **Children increasingly used to shifting for themselves out of school and increasingly aware of general democratization resent being powerless at school.**

The main reason children are reacting to subservience is that they are better informed than ever before. Chattelite insistence on keeping children ignorant/innocent is still officially in place but has been bypassed by television. Every child of ten has absorbed more mental images than his pre-television ancestors encountered in a lifetime. Children watching television now experience what adults experience, as they did before the present concept of childhood was invented: violence, war, death, starvation, flirtation, sex, infidelity, humour, hypocrisy, politics — everything.

A study at the University of Michigan in 1988 by Bradley Greenberg showed that in a year, the average fourteen to fifteen-year-old American girl encountered on television 1500 sexual acts or references to them and had virtually free choice of which shows she watched. Once again, differences between adults and children are blurring. Computers increase access to information and hasten blurring. Increased awareness brings increased reaction.

Worldwide, children are already reacting to their circumstances by behaving like adults, but their actions don't match the stereotype, so they have gone almost unnoticed, or have been misinterpreted, disparaged or dismissed as oddities. Predictably, among those chattelites who do notice, the usual reaction is alarm. They see no positive value in these early signs that **childhood is being redefined by children themselves**.

In some ways, the emerging new model of childhood resembles the medieval model and images of it often come via television from parts of the world where the ancient integration of children into the adult community never completely disappeared. We see children assuming responsibility, even leadership. The most remarkable example is children at war. They have always been as good at it as adults. Alexander the Great was a general at sixteen. At the same age, the distinguished international jurist and Nobel Peace Prize winner, Sean MacBride, led his own unit in the Irish Republican Army. The armies of Europe had large numbers of boy soldiers and officers aged eleven to sixteen until well into the seventeenth century. With the invention of childhood, we, in the West, have recast children as war victims instead of participants. But they are participants.

The intifada, the Palestinian uprising in Israel in the late eighties and nineties was fought in large part by Palestinian children throwing stones at Israeli soldiers who sometimes shot back. On July 3, 1988, children objecting to an archaeological dig near their school, attacked Israeli troops supporting the dig. Two days later, Israel closed schools to prevent their use by children as staging grounds for resistance to Israeli troops. By mid-1989, the United Nations estimated that a third of casualties were under fifteen years old. At least five hundred, mostly teens, lay dead.

Meanwhile, the main jungle troops of the non-communist Khmer Peoples' National Liberation Front in Kampuchea were thousands of boys twelve to seventeen years old. In Eritrea, photos of the sixteen thousand Ethiopian soldiers, held prisoners of war by the Eritrea Peoples' Liberation Front, looked like class photos from boys' junior high schools; the soldiers were fourteen to sixteen. In Nicaragua, all boys officially became soldiers at sixteen. Many were participants at fourteen. The Contra soldier with backpack and automatic rifle in a *Toronto Star* photo on April 6, 1989 was a thirteen-year-old girl. Iranian boys of fourteen to sixteen died by the hundreds of thousands in the longest-running obscenity of the eighties, the Iran/Iraq war.

At least ten thousand South African children from ages twelve to seventeen, and some as young as nine, were arrested and detained up to 1989. Vastly larger numbers were fully involved in demonstrations against Apartheid, often as leaders. Stompie Seipei, who was murdered at age fourteen, led the "children's army" of fifteen hundred in the protests of 1986. Both the cultural revolution and the student uprising of May, 1989 in China would have been impossible without massive participation by teenagers who supported older student demonstrators. In the Persian Gulf War of 1991, boys of seventeen and younger manned much of the Iraqi front line, and thousands were killed or maimed.

Strategists allow that young teens would probably be involved in a third conventional or nuclear world war — initially because of their computer and other support capabilities — but eventually because of superior resilience in a nuclear wasteland. With or without such a terrible conflict, it seems likely that as long as adults make war, children will be major contributors deserving the recognition accorded older soldiers.

Western chattelites are apt to dismiss child soldiers and child workers in developing countries, as regrettable exploitees. It is war and poverty that are regrettable, not the age of soldiers or workers. That exploitation exists is true. At least a million children a year are abducted or sold, and it happens in North America and Europe though mainly in poor Asian, African and South American countries. Women are similarly exploited. Such exploitation is usually a result of poverty and is an economic more than a children's or women's issue.

The reality is that pre-teen children are an important work force in all but rich countries, and most working children feel proud of their contribution. In Indonesia and scores of countries children eight to twelve are main caretakers of younger siblings. Millions of working children throughout the third world exude assurance, purpose and sense of accomplishment. Even when galling poverty makes their work as degrading for them as it is for adults, they do what must be done as well as adults do, in fields, sweatshops and streets.

Seven million, a third of Brazil's children, work and don't attend school. The child rug weavers of India are as industrious as their elders. The child drug peddlers of Bolivia are as adept as older dealers. Thousands of street children in the Ermita district of Manila are as good as adults at hawking, picking pockets, shoplifting, begging and prostitution. So are the half million street children of Sao Paulo who come and go in the Praca da Se. And those in Khartoum, Cairo, Calcutta. . . . Just as good as adults at adapting, surviving, making rules, cooperating, organizing. . . . And they are even better than adults at looking after each other. I salute them. They have shown the world that children can shift for themselves in the worst of circumstances.

It remains for all of us to accept that children can and do shift for themselves in the vastly better circumstances of the West. By conservative estimate, well over five million American children under thirteen manage their lives largely unsupervised because there is no adult in the house most of the time. A study by M-E Marketing Research, reported by the *New York Times Service* in spring 1988, showed that thirty-seven percent of children between six and eleven years of age do household chores such as laundry and cleaning; thirteen percent ages six through fifteen make their own dinners most of the time and eight percent make dinner for the family. Because these millions of children shop for food or influence the choice of household products, advertisers take them seriously.

As well as helping run households and attending school, many teens are also wage earners. By millions, they buy goods and services for their own use with their own money. The twenty thousand or more commercials aimed specifically at American children every year are not entirely from the thirteen-billion-dollar a year toy industry and the even more gigantic cereal and junk food industries. Increasingly, children are seen as a market for nearly all goods and services. And advertisers know that children don't always need special commercials; they watch "adult" commercials just as surely as they watch "adult" programs. In this respect, as in others, children have rejoined the adult world.

When broadcasters, advertisers and producers of goods and services acknowledge and court children as an emerging power group, chattelite society recoils. We can't yet conceive of huge numbers of self-directed children acting as responsibly as adults. Hardly anyone has noticed that, like Dorothy in *The Wizard of Oz*, children are the ones in many groups who pull things together for adults. **When millions of ordinary neighborhood fledglings fly on their own, nobody cheers. They are ignored altogether by the media, or worse, disparaged as "latchkey children." They are never praised for running households in place of absentee or disabled parents.** In Britain, the ten thousand or more children who, by themselves, look after chronically sick or disabled relatives are discredited in the press as "nursemaid kids."

Thousands of independent youths who make it on their own are either ignored or else sensationalized in the press as runaways, dropouts, or street children even though many

don't live on the streets and manage quite well in spite of adult prohibitions. When I was shopping for an inner-city house to renovate, I saw many run-down rooming houses. One room was spotless and more beautiful than all others. It had the ordered simplicity of a classical Japanese room: white walls, wood floor painted forest green, white futon, tatami mat, yellow cloth covering a box, lamp, vase of dried flowers, green plant, old chest of drawers painted sunny yellow, brick and board shelves, books and prints. The tenant was fourteen and living on his own half a continent away from the impossible home of his birth. The tenants of all the shabby, filthy rooms were adults.

All of these children who keep house for their families or live alone are admirable, low-profile pteropaedics. (Pteropaedes are birds able to fly shortly after being hatched, but I apply the term to capable children). Among the most hideous aspects of the childhood fabrication is the ritual wing-clipping of potentially high-profile pteropaedics. A few of the dazzlingly pteropaedic, in the tradition of Mozart and Chatterton, may still occasionally fly so soon and fast as to escape clipping, and others not quite so spectacular may keep enough of their wings to soar fairly high:

Nine-year-old Emma Houlston pilots a plane across Canada, eleven-year-old John Hill flies across America and eleven-year-old Christopher Marshall conquers the Atlantic (but the law doesn't allow any of them to have a pilot's licence). At age thirteen, Ruth Lawrence graduates with a first class degree in mathematics from Oxford University in England (but the law won't permit her to teach mathematics). Eleven-year-old Kristen Banerjee is a pre-medical student at Lee College in Texas and will have her medical degree at seventeen (but, Doogie Howser notwithstanding, law and custom won't let her practice in most places).

In Canada, fifteen-year-old Tony Lai studies for his PhD in computer science at the University of Waterloo (but even if companies want to hire him as a computer consultant, the law won't allow him to drive to meetings). Fifteen-year-old Mark Lawee of Toronto runs a successful construction business (but the law won't let him operate the bulldozers he commands).

At thirteen, The Artful Dodger is wanted for twenty burglaries in London, England while he hides out on the Costa del Sol in Spain and slips in and out of Britain in disguise on a forged passport (but the law won't allow him to manage his own defence in court or even to publish his own name). Fourteen-year-old Xiong Ni so astonishes the world with his diving at the 1988 Olympics that a *New York Times* editorial describes him as "spectacular" (but no country would certify him as a diving coach).

Seventeen-year-old Danny Stein surmounts all barriers to become a full-time registered stockbroker in Manhattan (but the competition immediately expresses resentment by dubbing his firm, Romper Room Securities). Nine-year-old Aaron Gibson capably and willingly takes care of his schizophrenic, divorced mother, the gifted Canadian writer, Margaret Gibson (but the courts debate who should have custody of Aaron, his mother or father).

Meanwhile, many others are so routinely and ruthlessly cut to size that masses of children who could be high- or mid-level pteropaedics in one or more ways are confined to cages: the skilled twelve-year-old is not allowed to drive; the inventive fourteen-year-old cannot sign a contract or borrow money to market ideas; the industrious ten-year-old is not allowed to hold a job; the fifteen-year-old fancier of literature and ideas is prohibited from reading significant books at school; the eleven-year-old stage lighting specialist is refused admission to the union; the politically aware thirteen-year-old is not permitted to vote; the four-teen-year-old stock market analyst is forbidden to invest her own inheritance; the avid sixteen-year-old film historian and critic is refused admission to major movies; the sexually gifted fifteen-year-old is denied any approved outlet for his talent; the self-directed nine-year-old is imprisoned by the standard regimentation of school. . . .

Because reports of their accomplishments remain individual and unrelated, high-profile pteropaedics have no more positive, cumulative impact on society's interpretation of them than do millions of low-pro-file pteropaedics. Media editors and social commentators have not yet recognized their *combined* efforts as stunning evidence that **children**

are proving themselves and should be welcomed into the world of human and civil rights.

There is a modest literature of children's liberation which has much to say to thought leaders including educators but most of which is ignored or ridiculed by the press and traditional academics. It rarely reaches teacher trainees or practicing teachers who could carry it forward for discussion in schools by faculties, students, and parents. Most teachers have not even read Richard Farson's compelling and readable book, *Birthrights*. So any discussion is usually about protection of children. If children's liberation is mentioned, it is usually disparaged on grounds that belittle children as unsuited for the human and civil rights of adults — the same specious arguments that were made against rights for women, blacks, immigrants, lower classes, etc.

There are indeed differences between ten-year-olds and thirty-year-olds. There are also differences between thirty-year-olds and sixty-year-olds, and between sixty-year-olds and ninety-year-olds. But that has nothing to do with human or civil rights. It is **needs** of different age groups that vary, not human and civil **rights**.

The liberation of children can happen only when that principle lights up adult minds. Should it happen suddenly, the immediate and significant difference would be in the attitude of adults toward children, not in the behaviour of children. Most essentials of children's liberation have to do with attitudes of adults. What is required is that every adult, including politicians, parents, teachers and preachers, accept every child as a **person** with every human and civil right. Appropriate legislation, where needed, will follow.

It remains to be seen how all this will flesh out after much public discussion, but the framework seems clear: **every individual has complete civil and human rights from conception (or birth, or some point between if pro-choice forces win the abortion debate); thereafter, it is the role of society, through advocates, to safeguard or exercise those rights and responsibilities on behalf of individuals until they choose to exercise their own rights and accept related responsibilities.**

All people, regardless of age, who are permanently or temporarily unable or unwilling to make decisions for themselves, have the right to advocates who protect and/or pursue their interests. When temporary incapacity ends, individuals have just claim to exercise their own rights regardless of age as they do regardless of race, religion or gender. Individuals will begin to exercise their own rights according to personal developmental timetables. At puberty nearly all people will exercise their own rights with or without benefit of counsel, whichever they choose; however, individuals may choose to exercise rights personally before puberty or may choose not to exercise rights after puberty.

It follows that long-standing assumptions about parent rights must be revised by mutual consent or legislation. The main specious assumption, and one that is reflected in common law, is the notion that parental rights over children are natural. That is a self-serving supposition generated by the chattelite belief that parents own children and hence are owed duties by their children. When such assumptions have been challenged and changed, the right to procreate will remain. But limitations will probably increase to include more than prohibition of incestuous procreation as caring societies become concerned about overpopulation, contagion, contamination, addiction, genetic disease and engineering, etc.

People who exercise their right to procreate automatically accept concomitant responsibilities of parenting which will have to be spelled out. Some begin before procreation: since a child has the right to be born whole, practices which cause birth defects such as smoking, drinking and eating inferior foods, must be discontinued long before procreation. All people who are parents and, especially, all people who may become parents, must know in detail, in advance, what parenting responsibilities kick in automatically for all people who choose to exercise their right to procreate.

Since sexual intercourse may result in procreation, a person who exercises the right to sexual intercourse is ipso facto accepting all responsibilities that go with the right to procreate.

Beyond procreation, all rights presently assumed to be parents' rights must be refocused as children's rights. In large part, parents' rights as regards offspring end with the creation of new life. From that moment, it is offspring who have all the rights regarding themselves; only responsibilities remain to be completed by procreators. Those responsibilities are so important to the well-being of the species that they over-ride some personal rights an adult enjoyed before exercising the right to procreate: if vaginal birth transfers a deadly virus from mother to baby, the child's right to be born free of disease demands Caesarian section even if the mother would prefer vaginal birth.

Many rights to be refocused are those that meet physical, emotional, intellectual, social and moral needs of children. If we previously said biological parents have the right to be primary caretakers of their offspring, the same statement refocused becomes children have the right to primary care by their biological parents, who have the responsibility of giving it well. If we previously said parents have the right to feed their children as they see fit, the same matter refocused becomes children have the right to good nutrition, and parents have the responsibility of providing it. Parents have the right to punish their children becomes children have the right to freedom from physical and other demeaning punishment, and parents have the responsibility of protecting them from such abuse.

Many rights to be refocused have to do with agencies, particularly schools. **The mandate of schools is to meet all needs of children not met elsewhere**. No schooling innovation has ever included that unequivocal statement, but it is essential for any new model of schooling.

Most rights that will have to be restated as children's rights are not unique to children but are instead, universal rights to enfranchisement; justice; privacy; self-determination; sexuality; information; economic equality; freedom of religious belief or disbelief, assembly, expression, opinion, etc. In all of these, children are just the latest of many minority groups to remind a complacent world that democracy without full constitutional rights for minorities is tyranny of the majority. To mark the anniversary of Dr. Martin Luther King's birth, a *New York Times* editorial said, "As long as blacks are diminished, so are all citizens and so is the American ideal of freedom and equal justice." True. Replace the word "blacks" with the word "children" and it is also true.

As children's rights are spelled out through debate and legislation, related parental **responsibilities** (and those of other adults such as teachers and social workers) will become evident and must be as clearly stated and, where necessary, legislated. And **we must clarify and specify the responsibilities that children will assume along with their rights**. All rights of all citizens should be legislated and stated in a left-hand column with related responsibilities as clearly legislated and stated in the right-hand column, and both columns must be thoroughly studied in elementary and high schools in obligatory programs such as children's rights, student government, law, current affairs, national history, international understanding, etc. It must be the legislated responsibility of parents and teachers to **teach** children, step by step, from the earliest possible moment, **how to perform their responsibilities** in regard to every right.

Teachers should lead the discussion that will redefine children's rights and hence our models of childhood and schooling. They have that obligation because children are their clientele; professional ethics demand that they put children's interests above all else and that they be proactive on behalf of children rather than just reactive or worse, inactive. To begin with, **it is the professional responsibility of education leaders, and their challenge, to acclaim publicly the collective accomplishments of pteropaedics, especially the masses of children who are showing they can help run households, care for younger siblings, look after themselves, hold paid jobs and attend school, all at the same time.**

But the responsibility goes unfulfilled; twentieth-century schooling is so infused with chattelite convention that instead of leading society in a positive interpretation of the redefinition of childhood that is beginning in spite of us, schooling authorities are likely to write memorial hymns to treasured chattelite traditions. Charles R. Lawrence 3rd, in his book, *The World We Created At Hamilton High* (Cambridge, Mass.:

Harvard University Press, 1988), bemoans what he should be interpreting positively, the general decline of adult-child authority relationships.

Professor Lawrence's theme is just a sophisticated version of the chattelite song of praise for authoritarian control of children that ran to enthusiastic applause throughout North America in Ann Landers' Father's Day column, June 19, 1988. A father wrote to his son:

> In our house we do not have a democracy. . . . You will do as I say as long as you live in this house. You are not to disobey me because whatever I ask you to do is motivated by love. This may be hard for you to understand at times, but the rule holds. You will understand perfectly when you have a son of your own.

Late twentieth-century captains of the education industry are so used to the model of childhood conforming conveniently to the model of schooling that they are left dumb by the recent reversal that puts the changing reality of childhood in advance of the model of schooling for the first time in recorded history. So children continue to lead education leaders. Educators say, "we must wait till society redefines children's rights and the model of childhood before we can create a matching model of schooling." They are wrong. A developing model of schooling (the present one) has already led to one model of childhood (the present one). Why shouldn't school lead again? All three redefinitions should go on concurrently and nourish each other.

No model of schooling will work till children are liberated from the double standard which now denies their human and civil rights to self-determination, information, political power, economic power, sexuality, justice, freedom from physical and other demeaning and arbitrary punishment, etc. **People can be educated only to the extent they have the rights and responsibilities of self-determination. Subjugated people can only be indoctrinated.** But indoctrination is an appropriate activity only when recipients are volunteers, never when captives. To indoctrinate captive children is to oppress and abuse them. It is the opposite pole from education. It is brainwashing.

Schools should defuse public concerns and aid redefinition by patiently raising consciousness about chattelitism and by demonstrating that children respond positively to rights and responsibilities. To get them moving, schools will have to be kick-started by rights-conscious thought leaders among parents, politicians, journalists, students and teachers. It is in the self-interest of educators to act. Their survival depends upon regeneration of their industry. The way out of the schooling dilemma will be lit by redefinition of children's rights.

CHAPTER 13

CHILD ABUSE

A distorted fatherhood is what a pathological patriarchy is all about.

— Matthew Fox, *The Coming Of The Cosmic Christ*
(New York: Harper & Row, 1988)

Very few people survive one mother.

— Woody Allen in the film, *Manhattan*

Every school teacher, parent or person standing in the place of a parent is justified in using force by way of correction toward a pupil or child.

— Section 43 of the Criminal Code of Canada

The abuse of children is as varied as it is universal. It ranges through murder, torture, beating, rape, exploitation, deprivation, rejection, detention, suppression, indoctrination, chattelization, tongue lashing, abandonment, neglect, over-indulgence. . . .

Some abuses are decried, others allowed, and still others approved by society. Those decried have been publicly aired and countered with as much reckless emotion as reasoned intelligence. Extreme physical brutality has been acknowledged and responded to intelligently. So has rape. But much that is tactile rather than sexual, or that is a child's sexual prerogative, has been responded to rashly.

Abuses that are allowed have occasionally been challenged but seldom with funding, determination and organization: physical punishment persists; so does neglect, particularly emotional, intellectual and nutritional neglect.

Abuses approved by society have rarely been broached much less debated. Instead, they are inviolable weed beds tolerated even by reformers, circled or tiptoed through cautiously. Rarely have they been trampled deliberately and never plowed under. Among the sacrosanct weeds are: arbitrary detention; denial of right to information, free speech, assembly, association and sexual expression; indoctrination; exploitation; disenfranchisement. . . .

Many matters that are discussed throughout this book as schooling issues are at the same time child abuse issues. The two are intertwined, so unsnarling the education mess will overcome abuse. And vice versa. People working for change in either area had better also be active in the other. So far, schools have usually followed society instead of leading it toward intelligent solutions to child abuse. The major innovations in schooling in the twentieth century have been almost silent on the subject. Even essentially humane initiatives such as open education have been grafted incongruously onto an intrinsically authoritarian and abusive model of schooling.

A useful contribution to public reconsideration of the status quo was a landmark 1986 project of the Ontario Teachers' Federation called *Breaking the Cycle: Child Abuse Prevention*. The title refers to the near-certainty that abusive adults were themselves abused as children and that their abused children will perpetuate the cycle endlessly unless prevention (rather than mere crisis intervention) becomes the response of society. The project was funded by the Province of Ontario, a jurisdiction that has been as reactive to child abuse as any in the world except for Scandinavia where response has been sooner and broader.

When I was called in, the knowledgeable committee in charge and the professional researchers had reviewed the literature and assembled information on five topics they considered significant for prevention: trends in childrearing and family life (Family Matters); parent education

(Learning Parenting); disciplinary practices in schools (Hugs and Hickory); role models and socialization patterns for children (Little Images); ethnic and cultural heritage (Multicultural Kids). My role was to unify the five batches of material with a concept and a common written introduction that would appear in each of the five books, and to title, edit and rewrite all the papers for publication, adding additional material where I thought necessary. I also wrote a discussion guide for each book.

I accepted the contract because I felt the committee in charge was willing to take some steps toward identification of chattelitism as the main source of abuse, and children's liberation and consequent redefinition of childhood as the ultimate prevention protocol. I considered writing the introduction and additional material deliberately and overtly in that vein. But I didn't. I knew the best I could hope for from the sponsors was exposure of outer layers of an onion that must be pared to the core later.

Following are some cuts into outer rings that I wrote into the five publications:

[There is] concern about the belief, residual in our culture, that violence is justified, that it can be therapeutic.

It seems inconsistent with the growing sense of professionalism within teaching to tolerate violence as an acceptable part of the continuum of ways in which people relate.

It is probably idle to dream of non-violent families in a violent society. That a violent society begets violent components is a compelling assumption that obliges teachers to think of violence prevention in global terms now rather than wait while researchers test bits and pieces of the assumption and proponents of violence go right on defending or condoning the arms race, capital punishment, screen mayhem, police brutality, pornography, sports savagery, and many more models of violence against people, not to mention models of violence against animals and the environment.

[P]revention to date has been in the crisis mode, particularly the unprecedented campaign to streetproof children. It is natural and necessary to act immediately when blood is flowing but spilt blood may elicit a knee-jerk rather than a reasoned response. The quick fix may provide immediate gratification at the expense of long-term deprivation. It may, like an unproven drug, relieve an epidemic but cause devastating side effects.

[Streetproofing] has created an alarmist response to touching by failing to adequately discriminate between touching as a vital part of healthy, everyday human interaction and touching for sexual purposes. The distinguished Princeton scholar, Ashley Montagu, refers to "massive tactile stimulation" to describe the use of the skin organ for sexual purposes. This contrasts sharply with the minor tactile stimulation that is a vital part of child nurture. If children do not receive a broad range of tactile experience, they grow up stunted in their ability to relate.

Emotional, intellectual, moral and social neglect will all require detailed definition and discussion before comprehensive prevention can be a reality.

When neglect receives the attention it demands as the most prevalent form of child abuse, society may at long last accept the blame it deserves for neglect inherent in poverty, inadequate daycare, restricted housing, minimal family support systems and under-funded schools.

It seems possible that the urge to preserve its image has spared the family from the microscope even though statistics tell us that violence thrives within families. It may be that some of the institutions of society have to be attacked before we can stop attacking each other.

[A]t least half of the abused children in Ontario are in school on a given day along with most of the next generation of potential abusers.

[W]e must eliminate sexist attitudes and practices which are imbedded in our heritage because they seriously inhibit the growth potential of both men and women and hence prevent the full development of mutual respect and mutually supportive relationships.

Cultural baggage centuries old from every corner of the earth is stored in the attics of our minds.

[T]he neo-conservative emphasis on parental autonomy is sometimes at odds with recognition of the obligations and rights of the community. It may soon be equally evident that what is proclaimed by some as protection is seen by others as infringement of the rights of children; protection from information versus the right to information is just one example.

[W]e must study the milieu of childhood in depth in order to plan prevention of child abuse. It is difficult, often agonizing, for all of us to scrutinize the customs and conditions of childhood that were unquestioned, idealized, held sacrosanct only yesterday. Yet it must be done — not as a witch hunt, not as an exercise in finger pointing — but rather, as an exercise in love and justice in which all of us who are responsible adults participate.

Modest beginnings, but enough onion peeling to make some eyes water in the mid-eighties. Now, we must cut deeper and confront over-zealous responses to decried abuses. **Murder, torture, rape and all such physical/sexual abuses of children are rightly decried, but kindly, affectionate, communicative touching, which is not at all related, has been glued to decried violence**.

Privately, psychologists and psychiatrists may suggest that the glue oozes from festering, repressed middle-class sexuality.

Affection is expressed in body language, words and deeds, but it is also, and most universally, expressed and understood in touching. Unfortunately, certain of our forefathers, either mistakenly or maliciously, confused the massive tactile stimulation of sexual intercourse with the minor tactile transfer of the psyche's élan vital from generation to generation. Hugs nourish the soul. Busses warm the heart as well as the cheek. Pats are building blocks of self-esteem. Life force is shared through touch communication.

The present model of schooling, having developed in the context of generalized Western repression of demonstrated affection, has always suppressed expressions of affection and has suffered from that failing. But a few good teachers have always defied the taboo. As the urgent need of children for affection became better understood after the Second World War, more teachers responded. Just when schools were beginning to meet the need, a self-righteous, increasingly alarmist, streetproofing movement swept North America. Sexual repression, always latent and seething in a sector of society and always in need of an outlet, had found one — a sensational sure thing — and took to the media to save children from strangers.

The streetproofers conjured a world of roving monsters bent upon sexual abuse. They distorted a serious matter that is essentially an aspect of family violence into a misrepresentation of public behaviour. The campaign created the false impression that children are in great danger on the streets when virtually all violence to children happens around home, usually within it. Except for the very real danger from drunk and careless drivers, children are in about as much danger from strangers as from lightning. Nonetheless, the campaign succeeded and many children were made fearful of strangers.

Encouraged by their streetproofing victory, crusaders hoisted the broader banner of child abuse and marched on to attack touching. Otherwise moderate matrons, reinforced by otherwise temperate men, became exterminators charging from platform to platform impaling all touchers on their rhetoric. They succeeded in misrepresenting the fundamental human need to touch and be touched as salacious. Every affectionate man risked roasting on their shishkabob of touchers. Fathers and male teachers became easy targets. Vindictive wives, disgruntled students, jealous colleagues, pious prudes and all manner of emotional cripples found it easy to ruin a man's career by merely accusing him of touching. No matter that he was quite innocent of anything but affection.

A report in the *Toronto Star* on May 8, 1988, began, "School children are becoming aware that accusing a teacher falsely of sexual abuse is one way to take revenge, a prominent forensic psychiatrist says." As widespread and as frightening as false accusation is, it is not as frightening as the perversion of young minds so that they actually believe touching is evil. Goaded and coached by zealots, they distort affection into sexual aggression and march to court. The evidence presented by a twelve-year-old boy against a long-service teacher was that the teacher had "patted his legs, touched the bottom of his spine and hugged him." To intelligent, stable people this is a little, everyday, incidental, healthy, unconscious, communicative part of a larger context of affection. To crusaders on a roll this is sexual abuse.

Three-quarters of formal sex abuse accusations are groundless and never go to court. Most that do result in acquittal. For every formal accusation there are countless malicious rumors. The wrongly-accused are shattered for life. Rumour mongers and false accusers go scot-free. Just in North America, and just in the teaching profession, thousands of careers lie in ruin. At any moment at least thirty cases, most of them groundless, are before courts in Ontario alone.

In the wake of career carnage, North American teachers have been warned repeatedly by school boards and teachers' associations not to touch. A typical article in the Toronto *Globe and Mail* on June 11, 1985, began: "Men who teach in Ontario's elementary public schools are being advised not to display affection with students so that they protect themselves from accusations of sexual assault." The article described sitting a child on his knee as a mistake in a teacher's judgement.

When I was a student teacher at an inner city school and taught a grade one class because the regular teacher was away ill, children often sat on my knee or hung around my neck. Sometimes I swung one up on my desk to be king of the castle when we played a number game. Occasionally, I carried a hurt, crying or weary child. I even gave horseback rides around the room whenever we made up more verses to a continuing poem about a little cowboy and a big horse who could hippity hop (clippity clappity cloppity clop, hippity happity hoppity hop). So much touching! Even legs and the bottom of spines! And hugging!

One might have hoped that school systems would mount a counter campaign against anti-touch alarmists; instead, they acquiesced and are now handmaidens to the repression crusade. Teacher's associations occasionally mumble publicly about ruined careers or threaten to sue false accusers, but they too lack the will and leadership to proclaim that **expressed affection is an unavoidable professional obligation of teachers, and touching is an integral part of expressed affection**.

In 1989, the Canadian Teachers Federation resolved to seek a change in the Criminal Code that would keep the names of those accused confidential unless found guilty. The federation should also have gone after all false accusers with lawsuits, and they should have mounted an all-out public information discussion to counter false assumptions of the anti-touch/streetproofing industry and their followers: police, and public prosecutors who lay charges that don't belong in court, and media reporters who mine the easy payload in touch-hysteria accusations.

Neither mental health professionals nor teachers nor any other responsible group in society has strongly objected to anti-touch crusaders, partly because everybody is reluctant to talk publicly and seriously about sex, and partly because the no-touch response reinforces chattelism, which is about as unassailable as sex. Prior to the invention of childhood and the related definition of the modern family, many adults in the extended family and in the community helped parents rear children and interacted directly and personally with the young. They touched. As families became more and more nuclear, suburbanized, isolated and withdrawn, it became less common for other adults to be closely involved in the care of children except in ritualized, formalized, institutionalized, impersonal ways.

This change served the chattelite drive to have complete control of offspring. Now that nuclear families and their offshoots, nuclear "fragilies" (fragments of families), are frequently dysfunctional and usually under stress, the defensive chattelite response of parents is to forbid anyone to touch their children. And they, in their paradoxy, are increasingly anxious about personally providing touching, caressing, stroking and hugging that is essential to healthy sexual and psychological development in children, lest a disaffected partner charge child abuse in divorce litigation that may lie just around the corner. As for uncles, should a modern child happen to have one within a hundred miles, only a fool would touch a niece or nephew even to shake hands unless accompanied by impartial witnesses.

A false assumption that is in itself abusive of children is that children are not sexual. Researchers say all children of all ages are sexual. Some are actively so, even before teen years. It is their God-given nature. In the middle years of childhood, between seven and twelve, the number is small but it increases yearly. Late in that period, many will have entered puberty and some will have passed it. By thirteen most children are actively sexual if only in fantasy. Observation backed by research reveals that some males of thirteen with surging hormones are horny six-foot youths six times as strong as other males the same age with dormant hormones who are happily celibate little boys of four feet eight. Yet we stupidly group them by age for everything from sports to sex.

Psychological literature confirms that voluntary childhood sexual activity has no negative effect and may have a positive effect. Yet, in the current canons of sex, not the slightest attempt is made to distinguish between use by children of their own sexuality and abuse by others. Instead, those opposite poles are combined as child abuse and made a metaphor for all that is evil. Susan Sontag said the way we talk about disease determines how we experience it. The same is true of sex.

The pressure to identify and label all sexually-active children as abused creates an anti-scientific, defilement syndrome. A class of pariahs is created by convincing non-victims they are victims. Children who are in some degree sexually active of their own volition, and have found it no big deal, or pleasant, or comforting, or just another experience in learning, relating, loving, expressing, being — are made to feel guilty, dirty, cursed, defiled, victimized. . . . Even masturbation is reviled as self-abuse.

The last thing children need is the heavy load of guilt that accrues from films and other paraphernalia of abuse hysteria which fail to affirm and validate their sexuality. That failure is in itself child abuse since it makes sexual children feel they must be bad because they are sexual. Each such child suffers solitary guilt since each believes he/she alone must be a monster. Much that zealots consider sexual molestation does not trouble or harm children; from the point of view of harm, loving closeness and affectionate touching are non-events compared to the physical, emotional, nutritional and intellectual abuse that violates so many children. **We dilute the bitter reality of actual sexual abuse when we throw into the definition the sweetness of chosen closeness.** Individuals who truly sexually molest children are those who rape, inflict physical pain, force, frighten, threaten, dominate, cajole, betray, mislead, entice, incestuously entrap, etc.

Such acts are selfish, unilateral and loveless, and must indeed be stopped. The commonest by far — more than eighty percent — are also incestuous (or involve a stepfather, baby-sitter or someone at home) and all are consistent with the persistent model of childhood that sees children as chattel, as possessions without human or civil rights. To be possessed is to be a victim. To be a victim is to be open to further victimization. Only when children cease to be manipulated possessions and become citizens with complete human and civil rights will they cease to be victims, cease to be abused.

The meaning of molestation is "to meddle with so as to trouble or harm." The hysterical reaction of organized alarmists (and the legal system they have influenced) to all child

activity that is somewhat sexual and to touching by adults, actually creates trouble and harm for children by persuading them they are troubled and harmed. The sexual abuser, then, is society: it "meddles so as to cause trouble and harm" to children.

The no-touch alarmists have promoted the myth that children don't lie about important matters and hence are supremely credible witnesses in court. Aware and impartial teachers could set the record straight. For fourteen years I counselled children daily and for half that time I was in charge of discipline counselling for entire schools. Some children lied to me and some told me of lies they had used on other teachers and parents. In this trait, as in others, children are about the same as adults: a few are consummate liars who perform frequently and convincingly; others lie only occasionally but artfully; still others, hardly ever and not well; some never. Most lie sometimes and well enough to be believed. Some older children and many younger ones convince themselves that their lies or fantasies are true.

Children are more likely than adults to externalize, verbalize and play out fantasies. In that sense, some children can be more overt liars than adults. Many can be coached to believe others' lies or assumptions as their own truth. About fifteen percent of children (and adults) have a detectable learning disability, a neurological problem processing information; and who knows how many more have a mild undiagnosable learning disability. One possible characteristic of even the mildly learning disabled is difficulty recalling events, sequence and details. They may be unintentional liars because they have faulty recall.

Another false assumption of alarmists is hurtful to unloved children because it makes them feel deeply guilty: print and visual streetproofing and abuse-prevention materials may tell children their abusive parents love them and that all children love their abusive parents. The unloved and unloving among abused children need acceptance of their loveless reality. They need to know they are not alone in being unloved by parents or in not loving parents who abuse them. And they need to know they are not to blame for the absence of love.

Perhaps as difficult as any of the many matters large and small that must be reconsidered in the abuse debate is multiculturalism. The false assumption of multiculturalism is that all cultures are created equal. In truth, **the triumph of the West was a triumph of culture and it triumphed over cultures that were and are antithetical to the West**. Yet, in a November 3, 1985, article for the *Toronto Star*, former deputy minister of the Government of Canada, Bernard Ostry, had this to say: "All traditions and cultures are valid ways of being Canadian." He was wrong.

All races are created equal, but not all cultures; countries should be unequivocally multiracial and multiethnic but they should be cautious about cultural elements that are welcomed into the national mix or mosaic. While it is wonderful and essential that various cultures of the world learn from each other and agree upon values to be shared so that together we can save the planet, we must not tolerate in Western countries aspects of old cultures that are abusive of children.

Cultures that regard a father's word as infallible and final are intrinsically abusive because they defy the right of children to self-determination, democratic participation and due process. Several cultures deliberately train boys to replicate the dominance role. Some cultures abhor the freedom of speech and expression which is at once the heart of democracy and an essential ingredient in the liberation of children. Other child-abusive cultural baggage that accompanies many immigrants includes: insistence upon compliance; rejection of autonomy and independence; practice of corporal punishment and ridicule; promotion of a double standard for teenage boys and girls with regard to freedom of movement and relations with the opposite sex; subjugation of females; demand for unquestioning respect to elders and enormous obligation to parents; relentless indoctrination; instillation of hatred toward other religious, tribal, racial or ethnic groups; continuance of unhygienic practices. . . .

Certain immigrant groups bring with them abusive traditions which are illegal in some countries and should be in all, but continue underground even if banned. Sexual mutilation of girls is one example. It is practiced so widely that the World Health Organization estimates that at least seventy-five million women are victims. The main abuses are circumcision (removal of the tip of the clitoris), clitoridectomy (removal of the entire clitoris and adjacent parts of the labia minora) and infibulation (removal of the entire clitoris, labia minora, and labia majora and the joining of the scraped sides of the vulva across the vagina). But there are other variations such as carving a cross with a razor blade on a baby girl's vagina as a good behaviour charm.

Another problem is that multiculturalism encourages immigrants to isolate from the mainstream by simulating another time and place in ghetto form. Ghettoizing diminishes opportunities for children. In that sense, it is more than just unfair to children of minority groups. It is abusive.

Punishment

A matter that needs public airing is the probability that most traditional punishments are more sexually motivated than is touching, more titillating for perpetrators and more damaging to children. Sadism means "getting sexual pleasure from dominating, mistreating or hurting a powerless or compliant person." Most punishments are forms of bondage: detentions, grounding, line-writing, spanking, strapping, etc. Children must surrender completely. Often they cry helplessly and their shudders cause pelvic thrusts and gluteal contractions. Approved instruments of punishment are of rubber and leather. A lone child kept imprisoned after-hours at a desk is at crotch level of a patrolling teacher.

The primitive notion lingers that violence is an appropriate response to anti-social behaviour. School and community leaders, even those who sense in their hearts that the present models of childhood and of schooling make children eternally restive, fear loss of control and imagine chaos as the alternative to punishment. Punishment to enforce obedience is equated with discipline. The establishment pressures each new wave of teachers to become punishers.

Vindictive people say punishments improve children and schooling. That is not so, but even if it were, it is not the issue. The real issue is that punishments violate children's rights. Since all punishment does violence to one or more rights, school people have a particular responsibility to take a stand against punishment; but traditionally schools have done just the opposite — they have set an example of negative control through punishment and coercion using sundry forms of physical and psychological violence. Consequently, they have turned out generation after generation of believers in violent response. The current generation of adults is no exception.

In the fall of 1988, a Toronto television station tallied phone responses and found that punishment was favored two to one over rehabilitation for abusers of children. This, from the upscale audience of an educational channel, the kind of people who must be aware that, nearly always, when a child is the victim of abuse, so is the abuser, the only difference being that the abuse is current for the child and historical for the adult. The same people must know that rehabilitation is a far more effective response to anti-social behaviour than is punishment. But they don't care. They have been conditioned to see punishment as the righteous revenge of the powerful and now that they are among the powerful, they insist on punishment, the more the better.

Schools are doubly at fault. Not only do they set the universal example of punitive response, they also fail to condition each generation to humane philosophy and methods of rehabilitation. If schools had succeeded in the latter, society would now prefer rehabilitation (along with reparation) to incarceration. Prisons would be two-thirds empty.

When I insist that school people stop fouling their own nest, PTA leaders, teachers, even community activists, sometimes say the continuance of punishment in schools is not their fault, that they just do what the system and society requires. Former liberals mutated into neo-conservatives believe that inexorable forces — which will never yield to enlightenment — define the boundaries within which social progress can be made. The inexorable forces are hard-line conservatives, rednecks, fundamentalists and camp followers of confused presidents who envision a kinder and gentler nation through household firearms, capital punishment and slashed welfare programs.

Such people are formidable opponents. Theirs is usually the official position. They are devoted chattelites who will resist enlightenment and will yield only slowly. But that is no reason to acquiesce to them. The Nuremberg principle says individuals have an obligation to oppose official injustice. Besides, there are shining examples of good beginnings. There have always been societies that seldom if ever used punishments against children. The western islands of Scotland and Ireland and the traditional Innuit of Canada are examples.

Sweden should give itself a Nobel Prize for having achieved an almost complete reversal of "inexorable forces" in eighty years. Pious punishers held sway in 1899 when a Swedish newspaper offered the following traditional wisdom: "Flog your son while there is still hope. Foolishness resides in the heart of a child. Flogging drives it out." Fifty years later (1949), Swedish law forbad extreme forms of child punishment. In 1979, a further law banned all "physical punishment or other humiliating treatment" of children by adults, including parents and teachers.

Meanwhile, most other parts of the world, including much of North America, still allow "physical punishment or other humiliating treatment." On June 24, 1988, the *Toronto Star* reported the acquittal in Kitchener, Ontario of a father for striking his thirteen-year-old daughter ten times with a belt. The judge thought the beating was not excessive since bruises on the girl's buttocks disappeared within a week. He said he was, "not going to dictate what parents should or should not do. They have the responsibility to raise their children and can discipline them as long as punishment doesn't exceed what is reasonable."

Such tragedies continue by the millions in almost every country. But they seldom reach newspapers or courts because routine strapping is not regarded as child abuse. Nor is most pain and humiliation visited upon children by parents and teachers. Strapping, switching, whipping, caning, rubber-hosing, paddling, spanking, striking, slapping, pushing, yanking, shoving, shaking, hair-pulling, ear-pulling, and nose-pulling are all in the repertoire of physical punishments rained upon children.

All are abusive but are not considered child abuse unless extreme — murder, bloodshed, broken bones, burns, battering, etc. Illegal child abuse is the tiny, publicized and publicly reviled abscess of a chronic plague of violence toward children, which rages, hidden and approved, mainly within homes. In a *Toronto Star* article on June 21, 1980, Lynda Hurst began, "If you're a woman or a child, you're much more likely to be punched, slapped, kicked or even killed inside your own home than on a dark street."

She quoted sociologist Norman Bell as saying, "The family has always been over idealized. In fact, it's a hotbed of violence and getting more so every day."

Peel Region is an attractive suburban community near Toronto and is probably representative of middle North America. In the mid-eighties it had 90,000 students in 160 elementary and high schools. A study of the region from 1977 to 1986 showed that perpetrators of confirmed, extreme physical abuse were: natural fathers 43.5%; natural mothers 30.5%; stepfathers 13%; extended family members, baby-sitters and others 13%. It seems reasonable to assume that perpetrators of much more frequent approved or tolerated violence against children are the same folks in about the same proportions. The usual estimate, based on research, is that eighty-five to ninety-five percent of American parents inflict corporal punishment on their children. Dr. Irwin Hyman, a long-time scholar of child punishment, told the 1989 meeting of the American Psychological Association, "It's an epidemic in America that people readily accept that hitting children is an appropriate way of changing their behaviour."

Schools are also significant perpetrators of approved or tolerated physical violence (and are as bad as homes when it comes to non-physical humiliation of children). New Jersey outlawed corporal punishment in 1867, but over a century later, in 1989, thirty-one states in America still allowed it. The U.S. Department of Education tallies at least a million incidents of corporal punishment in schools every year.

Throughout much of the world, the administrative equation is discipline = punishment = violence. Even where beating children in schools is forbidden by law, it is apt to continue. Everybody in Japan knows that at least a third of teachers use corporal punishment, often in the form of beatings with bamboo sticks known as rods of love. In 1986, a record 189 Japanese teachers were fired or suspended and nearly 900 were reprimanded for physical violence against students. As a teenager in the mid-eighties, Takeshi Hayashi wrote two popular books condemning violent teachers. He concluded that Japanese schools are regressing to the authoritarian style of pre-World War Two.

When education leaders pass the buck on corporal punishment, they may do so with rationalizations more intelligent than fundamentalist chattelites, but they fall short of condemning violence and leading the way to new, non-violent models of childhood and schooling. Writing in the early seventies, A.S. Neill said British teachers would rebel if caning were abolished by law. In 1989, a Gallup poll found fifty-six percent of American teachers in support of corporal punishment. Canadian teachers still lack the will to protest corporal punishment unequivocally.

In August of 1983, a major newspaper published a letter which I wrote for the president of a large teachers' federation to sign. It disapproved corporal punishment at home or school and reiterated an important point teachers make:

Schools are funded to provide good mass education not individualized education. The latter is an admirable goal but not a present reality. The strap is a fast, cheap deterrent compatible with mass education at the lowest possible cost. The alternative, which is compatible with individualized education, is broad and deep counselling requiring large numbers of psychologists, psychiatrists, social workers, therapists, counsellors, attendance officers and remedial teachers, all of whom are in short supply or missing entirely from most school boards. The counselling alternative is based on the clinical, one-to-one model, but the classroom is not one-to-one; it is anywhere from thirty-to-one to 150-to-one.

The funding argument is valid, but the underlying assumption is not — that it is permissible under any circumstance to strike children. It is a pervasive assumption that disgraces us no matter how artfully deployed. Teachers may say the strap is a deterrent, that it is not actually used or that it is rarely used and only dispassionately, never in anger. Fundamentalists who wallow in the joys of whipping may quote some ancient and vicious text that glorifies paternalistic violence. Others may calmly agree with George Bernard Shaw (in Maxims for Revolutionists): "If you strike a child, take care that you strike in anger, even at the risk of maiming it for life. A blow in cold blood neither can nor should be forgiven." All vow vehemently that they love children and have their best interests at heart.

Teachers' organizations sometimes use the specious argument that corporal punishment should be retained so that teachers reserve the right to use force against children who attack them or each other. Teachers must not confuse the right to defend themselves and others in emergencies with the right to attack children as a discipline procedure. It is not difficult to write laws that clarify the difference.

A growing segment of the otherwise punishment-oriented majority is more or less opposed to the most blatant of physical punishments: strapping. They are supported from an unexpected quarter, the strap-making industry. In Canada, the traditional purveyor of school straps stopped selling them because the main buyers by far were individual sado-masochists acquiring them as sadistic sex instruments for home use. Since institutional sadists — school boards and schools — already have a supply of long-lasting straps, the unavailability of new models will be slow to benefit children. Meanwhile, those adults who find gratification for their repressed sexuality by striking others can legally continue to strap children whether at home or (in many jurisdictions) school. It is not unreasonable to assume that all corporal punishment is sadism, and hence is sexual abuse.

A danger is that as physical attacks on children decline, other forms of legal abuse in schools will increase. Even the way most schools administer progress of students is punitive. Computer print-outs have not relieved the devastation that used to be delivered on hand-written report cards or posted on bulletin boards as typed lists. An electronic sledge hammer is still a sledge hammer. The student who fails at year's end is typically abused and then abandoned by the school system until the summer-school or fall term arrives and the additional formal punishment of repetition begins. During that period of lonely abandonment, self-image shrivels. Giving up, dropping out, running away, getting pregnant, turning delinquent, doing drugs, withdrawing from society and committing suicide are a few options open to failures.

Emotional abuse has always been present in schools; and unless it involves some extreme (such as locking a child in a closet) it is a legal alternative for abusive teachers. All coercive discipline is, potentially, emotional abuse and most is intrinsically so. Denial of affection, rejection, humiliation, belittlement, isolation from outsiders and peers, unfair pressure, low expectations — the weapons of emotional abuse available to teachers (and parents) are many and effective. The commonest punishments in schools worldwide are cases in point. I used most of them before I mustered enough guts to refuse. All are vehemently defended as therapeutic for children though all would be impossible to inflict upon adults because the injustice and indignity of such consequences for such "crimes" would not be tolerated in any civilized adult society.

The most mindless punishment is writing the same line a thousand times: I must not make rude noises in class. A modification is the after-hours detention where passages from a book are copied. Devotees may select passages of uplifting value on the assumption that purification takes place while detainees are learning to hate passages they are forced to copy. A variation features extra questions on some subject such as mathematics, to be completed by coming early or staying late in a designated room (prison cell). The unintended lesson may be that mathematics is punishment. Even when the crime is failure to complete regular mathematics assignments, a detention with more questions piled on is not likely to ameliorate causes.

Line-writing and detentions in all their variations have one thing in common — revenge by arbitrary imprisonment. The school system gets revenge by imprisoning the child, stealing his time, robbing him of freedom and always for actions that could not possibly lead to such drastic consequences for adults in a democracy. It can't be argued that incarceration in the form of line-writing or detentions keeps criminals from endangering the rest of society because the rest of society, the class, is not there to be disrupted before or after school when punishment takes place.

Nor can it be argued that the purpose of line writing or detentions is correction, because no correction takes place except perhaps a modicum of the negative kind based on fear, hardly the kind of motivation worthy of a sane society charting the twenty-first century. Positive correction would involve counselling, constructive activities relating to specifics of the crime and honest attempts to do something about causes within the child (such as undiagnosed dyslexia, nutritional deficiency, chemical imbalance, functional illiteracy, stunted self-esteem. . .), causes within the school system (such as a dysfunctional model of schooling) and causes within the home (such as abusive parents).

Deportation is another favorite punishment. The back of the room, the corridor, the bench outside the front office, or the street are Devil's Islands of choice. Arbitrary sentences range from minutes of ostracism to weeks of suspension. A semblance of due process is sometimes included (if anyone cares enough to invoke it) in cases where punishment will be the academic death sentence, expulsion. Here, the argument is indeed that the rest of society, the class, must be protected from danger of disruption. And given the present dysfunctional model of schooling, it is a substantive argument.

An individual teacher — always short of time, running from class to class, under pressure, dealing with scores of students every day, standing in front of thirty or forty students at a time (some hungry, some tired, some hurting, some bored, some illiterate, some sick, some neurotic, some lonely, some unloved, some abused), trying to peddle data for short-term retention and regurgitation at fast-approaching examinations — can hardly be expected to cope properly with one or more disruptive students and still fulfill professional obligations to the rest of the class.

Chronically troublesome children are in pain, but they are also a pain in the neck to distraught teachers. Teachers need a pain reliever, and punishment is the aspirin of education. It comes in all strengths and various formats, all difficult to swallow. Children have to swallow it and teachers get temporary relief. Teachers dispense most of the aspirin but refer the worst offenders to the front office for stronger treatment. For seven years, as chief dispenser of industrial strength aspirin on the administrative team of a junior and then a senior high school, much of my day was spent dealing with pains in teachers' necks.

I was conscious of the tradition that administrators are supposed to defend teachers and the system, but I just could not pretend that teachers and the system were always right. It seemed to me then, as it does now, a denial of children's rights and hence abusive. I considered what would happen if every child sent to me for discipline were represented by a lawyer. What if judge and jury were to hear each case?

No fair person could approve the list of crimes usually punished and the punishments usually given school children. Imagine any sector of adult society under school conditions of justice. Picture everyone working on a car assembly line in constant danger of being strapped, slapped, pushed, yanked, pulled by the ear or otherwise hurt or humiliated by any exasperated boss. All workers have to raise their hands and ask permission to visit the toilet. An inattentive or unresponsive foreman means distress and even messed underwear.

On any working day, dozens of workers are forced to stay after hours to write a thousand times, "I must not talk back to the foreman." Others have to arrive an hour early to assemble two extra cars as punishment for smoking in the loading bay or running in the cafeteria. A few are always on suspension for multiple crimes (usually skipping work with fake excuses, having too many detentions, and smoking in the toilet). From time to time, a worker is fired for having done all three twice.

The bench outside the manager's office is occupied by condemned workers awaiting sentencing: a woman caught in the cafeteria at the wrong time, three people who forgot notes from home explaining previous absences, two men late getting back from fire drill, a couple caught kissing on the assembly line by a supervisor they mistook for a production robot, a woman wearing a skirt too short, and one man who told a joke that caused several people on the assembly line to laugh while the production quota was being announced on the p.a.

The man currently on the carpet and likely to be suspended without pay or strapped, stands accused of calling a certain executive a mother-fucking racist. He is willing to withdraw the mother-fucking part because he lacks evidence but refuses to withdraw the racist label because he personally is a first-hand witness.

All workers are denied any say in conditions of employment. They must take bits of automobiles home every night as homework and bring them back assembled the next morning. If, as often happens, various management people assign different home assembly projects at the same time, workers must stay up all night to complete all assignments. Even when assigned work is trivial or useless (such as trimming and polishing running boards even though cars no longer have running boards), it must be done without question and on time.

As a condition of employment, workers are required to accept from management: tongue lashings, sarcasm, innuendo, put-downs, arbitrary evaluations, gossip, gratuitous insults, absolute orders, secret record-keeping, personal interrogation, search of personal possessions and lockers. . . .

Every employee is required by law to continue working at the factory without pay for at least ten years and is under community pressure to remain longer. Should a worker switch from one factory to another, secret records from management to management precede him.

Workers who join an organization created by management to deal with workers' concerns, are allowed to decide all matters up to but not exceeding what colour streamers will be used at a social event should one be approved by management. Those workers who write for the management-approved newspaper must not mention sex, politics, car criticism, management, social issues or religions (other than car worship, and that only in a complimentary way); however, they are allowed to publish largely uncensored articles on inter-factory sports, charity cookie sales and winners of production-output competitions.

Any worker not at the auto plant during work hours is in breach of law and may be arrested by an attendance officer and either punished or returned to work or both.

Ombudsman

Teachers and administrators are police, prosecution, jury, judges and prison wardens all rolled into one. Imagine police arresting an adult and then prosecuting the case themselves in the police station with a policeman as judge handing down the sentence. The cards are stacked against a student who runs afoul of any teacher or school rule, value, assumption, expectation or practice. In the child's world, nobody has time for due process. Everybody assumes that adult benevolence is an adequate substitute. No adult would trust the benevolence of other adults in place of due process, but we force that injustice on children. They respond differently: some become fearful of adults. Children afraid of other people often grow up to be authoritarian and replicate the cycle.

Other children become rebellious, especially in teen years. Still others internalize their resentment and shrivel into lifelong victims. Even children who seem unaffected have learned something, if only to give up. Passivity that marks many students in the present model of schooling — including many neo-conservative students — is a response to repressive, unassailable authority of teachers and administrators. In kindergarten, children are active and creative because they have not yet realized their powerlessness. Three or four and especially seven or eight years later, many have become passive and uncreative, the better to survive in an unjust, authoritarian model of schooling.

To prevent institutional injustice, every school should have, on site, an ombudsman whose unequivocal duty it is to advocate on behalf of every student. Most dictionaries define ombudsman as "a commissioner appointed and paid by an authority to hear and investigate complaints by private citizens against government officials and agencies." The school ombudsman should, in addition, be an advocate with the specific duties of advising students of their rights and of being pro-active instead of merely reactive on their behalf. Children must see the ombudsman as their champion.

The eminent children's rights advocate and professor of psychiatry, Robert Ollendorff, thought ombudsmen for adolescents should be psychiatrists specializing in adolescence. That would be useful background, but it is more important that ombudsmen for all ages of children be specialists in children's rights, justice and schooling. No child should ever be tried by a teacher or administrator without the ombudsman present and, in all but routine matters, the ombudsman should conduct the defence. In future, when schools have student government with power, ombudsmen must also protect individuals from that possible source of abuse. Though peer groups do a better job than adults of making and managing rules for children, individual Davids must still be protected from possible misuse of power by group Goliaths.

It should be the ombudsmen's responsibility to monitor all administrative and educational decisions to see that they are in the best interests of children. If a child seems to be wrongly placed in a class or grade, it is the duty of the ombudsman to question the criteria for placement. The ombudsman should show every child his/her school file, explain every item and advise upon possible action; when a teacher enters a report, the ombudsman might help a child write a response to go in the same file and a counter report to go in the school board's file on that teacher. Every student (or teacher) file belongs to the person whose name it bears and must be forever open to that person; it is the ombudsman's role to see that each child has as much power in regard to records as does any adult.

The state ombudsman for children is a separate but also important concept introduced in Sweden. The Norwegian state ombudsman for children is listed in every phone directory and stands ready to act on behalf of any child who calls about neglect or mistreatment. State ombudsmen do not deal with advocacy matters within schools on a daily basis. Though they could and should deal with exemplary cases and class action tests of school abuses, they are more concerned with the child at home and at large in society.

The education establishment is nervous about both types of ombudsman. They are in favour of preventing murder, rape, and torture of children but are not eager to have either a state or in-house ombudsman scrutinize their daily operations for violations of children's rights. In 1980, the board of a large teachers' organization passed a routine, righteous-zeal motion approving the concept of a state ombudsman for children. To see if they really meant it, I wrote a memo outlining possible outcomes and asked the secretary to put it before the executive of the organization. He did. It read in part:

> The Ombudsman for children concept was approved by the Board of Governors in the expectation that the Ombudsman would deal exclusively with problems of children outside of school in the social/institutional and family breakdown areas. However, there are groups wanting an Ombudsman to protect children from the authority of the school. Those who think the school system favors the middle class will bring forward cases of children from poor families in low level streams and terminal courses. Other critics will refer to the Ombudsman, actions of teachers and principals in school discipline including corporal punishment, suspension, expulsion and mental cruelty.

A committee was struck to study the matter. In due course, the organization had a change of heart and quietly shelved support for the concept of a children's Ombudsman.

School ombudsmen should be associates of state ombudsmen to enhance coordination of children's rights activities. And internationally, school and state ombudsmen should work together as a kind of Amnesty International for children's rights. All of this could happen and be window dressing if ombudsmen are conceived as puppets to be danced through ritual displays by establishment chattelites pulling legislative strings.

Internationally, ombudsmen should bypass the list of human needs erroneously called children's rights by the United Nations and go straight for the jugular of chattelitism by demanding the inclusion of children in the United Nations Universal Declaration of Human Rights. The aim has to be full political rights for children, but **a good beginning would be unequivocal support of the most significant provisions of the 1989 Convention of the Rights of the Child** *as they apply to schools*: freedom of expression, opinion, thought, conscience, religion; the right to privacy; freedom from mental, physical or sexual abuse, neglect, maltreatment, exploitation; the right to social assistance and to adequate housing and nutrition.

School ombudsmen could be kept fully occupied dealing with just those aspects of the Convention that refer directly to punishment and schools. Article 29.2 reads, "States Parties (countries party to the agreement) shall take all appropriate measures to assure that school discipline is administered in a manner consistent with the child's human dignity and in conformity with the present Convention." It is disappointing that an often forward-looking document still equates discipline with punishment; it takes the old paternalist, authoritarian, punitive approach that discipline is something negative, punishment to be "administered," rather than something positive to be developed within each individual. Nonetheless, the article recognizes the child's human dignity, and if children were accorded that dignity, most school punishments would disappear because nearly all abuse human dignity.

Article 37 of the Convention has profound implications for every school:

No child shall be subjected to cruel, inhuman or degrading treatment or punishment. No child shall be deprived of his or her liberty unlawfully or arbitrarily. Every child deprived of his or her liberty shall have the right to prompt access to legal and other appropriate assistance as well as the right to challenge the legality of the deprivation before a court or other competent, independent and impartial authority and to prompt decision on any such action.

Almost every school in the world violates Article 37 of the 1989 UN Convention of the Rights of the Child, and most will continue to do so until each has an ombudsman with muscle.

CHAPTER 14

EARLY CHILDHOOD EDUCATION

Early childhood intervention is an idea whose time has come.

— *New York Times* editorial, September 28, 1988

Had I written the Times editorial quoted above, I would have said "education" instead of "intervention." That the editor had education in mind is certain: the same editorial speaks of "the distinct need to educate, not just tend poor preschool children." But the editor sees intervention as the significant move, with education following along in its wake like a dinghy, full of rescued children, stoutly tethered to the ship of state as she slices through the sea of poverty. Children must be poor to be rescued. No editor of a North American newspaper would dream of universal "intervention" on behalf of middle- and upper-class children. That is not an idea whose time has come. But it should be.

Poverty exacerbates some and causes other conditions that should be met by state intervention; but most needs of children are shared by offspring of all socio-economic strata, and wealth is no guarantee that needs will be met. The huge population that lies above the poverty line but below freedom from burdensome debt may or may not choose to spend scarce money on private nursery schools, diagnosticians, clinics, tutors and therapists. And money in the pocket is no guarantee of parental good sense, stability, affection, availability, literacy, counselling skills, etc.

Unreformed middle-class alcoholics, for example, are just as damaging to their children as unreformed poor alcoholics, maybe more so since middle-class children may be more ashamed. Debilitating shame is characteristic of children of alcoholics. It withers self-esteem and often leads to persistent smothered feelings and compulsive compensations such as over-eating, obsessive sex, excessive shopping, gambling, thrill seeking, etc.

Developmental delays can happen to rich or poor children. Motor, language and social deficits that can be successfully identified and treated in three-year-olds are much more difficult and costly to treat three or more years later.

Almost everything about an infant has implications for education and should be part of early childhood education (or intervention). Consider emotional problems. Ontario is as good as most jurisdictions in services for children, yet studies in Ontario show that seventeen percent of children have identifiable and treatable psychiatric disorders, most related in some degree to inadequate parenting. But only about one in five is ever identified and treated by a specialist. The rest, about 135 walking wounded in a typical elementary school of 1000, are left to be behaviour problems, truants, misfits, failures, dropouts and delinquents.

Even if they were identified, it would be too late to treat them properly at age five or six. But **if they were in school as babies, children with emotional problems could be identified with ninety percent accuracy and most of them successfully treated long before the too-late age of five.** Total cost of successful treatment of an infant (about $2200 in 1992) is one 25th the annual cost of much less effective residential treatment for a teen. And that is only the beginning. The lifetime cost in welfare, delinquency, treatment, lost productivity and shattered lives is beyond calculation.

Or consider just one among several escalating negative characteristics among children — violence. In his February 2, 1989, column, Bob Hepburn, Washington bureau chief of the *Toronto Star*, wrote about "the dramatic jump in childhood violence." He added, "In the past two years, assaults with deadly weapons have tripled in U.S. schools and reports of violence have jumped 24 percent in the last year." But he thought it a ghetto problem until two sixteen-year-olds with semi-automatic guns wounded four students at Wilson High School in his own upscale Washington neighborhood. Everyone allows that such violence is likely to have some relationship to drugs. But Hepburn noted that a "reason for the rise in childhood violence is that many parents are lousy parents and, for whatever reasons, don't know how to raise kids."

Parents who use force or direct punishment (instead of suggestion and explanation) tend to raise children who are non-compliant, unreasonable, angry and violent in their responses. When force goes to the extent of abuse, stored anger is a certain consequence. Children who are not themselves battered but witness family violence may take on the pulped personality of the abused person or the explosive anger of the abuser.

About one family in ten, rich or poor, has one child that is less favored and feels rejected; a common response to least-favored status is fighting, smashing and other violence. And there are other causes of aggression.

We know that aggressive children tend to become aggressive adults. The longitudinal research of Leonard Erons at the University of Illinois shows that aggression in the third grade is highly correlated with, and is the single best predictor of, criminal and anti-social behaviour in adults. Erons points out that **if anything is to be done about childhood aggression it must be done before age six.** It would be fairly easy and inexpensive to identify and successfully treat most incipient aggression if infants were routinely enrolled in neighborhood schools with mental health professionals and specially trained teachers on staff.

Nearly all such intervention should be one aspect of universal, state-sponsored, early childhood education. The total domain includes everything necessary for optimum physical, intellectual, social, emotional and moral nurture of children up to six. Innovations in schooling from Dewey onward have been remiss in not insisting upon inclusion on a voluntary basis of all children from shortly after birth. A major reason for the education mess is that schooling starts too late. In many countries, children under five or six are the only citizens **not** eligible for education in state schools, clearly a case of age discrimination and a violation of children's rights.

Educational disadvantage starts at home. Many parents don't have the patience, energy, personality, equipment, talent, training or time to do the whole job of educational nurture even if they would like to. They need and deserve help. This has been recognized for years as it applies to impoverished parents and some commendable compensatory education projects have shown that the right kind of early childhood education (not just daycare) can be helpful in giving children from economically disadvantaged homes a better chance to succeed in school and life. Starting in the sixties, the Perry Pre-School Project in Ypsilanti, Michigan provided one or two years of education to poor three-year-olds. It was a great bargain. For every dollar spent, the country has received back seven dollars because as adults the graduates earn more and pay higher taxes; and they require less expenditure on remedial education, welfare and crime.

Most lower, middle- and upper-class parents, even if they are good people, can't provide optimum learning conditions for infants any more than they can for eight or twelve-year-olds. In the limited time they have with their children, the most parents can do is weld love bonds with affection and togetherness, help build self-esteem with praise and encouragement, and make such efforts as are feasible to plan and provide rich learning experiences. Few accomplish that much. Almost none are able to provide all the nurture for optimum growth, all the foundations for later success in school and life. Even parents who try hard need help. One danger for middle- and upper-class children is that their over-zealous parents are often unable either to plan experiences properly or to identify signs of stress when children are pushed to excel instead of being helped to enjoy.

In the early sixties, people talked about early childhood education. Daycare was seldom mentioned. Now it is the other way around. What should be one road, has forked. The daycare road is becoming a freeway. The early childhood education road is a byway falling into disrepair. There are now vastly more mothers and single parents in the work force.

They are demanding that somebody look after their children. This is understandable, but it is also short-sighted and unfair because it is based on needs of parents rather than needs of children. **Daycare is for parents; early childhood education is for children.** If a child is twelve instead of three, we think first of her educational needs and when we provide for educational needs we provide for custodial needs, daycare, as a spin-off.

The daycare movement may succeed, and we will end up with warehousing for young children instead of schools. It will be a costly mistake. In dollars, it will cost almost as much to warehouse young children as to educate them in schools. In human potential unrealized, the cost of warehousing will be staggering. **It is essential that early education be provided by the local school authority because that is the only feasible way to achieve early identification of individual needs and then the continuity essential to serve those needs as each child moves through schooling from birth to age eighteen or so.** This is difficult enough within the school system and impossible if the years before five or six are spent in a plethora of placements outside of school.

It is unlikely that a state-wide structure will ever be set up for intermittent showcase programs or for warehousing. Since the school system is already in place, it makes more sense to use it than to do without a unifying structure or go to the huge expense of creating a redundant second structure. Besides, we know that emphasis will be on educational programs in the school system, but in a warehousing system, any guidelines that might be enforced are likely to be more about plumbing, places and procedures, than about educational programs.

So long as we are stuck with the present model and mentality of school administration, placing an early childhood facility inside a school is no guarantee it will be integrated into total school program. Such facilities may still be seen mainly as care stations and mainly for the poor. All schools being built in New York now have an early childhood wing, but the state is far from achieving a universal, fully-educational, fully-integrated program.

Where appropriate, early childhood schooling should include extended-hours programs and be located in factories, office towers or malls, rather than in schools, but it must be operated by the local school authority. No matter what location is used, schools for very young children must meet their needs and that means mixed staffing, including professional teachers with special training, facilities that are different from classrooms for older children, and a well-developed curriculum.

Play is central to early childhood learning. But play includes much more than just the childhood equivalent of mindless, basic-level, adult recreation — playing bingo, watching wrestling, throwing frisbees, etc. Play is also the child's avenue for socializing, creating, producing, and learning. Infants are prodigious learners. By age three children are graduates of the most complex of all learning programs — learning to talk. They are already graduate students but are patronized by society as dummies unworthy of publicly funded education.

Young children should be in school because an enormous amount of planned teaching is possible within the play context. As psychologist Jerome Bruner pointed out, "high level intellectual activity" at school causes children to play "in a richer and more elaborated way" when they are on their own. The present model of schooling accepts a certain amount of play-centred learning in the first three grades but kills it off long before high school. The entire experience of schooling is, at worst and at present, a deliberate switch to work from play. At best, it should be the careful nurture of the natural, creative, investigative play spirit so that it survives early childhood and infuses all of life, including the work ethic. Open education in the sixties tried to preserve child initiative but met with failure because it started too late for many children (at age five or six) and ended too soon (because nearly all high schools rejected open classrooms).

A.S. Neill put his finger on one of the sad outcomes of a model of schooling that fails to understand and accommodate play needs of children; he said that football fans are people who never had enough play as children. Neill was wrong, however, in his belief that play is bastardized when used in a planned way to help a child learn something.

Spontaneous play remains paramount, but it can be facilitated. That takes planning. And it must be supplemented by guided play which needs even more planning. Such planning is really curriculum planning.

Young children who play at home are likely to lack physical exercise, but good school curriculum includes planned exercise. Three and four-year-olds who play at home are likely to lack social interaction with peers, but socializing is carefully built into the curriculum at school. Equipment, supplies, instruction and supervision for electronic, scientific, linguistic, artistic, musical, athletic and other types of learning are unlikely to be available except within school curriculum.

In the years before six, children should acquire much of the skill and knowledge that will eventually make them self-propelled, active rather than passive learners, doers rather than done to. **The main building blocks of self-propulsion are language mastery and self-esteem.** Good, individualized school curriculum intentionally develops motor and language skills and self-esteem as part of play. Children who acquire both are equipped to use the creative urge that is natural to all but which collapses in school if the two building blocks are missing. Unless language mastery and related knowledge are planned and then facilitated through play experiences and direct teaching, much of the learning may never take place. Concurrently, self-esteem must be successfully fostered, and that may never happen unless children are with adults who have the time, diligence and know-how to make it happen.

I am thinking of a six-year-old who could swim, dive, skate, ski, sail and also enjoyed pre-participation (readiness) groups in several other sports: tennis, martial arts, gymnastics, etc. He could sing, dance, fiddle jigs, play piano, and knew a lot about hundreds of operas, symphonies and show albums, all of which he could identify by sound or in their dust-covers at age four. He could and did engage other children and adults in conversation in two languages. He could cook several items and knew nutritionally acceptable ingredients and foods from unacceptable ones. He could identify hundreds of animals, birds, trees and flowers. He read incessantly and was provided with anything he wanted to read.

He had a room full of science experiments and another for painting, photography, puttering, writing and research. He also spent a lot of time playing in a third room, a recording studio in his own home. His grandmother was a retired teacher who spent much of her time teaching the boy and taking him to lessons and clubs to learn what she could not teach and to socialize with other children. She had the time to do all this, the knowledge to do it properly and the love to enjoy it. Grandmother and child lived a glorious learning game.

In vocabulary and every other language and academic skill, in social and physical skills, this confident, happy, talkative little boy could run circles around most children his age. Imagine the advantage he took with him to school. There are always a few such advantaged children and they tend to be school stars. It is time to provide all children with the lifetime advantage that comes from early childhood education.

In France, it has been available as part of the school system for over a century. It is not compulsory to attend, but most children begin l'école maternelle at two whether or not their mothers have jobs. From the beginning, it has been considered education, not daycare, and most people regard it as an essential part of education. The program is free, learning-centred, and provided by fully-trained teachers who are paid the same as teachers of older children in grade school. Most children attend full-day programs, but parents may opt for part-day programs. Extended-day programs are also available, and some children, whose parents work long hours, are at school ten hours a day.

Why has the French model not spread to all other countries? In North America we are reluctant to admit that most parents alone can't educate young children. We are willing to admit that such is the case with ten or fifteen-year-olds but not with two or four-year-olds. This, at a time when neurological studies suggest that earlier access to stimulation and information would allow the human race to use brain cortex presently wasted. The collective untapped cortex of humanity is the world's greatest natural resource, the raw material of refined thinking that will access the ultimate mystery.

Parenting

Some romantics say we should help parents provide early education at home. We should instruct and support all interested parents; but there is harsh evidence that many can't even do basic parenting, let alone provide optimum early childhood education. The family institution is not always the mother lode of inherited treasure that conservative romantics claim. Among legacies many people inherit from parents and then pass on to their children are these: superstition, bad manners, intolerance, prejudice, racism, dishonesty, body-insult eating habits, drug abuse, alcoholism, unemployment, welfare dependency, illiteracy, functional illiteracy, low aspiration, lovelessness, violence, wife beating, child battering and sexual abuse.

Some of these have genetic implications, but most are ugly gifts passed on environmentally from parent to child unless early intervention prevents transfer. We have passed the half-way point in a trend: more than half of today's children live in dysfunctional households that fail to provide essentials of either the extended or nuclear family concept.

Roman Catholic priest and scholar, Matthew Fox, thinks only about ten percent of families are "mom, dad and the kids" as idealized. In 1989, about fifteen percent of households in North America had a fully employed father and a mother who was a full-time home maker. Half of pre-school children will eventually see their parents divorce. A study in California funded by the Zellerbach Fund found that only a third of children were doing well five years after divorce. More than a third had behavioral problems, difficulty making friends, and trouble concentrating at school.

Through acting out, if not through conscious decision, we are reconceptualizing grouping and renewal practices. In the recent past, society renewed itself and satisfied the grouping instinct at the same time, using the family concept almost exclusively. Family consisted of father, mother, children, grandparents, aunts, uncles and cousins, all with understood roles in the renewal process and nearly all in close proximity. Even in its nuclear form in the first half of the twentieth century, the family provided children with two married-to-each-other birth parents and usually some fairly close-by relatives.

For many people today, neither the need to group nor the urge to procreate is met using the traditional family concept. It is not only grandparents, aunts, uncles and cousins who have drifted out of the family orbit; often one parent is missing, or both. About a quarter of people now live alone and single-person households are increasing faster than any other type. Another sort increasing rapidly is headed by a single parent with custody of one or more children. Mixed, unrelated households of children from two, three or many previous couplings are common and are called "blended" even if many are oil and water mixes. Often the adults in a household come and go through divorce, serial monogamy, promiscuity or changing economic imperatives.

A Herman cartoon in the Toronto *Globe and Mail* on November 14, 1983, showed a teacher handing out report cards and a small boy asking, "Which do you want to sign it: my natural father, my stepfather, my mother's third husband, my real mother or my natural father's fourth wife, who lives with us?"

Roles have changed radically, and some roles vital to child development are not filled at all. In the absence of adequate fathers or other important males, boys tend toward anti-social and delinquent behaviour and girls toward difficulty in sexual and marital adjustments.

Fragments of families that remain are not families; the fenders of a car are not a car. Perhaps we need a new word, "fragily," which combines the words fragment and family. That jarring word may make us realize we are playing a new game and need new rules. We can no longer focus social policy exclusively on families because that compels us to stuff everyone into the family mold where many don't fit. **Social policy must focus on the individual whether in a family or not.**

Instead of telling us how wonderful and sacrosanct the family is and trying to force everyone into that concept, governments should admit that part of society lives under the family rubric and part does not. It may turn out that some new forms are just as good as the traditional family form, perhaps better for many people, provided proper support systems are built. Research and creative planning are needed to help us understand what has already happened to the family, what new norms are emerging, and how to support future developments in the renewal and grouping processes.

Good pioneer work has been done in the last third of the twentieth century, but it is dismissed by frightened conservatives who barricade themselves behind covered wagons of wishful thinking and fight against what they imagine are attacks on the family. What they are really defending is the imminent collapse of their longstanding right to impose their belief system on everyone else. They hoist the icon of family as a rallying symbol and pretend every fresh wind will blow it over. In their hearts they must know that alternative lifestyles are no threat to family lifestyle. If some people walk or cycle, or if tax money is spent for public transit, is that a threat to the icon of private automobile?

And they must know that parenting training in schools for all teens, sex education for all children and early childhood education for all tots are no threat to the family; yet all three of these programs are attacked by conservatives as anti-family. A conservative minister of education in Ontario proclaimed unequivocally in the family section of the *Toronto Star* on June 3, 1978, "The greatest teacher is the kind of instruction kids get from their own parents. It (parenting) is not a subject you learn in school." With few exceptions, school boards in every country are assailed if they try to provide honest sex education. That, the conservatives insist, is the prerogative of the family; teach it in school and you somehow undermine the family. But we know that most parents do not, will not and cannot teach about sex because they know too little about it and because they are tongue-tied on the topic.

Similar knee-jerk conservative rhetoric erupts whenever educators recommend schooling for the very young. Early in 1984, I appeared before the Committee on Social Development of the Ontario Legislature, speaking on behalf of the Ontario Teachers Federation in favour of early childhood education in the regular school system. A columnist on government matters who attended the hearing wrote in the *Toronto Star* of February 8, 1984:

For all of Dixon's presumably right intentions, the assertion of a professional educator's right to identify "deficits" in a child's development and then "do everything that needs to be done" about them has some alarming overtones for the future.

— the idea of "early childhood education" centres run by the state on a universal basis, "in the context of life-long education,"is simply terrifying in its implications.

— such a system would amount to an extension of state authority over education and therefore a further erosion of the influence of the family unit.

That kind of ostrich reaction in 1984 echoed the 1971 attitude of Richard Nixon when he vetoed a two billion dollar daycare and child development program because of what he considered ominous, its "communal approaches to child rearing." It would make more sense to regard universally available and voluntary early childhood education in schools as a joyous return to the communal care of children that previously existed in extended family, tribal and village life. That sounds like a kinder and gentler nation to me.

Conservative, non-interventionist, rhetoric insists that families are effectively self-regulating; evidence is overwhelming that many are not. Intervention is necessary to provide optimum nurture. Conservatives, and former liberals metamorphosed into neo-conservatives, are quite right when they say government intervention has not always worked. But instead of cutting government programs, we should design new ones that work because they are based on a new model of childhood that works. The present models of schooling and childhood are built on a rotten, children-as-chattel base. All social policy dealing with children and families, and the child justice system, share that same crumbling foundation.

Ingrained, authoritarian ideas of parental sovereignty over children, of children-as-chattel, will die hard, and chattelite diehards will defend their right to ruin their children through failure to provide optimum nurture. **The rights of children and the rights of society must**

delimit the rights of parents and define their responsibilities.
Yet in most countries, rights and responsibilities of children are ill-defined, and so are those of parents. Since 1939, France has had its Code de la Famille which sets out rights and duties of parents and children. Few would find it a satisfactory code for the twenty-first century, but it was a beginning. All countries should by now have improved the French prototype. Instead, most have ignored it.

One premise of any Children's and Parents' Code should be this: **If parents can provide optimum nurture for children, they should; the family, where it functions well, is the ideal milieu. If parents can't or won't provide optimum nurture, society must, because optimum nurture is the right of children and vital to society.** Society depends solely upon children for regeneration. Parents hold children in trust. It is a privilege to parent. It is also difficult. Not everyone can do it. So it can't be mindlessly dismissed as a right. No adult has the right to abuse a child's right to optimum nurture.

The rosy haze of sentimentality about families obscures the harsh fact that nearly everyone can procreate, but few can parent well. To procreate, to **become** a parent, is mindless. It is physical. Nature takes care of everything. Birds do it. Bees do it. Dogs do it. Fleas do it. People too. For the father, it takes a few magnificent minutes — a mere carnal caper. For the mother, it takes a few magical months — even the stupid and indifferent perform the magic. To **be** a parent is not mindless. Maybe it once was. Maybe it was just natural. It still is for beagles and baboons. But humankind has thought its way into a uniquely complex condition, so parenting our species is uniquely complex. Instinct takes care of only a few fundamentals. For both father and mother it takes eighteen or more often anguished and exhausting years of intelligent and informed committment.

In an earlier era more people could parent successfully because society was simpler: children worked alongside parents or surrogates; job skills were learned by watching and helping; the family was a complete economic and social unit; literacy was unnecessary; change was almost non-existent; pace was slow; people lived entire lives in one place; support was all around in the extended family and stable village; parenting behaviour was learned by osmosis, observation and imitation.

Not any more. Society is now complex: parents and children are separated by work and interests; literacy is essential; jobs and job training are beyond family control; change is constant; the extended family is gone; people move often; neighbors are strangers; pace is frantic; there is no accessible model of parenting and no training.

Giving birth triggers for most women an automatic change in self-image which child psychiatrist Paul Adams described as "the most pervasive modification that occurs in human beings." Fathers usually feel something of the same change. But traits present before are likely to remain during parenthood. Copulation is not conspicuously a character cathartic. Parenting is no passport to purification.

There are parents who are and who will always be some of the following: absent, alcoholic, brutal, callous, careless, cold, conniving, cruel, devious, dishonest, disorganized, dissolute, hateful, ignorant, illiterate, incapable, inconsistent, indifferent, immature, lascivious, lustful, malicious, mean, merciless, murderous, neurotic, oppressive, overbearing, promiscuous, psychotic, punitive, selfish, slovenly, sluttish, unavailable, uncommunicative, unloving, unreliable, vengeful, vicious, withdrawn. . . .

Fortunately, there are also parents who are and who always will be some of the following: able, affectionate, available, careful, caring, capable, clean, congenial, controlled, compassionate, conscientious, considerate, constant, consistent, communicative, devoted, enlightened, established, fair, fond, forgiving, generous, gentle, honest, humane, judicious, intelligent, kind, literate, loving, mature, moderate, orderly, organized, reliable, respectful, responsive, steady, virtuous, unselfish, watchful, wise. . . .

Poor parenting is seldom intentional. The abuser, authoritarian, bully, indoctrinator, ice-heart, absconder, cloner, neglecter, over-protector — all are fuelled by their own childhood experiences stored in the unconscious, out of sight and out of (conscious) mind. The fuel is powerful and volatile. The subconscious knows how to leak it like an intravenous drip to drive the conscious mind. Adults are driven and can only try to steer. Some are less driven; some steer better than others. The outcome depends upon the fuel mix, education, intelligence, practice, talent, luck, chance distribution of obstacles, etc.

We must be tolerant of those who steer badly. They deserve help and understanding, not condemnation. But that is not to say they should be allowed to raise another generation of poor parents by mishandling their children. We must admit that many adults will never parent successfully, probably at least twenty percent; and alternate provision will have to be made for their children. Another twenty percent will need constant monitoring and help. Surely this is, in the best sense, Abraham Lincoln's precept that government should do for people what they can't do for themselves.

We must admit that **no current generation of children can ever be saved by changing their parents**. Adult education affects too few parents and is always too little too late. It works best for those who need it least. For the small minority of current parents who are willing and stable, parenting training is valuable, but it will never be anything more than a minor aspect of a proper parent training program. The emphasis should be on the next generation of parents. Much that constitutes good parenting is learned behaviour, and we must see to it that everyone learns it.

Parenting Training

Most countries require prolonged training to be a plumber, mechanic or social worker, even if one has demonstrable natural aptitude, but require no training whatsoever to be a parent, even if one demonstrates no natural aptitude. Workers not required to make crucial decisions about the lives of others are given pre-service training: secretaries, bank tellers, sellers of real estate, etc. But people who will as parents make daily crucial decisions about the lives of their children are given no training at all. Nor are they examined or tested for suitability. Our society examines everyone who wants to drive a car but nobody who wants to parent (except adopting parents).

Some European countries have taken important steps in parenting training but most of the world lags behind. In North America, a few high school students study parenting by working, under supervision, with young children. A few more study parenting theory in regular classrooms, often in family studies or life skills courses; but most people still pass through the school system and into marriage with no training for parenthood. We need compulsory hands-on courses for all teenagers.

Teens who work with very young children are more likely to understand and welcome the challenges and rewards of child rearing. That will help counter the anti-child attitude expressed overtly or subtly in most of society. Movies of the eighties that seemed to be about babies (*Baby Boom*, *Three Men and a Baby*, *Raising Arizona*, *She's Having a Baby*, *Mr. Mom*, etc.) were really about adults and the effects, mostly negative, of babies on their careers.

Other negative attitudes to children show up in restricted housing and child-unfriendly urban design. The ugliest attitude of all is the universal rejection of individual children by individual adults. When a baby cries in public or a toddler throws up, nearly every adult, except the parents, is annoyed. Instead of helping, individual strangers complain or retreat. Over-zealous, beware-of-strangers fear-mongering by child protectionists has exacerbated the problem. Parenting training for all students will teach the next generation of adults that they have a responsibility to help raise all children.

By putting all teenagers in intimate, continuous, caring communication with young children, compulsory parenting courses will go a long way toward overcoming another serious social problem, the generation gap. Schools must also see to it that all teens are in continuous, caring communication with old people. Much current curriculum is trivial compared to inter-generational caring and communication skills. The early childhood classroom is an ideal place to bring teenagers and old people together as volunteer teachers' helpers.

Parenting education is not synonymous with sex education. They relate to each other, but each stands on its own as essential information that must be provided for every student. Sex education deals mainly with anatomy, physiology and biology — all about human plumbing and how it works, and especially with social values, ethics, psychology and politics that surround sex. Parenting education deals mainly with child development and how parents can facilitate development. They could be seen simplistically as a continuum with sex education covering everything up to conception (or prevention of it) and parenting education dealing with the pre-natal period through age eighteen.

In practice, they should be separate so each will be properly emphasized and taught by specifically trained teachers. Sex is not exclusively or even largely a family matter. It never was. It is necessary to deal with sexuality as sexuality. It has its own integrity inside and outside of marriage and family. When sex education and parenting training are mixed under some rubric such as family life, sex, as it is, often gets lost in the golden glow of family sentimentality and becomes sex as we wish it were. **Parenting training must be compulsory for all teens; sex education must be compulsory for all ages from infancy through eighteen.**

Existing parenting courses deal largely with needs of children under six. But even parents who manage well with young children often run into difficulties with teens. It is largely since 1900 that society has forced prolonged childhood on teens and parents have had to cope with teenage sub-culture at home. Fifteen-year-olds of the nineties are far more mature and sophisticated than fifteen-year-olds a hundred, fifty or even twenty-five years ago; but the adult mental image of teens is caught in an Andy Hardy time trap, circa 1940. Not every parent can adjust to reality. It is often difficult for a father to accept the presence in his domain of a sexually active, well-informed, money-earning, self-directed male.

A false argument holds that while it is easy to teach teenagers about parenting tots, it is impossible to teach them about parenting teens since they are themselves teens. All adolescents can and should study adolescent psychology and children's rights in order to understand themselves. If they do so in the context of how to parent teenagers, so much the better: they can look at both sides. Teen programs should include seminars to which their own parents are invited. Many parents would not show up even if invited months in advance, but enough could be recruited to have good, two-generation interaction.

Such seminars would be useful in teaching conflict resolution to two generations at once. Many parents fail because they are incapable of democratic family conflict resolution through parent-child discussion. The techniques have evolved from family therapy counselling. They must be learned by all who parent if we are ever to get past authoritarian, aggressive and abusive alternatives that now paralyse many families. No entire current generation of parents will ever learn the techniques so they must be compulsory in schools for the next generation of parents.

Some willing parents could also be involved in another area usually missing from parenting courses for teens: parent development. There should be more study of behaviour and misbehaviour patterns that characterize parenthood. The universal stranglehold of children-as-chattel mentality should be examined as should repetition compulsion which drives parents to re-enact unresolved conflicts from their own childhoods.

Class discussion in parenting programs should include definition of parents' responsibilities, a matter that must be clarified and legislated. Today's students may become the first parents held accountable as professional parents whose role is defined in law. Professionals are subject to malpractice suits. Malpractice is dereliction in professional duty and may result from: criminal intent; negligence; lack of skill or learning; or incompetence. We can expect malpractice suits against parents to be laid by society as well as by individual children.

Parenting training won't eliminate all bad parenting. That everyone knows how to do it does not mean everyone will do it; however, we can expect dramatic improvement following universal parenting courses and the success rate will increase with each succeeding generation of trained parents.

Divisions of Childhood

To help overcome misunderstandings and facilitate parenting training and early childhood education, we need to agree on names that describe natural divisions of childhood. There are three periods which I call **infancy or early childhood or junior childhood** (birth through six), **middle childhood or intermediate childhood or pre-teenhood** (seven through twelve), and **late childhood or senior childhood or teenhood** (thirteen through eighteen). Jean Piaget used similar divisions when he described mental development except that he designated birth to age two as a category and called it the sensorimotor stage. Three to seven or so, he called the age of symbolic thought. From then to about twelve he named the stage of concrete operations. The teen period, Piaget labelled the stage of formal or propositional operations.

Each of the three periods I propose divides naturally in half, so the schooling continuum for people up to age eighteen or so divides into six natural groupings based loosely on age. Though individual children may progress at quite different rates, there is sufficient similarity within three-year age groupings to justify organizing schools along those lines, provided the **norm** is that individual children move freely within the **entire** structure according to need rather than chronological age. **Separation into grades must disappear entirely in a new model of schooling** but grade names are listed in the middle column of the chart below as temporary reference points to the present model of schooling.

NEW GROUP NAME	OLD GRADE NAME	AGE
Infant A or Junior A }	Preschool 1	1 and less
	Preschool 2	2
	Preschool 3	3

NEW GROUP NAME	OLD GRADE NAME	AGE
Infant B or Junior B }	Jr. Kindergarten Sr. Kindergarten Grade 1	4 5 6
Preteen A or Intermediate A }	Grade 2 Grade 3 Grade 4	7 8 9
Preteen B or Intermediate B }	Grade 5 Grade 6 Grade 7	10 11 12
Teen A or Senior A }	Grade 8 Grade 9 Grade 10	13 14 15
Teen B or Senior B }	Grade 11 Grade 12 Grade 13 (college prep)	16 17 18

Some would prefer to organize three-year-olds with four and five-year-olds; and they would place six-year-olds with seven and eight-year-olds. And so on. So the age groups would become: 0, 1, 2; 3, 4, 5; 6, 7, 8; 9, 10, 11; 12, 13, 14; 15, 16, 17+. Fine. All I am saying is that children as learners fall more or less into six groups approximately as outlined above. I prefer the groupings in the chart because the oldest children within each sub-group are a year older and hence more ready to move upward individually at some time **during** their last year in each age group. That is an important consideration in getting rid of the foolish lockstep norm which moves all children because the school year has ended rather than because the individual is ready to move upward.

CHAPTER 15

TEACHING

Always and everywhere, "He is a schoolteacher" has meant "He is an underpaid pitiable drudge."

— Jacques Barzun, *Teacher In America*
(New York: Doubleday Anchor, 1954)

At sixty, after a lifetime around bullfighting, Ernest Hemingway resolved never to have a bullfighter for a friend because he had suffered too much for them and with them. For the same reasons, I have resolved never to have a teacher for a friend. But I shall continue to interview, admire, bemoan, praise, and reproach them. I expect Hemingway did the same with bullfighters and for the same reason: they are epicentral in an elemental drama. Whether in bullfighting or teaching, the sphere of vision broadens and clarifies with detachment from the hero and the field of battle — the better to see what is really going on. I see my hero is in trouble.

Even his name has been stolen. The title teacher is no longer of much value because it means everything and nothing, having been usurped for its aura by everyone with a doctrine or skill to peddle. When I use the word I refer exclusively to people certified to teach students ages five or six to seventeen or eighteen, with extension of those traditional limits to include children from birth through five and adults who return to school.

I exclude: Jesus, Mohammed, Buddha and other religious figures and their professional proponents; those who show others how to tap dance in church basements, play piano in their own living rooms, do the breast stroke at the YMCA, or look suitably vacuous modelling clothes at fashion "schools"; academic coaches who, as private entrepreneurs, either individually or collectively, sell their expertise in subject disciplines to desperate parents of desperate children. All are either separate from or peripheral to the schooling industry where school teachers labour. I particularly exclude everybody who works in tertiary education.

Rarely are university faculty trained and certificated teachers. They are professors, lecturers, instructors, demonstrators, etc. They are trained in subject disciplines but not teaching methods. Many do not perform well before an audience of students even in the limited sense of professing orally (as contrasted with teaching). Their reputations and rewards are based mainly on scholarly research and writing. Since they are almost certain to confuse school teaching with professing, academics are suspect as schooling commentators. But the media have never figured that out: whenever they want comments on teaching or the school system, they run to the faculty of the nearest university.

There is a sub-species of university academic that should have something relevant to say about school teaching — the hardy types who staff faculties of education, teachers' colleges, colleges of education, graduate schools of education and departments of education. The part of a university that deals with schooling and the academics who work there are likely to be regarded by their colleagues in the rest of the university as second rate, mainly because education is a late arrival among disciplines and not yet respectable.

It never will be, unless universities change their notion of what is respectable. In universities, any respectable discipline which has a strong practical side (medicine, engineering, computer studies, etc.) must also have a highly developed scientific side. School teaching is an art with practical application. The scientific side had to be largely appropriated from psychology, sociology, statistics and other disciplines. The artistic core of teaching was almost forgotten in the rush to be respectably scientific. "Quantify to qualify" became as much a requirement of academics in education as "publish or perish." They got busy counting what exists and now most universities have education academics who know all about statistical manipulation of empirical data and can talk and write about it in scholarly language. But they ignore the art of teaching and the art of conceiving whole new models of schooling.

To make schooling a safe haven for their scientific careers, academics in education have created the false impression that teaching is a science rather than an art. The school-teaching establishment has been taken in by the ruse. Schooling mandarins are busy in consort with research academics extending the felony to its logical conclusion: they are scientizing every aspect of schooling from teacher training to the final exams those trainees will set for their future graduating students. Some aspects of schooling do indeed lend themselves to scientific investigation, but science is an interloper and usurper as leader in an essentially artistic domain.

It is the very nature of science to deal with fragments, one at a time, putting each under the microscope. It is the very nature of art to create and improve whole pictures.

Some professors of education were once school teachers though not necessarily good ones. Some remember what it means to be a school teacher, and they sometimes also have the necessary integrity, courage and creativity to put aside academic games and do relevant work such as training new teachers and writing readable papers. Among academics, they make the best commentators on school teaching (but usually not as good as gifted teachers).

Conventional usage is correct in saying of every teacher "he/she teaches school." I was a career school teacher who used to say, "I teach children not subjects." I was wrong. What I taught was **school**. Whatever the school was, that was what I taught. I taught it **to** people **using** subjects. But **what** I taught was school. School is the medium of education and the medium is the message. Teachers are the most apparent component of school as a medium just as performers are the most apparent aspect of television. But the whole is greater than the sum of its parts. It is the whole that impacts students and society. And schooling as a whole is a mess. So teaching is a mess.

That is why the teaching profession and the public image of the teacher have been in decline for two decades — since it began to be evident that school had atrophied for want of creative nurture, that it had stalled at the toddler level of maturation in system redefinition, that it suffered from stopped action in a world charged with change. In the late fifties through sixties, it looked as though schools, like most of society, would really change; but it became increasingly clear that all proposed changes were too narrowly conceived to affect the whole. Throwing in a little open education, team teaching, cooperative learning or any other innovation never made much difference. The new concepts never changed enough elements of the old model to transform it. Instead, it killed them off or else beat them into submissive decorations. The present model of schooling is entrenched, an icon, even though the icon is hollow, gutted by worms of obsolescence.

It is disheartening to be a good teacher. Who wants to propagate the faith when the icon is empty? Even the most zealous become jaded. They feel powerless to make necessary changes. That is why burnout is epidemic, why teaching is the most stressful occupation except for air traffic controlling.

In 1983, I was having tea with five of the highest paid teachers in the world — certainly in the top two and probably the top one percent. All six of us, two women and four men, were executives. I asked how many would choose education if they had it to do over. Only one hesitated. The rest said no. Instead, we would choose business administration, law or some combination; or possibly another profession or something in media or arts. Anything but teaching school.

Yet not one of us disliked teaching early on. I expect the others were more or less like me — consumed with it. From the time I began to read the literature of schooling in the mid-forties till I started teaching in the fall of 1953, I was working up a head of steam that sent me whistling through schools for years. John Dewey died in June of 1952 when I was about to enter teacher training, and I had visions of the torch being thrown from his failing hands to mine. Not that I agreed with him about everything. Just that I was so earnest and starry eyed!

The analogy to steam is intentional. Steam power was then already dead, but schools were still running in the old way. I thought they would soon switch to diesel, jet, even rocket power. They never did. But I did; and I ran out of residual steam.

Conventional wisdom says some people outgrow their early interests, that old careers no longer suit the people they become. Quite so. But even allowing for the usual amount of that phenomenon, I think it true that many of the brightest and best who teach burn out from kicking a near-dead horse. School is almost dead. The model we use has been brain dead for years and sustained on a life-support system made of band-aids, hypocrisy, rhetoric, residual glory and the sweat of millions of teachers who close classroom doors every Monday morning and kick the near-cadaver into some semblance of life. The good ones kick the hardest. They boot away day and night, year after year. That is why they burn out. Or get out.

Getting out means all the way out. Business and industry, the arts and professions are blessed with an astonishing number of successful people driven out of teaching because they could no longer boot a dead horse. Add to that, successful people who never entered teaching because they knew doctors, lawyers and businessmen, not to mention plumbers, make lots more money. Now you see why education lacks its fair share of the best, brightest, and most creative and why the few bright, creative teachers are awash in a sea of mediocrity.

Getting into education administration is getting up but not out. Executives in education, whether in schools, school board offices, government departments or teachers' associations, spend nearly all their time manning life support systems. Like talented classroom teachers, the few bright and creative education executives can't escape either the daily chore of pumping life into a near cadaver or pedestrian pumpers as colleagues.

I am not going to dwell on low teacher salaries, but teaching is still a life of genteel poverty except, perhaps, in Japan where teachers are paid about as much as engineers. In 1991 the average salary in America was about $33,000. Even in countries like Switzerland and Canada where teachers are relatively well-paid compared to, say, Britain, they have risen only to parity with tradesmen. There are lots of Canadian policemen, postal workers and city bus drivers making more than teachers. In China and most poor countries, factory workers are better-paid than teachers.

Because salaries are low, teachers are forced into moonlighting to make ends meet. No other profession, no other category of worker, comes close to teaching in the extent of moonlighting. According to a 1982 survey by the National Education Association, about half of American teachers have second jobs. The jobs may be inside the school system and range from teaching night school to driving school buses, but vast numbers of teachers supervise camps, tend bar, deliver pizza, sell door-to-door, operate businesses, tutor, edit, drive taxis, guard buildings at night, cut lawns, pump gas, wash cars, etc.

Even if one assumes that present teacher salaries in the best-paying countries are fair compensation for mediocre people, there is no denying that the same ceilings are too low for superstars. Any bonus or merit pay plans that exist, and there are not many, are penny ante. What is great about a ten percent merit bonus based on a disgracefully low salary? Especially when the bonus is given to three-quarters of teachers. That is just a general salary increase withheld from some. It is a demerit scheme for the bottom twenty-five percent. Besides, merit schemes are usually based on test results of students and ignore the higher contributions good teachers make to schooling and to young lives.

I am concerned about the top ten percent, even the top four percent, the whizzes. What about the gifted, forty-year-old teacher who could be making a million dollars a year as a corporate executive, $150,000 a year at a walk in any one of a score of jobs or professions? In 1990, Rochester, N.Y. and a sprinkling of other places offered a possible $70,000 or so for a few teachers. Meanwhile, star teachers were making under $45,000 in New York City and under $40,000 in Los Angeles! Compare that with paychecks of other stars in town: movies, television, hockey, baseball, etc.

Even in education management, salaries are low, and anyone who walks tall has a lifelong headache from bumping the salary ceiling.

My brother is a year-and-a-half older. He dropped out of university to go into sales while I persevered through three degrees and more. From day one, he made so much more money selling rubber than I made teaching school that I could never keep up with him socially. By the time he was forty, he was a millionaire and I was making $12,000 a year. As president of a corporation, the gardening bill for his estate would cover most costs for my lifestyle in education. In his house, the room that contained the indoor swimming pool was larger than my living quarters. People in education thought my place was upscale.

Or consider what happened after graduation when my Psi Upsilon fraternity brothers went into law, medicine, diplomacy, or business and I into teaching. They were in social strata beyond my means, and as they climbed to the rewards of corporate board rooms, law partnerships, supreme court benches and other lofty perches, I was down below in the top echelons of education counting my share of the droppings, a net discretionary income for all purposes about equivalent to the annual fee at one of their clubs.

If other professions and big business are much more promising, why should a talented person go into teaching? I am reluctant to recommend it. Human beings are driven by the need for self-actualization. Teachers are supposed to reach that zenith through the joy of helping children. There may be satisfaction from daily immersion in the fountain of youth, but it has been sentimentalized to mythic proportions. One does not automatically emerge from the fountain immortal, or even energized and certainly not gold plated. Many drag themselves out of the daily dip emotionally drained and physically exhausted. Unfulfilled.

I have taught wonderful children. I passed their way. They passed mine. Passed. Past. Gone. A few keep occasional contact. Chance meetings with others touch the heart.

I was walking on a crowded sidewalk in Mexico when a middle-aged woman got up from an outdoor cafe and addressed me almost reverently by name. She wanted to tell me I had made a difference in her life almost a third of a century earlier. Amazing that she should recognize me in a crowd after all those years. Especially since I had taught her far away in Canada, only two periods a week, only art and only one year. Then she moved away to Virginia to live with an aunt. In nine years she attended nine schools. A difficult life. But she remembered me because I often said her paintings of mountains were interesting and I liked them even though she felt she had no talent.

That kind of residual royalty comes along once in a while like a windfall and there are occasional memories of special students and events to savour for a lifetime, but mainly the army of students marches past endlessly and, from the teacher's point of view, there is never enough time to accomplish much with even one student let alone all. I could have done much more for the mountain painter in a better kind of school. There is no self-actualization when you are not allowed to do your best. It is only mediocre people without much self to be actualized who can find enough scope in the present model of schooling.

Teaching is a viable career choice for a certain kind of mediocre person. I don't mean to disparage mediocrity. It implies a middle degree of talent. Not bad. A middle degree of talent can't be expected to have dazzling pedagogic or administrative insights but should be able to maintain the status quo. That is exactly what happens in education. But maintaining the status quo in education means stagnation from standing still while the rest of the world rushes ahead.

Mediocrity is acceptable as long as a fervid phalanx of brilliantly creative people, marching in front, leads the enterprise forward. No such phalanx exists in education. The brilliantly creative are few. Mediocrity is okay provided the middle does not swell grotesquely like a midriff out of control. In business and industry they cut that kind of fat. In education we shroud it with the ancient gown of academe and prop it up in front of a class or give it an administrative office in which to grow routinely rancid.

Half of any population, including teachers, must be below middle level in ability. They never achieve mediocrity. Some don't even aspire to it. Teaching has its drones marking time behind the mediocre minions.

I discourage young drones from entering education because they will do less harm and find more satisfaction selling gizmos or renting cars. I discourage young dazzlers because I believe they will do more good and find more satisfaction leading multinational corporations or discovering cures for cancer and AIDS.

That leaves the mediocre. I encourage the ones who, though they lack creative brilliance, have a fair measure of other qualities a teacher should possess (see chapter 16) and also characteristics necessary for survival in the present school system: herd instinct, docility, and modest aspirations if any.

Herd instinct is important because the teaching profession in most countries is dominated by unions, and if you don't run with the pack you get cut from it. In most jurisdictions, no individual teacher can negotiate personal compensation or terms of employment. Collective bargaining applies in all provinces of Canada, thirty-three states in the U.S. and many other countries. No matter how good or bad, every teacher gets paid according to an agreement negotiated by the union. Such agreements acknowledge seniority and paper qualifications, not ability.

To give unions their due, the thundering-herd approach has been vastly more effective at breaking barriers to better salaries than all the individual barrier butting that preceded it. But it is equally true that the thundering herd tramples the individual's right to determine his own destiny. The brilliantly creative find it galling to run with the pack when they could and should run on ahead. Individual barrier butting is now a more sophisticated matter than it was in pre-union days and the best people in every field demand the right to do it. Denied the right, they go where they do have the right even when it means changing professions or countries. Teaching should be like other performing arts: the union should negotiate scale (minimum) payment and leave to individuals the decision whether to work for scale or negotiate payment above scale. Stars command payment beyond scale.

The herd also influences decisions about qualifications to teach. Unions, with the grip and insight of bulldogs, fasten upon university specialization and complementary teacher training courses as the prime and usually the only measure of qualification. But everybody knows the best teacher, even of a particular discipline, may not be the one who specialized in that discipline years before as an undergraduate. The brilliantly creative may be generalists capable of ranging over several subjects and able to relate and intertwine them, a quality of great value to this and coming generations because the borderlines and barriers between "subjects" have already crumbled in the real world of politics, economics, sociology, science, business, industry, ecology, etc. Subjects are merging. Yet the gifted generalist, if he is allowed at all to teach a given "subject," will likely be paid less than the plodding specialist. There is no place in the herd for a maverick lacking standard branding.

Another thing the union does is affect tone in the work place. It used to be principals, outstanding teachers and unique customs that determined the ethos of a school, but now union power joins the list and may be the strongest influence. Responsibility for militant-worker atmosphere wherever teachers congregate in some schools lies entirely with unions. Many teachers' associations have opted for militancy over professionalism and no amount of obfuscation in the form of token seminars, research or publications on educational issues should fool anybody. Some associations tolerate a measure of real professionalism, usually at the head office level, but only as long as it does not interfere with militant unionism. Back at the school, the herd shuffles up and down the street carrying strike signs. That is the tone the work place must try to rise above between strikes.

Herd instinct assures survival within the union. Docility assures survival within school-system hierarchy. Teachers who contentedly shut up, follow orders and don't rock the boat get tenure, are promoted, enjoy security and don't burn out. Docile teachers accept mindless curriculum handed down from on high, busywork directives from department heads, marching orders for yard duty from principals, pseudo-supervision from superintendents, irrational budget cuts from school boards, gratuitous insults from the media, everything from indifference to invective from parents. All without losing a wink of sleep.

Anybody who wants to teach must be able to tolerate fools. It is not students who are fools; it is adults. Education attracts an inordinate number of pompous martinets, vacuous politicians, and an assortment of roadblocks disguised as teachers, principals, members of school boards, presidents of teachers' unions and school system administrators. Many have not bothered to study the broad spectrum of schooling and are content, nay confident, operating from ignorance.

For the uninitiated, I feel obligated to detail the degradation too many teachers endure at the hands of incompetent mandarins. I have heard similar accounts all over the world but will settle for an experience of my own.

A superintendent inspected my developmental reading class. He seemed to regard an undistinguished book called *Better Reading* as divine revelation, second only to the ten commandments in unimpeachability of origin and sacredness of content. An encyclical had been issued requiring that revelations according to *Better Reading* be the text for lessons. I had received the message and was awaiting conversion by transcendental intervention, a careful study of the text having failed to save me. Meanwhile, I took the book home and spent a vacation writing original replacement stories and exercises because my incoming students had used the same book the previous year. Besides, I could make the material exactly relevant to them and their community. At the time, I was studying reading at the masters' level so I knew a thing or two.

The superintendent asked a student if the class was using *Better Reading*. She answered, "no," whereupon the super flew into a rage and paid not the least attention to the substitute, original materials I tried to show him. Instead he shouted negative opinions about my attitude and aptitude. I had to invite him into the corridor — not quite the same thing as inviting him into the alley. I just wanted him to vent his spleen where it would be less likely to splatter students.

There being nothing much one can say to that sort, I said nothing and instead looked him over carefully in case I should ever want to write a Dickensian description of the quintessential quack. He was a study in rusted-out red. Perhaps it was the ruddy glow of rage flushing his face that made even his hair, spectacles and suit look rusty. Or perhaps he was dusted with the dried blood of hapless teachers.

When he seemed more or less in control of himself, I returned to my classroom and closed the door leaving him in the corridor muttering something about my being too big for my britches. My britches were the bottom half of a custom-tailored suit. His had the baggy aura of a warehouse sale, a uniform affected by so many supervisory officers that one suspects it is the secret insignia of a worldwide brotherhood. Shortly thereafter, this sartorial sadsack showed up in another class and demanded to know why I had not recorded in the appropriate place on the appropriate form, the temperature in the classroom. I told him, "because there's no thermometer in the room, a fact that I duly reported on the first day of last term."

Again he flew into a rage. I tried to assure him that if the room got too hot or cold, I would open or close a window and would be sure to let him know. But he was beyond reassurance. In front of the class, he fired me. His exact words were, "You can start looking for a new job." I took him at his word and went to the principal's office.

"Mr. Blank just fired me," I said.

"He what!" the principal exclaimed in a gasp of disbelief that sent a sirocco of dragon breath clear across the wide Mediterranean of his desk. That particular principal, though a courteous, conscientious fellow, always quaintly dapper in styles of yesteryear, brought with him every morning to his high office an amalgam of sour smells, consisting mainly, I believe, of stale pipe smoke and certain bilious byproducts of nightly insomnia, sometimes sharpened with Sen Sen.

"He fired me," I said, "and I'm wondering if I should leave now or finish the day or the week or the month or what."

"By Geez!" the principal cried. He was gentlemanly and never resorted to profanity. "By geez" was the ultimate expression of his exasperation.

"Go back to your class," he added.

"Am I fired?"

"No. Just go on with your class. I'll look after this."

He adjusted his tie pin and brilliantined pompadour and set off to do battle. A few days later I was called to a stand-up meeting in the back of the deserted teachers' lunch room. The super apologized for firing me but assured me it was because I had provoked him. I had provoked him? I had never raised my voice. I always spoke plainly and politely to him. That, in itself, may have aggravated but it did not provoke. What provoked him was unaccustomed confrontation with shortfall of sheep-like submission. That threatens second-rate, authoritarian administrators. Their teachers had better be obsequious.

And they had better have modest career aspirations or none. The top in education never provides the scope enjoyed by people at the top in other fields — captains of industry, financiers, entrepreneurs, surgeons, corporate lawyers, politicians, authors, etc. Leaders in most fields have more power and autonomy than leaders in education and hence more freedom to act. I confirmed that perception during the year I spent designing a proposal for a crown corporation to export education expertise, and again during the three years I represented the teaching profession on the board of directors of such a corporation. Teacher executives, even the few who are just as good as the best in business and industry, are always under the control of school boards made up of amateurs, education secretaries or ministers who are usually amateurs, or boards of directors of teachers' associations made up largely of militant unionists and political plodders.

Even if a career teacher's aspirations are to break new ground in teaching rather than management, present school systems are not responsive. Innovations may be tolerated, even encouraged. It makes the system look progressive. Over the years, teachers aspiring to push out frontiers have pioneered an astonishing array of innovations. All of them have shone like beacons in the darkness for a few months or years and then faded like toys forgotten when the batteries wore out. Or else they have become exotic fixtures in a few favored corners of education but have not generalized.

The literature of education and the archived minutes of school board meetings abound with examples of both; and many more great ideas have lived and died within schools or even single classrooms without so much as momentary recognition by boards or media. If the silicon chip had been an innovation in education instead of electronics, it would still be performing its magic in one school of one school board of one state of one country; or, more likely, it would have performed its magic as a pilot project and then been abandoned to the sands of time with nothing more as a memorial than a dusty report on the reject shelf of the school board budget committee.

Open education is just one example of an important innovation of creative teachers that never generalized beyond elementary grades in a few jurisdictions. It was British primary teachers who pioneered open classrooms and their North American counterparts who pushed the concept as far as it could go in the absence of major additional money and creative thinking to supplement its limitations. Open education was too small a concept to carry the load heaped upon it. It was a fragment of a new model. There should have been concomitant and integrated initiatives in teacher training and retraining to make open education workable, greatly altered forms of school administration to allow student and parent participation, new concepts in differentiated staffing to complement open classroom teachers, student self-government to extend student decision-making from the open classroom to the whole school, major changes in curriculum content, an end to the separation of elementary and high schools, etc.

My personal, buried, silicon chip of education was in the open education domain, and it performed its magic in the late fifties and early sixties, several years before open education burst broadly upon the North American scene. My chip lasted five years, a bit more if you count residual convulsions that continued a while after it was buried alive. Even while fully operational, it affected only two schools and never generalized beyond pilot-project classes within those schools.

A creative consultant working with parents and talented teachers had conceived a unique program for gifted students. It was my good fortune to benefit from their brilliance when pilot-project students progressed from elementary school, and I became their main teacher for the two years it took them to complete a three-year junior high program plus a lot of work usually done at senior high school and a lot more that high schools never get around to.

During those two years, it was clear that ingredients for a new model of schooling had come together, that a quite extraordinary event was taking place. Visitors recognized something significant. But they usually could not put a finger on it because the ingrained traditional model of schooling formed a mental block. They always found ways to relate what they saw to the old model: these children write tougher exams and better essays; they read more difficult books, make better speeches, do more homework, know more, make more decisions.

All true, but not the substance of the happening. The revolutionary crux was that student self-propulsion had kicked in and taken off like a rocket, trashing traditional classroom practice in its wake. The students were active agents in their own education instead of passive recipients as was the case in every other classroom in the school, in the country, in the world — except, perhaps, for a few other aberrant flash fires of educational innovation concurrently lighting up other dark corners for a brief moment.

It was awesome. We had actually found out how to do it! How to turn a key component of the traditional model of schooling from upside down to right side up. It seemed clear enough that the approach would work for all children in all places at all levels. Yet it did not even survive to the next level in the school board of origin. A myopic senior high school principal surrounded by equally short-sighted dinosaurs on his teaching staff, backed by a brontosaurs board of education, rejected and deflected the warm wind of change that would have melted the ice age of obsolescence already creeping over them. The class was disbanded at the end of junior high. A half-hearted attempt to run other classes that far fizzled slowly into quiescence and then evaporated.

So it is important that people considering a career in the present model of schooling not aspire to real innovation. It is alright, even stylish if not de rigueur, to talk about change so long as you make it clear to the establishment that it is only talk and you won't actually do anything to rock the tight ship of education. Scrape a barnacle or two and they will promote you to captain. Actually go about redesigning and rerouting the ship and they will hang you from the yard arm or send you below to wade forever in the bilge.

Anyone considering a teaching career in the late twentieth century needs one more quality. It takes either foolhardiness or else lack of integrity to teach in schools where teachers are forbidden to touch students at a time when the greatest need of many students is for emotionally available adults (see chapter 13). No person of character should enter the profession until it takes a firm stand in unequivocal support of children's right to affection from teachers.

CHAPTER 16

GOOD TEACHERS

Teaching involves emotions, which cannot be systematically appraised and employed, and human values, which are quite outside the grasp of science.

— Gilbert Highet, *The Art Of Teaching*
(New York: Knopf, 1950)

Two assumptions with the ring of truth are false: that young teachers are best and that experienced teachers are best. Youth is not synonymous with health, talent, reliability, compassion, affinity, affection, etc. Experience can mean the same failings repeated. My best teaching years were the first and second and the sixth and seventh. I expect equally good ones in the fortieth through fiftieth if I return to the classroom.

In his book *Teacher In America* (New York: Doubleday Anchor Books, 1954), Jaques Barzun wrote, "young teachers are best; they are the most energetic most intuitive and the least resented." Not necessarily. Intuition is an aspect of creativity, and if you have it, you keep it as long as you stay healthy. Not being resented by children depends on a teacher's personality and character, not his age. As for energy, older teachers who maintain physical fitness are just as energetic as young teachers.

The first quality a teacher needs is robust health. Teaching is lonely — lots of friendliness but little friendship — emotionally draining. And it is physically arduous. Only the strong do it well enough, regularly enough, long enough. Everything that goes on between teacher and pupils is cumulative and depends upon continuity. When continuity is shattered by teacher (or pupil) absence, the stream of process drys to puddles of busy-work. For years, I kept tabs on attendance of teachers and found what you would expect: the best teachers had the best attendance. No amount of scholarship or organization or panache is worth a whit home in bed when children are at school.

Apologists mask the epidemic of teacher absence with a smoke screen of rhetoric about quality of teacher time being more important than quantity. The education industry has spawned an underground army of substitute teachers who rush in to stand guard while the regulars are awol. They may be called occasional, supply, stand-in, temporary, replacement, fill-in, substitute, or visiting teachers. They cost a fortune and deserve every cent. Some work hard to create a semblance of continuity even though it is impossible when they bounce from class to class and school to school every few days. Others maintain a grim holding action with busy-work as the weapon of choice. Either way it is hard slugging.

Other industries also have absentee workers, but none has to supply body-for-body replacements in such huge and financially-crippling numbers. That in itself justifies making robust health a qualification for teaching. Another reason is that no other industry telegraphs such a powerful negative-value message about absenteeism to an entire generation of potential abusers.

Paid sick leave should be for unavoidable accident and illness, not for largely discretionary complaints indicative of inadequate self-discipline and stamina for a career in teaching: headaches, stomach aches, fatigue, colds, malaise, cramps, tension, indigestion, hangovers, etc. The frail should look to a less demanding occupation. So should those who refuse to remain physically fit through proper exercise and diet.

I am not talking about Spartan diets or rigorous training for marathons — just basic body maintenance — the kind that sustains energy, stamina, good spirits and resistance to illness: caloric intake which normalizes body weight; regular consumption of nutritious, low-fat, low-sugar, low-salt, whole food; avoidance of body-insult junk food, drugs and chemicals; and half an hour of vigorous exercise at least three times a week with some brisk walking most other days. Not much to expect of a professional, young or old.

Teachers' associations are remiss in not taking diet and exercise, and hence the health of teachers, seriously. In the face of overwhelming evidence that avoidable illness caused by careless lifestyle is crippling national economies and killing far more people than wars, it is still fashionable in many teachers' associations to pooh-pooh sensible diet and exercise or give lip service while serving another round of donuts or liquor at meetings.

In most countries, it is difficult to prevent either the physically or emotionally unfit from entering teacher training or from being certified to teach. In 1988, a young man who had just been trained as a high school teacher, certified by the government and hired by a Toronto area school board, was charged with brutal sexual assault and easily diagnosed as paranoid schizophrenic. If nobody in education could identify such a serious disability, imagine how many less serious ones are overlooked. We are more careful in selecting policemen, soldiers, astronauts and airline pilots. And that says something about our regard for children.

Nor are we good at removing the unfit from classrooms. The best teachers' associations and school boards have counselling for crisis cases but rarely for the sub-clinical, walking wounded. My guess is that health/fitness factors are central in most and implicated in nearly all walking wounded as well as crisis cases. Yet those factors are virtually ignored (except where drug or alcohol abuse is flagrant) especially in walking wounded who manage to show up fairly regularly. It seems likely that counselling and therapy by an orthomolecular physician might get many sub-clinical and quite a few clinical cases back into classrooms. Some people need more of certain nutrients and the role of orthomolecular physicians is to identify and eliminate deficiencies.

Governments and teachers' associations have to take teacher and student attendance seriously and confront causes whether inadequate nutrition and exercise or equally dangerous negative values — many absentee teachers pretend to be ill and skip school for the same reason as many students: they think cheating is alright. A fudging front is burgeoning under the banner of "mental health days." The battle cry claims everyone is under such stress that days off are more than just alright — they are admirable. The real purpose of the campaign is to justify slacking. Anyone who is truly in need of days off because of stress is more in need of stress management counselling than dereliction of duty.

To clean up this aspect of the education mess teachers absent more than four days in any school year should forgo salary or else report to an attendance committee made up of faculty, administration, parents and students. If there is reason for compassion, the committee should be compassionate. The allowable limit for teachers (and students) should be two percent, or four absent days in a 200-day year. That is generous. It totals 140 days or seven months of school days over a 35-year career. The shameful reality is that teachers in many countries are paid full salary to stay home twenty or more days a year. That totals a staggering 700 days or 3.5 school years of absence with full pay in a 35-year career. Ten percent of a "working" life!

There is a caveat: all teachers are under stress because the present model of schooling denies them meaningful control over their professional lives. The most stressed are those with the heaviest load of extra-curricular activities such as music and drama teachers. They share with all teachers a heavy classroom load and inadequate pay that often requires a moonlighting job to make mortgage payments; but they are expected to put in additional hours without pay after most teachers have gone home weary. Some work twenty-five percent longer than usual. They should be compensated with matching reductions in classroom load or else full overtime pay. If after-hours activities at school are worth doing, the teachers in charge deserve that kind of recognition.

When a new model of school administration gives teachers control over their professional lives, they will address overload problems and teaching will be less stressful. When an adequate job description for teachers is written and implemented, it may not be necessary for them to be so extremely healthy because workload will be better managed.

Presently, everyone just guesses at real workload and keeps piling on more each year. In that kind of career milieu, there is no place for the weak and no choice but to discriminate on health grounds in selecting and endorsing teachers.

I include mental health grounds. Teaching attracts its share of psychologically maimed, and stress on the job weakens others whose personalities were only tenuously integrated. There are too many emotional abusers in classrooms who habitually belittle, ignore, embarrass or otherwise victimize children they dislike. And they do it with impunity because the present model of schooling is based on the ancient assumption that children are chattel and teachers *in loco parentis* are always right.

The great fear is that any move to regulate on health, especially mental health, grounds might stimulate a witch hunt by fundamentalists out to burn liberal thinkers who keep education from becoming indoctrination. That is a real problem but not insoluble. The same lot has been out to burn books for decades. We need to confront them, not avoid them.

The second essential quality in a teacher is committment that expresses itself as genuine interest in schooling, devotion to duty and total reliability. It is not unusual to find that half of a surveyed group came to teaching because they could not get into preferred work or could not think of anything else to do. Some can't commit to anything. When they lack interest in schooling, teachers don't read the literature: curriculum development, innovations, research, philosophies of education, organizations of the teaching profession, child development, children's rights, etc. When they lack devotion to duty, teachers arrive at the last possible moment and leave before the buses are loaded.

A teacher must be able to communicate with children. Any manner of speaking difficult to understand is likely to cause learning problems for students and discipline problems for the teacher. One barrier to easy understanding is heavy accent. I represented the teaching profession on a government committee that assessed teachers from other countries applying to teach in Ontario. Problems of inadequate academic standing or teacher training were easy to deal with by identifying necessary make-up courses. Problems of inadequate command of English were frequent and much more difficult to resolve. Even people who were fluent, often had accents that were impossible to understand. Too many marginally understandable people were accepted and sent into schools to make their own and their students' lives miserable. Some of them might have made admirable teachers of immersion courses in their native languages or ambassadors-in-residence at schools, interpreting the cultures of their homelands, but as regular teachers they were failure fodder.

All teachers should be screened and trained to speak clean English. Their constant good example is the least we can offer students in a school system which rarely teaches oral language skills. Teachers who use sloppy, local or personal modes of speech telegraph the message that anything goes. "Ah reckon them thar taters ain't no good fur nothin' 'ceptin" seement ur hawg slops," may reflect local speech, but it does not open most career doors or enhance international understanding. When I was in Beijing discussing terms for contracting Canadian teachers of English, a senior official of the Bureau of Foreign Experts lamented poor pronunciation of English by Australian and British teachers. His examples included york and yoke pronounced alike by teachers from England so that Chinese students had a vision of a big American city named after the yellow of an egg.

This is not to say that all accents are unacceptable. Some are as understandable as they are charming. No problem. But the teacher is not acceptable who persistently pronounces ask as axe, bail as bile, nothing as nothin', etc. Nor is the one who uses fillers excessively: I mean, basically, you know, like, well, eh, etc.

Every teacher must be articulate. I have heard teachers give garbled instructions, illogical and disorganized arguments, inaccurate descriptions and confusing explanations. Not that they are at a loss for words. Many are verbose. What is teacher training for if not to screen out the inarticulate and train the rest to speak with precision?

An aspect of being articulate is having something to say. It seems little enough to expect of teachers reasonable ad lib explanations to the public of matters relating to their disciplines, pedagogy, child development, curriculum, education issues, etc. And to their students on world and local cultural and political matters. But a surprising number seem unable to get past "yes," "no," "I don't know" or some other guillotine of ordinary, intelligent discussion. Teachers need to be exceptionally culturally literate.

"Good sentences and well pronounced" are useless if they can't be heard. Whether the space is a small seminar room, a theatre, a gymnasium or a cow pasture, every teacher has an absolute responsibility to be heard. People without the natural gift must be trained to be heard or get out of teaching. Instead we put up with excuses about "tiny voices" and "modest personalities." All such excuses are self-indulgent and unacceptable.

Another essential quality in a teacher is genuine affinity with a broad range of children. I say "affinity with" instead of "affinity for" to emphasize that mutual affinity is necessary. It is often assumed but not true that children like every adult who likes them. I say "a broad range of children" because a career in school teaching is bound to include a range of types and ages of children. It makes sense to work mainly with the age group one prefers, but teachers too confined to a narrow age range, lose their grasp (if they ever had one) of the whole spectrum of schooling. A fault of the present model of schooling is its fragmentation by age grouping into several solitudes. Any new model must integrate all ages. In anticipation, every teacher must make it a point to keep in touch with all ages.

I taught children from six to eighteen during training and on the job; but when I began writing television for tots, I had to get acquainted with all ages below six. Only when that last piece of the picture was in place did lights go on and for the first time I could see the whole. Child-development courses are useful provided they cover the span from birth through adulthood, but they can't substitute for first-hand experience with all age groups.

In the model of schooling I propose, campus schools accommodating all age groups from infants to late teens will broaden teachers' grasp of schooling as an organic whole; they will constantly exercise rapport with children of all ages. It might be possible to improve affinity through therapy: some interpersonal skills can be taught to adults. But real rapport is a gift; it is palpable in a classroom in the first year of teaching or the forty-first. So is lack of it. A truthful adult should recognize lack of affinity and stay away from teaching. Unfortunately, love of a subject or dearth of other career opportunities too often convinces people they should be teachers even when their love of children is weak.

Teachers must have a genuine feel for the condition of being young and for the ever-changing culture of youth. In some ways, childhood and youth are "other countries" and teachers must know the language and culture of those countries. Most teens, and many preteens, spend almost as much time listening to music as they do watching television, mingling with the family or going to school. Most children don't get direct instructions from records and videos, but they do absorb general conditioning to cultural norms. Music lyrics should be studied and discussed in school (but usually are not) and at the very least, teachers must be familiar with them.

Many children can "talk adult" and nearly all give it a try when confronted by teachers who don't speak their language. Ritual dialogue results, rather like polite conversation with the vicar over tea. In day-to-day classroom encounters, especially the fleeting ones in high schools, such shallow exchanges rarely reveal signs of trouble brewing. That is intolerable since classroom teachers are ipso facto the front line of surveillance for internal bleeding of the second kind.

Unless classroom teachers spot sub-clinical problems and either deal with them or arrange referral, it is often too late by the time routine guidance counselling cycles an internal bleeder into the overcrowded schedule of the guidance department. Even then, there is no guarantee the counsellor will get past "talk adult" formalities. I checked files of several students with incipient problems, all of whom had been through recent, cyclic, private interviews with school counsellors. Among matters missed were home neglect and even abuse, negative or anti-social attitudes, inadequate self-image, heavy smoking and an all-night job.

Only writers of fiction equal teachers in the need for intense emotional responsiveness to other people and their problems. Call it activated compassion. My unabridged Webster's dictionary lists as synonyms for compassion: pity, commiseration, fellow feeling, sympathy, kindness, tenderness, clemency. I mean all of those things when I say **compassion is an essential quality in a teacher.** For even the most fortunate children the first eighteen years of life are so full of rapid changes, mysteries, uncertainties, and contradictions that nothing less than unconditional compassion in teachers provides sufficient support for the daily tremors and periodic earthquakes of growing up. Children know when teachers have it, and with such teachers, they feel supported.

For the least fortunate children, compassionate teachers are tenuous umbilical cords providing stabilizing nurture until they are able to make it on their own. Such compassion requires knowing each child, an impossible task in the present model of schooling. I found it difficult just to read the office files on every child I taught; some years I had to study over four hundred. Just memorizing the names was arduous. I cheated by taking piles of files home to read on weekends, a practice forbidden by management.

I always tried to be available at all hours to children who wanted to talk, to visit at home those with family problems and those long absent with illness, to find alternate housing in emergencies, to go to police or court in support of students, to give or lend money for necessities like bicycles and dentistry. . . . But I know I failed too many because I didn't know about their problems or didn't know what to do. Still, compassionate teachers reach an extraordinary number of less fortunate children, usually with words and affection, but also with actions.

Affection is related to compassion but is not the same. Compassion, or at least pseudo-compassion, could derive from mere sense of duty. Affection implies the added dimension of love, liking and fondness, and it implies that all three are expressed rather than repressed. Everything I have studied and observed tells me that **teachers must be affectionate** because affection is essential for children of all ages; if teachers don't supply it, many children never get enough to avoid becoming emotional cripples. Their self-esteem withers for lack of nurture.

Teachers must be trustworthy. A combination of qualities mentioned above — health, affinity, ability to communicate, compassion, affection — should assure trustworthiness but doesn't always. Some otherwise admirable teachers routinely betray confidences of children: they gossip in the faculty lounge. Others are only occasionally indiscreet: they pass along confidences in good faith, even record them in files. But children must be able to trust teachers all the time. They have that right. In the medical and legal professions, ethics of client confidence are well-developed as regards adults and are being extended to children. Not so in the teaching profession because teaching had no tradition of an adult model.

Fortunately, many children know intuitively which teachers they can trust. But in the absence of such a teacher, a child in need may blurt out confidences to any teacher who will listen. Another will conceal everything and suffer alone. My own ethic is that any information from child to teacher is confidential if the child expects confidentiality or if information is the kind a physician or lawyer would regard as private. I will go to my grave with hundreds of such confidences locked in the privileged information vault of my mind. **The trustworthy teacher never gossips about children and never writes anything in a record or otherwise passes on information even to parents without first sharing the proposed report with the child and receiving unqualified approval.**

The trustworthy teacher should also be open. This is not to say teachers should pour out their hearts to students. The focus should always be on concerns of children. But open teachers share enough of themselves to diminish the yawning chasm that so universally distances aching children from caring adults. The strong, silent teacher, no matter how well endowed with other qualities, remains forever out of reach. Openness is a form of touching; it touches the heart.

An aspect of openness is humour and **teachers need a sense of**

humour. I have known joke-telling teachers who lacked the openness that goes with a real sense of humour; they hid behind jokes. A joke teller can be just a ham, a bore. What is important is to see humour in everyday life and to laugh, especially at oneself. If in addition, a teacher has the wit to be amusing about everyday life, students are enhanced. Vinegar vibrations from dour teachers sour the atmosphere and shrivel students. It is time we weeded the humorless out of every batch of applicants to teach.

We should also weed out people lacking exceptional ability to organize. **Even in the present model of schooling, teaching requires organization, and in the schools of tomorrow every teacher will need organizational skills on a par with generals and chief executive officers.** In some countries, the widespread inability to organize even the short-range, much less the long-range, is a national impediment. A valuable aid project would be a thorough training course in planning and organizational skills for teachers in poor countries. The multiplier effect organized teachers would have upon their students should positively affect third world development. But it is difficult to teach adults complex organizational skills and can only be done longitudinally with much practice and coaching along the way. It makes sense to identify applicants for teacher training who already have such skills. The same is true of **other qualities teachers need: self-propulsion; leadership; and interpersonal skills**.

As performing artists, **teachers need a touch of class, panache, charisma**. This is not to say that great flair is needed or that only larger-than-life characters need apply. A touch of class is just that: a touch. But it lights up a classroom as surely as it does a Broadway stage and for just as discriminating and appreciative an audience.

A minor but important aspect of style is dress. Teachers are role models; from them, students absorb concepts of dress and grooming. This does not mean teachers should be fashion plates, clothes horses or faddists. A few well-tailored suits will do for both men and women, but there is plenty of scope beyond suits to accommodate free expression of good taste. There is nothing wrong with casual clothes, but it is more difficult for people lacking taste to look good in casual clothes. They often look either flashy or sloppy, and the ones who imitate teenage fashions look foolish. Since some teaching chores are best done in casual clothes, teacher trainees lacking natural taste need guidance to keep them from showing up in classrooms unshaven and unshorn, in old T-shirts and run-down sneakers.

All qualities needed should be assessed before admission and during teacher training. Instead, the only thing usually considered seriously for admission is paper qualification. Degrees and certificates are seen as proof of mastery of subject matter and mastery of subject matter is seen as proof of fitness to teach. Both assumptions are incorrect. Mastery of subject matter can be acquired without attending university, so if mastery is to be **the** criterion for admission to teacher training, there must be provision for people who have come by their expertise independently. The present exclusion of such people from training is contemptuous of the very thing education claims to champion — independent learning.

Mastery of subject matter is necessary in some situations: mathematics, various branches of science, foreign languages, etc.; where delivery of data is the teacher's role; where accumulation of precise data is the goal for students and that data is not available except in the heads of teachers. But there are or should be many more situations where data delivery and accumulation are not the intent or where data can be found by students.

This is not to disparage mastery of subject matter by teachers; it is useful in all situations and essential in some. But it is not synonymous with good teaching even in situations where precise data are critical. It is an ingredient in the mix. An abundance of other ingredients can outweigh the value of mere mastery in many situations. Especially so when schools move, as they must, from the dead notion of teacher as repository of knowledge to teacher as orchestrator and conductor of learning opportunities. **In any new model of education, schools will need brilliant generalists to knit together the ravelling cloaks of old-fashioned subjects. They won't be found by**

emphasizing mastery of separate packages of subject matter.
But even when generalists are the driving force, there will remain a
need for specialists as support personnel, especially in high schools, but
also in elementary. For these people, it is appropriate to give mastery of
subject matter more weight in selection and in evaluation of teaching
performance; however, even for subject specialists, it is true that teaching skills and the other essential qualities in a teacher are fundamental.
Without them, all the subject-matter mastery in the world is useless.

**When teachers fail, when they are incompetent or ineffec-
tive, it is rarely because of inadequate scholarship in a subject
discipline; rather, it is because of inadequate stamina, energy,
physical health, mental health, commitment, self-discipline,
personality, character, organizing ability, leadership, self-
propulsion, interpersonal skills, teaching skills, etc.**

Since teaching, especially in the present model of schooling, is a
performing art, **the ultimate essential quality a teacher needs is
talent**. It is a gift. No amount of training will produce it. But the right
kind of training or practice or both can hone talent into artistry. This
applies to baritones, pianists, painters, actors, teachers and all other
performing artists. Nobody expects the untalented to be given stage or
screen roles, and when it happens, corrective mechanisms usually
remove the untalented; so career performers generally have both talent
and artistry. Printed public criticism of specific performers and performances is one of the corrective mechanisms. Patrons choosing not to
attend performances is another. Neither of these admirable correctives
is common in education, so weak performers remain on the job before
captive audiences.

Another corrective mechanism removes untalented actors: common
sense. After looking at television shows in which I was required to
deliver memorized lines on cue, my common sense told me I was not
an actor, so I stopped doing it. Many teachers without talent for teaching
lack the common sense to realize it. But we should not have to depend
on the common sense of the untalented to keep them out of teaching.
Talent and all other qualities needed by a teacher can be identified well

enough before or during teacher training and extremely well during internship. If teacher training were done properly and failures screened out by the end of internship, we would have a professional teaching force that would lead the world into a vibrant new model of schooling instead of ministering interminably to death throes of the old one.

CHAPTER 17

TRAINING, MONITORING & ORGANIZING TEACHERS & AIDS

[T]eacher education should be founded on the idea that there are forms of professional and personal knowledge of teaching which may be taught and learned and which, therefore, confer specialized professional status on those who hold the knowledge.

— Michael Fullan & F. Michael Connelly, *Teacher Education In Ontario: Current Practices and Options for the Future* (Toronto: Ontario Ministry of Education, 1987)

The public takes seriously the training of physicians, dentists, engineers, airline pilots, etc. But teacher training has never been taken seriously. People believe: that teachers know a lot of facts because they went to college or because they are smart; that anybody who knows facts can tell them to children; that it has nothing much to do with "training." Training for what? How to write on a chalkboard?

Most teachers believe their own training was a waste of time but that other people need a lot. And deep inside they believe there must be a way of preparing people to do with professional certainty what they personally must improvise every day for forty years, all the while trying not to be found out. Their anxiety is born of inferiority feelings which I attribute to the misconception that teaching is a science when it is three-quarters art. People who are essentially artists look into the mirror of their working days thinking they should see scientists, but instead they see artists pretending.

Teachers' associations institutionalize the misconception, the pretense and the anxiety; they think more teacher training should make the next generation of teachers what the present generation only pretends to be. And they have an additional reason to promote longer teacher training: training broadly perceived as more rigorous should carry with it higher status and salary.

Presidents, Prime Ministers and politicians can be counted on for occasional lip service to teacher training. It has a nice ring — nothing but the best for our children. And it may win teacher votes. But politicians have never taken teacher training seriously. One proof is their unconcern when cyclic shortages of teachers are accurately predicted years in advance. They never act early to train more teachers. They wait till the shortage is catastrophic and then, claiming an emergency and banking on public indifference about training, they undermine the profession by handing out teaching jobs to crash recruits after a few weeks training.

In the early nineties, twenty-three states in the U.S. had shortcut training schemes and only eleven states were not contemplating them. In Texas, people with three weeks training were being hired as teachers. Some additional course requirements for certification later on were tagged to the deal, but the "teachers" in front of hundreds of students on Monday morning had three weeks training. The citizens of Texas did not take to the streets. But imagine the furor if they had been assigned physicians or airline pilots with three weeks training.

In the early nineties, no province in Canada was operating a quickie scheme; but individual school boards were legally hiring untrained, unqualified persons in the absence of qualified applicants for duly advertised teaching jobs. Such boards were not even obliged to provide quickie training and most didn't! But the looming teacher shortage of the later nineties was getting some press attention and proponents of quickie courses got busy preparing the public to welcome stopgap teacher training. Ontario was reminded that it operated quickie courses during the late fifties and sixties and that graduates were among administrators still in office. But little mention was made of the many quickie-course teachers who failed or became plodding survivors. Instead, trendy new supporting arguments were offered. One in the Toronto *Globe and Mail* on March 27, 1989, proclaimed, "Not everyone can afford a full year at a faculty of education, a requirement that discriminates against working class students." The author did not, however, proffer the same argument for cutting medical training to a few weeks. Why not?

Shortcut proponents assume that natural genius for teaching exists. It does. But they must also assume that quickie-course organizers have divined some way to identify and recruit only natural geniuses and that lots are just treading water, waiting for teacher shortages. Both are false assumptions. Recruiting for quickie courses is mainly on the basis of paper qualifications and, usually, a bare minimum is required. And people treading water are likely to be: chronically unemployed or underemployed failures from other jobs; or people without the committment to take longer training; or people who couldn't think of anything else to do. However, some real talent swims into the net while it scoops up the dregs.

Another favorite political game is to raid other jurisdictions for teachers instead of training enough to meet a long-predicted shortage. Politicians in the jurisdiction being raided can be counted on to be as delinquent as the raiders: they give away teachers they will need to meet their own coming shortages. In 1986, California raided British Columbia and Ontario and hired away several thousand teachers when it was evident that both provinces would soon have teacher shortages of their own. But Canada is just as good as California at raiding other jurisdictions and just as good as Texas at quickie courses, so why worry?

Perhaps the message is that teacher training has always been so inadequate that conventional wisdom is wise to it. The general public knows intuitively that an eight-month year of teacher training has never amounted to much more than a few weeks of ritual imitation called practice teaching, interspersed with a segmented quickie course bloated to fill the time.

From country to country and within countries there are variations on the common, one-year period of teacher training. Some have lengthened it. But they all prepare teachers for the present model of schooling. Creative teacher trainers, who look ahead and train teachers for schools as they should be, are accused of leading neophytes down the garden path. Student teachers prepared for future schools must walk into present schools and survive. So most teacher trainers teach survival skills young teachers need; they train obsolete teachers for obsolete schools.

The best trainers manage also to impart at least a vision of things to come, but the vision slowly dissolves and trickles away from many young teachers, squeezed out by the pressures of manning life-support systems that pump some semblance of life into schools. Most new teachers teach as they remember being taught. When a promising innovation comes along — such as open education, or an even smaller fragment such as student-run seminar/discussions within otherwise regular classrooms — most teachers are incapable of participating.

All major schooling innovations have failed because proponents have not specified and insisted upon universal teacher training (and retraining) prior to implementation of the innovation. Late in 1971, long after open education had arrived, a proponent, Joseph Featherstone, wrote in a booklet for Scholastic Magazines Inc., "it is far from clear how to improve it (teacher training)." I disagree; everything in this chapter (along with related matters elsewhere in this book that have implications for teacher education) must be an integral part of any new model of schooling before it is implemented.

Whether a one-year program of teacher training follows graduation from university or is spread out and done concurrently with a basic university degree program, the time is too short for real teacher training. **The ideal is a three-year, post-graduate teacher training program yielding a doctor of education degree** and an opportunity to audition for teacher certification and licencing by successfully completing a further internship of six months. Two years plus two or three summers (instead of three full academic years) might be enough time. Nobody knows since a proper teacher training program has never been done.

The program I favour is based on one I offered the dean of a teacher training college in 1969. I suggested he hire me and give me a studio group of twenty to thirty of his students who were willing and who could pass my screening. In two years including two summers, I would turn them into first-rate teachers as judged by the college's criteria and my higher criteria too. My group would plug into some lectures at the college but otherwise would operate as a roving band, mostly in schools and in our own seminars; I would make all arrangements. I intended using the living room\hi concept (chapter 21) adapted for teacher training. The trainees themselves would operate as a living room group and would invite children into their midst; both summers, they would "teach" living rooms for volunteer children. My offer was never accepted. The dean was intrigued and for a moment his face lit up, but he soon regained his composure and settled back into the tried and untrue.

People applying to study art or architecture submit portfolios of their work. Those applying to study music, acting or dancing audition. The folks who train teachers don't usually bother with either. They claim the number of applicants is too great. The truth is they prefer to use high marks in the previous year as the main entrance requirement even though there is no correlation between high grades and talent for teaching. A token screening interview may be added. A resume, which nobody checks (too many applicants) and a letter of praise from somebody back home which nobody checks (too many applicants) are the only opportunities for aspiring teachers to show creativity.

Let's assume that teaching is unique among the arts in that it is impossible because of sheer numbers to audition all applicants for training, or even to require of them a comprehensive portfolio. (It is not impossible, but it would be expensive — not expensive in the realm of cigarettes or adult war toys or cosmetics, but expensive compared to what we are used to paying, practically nothing.) There is a way to reduce the numbers being auditioned: **do auditions after teacher training instead of before**.

Lee Shulman and associates at Stanford University have done important work on the portfolio concept as a way of assessing practicing teachers. It holds just as much promise as a way of assessing trainees. Throughout teacher training, each student should prepare a portfolio for presentation to an official licensing body. Those with good portfolios are allowed to proceed to an audition lasting six months in the same school assisting the same computer-matched teacher. The licencing body, having closely attended auditions, admits to teaching only those people who perform well enough, the talented, the artists.

Teachers should be trained as performing artists. Related concepts have drifted around the fringes for years, and some training centres have adopted minor characteristics without going far enough to make much difference. Even the best concepts have been weakened by their devotion to the present model of schooling. Still, a concept offered by Harry A. Dawe in the April 1984 issue of the *Kappan* was admirable and should have set the world of teacher training on its ear. It didn't.

My concept goes further; it anticipates a new model of schooling and prepares teachers for it as well as the final years of the old. It resembles the workshop method of training actors; students form studio groups for long-term study and then alternate performances and evaluative seminars. Master mentors work with them. The trainees perform and then analyze, perform and analyze, and then perform some more. It is exhausting. But it works. Practice, followed by peer and mentor evaluation, makes perfect, or as near as humans can get.

The establishment in all performing arts except teaching seems to know this. Many people in the education establishment think improvement in teacher training will come from getting teacher trainers to do and read more research and then get their trainees to read most of it. They have fallen into the trap of thinking teaching is a science. It is true that teaching, like other performing arts, can be broken down into many parts and that certain parts can be examined in detail using scientific or quasi-scientific methods. Some of the information so derived is useful. Some is not. Much of it is written in confusing academic language, and most reported research lacks a clearly-written final section on "applications for teachers."

What teachers, teacher trainers and teacher trainees need is short reports that answer the question "so what?" about any and all research. That would be useful, sometimes important, in seminar discussions as trainers and trainees go about their real business of workshopping raw talents into artistry. Research on learning styles and teaching styles is a case in point: a group of trainees should practice different teaching styles and discuss the research. They would find out that children vary in the ways they learn best: in groups, alone, from abstractions, from practical applications, etc. Through workshopping, trainees should learn how to vary teaching styles to match learning styles. And when and why to do it. Research findings could hasten the discoveries and sharpen the focus.

But much research on schooling would still be of little value in teacher training even if written in understandable English because researchers limit themselves almost exclusively to examining what presently exists. They assume they are examining and clarifying aspects of a vital organism, but in fact their work is more akin to post mortems. On rare occasions when researchers create situations to examine (instead of examining what already exists in schools), they create only fragments instead of whole new models of schooling. Fragments do not graft easily onto mother school in her weakened condition.

It is not only teacher trainers and researchers who cheat trainees by examining and hence replicating what already exists. Producers of print, computer and audio-visual materials for teacher training make the same mistake. For years I represented teachers' associations as consultant to an educational television network. I tried to persuade network executives to create school situations instead of always filming what already exists. They refused. The films we made for teacher training, though among the best in the world, were always case studies of dead schooling, more useful as eulogies for yesterday than as models for tomorrow.

Though they were intended and are still acclaimed as examples of how-to-do-it, I always think of them (and could use them) as examples of how-not-to-do-it.

There is an urgent need for good audio-visual and computer materials to be used directly by self-propelled trainees. A few lecturers and specialists, particularly in the various literacies, will serve many studio groups of trainees, and some will serve more than one college. But much of what teacher trainees study over three years (while they concentrate on practice teaching and evaluation of performances) will be learned in seminars with trainees making all of the individual or group presentations (see chapter 22).

Much of the mastery required of a teacher is acquired during teacher training, not before: **how** to teach reading, writing, speaking, ciphering, problem solving, researching, interpersonal skills, conflict resolution, discussion skills; **how** to diagnose and remedy specific problems in all those skills; **how** to evaluate students and how to teach them to evaluate themselves and each other; **how** to turn over to students most of the chores now performed in front of classes by teachers; **how** to counsel individual students.

At this moment, hardly any teachers know how to teach reading, and those who do are mainly at the early primary level even though students leave early primary long before most learn to read well — or write, speak, listen, cipher, solve problems, etc. Hardly any teachers know how to diagnose problems in skills development or how to evaluate students. Most have no idea how to change classrooms from student-passive to student-active. Even people who are potential jewels remain undeveloped as teachers unless their talent is polished with such knowledge.

All elementary school teachers in the present model of schooling and all full-time elementary-level mentors (called hies in the new model I propose) must study content as well as teaching strategies in language, mathematics, science, and other literacies. Many trainees will not have studied any of these previously at university and may or may not have adequate knowledge. Those with adequate knowledge should be excused from further study by testing out. Elementary and high school teachers who will be subject specialists (called consultants and lecturers in the new model) should have adequate background in their specialties before being accepted for teacher training or else acquire it before being licenced to teach. But even a candidate with a Ph.D. must also acquire the teaching degree by completing a full teacher training course.

Most recommended curriculum for teacher trainees (mentioned above and implicit in all chapters of this book) differs considerably from the usual content of teacher training. All aspiring teachers will become versed in children's rights, the history of childhood, student government, the various literacies — topics seldom even mentioned during traditional teacher training. But some of the curriculum will resemble what is or should be in present curriculum: six aspects of education (history, philosophy, law, psychology, sociology and politics of education), details of professional organizations of teachers as they are and as they might be, measurement and evaluation, etc.

In any workable new model of schooling, so many teachers will cycle in and out of supervisory and administrative roles that they must be trained from the start for that aspect of their work. Much of the study of education management should be done in the studio workshop mode.

Every trainee must be assigned as "education friend" to a housing development, apartment building or individual family for the duration of training. In countries with immigrants, a teacher trainee could be assigned to an immigrant family or group as education friend. This model is used in Ankara, Turkey by the University of Hacettepe except that student physicians are assigned to slum families as "medical friends." The log of such a relationship would be an important addition to any aspiring teacher's portfolio.

The studio model of teacher training requires the trainer in charge of each studio (or else administrators of the teachers' college) to round up children to populate practice teaching living rooms. As a start, summer schools would do. But eventually, teachers' colleges must contract with school boards to operate designated schools as new-concept schools on behalf of boards; or else new-concept schools must be run by colleges on their own campuses. Either way, children will volunteer in droves.

At the start of teacher training, all trainees will create personal growth profiles in consultation with mentors. Each profile will begin with a full account of health and educational background from birth. It will detail studies and experiences completed throughout teacher training and will look ahead outlining intended growth activities. Since pre-service teacher training is only the beginning, much growth activity will be undertaken while working as a teacher and will continue for a lifetime. **Though it must be maintained as a condition of certification and licencing, the growth profile must be a teacher's personal property**.

After three years, a teachers' college will award the doctor of education degree to trainees it considers successful. Those who want to teach will present to the licencing authority their new doctorates, their growth profiles and portfolios of their accomplishments: video tapes of their teaching and counselling; classroom planning records; projects; essays; computer programs; curriculum designs; research; professional writing; original learning materials; evaluation records, etc. Those accepted will be matched with one or more experienced teachers and embark upon a teaching internship/audition of six months. If the licensing authority applauds the audition, a certificate and licence will be granted.

Those not admitted to the audition and those who fail it, along with those who do not apply, may seek careers in the support network of industries that surrounds the education industry: publishing, television, computer program design, research, etc. Or they may go into other industries as trainers or become academics. But they may not teach in schools.

Much fuss is made about allowing mature people with advanced academic degrees or rich experience to switch into teaching as a career after years in research, tertiary education, the arts or industry: historians, biologists, psychologists, musicians, accountants, automotive engineers, etc. They should be allowed to teach provided they know how and know about the schooling industry. A forty-year-old research scientist (or a twenty-year-old prodigy) may be a born teacher, a genius artist who knows the art of teaching without having been taught. In the best of worlds, he should be able to bypass teacher training. But that could only happen if there were a first-rate screening process in place. There isn't.

Such a screen might evolve from the work of the National Board for Professional Teaching Standards, a sixty-four member panel established by the Carnegie Corporation of New York to offer (from 1993 on) a new, prestigious, voluntary teaching credential for American teachers. There will be separate tests and credentials for many specialties from early childhood education to senior physics. As conceived, the new credential, "Board Certified Teacher," is for experienced teachers who opt for close classroom scrutiny of their teaching and a battery of pedagogical tests more sophisticated than any presently in use by school boards or teacher training colleges. The intention is to test everything teachers should know and be able to do.

National Board tests could be adapted to screen exceptional persons who lack a teaching degree or equivalent training but seek a licence to teach on the basis of alternate training or natural gift. If that ever happens, it could be a model for a new era of rational openness in all professions. Can we look forward to tests for the alternately qualified or naturally gifted who seek untrained entry into law, accounting, medicine . . . ?

Monitoring Teachers

Competent professionals tend to be self-regulating. They are driven to stay in balance. With a little help from their colleagues, good teachers are constantly checking up on themselves, examining experience and learning from it, forming and reforming themselves. With a lot of help, they can do it very well. That kind of help is sometimes called formative evaluation, especially when it is part of formal supervision and tied to professional development and personnel management policies of a school board. There is nothing punitive about formative evaluation. The aim is to help teachers.

This type of evaluation in school systems is usually too occasional to be of much help and is done by principals and other supervisory officers who lack the training or talent to critique teaching performance even when equipped with the latest fifty-page observation instrument. Occasional visits by supervisors for an hour or a day encourage teachers to put on shows. They know what impresses and how to rehearse students if visits are scheduled in advance. For surprise visits, teachers reach into their bag of tricks and go into their acts. They are, after all, performing artists.

Teachers know that every evaluation touted as formative is likely also to be used as summative evaluation when administrators talk tenure and promotions. So it is worth playing the game. If today the principal visits, give lots of ritual teacher talk from the front of the room because that is what he or she likes. But if the area supervisor shows up tomorrow, stay away from the front and use lots of contrived seatwork because that is what he or she likes.

Principals can identify basket cases long before visiting them. They hear the news from students, parents, other teachers and privileged sources such as school secretaries and janitors. **Children identify bad and good teachers accurately.** They can hardly ever be fooled and no teacher can fool all of them all the time or even most of them most of the time. Children know which teachers: care passionately about schooling; give completely of themselves all day, all year; are trustworthy, understanding, open, affectionate; accept them unconditionally. They know if they are loved, if they are growing and blossoming in the care of a teacher. **Group response is the quintessential evaluation of teacher performance.**

Individual children may spread false reports about a teacher's competence just as individual adults may do and for the same reasons: some are liars; some want revenge. But most children who report a competent teacher as incompetent are really reporting incompatibility. When teacher and child are incompatible, they should be separated and neither blamed. If several children report incompatibility with the same teacher, thorough evaluation of that teacher must be documented by the administration.

Parents learn about good and bad teachers in bits and pieces from things children say and do. They form a fairly accurate second-generation picture and pass it over garden fences to become the third-generation picture a community has of its teachers — a bit fuzzy but good enough to admire or abhor. So principals and supervisors go about their supervision with bad and good teachers already sorted by hearsay. But "good" teachers range from the barely competent through the dazzling. Too often, supervisors and principals mistake the mediocre for the best and fail to recognize stars. Sometimes stars are so unorthodox, so far ahead of supervisors, that they are mistaken for troublemakers or weak teachers.

When I was a vice principal, I was surprised to hear from the principal that a young teacher whom I rated highly was "having a hard time of it and not working out." He based his judgement on what seemed to him "disorder in the science lab." In fact, it was the hum of self-propulsion as students actively explored science while the young teacher circulated inconspicuously, a powerful catalyst in every experiment. He went on to become a successful teacher trainer.

Even if they happen to be good at it, principals and supervisors haven't the time to do proper formative evaluation with the ninety percent of teachers who are competent. They need every available moment to deal with the ten percent who are incompetent and to do the myriad other chores expected of them (see chapter 19).

Another problem is that the very nature of occasional, drop-in evaluation by superiors perpetuates teacher-active and discourages student-active classrooms. Teachers are doing their best teaching when students are productively self-propelled and teachers are relatively inconspicuous. But many traditional "superiors" dropping in briefly are unable to tell much about a teacher if students are "performing" instead of the teacher. They are apt to say, "I'll come back some other time when you're teaching." I swear this is true. It happened to me, and teachers tell me it still happens.

The question then, is how to do formative evaluation that keeps good teachers developing professionally for a lifetime. Some jurisdictions have opted for no formative evaluation worthy of the name, others have developed peer review methods and others keep trying to improve their checklist instruments and their checkers. **Responsibility for formative evaluation of teachers (and hence routine supervision that is implicit in formative evaluation) must be taken away from principals and supervisory officers and given to counsellors employed by every school board to help teachers plan professional growth and to advocate on behalf of teachers, especially for growth opportunities.** A teacher and his counsellor should meet regularly in the classroom and in private to assess daily performance and plan appropriate professional development.

Teachers and their growth profiles will be the focus of attention for counsellors with expertise in professional development, counselling, and assessment of classroom activity. Their responsibility will be unequivocally to their clients, teachers, and no information about a client will be revealed by a counsellor except with the express agreement of the client. Still, counsellors and growth profiles of their clients could provide input for personnel decision-making by the school board; where opportunities for professional development training or for promotion are at stake, teachers will usually authorize release of relevant information.

Teachers and their counsellors will welcome and make use of input from peer review teams or administrators though such information is unlikely to tell them much they have not already figured out. Peer review will be particularly welcome when it is linked with peer coaching and is part of a good professional development program (see chapter 18).

With ninety percent of teachers taken care of by counsellors alone, principals and supervisors will attend exclusively to the ten percent or so of teachers who are in such difficulty that counsellors have not been able to save them and arduous documentation leading to termination must be undertaken. That is the kind of summative evaluation that is appropriate work for administrators. Inadequacies must be summarized clearly while libel, slander and malice are scrupulously avoided. This is crisis intervention as demanding as any police investigation and administrators must not shirk responsibility as they have in the past by sloppy preparation of cases or by turning a blind eye to incompetence or by giving letters of recommendation in return for resignations.

Since there are many borderline or complex cases (perhaps as many as three-quarters of the bottom ten percent) and since all people have the right to due process in the best sense, counsellors must advocate on behalf of their clients and should be supported in that task by teachers' unions and their lawyers. It is up to administrators to show cause for dismissal. If cause exists and they are competent administrators, inadequate teachers will be dismissed even in cases that go to court.

In assisting such teachers, unions and counsellors are not championing incompetence; rather, they are protecting the individual's right to due process. Nor is it their fault that incompetent people were graduated from teacher training and then certified to teach, or that they were hired by school boards. Usually, teachers do not turn bad as members of unions or clients of counsellors: they were bad in the first place. If teachers' organizations are at fault it is for not demanding better screening and for not insisting upon professional status that would give them meaningful quality control through significant (not token) participation on licencing bodies.

Major participation in licencing of teachers should be an obligation of the official professional organization of teachers, probably using a mechanism such as a council run by (but at arms length from) the teachers' organization. The public, government, and teachers' colleges should be represented. Or government itself could create an arm's-length licencing board and ask the teachers' professional organization to name most members. Either way, government must bear the cost and the licencing authority has to have a secretariat and support staff that enable it to operate independently and effectively.

Teachers fired for incompetence or inadequacy should be reviewed

by the licencing body and licences revoked, suspended or made condi-
tional in keeping with circumstances.

Organizing Teachers

**There are three separate activities for which teachers must
be organized: most important by far is professional leadership on education issues; a distinct and defined aspect of
leadership is licencing; least important, though always a
necessity, is protection of teachers' financial and related
interests.**

Teachers as a group don't yet see themselves as professional artists or
as professionals of any ilk. In their collective heart of hearts there
remains a debilitating tumour of inferiority feeling nourished by long
years of genteel poverty, middling status, hack mentality and lack of
leadership. The malaise has been exacerbated in the last half century by
the success of empiricists in convincing teachers of the false notion that
teaching is a science, and hence, scientists or quasi-scientists at universities are the leaders in education. Such leadership as exists among
teachers is largely within the union movement and usually limited in
reach and grasp to protective issues.

Teachers who rise to union leadership are the best politicians, not the
best educators. Often the best teachers eschew politics in favour of
classrooms. If they participate in union activities, it is at the committee
level and only committees dealing more with schooling than with
protective issues. A union leader who is also a brilliant educator is rare.
And yet it is often unions that deal with government and other agencies
on professional issues because, in most jurisdictions, there are no
powerful teachers' organizations with a professional rather than a union
bent.

Associations of English or mathematics teachers (and many other
job-alike groups) exist, but they reflect the fragmentation of the present
model of schooling and rarely combine to achieve sustained political

clout. Too often, they become accessories of unions, tolerated for legitimizing value. Attempts to form colleges of teachers or similar professional associations with power have generally been unsuccessful, and where they have had some success, as in Scotland, the concept has failed to grow and generalize.

Nearly all teachers' unions have a professional veneer. But their sponsored research, conferences, workshops, curriculum committees and publications on professional issues are likely to be ritual finery trotted out for fashion shows and then routinely put aside in favour of dungarees for militant marching, breast thumping and barricading. Such professional work as is done by unions derives more from the leadership and creativity of a few salaried staff than from elected officials. It is characteristic of teacher unions worldwide that they occasionally hire for their secretariats a few real professionals along with a plethora of political plodders and other yes-men and women. From those few professionals comes an astonishing amount of work some of it educationally important. Much of what they generate is killed off or diminished by lesser lights elected to executives and boards of governors of unions. But enough survives to become part of the glacial drift that passes for progress in schooling.

Staff officers of unions constantly spread progressive ideas, sometimes surreptitiously sometimes openly, to each other, teachers on committees, academics, government officials, thought leaders, the media, foreign colleagues, etc. They do so in spite of union leadership and at the risk of being humiliated, vilified, castigated, and harassed by those leaders if found out. Union staff officers who have real educational credentials, reputations and interests are always under suspicion of being secret agents whose loyalties to children and educational progress might compromise militant unionism on protective issues.

I learned early on about union mentality. In 1967, shortly after I was hired to the secretariat of a large teachers' federation, the *Toronto Telegram* interviewed me and published a story mentioning some of the ideas in this book. Instead of welcoming the ideas for discussion, the executive of an affiliated union gave me a hard time. Their office and their representatives on the governing board of my employing federation were frosty toward me for years. On August 24, 1983, the Toronto *Globe and Mail* quoted me as saying:

> The profession is becoming more professional and sees its obligation to be concerned with curriculum. It indicates the way of the future. For the first time, the federation has policies on curriculum development. The era of political activity (my word "exclusively" was omitted) on protective issues is over. Curriculum is becoming an area where teachers will insist on taking a leadership role.

Some representatives of the same affiliated union hauled me on the carpet to answer for my optimism. Perhaps they were nervous that teachers might be wooed by such hopeful words into thinking first of curriculum issues instead of protective matters, that they might reject politicians in favour of professional educators as leaders. Luck was with me. The president of the moment was one of the occasional teacher politicians with professional as well as union insights. He calmed the waters.

It is important for teachers to protect their financial interests through organized (union) activity. School boards and governments throughout the world were among the most repressive of employers in the early twentieth century. It is only because of the tenacity of union leaders that teachers have risen from galling to genteel poverty, from floor-scrubbing flunkies to semi-professionals, from victims to victors in wrongful dismissal battles. And **many school boards are still capable of sacrificing teachers' rights to political expediency.**

But it is wrong for teachers to make protection the main activity of their organized representatives. It should be a routine departmental matter, in a professionally oriented political organization that spends three-quarters of its time and money on curriculum, teacher training, professional development, licensing, etc. The alternative is to have two organizations, both properly funded, one a union to deal with protective matters, the other a professional society to deal with educational matters. Either way, the public has a right to expect educational and even broader, societal leadership from teachers' organizations.

It may be true that physicians' organizations provide little leadership to society in matters of health, or architects' organizations in matters of housing. If so, the public should demand more of them, and they should demand more of themselves. The same with teachers. The most obvious leadership teachers should provide is in curriculum development (see chapter 20). To be community, national and international leaders in curriculum and other educational decision-making, teachers organizations must be diplomatic, cooperative and conciliatory rather than militant and confrontational. They must bristle with creativity rather than rancour.

Typically, official organizations of teachers exhibit siege mentality on educational issues, usually defending the present decrepit model of schooling, usually wanting additional money spent to do more of the wrong things better. Picture a nineteenth-century factory — full of old belts, pulleys, gears, hand-brakes, fly-wheels, pistons and monkey-wrenches — wheezing and puffing to turn out a product that no longer matches market demand. No official teachers' organization has ever designed or even condoned a new-model factory. Instead, they talk of: more belts and gears; better training and certification for hand-brake, fly-wheel and monkey-wrench operators; tinkering with this pulley or that piston; addition of more displays for public show-and-tell tours — the odd computer, a picture window on the world — anything to pretty the place up without actually changing it.

Or, picture school as a nineteenth-century carriage designed to transport a selected few youngsters from childhood to adulthood within the local village. Now, a hundred years later, all children must be aboard and must stay there for years longer, and they must reach adulthood in the global instead of the local village. Teachers' organizations feed the horse more oats, add a fifth wheel, spruce up the upholstery and ride shotgun to protect the vehicle from attackers.

Driven as they are by union priorities, teachers' organizations have hardly begun to realize their potential for educational leadership locally, nationally or internationally. I attended a meeting of The World Confederation of Organizations of the Teaching Profession in Singapore and wondered why I travelled halfway around the world to hear unionists waste precious hours on platform bombast. Such modest forays into educational thought as were attempted were perfunctory, trivial and firmly rooted in the present model of schooling. The occasional educational insight almost always came from staff officers of w.c.o.t.p. and its member organizations, yet delegations consisted almost entirely of politicians.

Teachers organizations think they are protecting teachers when they protect the present model. They are wrong. **All great opportunities for teachers lie in redefining the model of schooling.** Redefinition should be a perpetual obligation of every official teachers' organization. Teachers have a right to expect it. So does the public.

One thing teachers' organizations must do is sensitize the public and the corporate sector to education as an industry that is crucial to the economic success and survival of any nation. Because education is the primary industry that feeds all others, one would expect to find teachers on boards of directors of all companies. But there are almost none: partly because big business does not fully appreciate the relationship of schooling to its bottom line; partly because teachers have failed to engage the business community, to attract its attention, to promote schooling and hence teachers as an economic force.

Because of their large numbers, teachers will be a political force to be reckoned with once they have something to say besides, "gimme." They are potentially an even more powerful cultural force. By the early twentieth century, school had become the primary transmitter of culture from generation to generation. It superseded family, tribe, church, government and all other agencies in that role. But **radio, film, television and computers rushed in to challenge schools and succeeded within fifty years in changing childhood enough that it was out of sync with schools. In the twenty-first century the trend will continue unless teachers and their**

schools change enough to reclaim leadership.

A big and burgeoning group of teachers that urgently needs reorganizing is retired teachers. Worldwide, they number millions. Just in Ontario, there are always fifteen thousand healthy teachers officially consigned to rocking chairs. Some do the traditional good turn in hospital flower shops. Many live seven-day weekends of bingo, golf and bridge. Such organizations as exist are usually led by retired politicians from unions and are self-serving, devoted to pension improvements and packaged tours.

Retired teachers must organize on a large scale to be and to train volunteers for schools. They should also organize to lead the world toward a new model of schooling. They have no jobs to jeopardize through challenging the establishment. **Retired teachers are in a perfect position to organize the transition to a new model of schooling and of childhood through a community discussion process on a scale unprecedented in history.** Mercy killing of the present diseased model of schooling seems a reasonable cause for retired teachers, but they don't espouse it. Some are too neurotically attached to the near-cadaver to pull the plug. All are too unused to educational leadership.

Paid and Volunteer Assistants for Teachers

Education is the basic industry that supplies all other industries. As an industry, it must use labour cost-effectively and that means intelligent use of paid teacher aids. Education is also the basic social service that comprehends all other social services. As a social service, it must make optimum use of volunteer aids.

The picture of "teacher" now emerging is of a busy executive who oversees complex operations. Paid teacher aids and volunteers are valuable helpers as huggers, nose-wipers and film-threaders. But they are much more: secretaries, computer and word processor operators, markers, testers, monitors, readers, listeners, researchers, record keepers, etc. Community colleges can and do offer two and three-year training courses for teacher aids. Either colleges or school boards should be funded to provide courses of a few days or weeks to train various kinds of volunteers.

The real potential of assistants for teachers has not been exploited, particularly in high schools, partly because of the overuse of recitation teaching. A teacher holding forth in front of thirty students or working from handouts is not likely to delegate and supervise high-level teacher-support tasks. Even highly skilled assistants are likely to be idle or relegated to running errands or marking simple assignments.

Most high school teachers are not used to long-term classroom planning and don't know how to organize teaching and learning for small groups and for individual study; they grew up being taught by teachers talking in front of thirty children and that is all they know how to do. It is part of their belief system. Even when teachers work in teams they usually maintain the teacher-driven tradition that finds little use for aids. Only when schools are student-driven, when classes are divided into smaller groups, each working on different chores, or when students work individually at different projects and levels, can paid assistants be really useful.

Teachers must be retrained before they can use assistants effectively. We should get on with it because eventually, when a new model of schooling is in place, paid and volunteer assistants will be an essential part of the system. Meanwhile, even promising fragments of a new model, such as open education, peter out partly because assistants are not provided or because teachers have not been trained to use them.

CHAPTER 18

RETRAINING TEACHERS

*Professional development programs should include the general compo-
nents found by Joyce and Showers (1981) to be necessary for change in
practice: theory, demonstration, practice, feedback, and application with
coaching. Follow-through is crucial. A series of several sessions, with
intervals between in which people have a chance to try things (with some
access to help or other resources), is much more powerful than even the
most stimulating one-shot workshop.*

— Michael Fullan, *The Meaning Of Educational Change*
(New York: Teachers College Press;
and Toronto: OISE Press, 1982)

At the end of the twentieth century, **schools must teach everything
that parents don't**. Obsolete schools are groaning under the weight
of responsibilities never dreamed of when our Victorian school model
crystalised. It is not just subjects that have been added; schools have had
to take over services that don't fit into any one subject and can't be
managed for all students unless all teachers assume new roles.

**Society is right in giving added responsibilities to schools
because there is no other agency available, but society is
wrong in not reconceptualizing schools to meet the
challenge.** There should by now be a new model of schooling that
includes much-improved teacher training for new roles. But there is not.
So we have to make do by constantly retraining teachers on the job. And

even when teacher training is improved and extended, there will remain a need for continuous on-the-job training. If student-teachers were trained to do all things society expects, training would take ten years. Much of it has to happen in the work place and be specific to particular teachers undertaking particular responsibilities as circumstances change.

Additional training for practicing teachers goes by many names: professional development, staff development, in-service training, retraining, continuing education, further study, etc. It is difficult to think of another schooling issue so shallowly conceptualized and analyzed in the media. A typical example of press confusion was a full-page report on professional development in the *Toronto Star* on January 1, 1986, followed by a lead editorial three days later. Both were naive; the writers did not know **there are two kinds of professional development, personal and corporate,** and that the latter is synonymous with curriculum implementation and hence must be provided by school authorities as part of the teacher's working day. The editor wrote:

> As for professional development, we encourage teachers to take courses and seminars at night or during summer. And we expect them to do it on their own time.

Personal professional development is for career and personal growth and is indeed done at the teacher's own expense in time and money. Teachers' associations may be involved in planning or providing opportunities for renewal credits, but individual initiative remains the norm. As associations become more professional, they tend to set standards and urge members to continuously upgrade.

The main personal PD activities are: graduate courses for advanced degrees; additional qualification courses for certification or higher standing on salary scales; refresher courses; special interest workshops and seminars; experimentation; educational travel and reading the literature to keep abreast of one's discipline and of education generally. All are done at the teacher's own expense. The median length of time it takes American teachers to complete doctoral degrees in education is eight years and they finish at a median age of forty. The reason it takes so long is precisely because most teachers do advanced degree work evenings, weekends and summers while fully employed as teachers.

There are some slackers, but the teaching profession is exemplary in the amount of personal time and money members spend individually and collegially on professional self-improvement courses, seminars and workshops. Teachers should not be expected to do more, and the public should get off their backs. Teachers are remiss in not making their record better known. Few individual teachers or their associations bother to issue local press releases or arrange media interviews to inform the public.

Teachers share with most other professions chronic neglect of the literature of their calling. Neither doctors nor teachers usually get beyond journals and newsletters of their associations. Some don't even bother with those. Doctors make do with pitches and perks from drug companies. Teachers get by on handouts and what they hear at meetings. Part of the problem is that much education literature is unreadable. Academics usually talk to each other in print. There are few writers on the art of teaching and schooling, and there are few journal editors interested in anything more than empirical aspects of schooling or union aspects of teaching. A page of footnotes is to journal editors, if not the measure of a good education article, at least the measure of respectability.

Every teacher should regularly plan and try out new ideas and evaluate results — a creative rather than a scientific process. Teachers who do informal, creative experimenting deserve more attention. Too few contribute to the literature by reporting their experiments or their creative thinking.

This is not to suggest that teachers ought to avoid "scientific" experimentation. Teachers should occasionally test an hypothesis and document the process using the natural laboratory that every school provides. Most don't. I am not suggesting rigorously structured research with slavish adherence to scientific method (though such research has its place and some teachers do it very well); rather, I am suggesting enough planning and documentation to clarify rather than to prove. Since all teachers should know enough about statistics to understand measurement and evaluation, all should know enough to do classroom research.

Teachers do more educational travel than any other group. Unfortunately, they don't do it well. All travel is in some degree educational. At the low end of the spectrum is fun-in-the-sun for a week or two in winter at a palm-fringed tourist ghetto. An occasional foray away from the beach for shopping and picture-taking at the market and quick chats with busboys is about the educational apex of such travel. Slightly better is the typical historical walkabout that teachers so enjoy in summer. The best such tours might rate four on a scale of one to ten. Not only are they limited in scope, they are invariably undertaken in pairs or groups, and teachers cocooned in the security of company from home are more protected from real involvement in foreign cultures than from imagined dangers.

Few teachers ever do educational travel that rates a ten or even a seven or eight because such travel involves confronting people more than churches and galleries. It is dirty, difficult, lonely, and gloriously enlightening. Not many teachers will forgo high-rise hotels, air-conditioned buses and shopping escapades to really find out what is going on with people in a foreign country, especially a poor country or one culturally quite different. I led an educational tour of teachers in the Orient. A group visit to a Japanese school was prearranged. Several Japanese teachers remained at school during vacation just to meet us and had thoughtfully prepared food and an informative program. Two-thirds of my group failed to attend the seminar and instead went shopping.

Teachers rarely visit schools in foreign countries even though it is easy to do, always informative and frequently evokes invitations to teachers' or students' homes. When school is in session, visiting teachers have only to present themselves at the schoolhouse door and convey with smiles, gestures and as much mutually understood language as can be mustered, that they are teachers from X country and would like to come in. A calling card printed in the local language on one side is helpful but not essential. A little kit of school photos from back home is invaluable. But the only necessary credential is the magic word "teacher" accompanied by a finger pointed at oneself and the name of one's country on a jacket or bag. I say, "Teacher. . .Canada," and smile. The red carpet is rolled out, tea is brewed, children are thrilled, and both hosts and guest feel honored. Any teacher who wants to know what it feels like to be visiting royalty should stop by any local school from Portugal to Pakistan to Paraguay.

If you are alone and show an interest in the locality, some teacher is likely to offer you a walking tour. I often ask a teacher or student who is studying English if I can help with English and if he/she would help me by showing me around. Usually, I am the first native speaker of English the learner has ever met and we have a constant excited lesson on pronunciation, idioms, vocabulary and grammar as we explore back lanes, back streets and back yards tourists never see.

The second type of PD, **corporate professional development**, is the **only** way to implement changed curriculum. Any change in education requires changing the skills, knowledge, beliefs and practices of the people who implement the change — teachers. **Since change in program is the employer's responsibility, changing the implementors must also be the employer's responsibility**. It can't be done in a day. It is not an event. It is a process, and it takes weeks or months rather than hours or days. **Since change is constant, corporate professional development must be constant.** It has to be part of the model of schooling.

But it is not part of the present model of schooling. Imagine the transportation industry without fuel for its engines or the banking industry without money to invest or the agriculture industry without seeds to plant. That is what the education industry is like without major corporate PD to implement the constant program changes which are the life blood of relevance. In any new model of schooling, the job description of every teacher must include on-the-job corporate professional development provided by the employer, either the government or the local school authority. Every teacher's timetable must have time blocks for **major** corporate PD.

Major PD is presently virtually non-existent. Instead, employers provide **minor** corporate PD, usually one- or two-day workshops that introduce teachers to change but don't change them. Such events teach new catch words and are a useful first step. Unfortunately, they are usually also the last step, so teachers are left with the vocabulary of change, but their beliefs, practices and skills have not been altered to accommodate the change.

Minor corporate PD also includes inspirational speeches by high-profile people, usually to large audiences. At worst, such events resemble bullfights. An expensive toreador is flown in to dazzle the locals. With a final swish of his verbal cape, the visiting star is gone, cheering subsides and life goes on as before. At best, the big speech raises consciousness. But it doesn't change classroom practices.

Other variations of minor corporate PD include: job-alike discussions, demonstrations, mini-refreshers, theme panels, etc. All are useful and necessary. So much so that content for programs is always in demand and colleges of education, teachers' associations, and private enterprise have become providers. Nearly all have improved their packages and some make brilliant use of the one or two days at their disposal.

Sabbatical leave must be considered minor PD because it applies to few teachers. Since recipients usually pay for it in reduced salary, it is a hybrid of personal and corporate PD. Despite its beauty it remains exotic with little chance of becoming garden variety. Less admirable are alternatives to sabbatical leave which amount to little more than consecrated moonlighting. School boards, universities or corporations act as procurers providing teachers for industry jobs during teacher vacations. Rhetoric says teachers learn lessons about real-world business methods and problems which they can then use to vitalize classrooms. No doubt. But that seems rather like saying people who get out into the world as prostitutes during vacations bring back information about methods and problems of the real world to vitalize home bedrooms.

Even if such liaisons are informative, they are demeaning. Nobody would suggest other professionals give up vacations to take paid employ-ment even if somewhat related to their professions: doctors working at drug companies, lawyers in jails, pilots in aircraft factories. It is only because teachers are underpaid that they submit to such humiliation. If projects such as the San Francisco and Los Angeles programs called "Industry Initiatives for Science and Math Education" are sincere, they will move on quickly to arranging working visitations as part of teachers' work time, not their vacations.

Teachers on loan/leave to business and industry should be paid full salary by school boards; and corporations should reimburse boards and pay whatever related expenses befall either teachers or boards. Periods of employment should vary from a few weeks to a year. Since loan/leave benefits everybody and is virtually cost-free to all parties, it is more feasible for widespread use than is sabbatical leave. Because so many teachers and principals plateau or burn out after seven to ten years, a universal refresher is needed.

Timing is mismanaged in nearly all manifestations of minor corporate PD. Years ago most of it was scheduled outside of school hours. To the burden of personal PD programs already being taken by large numbers of teachers, an ever-increasing load of minor corporate PD workshops was piled on. To relieve the pressure, many governments and school systems, often at the urging of teachers' associations, made the foolish decision to close schools and use the time for minor corporate PD. The young were robbed of schooling to provide schooling for teachers. That, in itself, is so irresponsible as to be unprofessional. But there is more to it. By closing schools, educators weaken a social system that is already barely coping with strains of family change. The last thing working parents need is the collapse even for a day of the custodial function of the school. No wonder they have turned against teachers and admini-strators.

Unfortunately, the solution suggested by irate parents and the media is as foolish as the closures they abhor. They say, "keep schools open and let teachers bear the burden after hours." They are right to demand that schools be kept open, but they are wrong to make corporate professional development the responsibility of teachers. It is not. It is the responsibility of the corporation, the school board (or, ultimately, the government). **All corporate PD whether minor or major must be scheduled during the teacher's working day, and the school must remain in full operation**. Professional development activities don't require that large numbers of teachers from one school be involved at the same time. Schools can be kept fully operational while one or two or a few teachers at a time are doing PD during regular school time. Itinerant or substitute teachers, teacher aids, and trained volunteers can and should be used to free teachers.

To change a teacher's beliefs and practices takes time. The first steps are: **presentation and explanation of theory**; detailed and repeated **demonstration (or modelling)**; plenty of **practice** by each learner; and individual **feedback** to each learner. If nothing more is done, only five percent of teachers will successfully incorporate the change in daily practice; however, with one further step, nearly all teachers can internalize and practice the desired change. The additional step that successfully changes beliefs and habitual practices is **application with coaching** over a period of weeks and months. Each teacher must perform twenty or thirty trials of the change in the classroom with a supportive colleague coaching. Teachers may coach each other or talented and trained counsellors can coach.

All of this has been understood since the late seventies by which time the distinguished American researcher Bruce Joyce and his associates had developed and widely publicized the concepts and implications. Governments and school boards have yet to comprehend the ramifications. Two teachers coaching each other must each have at least thirty hours of coaching on their timetables for each major professional development activity. And that is in addition to the hours timetabled for both, in advance of the application/coaching phase, for theory, demonstration, practice and feedback stages. Coaching by teacher counsellors rather than fellow teachers eliminates the need to take teachers away from their own classrooms to act as coaches for other teachers.

There are three main divisions of major corporate

professional development, all of them essential to the well-being of the system: implementation of curriculum policy documents; implementation of massive additions to curriculum; and implementation of public expectations that have not yet become outright bandwagons and so might be considered lesser rather than massive additions.

Curriculum policy documents are guidelines, bulletins, courses of study and other publications of government and school districts which specify frequent changes in goals, content, methods and all other aspects of school programs. Each guideline is likely to affect a particular group of teachers: all teachers of senior mathematics, or all kindergarten teachers, or all guidance counsellors, etc. In some jurisdictions, there are so many new guidelines or courses that most teachers are involved in implementing one or more at all times and hence in need of the major corporate PD which is synonymous with curriculum implementation.

Massive additions to curriculum are waves of change that wash over most teachers at once. Integration of computers and paper-book technology is an example. Few experienced teachers are computer literate but soon computers will be as important as paper in most classrooms at all levels of education. Even if teachers learn on their own how to operate computers, that does not show them how to teach with computers. A teacher used to standing at the front of the room and talking all day will find it difficult to teach with one, ten, or especially, a roomful of computers. Such a teacher must learn a whole new belief system and way of teaching.

I spoke to two teachers just finishing thirty-hour courses learning to operate computers. Both wanted thirty more hours on how to teach with computers. Every teacher needs at least that. So the minimum amount of on-the-job training to get a teacher up and running as a computer literate teacher totals ninety hours — thirty about operating computers, thirty on how to teach with computers, and thirty on application with coaching. And after all that, they need at least ten more hours on the principles of computer program selection.

Examples of other massive additions in many jurisdictions are language-across-the-curriculum and guidance-across-the-curriculum. Both concepts require that all teachers assume responsibilities for which they were never trained. It is wishful thinking to suggest that teachers of science or mathematics have the skills to teach reading, writing, speaking and listening or that they can acquire such skills in a two-day workshop. Even teachers of English Literature almost always lack the skills to teach reading, so it is unrealistic to expect teachers of mathematics to pick up the skills in a hurry or to change their practices easily.

It is equally idle to expect all teachers to become instant guidance counsellors. To be effective in personal counselling, teachers must possess or acquire superior interpersonal skills and must practice using them in the one-to-one counselling situation. Counsellors also need considerably more knowledge of child development and the sociology of childhood than teachers usually have. To do career counselling requires a broad knowledge base about thousands of careers that are new and many more that are expected soon. And it requires practice using computerized career data bases as a teaching tool.

It is also foolish to expect that all teachers can become instant social workers. Yet that is what happened in Rochester, N.Y. in 1987. The city thought by improving salaries they could suddenly transform teachers into social workers who could take on home visitation, counselling, therapy, and coordination of other professionals. And at the same time, teachers were expected to redesign curriculum. All without retraining! The concept was brilliant except that it lacked at least two years of on-the-job preparation for all teachers to change beliefs, behaviour and skills **before** beginning the program. And thereafter, there should have been a continuing retraining component built into the work routine of all teachers.

Special education is a classic massive addition to curriculum without adequate preparation of teachers. Special education means schooling for people with learning disabilities, physical problems, behavioral disorders and other exceptionalities including giftedness. Except for the gifted, many special children never attended regular schools till recently, and those who did were taught by specialist teachers in segregated classrooms. Now, the trend is to mainstream most of these children in regular classrooms in regular schools with regular teachers most of the time (see streaming in chapter 21).

The fifteen percent or so of students called special are carefully assessed to pin-point individual needs. The other eighty-five percent don't receive either testing to identify individual needs or meticulous attention to placement in programs that will meet those needs. The assumption is that the general school program is good enough for "average" children so they can be sent to the nearest empty seats. Of this eighty-five percent, at least half have problems with reading, writing, speaking, listening, ciphering or some other skill that will adversely affect their entire lives, but identification and remediation for these "normal" children are not included in special education.

The same kind of unfair discrimination is inflicted upon gifted children whose gifts are other than intellectual. The most creative individuals are not necessarily those who have the full spectrum of exceptional intellectual gifts needed to score as "gifted" on IQ tests, so the very creatively gifted are often ineligible for special programs and are left to wither in regular classrooms. The same applies to people with one outstanding gift (mechanical, technical, mathematical, interpersonal, verbal, athletic. . .) but not the range of gifts that would put them in the gifted grab bag as packaged by most schools.

Arguably, there is no such thing as an average child. Each is unique and has special needs. School systems pay lip service to that reality but do violence to it in practice. Providing for fifteen percent of the population while denying individualized services to the other eighty-five percent will surely compound the education mess. Teachers are caught in the middle. They were trained to do mass education and they work in a mass education system. But now they are expected to individualize education for fifteen percent of students in regular classrooms and still run a mass education program for the rest. No significant professional development with application and coaching has been provided.

The whole mainstream special education house of cards would have collapsed already except that many teachers took it upon themselves to do personal professional development in special education. They attended courses on their own time, some altruistically, but most to advance their careers. They saw the wave coming and learned how to ride it. Some became specialists or consultants, but many just took a course or two for classroom survival. Such courses provide theory and perhaps a bit of practice, but they never provide enough on-the-job application with coaching to really change a teacher's beliefs and practices.

Those who take special education courses usually study only two or three facets, so most teachers find themselves in the classroom having just brushed the surface or without having taken any special education courses. **The need for major corporate PD in special education for all teachers is enormous**. Almost all need at least a hundred hours — a lot more if we expect real proficiency at an addition to curriculum as complex as special education in the regular classroom. We should remember what happened to open education. It was a massive change introduced in the sixties without corporate professional development for **all** teachers. Most would have needed more than the minimum hundred hours of retraining to make the dramatic change in teaching belief and behaviour. Most got none. So open education failed.

A **lesser** addition to curriculum affects fewer teachers than a massive addition because it has not yet achieved bandwagon status. Cumulatively, lesser additions can be just as demanding as any massive addition and require just as much corporate professional development.

It is easy to list dozens of issues affecting many schools as minor thrusts (and already escalating to massive thrusts in some jurisdictions): race relations; multiculturalism; global studies; peace education; media literacy; fitness (health, prevention, nutrition, exercise); values; street-proofing and abuse prevention; sex; sex-role stereotyping; parenting; drug and alcohol abuse; personal finances (banking, tax, budgeting, credit, investment); consumer studies; behaviour (manners, discipline, dress); delinquency; self-defence; aesthetics; home maintenance; home management; law; road safety; generic job skills; rights (women's, old age, gay, aboriginal, children's. . .); urban/rural development; abortion; capital punishment; gun control; economic developments (unemployment, trade, etc.); nuclear proliferation; environmental matters (conservation, pollution, animal rights); problem solving; measurement and evaluation; needs assessment, etc.

To meet corporate responsibilities for professional development, school boards must make detailed long and short-range plans which are published and revised regularly. As a matter of public accountability, every school district and every school should be required to maintain a detailed institutional **growth profile** to help them see where they have been in professional development, where they are going and what they have to do to get there. And every teacher must have a detailed, personal growth profile. Basic training and certification should be just the beginning and should fade in importance with time, superseded by an endless flow of personal and corporate PD, all recorded.

Teachers must have continuing access to expert career and life counselling to help with growth profile management. A sensible employer would see it as a cost-effective investment in personnel to provide such counselling; however, counsellors must be, and be seen to be, separate from summative evaluation officials who stand in judgement of teachers' competence.

There should be a close relationship between formative evaluation of teachers and professional development, but it can't properly develop in a punitive climate. Unfortunately, there is a punitive climate in many jurisdictions. The notion that teachers should requalify periodically is punitive. It seems to say, "We're out to get you. Measure up or get out." It is crisis-oriented, based on confrontation, the negative end of a spectrum. The positive end of the same spectrum is professional development. Instead of being out to get teachers with the bludgeon of a test, employers should be out to help them with further training. Professional development provided by the employer can be therapy and it can be prevention.

The role of government is to fund all corporate profes-

sional development, describe in detail corporate professional development that must be done to implement changes in school program, and require all school district authorities to produce detailed plans for carrying out each item of corporate professional development. Government must also supply basic training materials and travelling teams of resource people to avoid the cost of reinventing presentations in each locality. **The role of each school district is to create detailed plans for corporate professional development, and to carry out plans during regular school hours while keeping schools in normal operation.**

Government and school boards must involve teachers meaningfully in all decision-making about professional development. Policy-making and working committees at all levels must be made up largely of teachers selected by teachers' associations. Unless teachers feel they have been properly involved, the desired results won't be achieved. Central government authorities and school district authorities often make the mistake of putting the wrong people on committees dealing with professional development (and curriculum), or else they welcome representatives of teacher's associations too late, after critical decisions have been made.

Why governments are so obtuse is difficult to explain. It would be to their political advantage to have the teaching profession on side and it would be cost-effective to tap the pool of expertise that is the teaching profession. Perhaps staff officers of government agencies and school boards are jealous of the superior expertise likely to exist beyond the inner sanctum. They should welcome it. After all, final decisions remain with governments so they are only availing themselves of the best ideas from which to choose.

A rule of thumb is that more than half of any professional development (or curriculum) decision-making group should be appointed by the teachers' associations to which most teachers belong. There will still be plenty of room for appointees from all other sources.

Teachers' Centres

A mechanism has to be found to give credibility to management of PD (and curriculum) committees. Provided they are properly conceived and funded, teachers' centres can do the job. I am not talking about a place teachers go to shoot pool or make visual aids. **A teachers' centre is where teachers manage their own corporate professional development**. The three essentials of a teachers' centre are: the board of directors is made up mainly of teachers elected directly by all teachers or appointed by the official teachers' organization; all costs are paid from the public purse by state government through grants to school boards; the purpose is to implement curriculum through corporate professional development.

School board administrators must also sit on the teachers' centre board, and the senior curriculum official, should be its permanent adviser. Other board members should be from nearby teachers' colleges or similar sources. A curriculum representative from the government department responsible for education would be useful, perhaps essential. A representative of the local curriculum council (see chapter 20), probably the chair, would certainly be essential.

Funding must be a state responsibility since curriculum implementation is a state responsibility and corporate professional development is synonymous with curriculum implementation. Though the local school board is the logical conduit for state funds, it is advantageous to put the teachers' centre at arm's length from the board by giving it autonomy, with only routine, minimal accountability.

While funding of corporate professional development must always be the responsibility of government, there will be occasions when the teachers' centre can facilitate personal professional development and in that case, teachers individually or collectively should pay program costs. If a university agrees to provide graduate courses for interested teachers using teachers' centre facilities on weekends or evenings, teachers should pay the university fees and other costs.

Though the purpose must be unequivocally to facilitate curriculum implementation through corporate professional development, the teachers' centre will necessarily be involved with closely related matters, particularly acquisition and development of curriculum materials ranging from text books to computer lessonware. It will also act as liaison with other teachers' centres and with state education authorities to share information and resource people and avoid duplication. All teachers' centres, nationally and internationally, must be networked by computer.

Teachers' Counsellors

Aside from the administrative secretariat, the staff of a teachers' centre should be mainly counsellors who work with teachers individually and collectively: counselling (personal and career), evaluating formatively, coaching, improving performance, reviewing growth profiles, arranging appropriate professional development activities, etc. Counsellors, not administrators, should work with the ninety percent of teachers who are competent. (They should also work with the ten percent who are incompetent, but principals and other supervisory officers will be active concurrently with the incompetent doing summative evaluations that lead to dismissal).

It would be helpful to make counsellors employees of teachers' centres rather than of school boards. Counsellors of teachers must be and be seen to be advocates for and loyal to the teachers they counsel. They are nursemaids, talent scouts, talent managers, mentors, monitors, confessors, agents, therapists, analysts and friends. They are the people who nurture the most precious resource in education — teachers.

Counsellors should not be the only or main resource persons for group professional development activities. Leaders should also come from schools, teachers colleges, universities, government agencies, school board staffs, teachers' and other professional associations and private industry. Counsellors should, however, routinely coach their clients in the classroom application of what is learned during professional development programs. When a school is big, its counsellors should be housed there, not centrally at the teachers' centre. This would help overcome the residual suspicion that anyone from outside a particular school could not possibly know enough about its unique characteristics to counsel or coach there.

Since there are presently no teacher counsellors, it is difficult to estimate case load. It depends how much coaching is done by teachers for each other and how much counsellors do. My guess is that a counsellor should serve twenty-five but might manage up to forty-five teachers, that a counsellor would burn out with sixty-five, and that school boards and governments will claim a counsellor can easily handle a hundred.

CHAPTER 19

MANAGING SCHOOLS

Educational leadership by the principal is at present rare. Things being as they are, the principal has neither the time nor the inclination, even supposing the competence, to provide the leadership so sorely needed.

— Mortimer J. Adler, *The Paideia Proposal*
(New York: Macmillan, 1982)

In November 1959, the earliest published version of my proposal for managing schools without principals appeared in the American education magazine, the *Phi Delta Kappan*. Under my title, "Are Principals Obsolete?" the editor's headline read "an ingenious reform that would put teacher leaders in the principal's office." Little did he know that I sent him a watered down version. Colleagues had advised me to remove certain suggestions or else the piece might be rejected as too extreme, or if it were published, I would be pilloried by the establishment as subversive.

From the 1959 version, I removed proposals that parents and students be represented, along with teachers, on committees elected to administer schools. But in subsequent versions, I reinstated both parents and students and in the fall of 1968 was indeed targeted by the establishment. My subversive thesis was and is this: **students, teachers, parents and most other adults are disempowered by the present model of schooling**; they have almost no control over their schools and hence an important part of their lives. They feel frustrated because they are diminished and subjugated. The frustration is there whether it is realized or not. **Wherever subjugation exists people react in ways that range from apathy, through mindless obedience, to violence and revolution. All of those reactions are characteristic in schools**.

Education is an industry, and the present model of schooling along with other industries was shaped by the industrial revolution in the eighteenth and nineteenth centuries. It is common, when examining school administration problems, to look at parallels with other industries. Principals are likened to branch plant managers, area superintendents to district heads of several branch plants and so on up to senior superintendents or directors who are likened to company presidents. School boards parallel corporate boards of directors. Both must abide by government regulations. Within each branch plant, teachers are assembly line workers and students are products moving on an assembly line from period to period, subject to subject, room to room, grade to grade, year to year.

Practices in school management in North America are said to be imitating late twentieth-century innovations in manufacturing industries. The reverse is also true. It would be accurate to say that worker participation in decision-making was pioneered in education and copied by Ford and other corporations, rather than the reverse. But the much-touted school administration innovations in Hammond, Indiana, Miami, Rochester and several other places are modest innovations if they are innovations at all. Calling committees of teachers management teams changes little. Teachers have been serving on such committees for half a century to deal with every matter the so-called management teams now consider. As a teacher in the fifties I sat on committees and in faculty meetings that dealt with textbook selection, staff deployment, discipline, curriculum implementation, professional development, evaluation of students, public relations, school budget, etc. And so did thousands of other teachers. And they still do.

Nonetheless, the perception of journalists is that school boards are doing what Ford and a lot of other corporations did when they found the Japanese outpacing them: they are modifying the traditional top-down management style to give workers more participation in decision making. The worker committee route may be significant in manufacturing industries, but fifty years of it has had little effect in schools partly because of three important differences between the manufacturing and schooling industries:

1. The schooling product is not goods; it is children who should have all the human and civil rights of adults.

2. Parents, and other taxpaying adults have a more compelling stake in schools than in any other industry; they care more about the future of children and the human race and about the cost of education than they do about widgets or corporate profits.

3. Teachers are far better educated than factory workers and, unlike people on factory assembly lines, teachers are just as qualified as anyone above them; yet the public notion of participation that should be accorded teachers suffers from the same suggestion-box mentality which patronizingly allows that assembly line workers on committees might have a suggestion or two about improving output.

Because of these three decisive differences, there may be more validity in equating schools to towns rather than manufacturing industries. Principals of schools must deal with learned faculty, and mayors must deal with astute town councillors. Both towns and schools have human constituencies. Individual schools fit into a hierarchy of school boards, state education departments and federal offices of education, and individual towns fit into a hierarchy of governments that includes regional, state and federal levels. The telling difference is that individual towns are run democratically but individual schools are not.

Mayors are elected but principals are appointed. Mayors have elected councils to contend with, but principals have teachers who are appointed. Townspeople vote for councillors and mayor, but children have no say about either teachers or principals. Should one person administer a town without direct decision-making representation of the people who make up the jurisdiction? That is exactly what happens in schools. Worse, the one man or woman is usually picked by relative outsiders (the school board) and parachuted in.

Autocratic administration of schools derives from the old European concept of authoritarian headmaster. It suited pre-Victorian and Victorian times when democracy was narrowly based and defined. It has lasted, largely unassailed, in an otherwise democratized world because the clientele happen to be the last subjugated minority, children. It is only because teachers, parents and other citizens have realized recently that they (adults, not children) have a stake in schools that the administrative method is being questioned. Unfortunately, most activists, unable to conceive of a different model, want to retain the role of principal but have a say in who plays it. But the role is unplayable.

No veneer of democratic pretense will alter the fact that the headmaster model is the military model and the imperative of that model is obedience in the ranks to an autocratic commander. It is no accident that the commonest description of a good school principal is that he runs a tight ship. True, both admirals and principals are accountable to some distant authority but, on their flag ships, both are supreme commanders. The blind obedience that is the foundation of the military model may be compatible with military goals, but it is antithetical to educational goals. It is the ugliest of hypocrisies to claim in all our statements of curriculum goals that we are preparing children for life in democracies and then subject them to authoritarianism in schools.

Safe little pretenses of participatory democracy that have been trotted into schools for show and tell in the last half century exacerbate the problem. Every school has its impotent student council, its ebb and flow of discretionary teachers' committees, its token town meetings of parents, its hand-picked advisory committees, all carefully manipulated to keep underlings in their places — out of the major decision-making arena. Out of power.

Even the best excursions into participatory school administration are mere day trips, intermittent and fleeting, usually without legal status, dependent upon the passing whims of local and state authorities. Those that are briefly acclaimed locally and trumpeted internationally usually exclude meaningful student participation, and that gaping hole in the hull, alone, dooms most of the excursion ships to head for the safe old dock or causes them to pump furiously just to keep afloat. Either way, eventual committment to the depths seems likely.

In most jurisdictions, **policy-making** remains in the hands of school boards and **policy implementation** in the hands of principals. Teachers remain essentially **powerless**, even if a large part of their work is administrative and of great value to management. Parents remain largely powerless except for occasional pressure groups that promote their own interests with some success before burning out like spent comets. Some parents are appointed to advisory committees but have no real power. Adults other than parents are usually forgotten. Yet seventy percent of taxpayers have no children in school. Expecting only parents to participate in school governance is like expecting only kin of sick people to participate in hospital governance.

At the school board level, citizens are powerless where the board is appointed, not elected. In jurisdictions with elected boards, parents and other adults may, by law, vote, run for office and otherwise be involved if they have the skills, time and money. Most are unlikely to participate because they never learned the skills of democratic participation while in school. Teachers and children are largely excluded by law from participation in their own school boards. That situation will be improved when children are enfranchised, and when laws are changed so that student governments and teachers send fully accredited representatives to school boards to have a voice in policy-making.

At the school level, where policies set by governments and school boards are implemented, teachers and students are also usually without legal right to decision-making power. And children remain the most powerless of all. The longstanding inclination of British schools to involve teachers in decision making has not grown to include students. The Dade County, Florida plan (and similar plans that require principals to share decision-making power with teachers, parents and others) does not include students on management teams, nor does the Chicago innovation that gives elected community committees virtual control of schools.

In most jurisdictions the policy-implementation power of principals is so great that all but a few milquetoasts put their personal stamps on schools. The principal's style becomes the ethos of the school. There is no greater power for big fish in little ponds. The traditions of a school, the strength of certain maverick teachers, political circumstances, union militancy or other factors may modify the vibes, but the principal is the tuning fork that makes the building resonate. I went from teaching in a junior high school run like an adventurous summer camp to one run like a modified prisoner-of-war camp. The two schools were a few blocks apart and under the same school board! The policies that had to be implemented were identical. The only difference was in the style of the two principals, yet I felt I had gone from West to East Berlin when the wall was up.

The chance for that much power attracts lots of aspirants for every vacancy. But an even stronger attraction, is the principal's salary, the only half-decent pay packet at the school level. The average 1990–91 salary for principals in the U.S. was $55,722 in high schools and $48,431 in elementary schools, disgracefully low figures for busy executives in any industry but better than the average pittance handed out to teachers. Then too, a principalship is the only route to an even better salary in top management.

Applicants don't apply for principalships thinking the job easy. Teachers know better. It is true that some principals arrive late, leave early and in between do as little as possible. They strut and fret their hour upon the stage and then laze away their several hours safely hidden off stage. The commandant of the modified prison camp mentioned above was a great reader behind his closed office door but not, it seemed, of education literature. In six years, I was never able to engage him in conversation about education literature, issues or policy documents.

But most principals are frantically busy. Some competent people knock themselves out trying to cover all bases. The leader of the adventurous summer camp referred to previously was not himself creative, but he was willing to take chances on creative teachers and new ideas; so his school was dynamic. He was only saved from the exhaustion of exploration by his ability to give creative teachers freedom to run and to shoulder the load. Less adequate principals thrash about trying to stay afloat and pass themselves off as good swimmers.

When the masses stayed respectfully in their places, the principal ran his domain unassailed. Today, the masses are restless from powerlessness, and the principal is vulnerable. If he can't quell discontent, the same distant authority that dropped him into power may yank him out. Consequently, many principals spend too much time stamping out fires, too little managing the plant and hardly any providing educational leadership. The public perception is that stamping out fires and managing the plant are what count most. William Bennett, speaking as U.S. education secretary in 1986, reflected that myopic point of view when he said retired army officers, experienced business people and heads of government bureaus should be eligible for school principalships.

Somebody has to handle emergencies and run the building, but that is about a quarter of the school principal's job. The other three-quarters is strictly professional, and I have never met a business person, a colonel or a government bureaucrat (except in departments of education) who knew the first thing about curriculum development and implementation, professional development of teachers, teaching methods, learning styles, learning process analysis, teaching performance assessment, measurement and evaluation of student achievement, and about two dozen other essentials of the principal's job. An incumbent must be forty-dimensional.

The hero-principal is usually seen by movie producers and the public as having one, maybe two dimensions, the obligatory one being an iron fist, the optional one being a velvet glove for dress occasions. This managerial thug uses some strong-arm method to raise test scores temporarily by one point or else cleans the corridors of graffiti, gangsters and groupies. The 1989 movie, *Lean On Me*, lionized such a demagogue. But when Mr. Rambo retires, transfers or just gets tired of wielding his baseball bat, the cleaned-up school dirties again. And even while he remains, a thousand other schools are unchanged because, fortunately, the model has little replication potential.

Sometimes a principal becomes a local hero, even a legend, on the strength of his humane personality and character. Such a person cares deeply about children and it shows. Children, teachers and community are moved. They love in return. But such a principal often lacks educational vision, or creativity or some other personal quality, or the deep knowledge of curriculum and professional development or some other professional quality that is essential to school health. Those fatal flaws are not easily evident to a devoted public. But a bungler is a bungler even if benevolent and much loved.

The real hero-principal is one who has all the qualities of a good teacher and a broad and deep knowledge of all the bits and pieces that constitute schooling. That sounds easy. But most teachers know only their own classrooms. They know little of education theory, child development, other schools, other levels of education, world developments in education, their own professional organizations, the politics of education, social developments that influence education, etc.

Aspiring principals must be especially expert in curriculum (planning, development, implementation, evaluation. . .) and in professional development (further training of practicing teachers) and should have a proven record in both. But most applicants know nothing about curriculum beyond the subject and grade level they teach. Few know what real professional development is or how to do it. It must be made clear to all teachers in training that **the only route to promotion is through knowledge of and experience in curriculum development and professional development.**

Unless the principal regularly generates ideas, he is too dependent on input that may not be forthcoming from others. However, when ideas do come from other people, the creative principal is good at incorporating them and encouraging creators, giving them their heads. School boards are more likely to promote uncreative than creative teachers because the uncreative don't rock the boat. A truly creative principal is a rarity. Some have just enough creativity to recognize and foster the quality in teachers. Many dowse for fresh wellsprings of education, waving as divining rods whatever wands they have plucked from the thicket of fads.

Creative principals should have a vision of future schools which they express orally and in writing in a way that inspires teachers, students and community. Such vision is rare, so we seldom have articulated for us models of schooling that differ from the present ubiquitous model. Hardly ever does a school board ask an aspiring principal for his vision of tomorrow's school. Most boards don't even bother to find out if applicants could write it well if they did happen to have such a vision. Too many principals can't write.

Principals must be comfortable with change and taking risks. Most are not. If the principal is not an active change agent, the school doesn't change. It doesn't even stand still. It decays. School boards tend to promote conservatives who play safe, who don't want to change themselves or the familiar environment.

Anyone leading people through constant change must be, and be perceived to be, trustworthy. Principals must remain faithful to their visions. Their teachers, students and communities will understand the necessary compromises of the real world, but they demand and recognize integrity: principals are expected to stand up for what they believe. Too many principals say one thing but do another. They learn the vocabulary of change but don't understand the substance and would never dare take the risks involved. They just pretend. School boards often anoint pretenders.

Other qualities are also essential: courage, stamina, health, political acumen, human relations skills, planning and organizational skills, confidence, affection. . . . And I think it reasonable to expect a touch of charisma. Virtually all of these essentials or the lack of them could be documented in detail for all potential principals. They never are. Far too many people are promoted on the strength of having been: a football coach; a hail fellow well met; a bootlicker; of the right religion, family, political stripe, sex or race; a tough taskmaster in the traditional classroom. None of these is any more indicative of educational-leadership potential than is red hair. Nor is a degree from this university as opposed to that. Or a certain type of teaching certificate instead of another.

Most countries require aspiring principals to have a graduate degree and/or certification from a training course for principals. And most jurisdictions require a stint as assistant principal. All to the good but still no guarantee of educational leadership. Mediocre pluggers lacking essential personal qualities can and do get paper qualifications and principalships. Training courses for principals and course requirements for some graduate degrees in education are trivial and irrelevant. Experience as a vice-principal can be nothing more than an apprenticeship in tyranny or administrivia or both. Most people climb to principalships after exposure to few role models. They may vaguely recall two or three principals from childhood and have taught under two or three. Teachers lead surprisingly insular professional lives.

If the present model of schooling included a functional mechanism for curriculum implementation and a satisfactory professional development plan, the seventy-five percent of the principal's role that is curriculum and professional development management could be done by a mere mortal with a sound knowledge of both and a fair measure of the right personal qualities. But there are no such standard mechanisms. The creaking old model of schooling was never made for constant curriculum change and integrated professional development.

It would take a genius, superman/woman principal to make something significant happen. No wonder even the best burn out in a few years. Principals don't get out when they burn out. They hang on because there is no place for most to go. There are so few jobs above principal that over three-quarters who make it that high are stuck there till retirement. They can't go up because there are no jobs, they can't go back to teaching because the loss of pay and face would be intolerable; they can't get out because they are not qualified for any other career, are too old to start over and could not survive on entry-level salaries in other fields.

Museums occasionally rearrange fossils in a showcase; school boards shift principals sideways from school to school. Sometimes they play all-switch, a venerable administrative version of musical chairs intended to show citizens that school boards know how to change with changing times. Every principal moves one school to the right and life goes on as before except that the style of each principal moves with him. A short period of adjusting trivialities passes for real change and takes everybody's mind off general putrefaction in the system.

Teachers, students and parents quickly adjust to the style of a replacement principal and line up in support, in opposition or in the middle. Most teachers line up in support out of self-interest. The principal is likely to stay on for years, so teachers bow down — it makes their lives easier. They will get away with more absences and can expect: a break or two on hall-patrol assignments; more support when they report troublesome students; more backing when parents complain; an occasional perk, perhaps an all-expense trip to some plum conference. But the main reason teachers go along with principals, even ones they despise, is that they hold almost complete power over all routes to tenure and promotion.

With or without formal performance review, principals evaluate teachers and keep memories and records which determine whether or not a teacher gets an approving nod from the school board. Principals disclaim power to promote. But their superiors have little to go on in deciding promotions except the word of principals and data that one way or another filter through the principal's sieve. Teachers know all this, so they either conform or risk the exhausting, lonely, dangerous, often futile route of the maverick. Those who line up somewhere in the middle are generally teachers who have little hope or ambition for promotion or lack the conviction of the activist.

Students fall into the same three groupings as teachers — most, by conditioning, into the neutral middle group. They hold no particular position or opinion and just drift along. Perhaps a quarter of students actively curry favour with the principal, directly or through teachers. Their purpose is to win prizes and plaudits for resumes. A few students resist the principal. Most of these are characterized as bad actors lashing out against the system with antisocial behaviour. Usually the system breaks or expunges them. Few successfully buck the system as creative, political activists. Principals love favour-curriers, appreciate the silent majority, loathe disturbers and manipulate all three groups with impunity — provided they steer clear of occasional activist parents or groups.

Most parents haven't the time, energy, know-how or courage to fight the system. They line up along with their children as either favour-curriers or silent majority. The few individuals and groups who confront the principal and the system he or she represents are sometimes successful whether the issue is reinstatement of an expelled student or admission to classes of hitherto excluded exceptional children. But such individuals and groups are universally, and perhaps necessarily, limited and focused in their activity. They rarely attack the principal and his or her total system because they lack any vision of a new model.

A.S. Neill demonstrated a new model of democratic schooling that worked in his very small private school. Summerhill usually had forty to sixty students, more like a large classroom than a school. Governance was by direct participation of all staff and students rather than by elected representation. That model is useful for classroom administration, especially since it offers opportunities for consensus rather than adversarial methods. But for school administration in the real world of big schools, it is unworkable. Some kind of representative governance is necessary.

The *Toronto Star* of May 16, 1969, reported a proposal by Tim Reid, then a member of the Ontario Legislature:

[T]ake a high school of 1500 students with between 75 and 90 teachers. Have the teachers elect (by secret ballot) 25 of their number to a High School Governing Council. Have all the students elect (by secret ballot) 10 of their number (perhaps restrict these representatives to students in grades 12 and 13) to this governing council. The principal (appointed by the board) would be an ex officio member of this council and could be its chairman (or he may wish to have the members of the council elect someone else so that he could be freer to argue for the policies and programs which he wants in the school). There might even be one or two parents on the council.

This council would be the supreme decision-making authority in the school. The principal would remain the chief executive officer of the school: he would carry out the policies of the council.

Reid's proposal and others like it retained the appointed principal but gave responsibility for internal matters to a governing council. I doubt he intended taking from school boards any of their policy-making prerogative. But he was suggesting that implementation of board policy be done by principals as directed by governing councils. That would partially democratize administration, though a principal could still be ensconced for life and could still lack professional and personal qualities necessary to lead. With some modification, the model might be workable: a smaller council would be more effective; grade level requirements for student eligibility to serve on the council would have to be removed; term appointments for principals would have to be standard.

Even in the liberal late sixties the proposal garnered little support from an apathetic public or response from the education establishment. Reid was just a politician, and sitting in opposition at that. What did he know? But that same establishment is ferocious in protecting the status quo if the attack is taken seriously. Seven months before Mr. Reid made his proposal, a Toronto newspaper carried a story about what it called my "revolutionary design for school administration." Since I was a member of the establishment rather than a mere opposition politician, I was perceived by some principals as dangerous. The *Toronto Telegram* report of October 8, 1968 included these statements:

[I]t's unlikely the establishment of the education fraternity will stand up and cheer.

The Dixon Plan, as it has become known in high school staff rooms, sounds a great deal less drastic than it might have five years ago — or even one year ago.

Permanent principals would be abolished and in their place would be a three man Adcom (administrative committee) elected by the teaching staff of the school.

At least two students would be elected each year to work with the Adcom administrative team, reflecting students' views while learning how democracy can work in action.

Elementary school principals contained their concerns, possibly from a misconception, generated by the wording of the press report, that my proposal applied only to high schools. But high school principals reacted angrily. Their affiliate of the provincial teachers' organization for which I worked, complained to my employer. Their purpose was to silence me, to make my life uncomfortable and perhaps to get me fired. They failed; but leaders of that affiliate were cool to me for a decade. Worldwide, the administrative establishment still resists innovation. We need a new structure to which change is no threat.

All innovations in schooling including major ones such as progressive education and open education failed to specify a different administrative structure so they failed to change the model of schooling and were swallowed and dissolved by the powerful stomach acids of mother school. **Adcom (for Administrative Committee) is a new administrative structure; it carries out school board policy; it runs the school; but unlike a principal, Adcom is responsible to an electorate.**

Three teachers, elected by teachers, serve as the executive of Adcom. In the first year, an elected teacher serves half-time and teaches half-time. The next year, he/she serves full-time as president of Adcom. In the third and final year, he/she again serves half-time and teaches half-time. While on the executive, a teacher is paid additional salary for additional responsibility. After the three-year hitch, a teacher must return to the classroom for at least a year before being eligible to run again for the executive of Adcom.

In addition to the three-person executive, Adcom has six other members: two teachers, elected by the school faculty (including paid

aids as well as teachers); two adults from the immediate school community (one a parent of a child presently in the school and one not) both
elected by the community; two students elected by students. Very young
students are represented by advocates. Non-executive members of
Adcom are elected for one year and may serve a maximum of two
consecutively. So Adcom has nine members with nine equal votes: five
teachers, two community adults and two students. The executive meets
daily and the full Committee weekly, the latter usually at night because
community-adult members are likely to have day jobs.

Teachers know better than anyone else who among them has the
professional and personal qualifications to lead. If a dud slips by, he/she
is only in the president's chair one year; and every move of the president
is monitored by the other two teachers on the executive and by the rest
of Adcom. Any teacher or aid on contract who has been on staff for
nearly a year is eligible to run for the two non-executive posts in
elections held toward the end of each year. Any teacher who has served
at least a year in a non-executive position on Adcom is eligible to run
for the three-year hitch on the executive. Any teacher who runs for the
executive must already have completed an approved school administration course (usually the case) or be able to finish it not later than the
summer before the presidential year begins.

If there are more than two candidates for the entry-level position on
the executive, there is a preliminary election to eliminate all but the top
two candidates. For non-executive positions, the preliminary election
is less critical, but has enough advantages that the inconvenience is
justified. There is no limit to the number of three-year terms for which
a teacher may be elected, but there must be a teaching year or more
between each term. All credit for Adcom service goes with a teacher
who transfers from one school or school board to another.

To be eligible for promotion to any school-board administrative
position, a teacher must have served two terms on the executive of
Adcom. Eligibility for promotion to all other positions within a school
or school board (department head, subject discipline coordinator. . .)
require, in addition to teaching qualifications, only one term as a

non-executive member of Adcom though a term on the executive should be regarded as an asset.

Incoming and outgoing members of the executive function as vice-principals with the title vice-presidents. If a school is so large that full-time vice-principals are required, one or both may be full-time administrators instead of teaching half-time. This should not be necessary if the school has an ombudsman, a real student government and a committee structure to deal with many student concerns, and if it has an office (business) manager empowered to deal with routine administrative chores that steal the time of principals and vice-principals in the present model of schooling.

A young teacher with one year of experience could be elected a non-executive member of Adcom. The following year, with two years experience, he/she could be elected to the executive and might be elected to a second term (after just one obligatory full year of teaching between hitches) and so be eligible for promotion to superintendent after nine years in the profession. Good. There should be a chance for the young and brilliant to rise quickly.

All posited weaknesses of Adcom seem to be the strengths of democracy. Some say Adcom could turn a school into a political arena with individuals and factions battling for office. Maybe so, but the politicking is likely to be low-key since most teachers are, in their daily work, more professionally than politically oriented. Indeed, one could complain that, with the singular exception of union negotiations for better benefits, teachers are insufficiently involved in the politics of education. Adcom will add the necessary political dimension.

An important thing the Adcom concept does is say to teachers that the public trusts them, that they are expected to make educational decisions on behalf of society, that they are professionals. Public trust and the public scrutiny that goes with it will keep the political process on a high level.

As for community representatives, the maximum hurly burly of politics may apply, but more likely residual apathy will make it difficult in the beginning to stir up broad interest. Parents who are presently active in school organizations will run for Adcom and so will candidates of special interest groups and some outstanding citizens. Good. The limitation on possible length of service will make it impossible for any one person to become entrenched. The present generation of disinterested parents and other citizens will be only marginally more involved in schools than they are presently. But as time goes on, the community will become more committed. The real challenge for any model of schooling is to involve adults without school-age children. Adcom will help because half the adult incumbents must be from the non-parent group.

With most innovations in education it is possible to point to successful pilot projects. They shine in some dark corner but never generalize to brighten the world. When the Adcom concept was first published in 1959, it brought a flurry of positive reaction from aspiring innovators. I anticipated trial runs. In 1969, ten years after my proposal appeared in the *Phi Delta Kappan* magazine, I received a letter about it from Professor Roman Bernert, director of the School Instruction Improvement Program in Milwaukee. He wrote, "I think it holds the key to many of the perplexing problems confronting American education. To your knowledge, are there any schools in Canada or the U.S. that have the Adcom arrangement?"

My answer was no in 1969 and it is still no in 1992. But I am hopeful for 2002. Dade County, Florida, Chicago and a few other places are showing signs of awakening.

CHAPTER 20

DEVELOPING CURRICULUM

[S]chools are currently doing an excellent job of preparing their students for life in the 1960s . . . because those who control curriculum (ultimately, newspaper editorialists, Chambers of Commerce, political fund raisers, and those academics who determine university admission criteria) have not yet taken the implications of the future seriously.

David Pratt, "Curriculum for the 21st Century,"
Education Canada (winter 1983)

Inherent in the present model of schooling is the fixed notion that teachers **deliver** curriculum. Nobody on the street has the mental image of teachers as **developers** of curriculum. Nobody envisioning the working day and year of teachers sees them bent for weeks over boardroom tables "developing curriculum" without a student in sight. No film, television or newspaper images of teachers convey the curriculum-development role. Plain folks believe nobody develops curriculum. It just exists. Mathematics is mathematics. Chemistry is chemistry. What is there to develop?

But schooling can't stand still. Every change in society has, or should have, implications for schooling. What, why, when, where, for whom, by whom, and how are constantly re-asked curriculum-development questions. Teachers could help supply better answers if they were used properly in curriculum decision-making. The teaching profession has an unavoidable obligation to serve society with curriculum leadership and government has an obligation to mine this renewable natural resource for the public good.

Where teachers' associations have been asked by governments to wear their professional hats and the associations have chosen to comply, their contributions to curriculum policy-making have been considerable. But such cases are uncommon. Except for militant confrontations over salary and pensions, official associations of teachers are apt to have only ritual dances with governments. In curriculum matters, the bows and curtsies and other niceties are observed. There may be occasional flirty winks, even a naughty pinch or two. Perhaps a well-aimed elbow now and then. But when the dance is over, there has been no significant improvement in curriculum.

Only marginally more effective is the ritual fencing between teachers' associations and government that is the norm in some jurisdictions. Everyone knows the rules and all thrusts and parries are by the book. If a bit of blood is occasionally let, the cut is superficial. The bout over, everyone bows and curriculum goes on as usual. All of that must change. Teachers' organizations must field professional curriculum corps at the local, state, national and international levels. Even in America and Canada where there have never been national curricula, the realization is dawning that no nation can establish and maintain an identity without national curriculum, and there are glimmers of recognition that international curriculum is synonymous with international survival.

In every country, in every school district, in most schools, there flourish or wither a few precious resources — truly creative teachers. Not nearly as many as there should be, but some. My guess is that four percent of the teaching force is star quality. In the province of Ontario that amounts to over four thousand exceptional teachers. Worldwide, it amounts to millions. During their careers, they develop lighthouse landmarks that blaze briefly in the black night of tradition and are snuffed out by ignorance, stupidity, parsimony, administrative ineptness or public indifference.

Nearly everything we should do in schools has already been done by some talented teacher or administrator. Many of these international treasures have died unsung. Some have retired. Others have given up in disgust and moved to greater rewards and recognition in other professions, business, industry, and the arts. But some are in schools shining like gold among the dross or buried under it. They must be recognized and named to an array of new curriculum agencies.

In most countries, neither official teachers' associations nor government has an accurate and complete profile of every teacher, so it is difficult and often impossible to find the right person for a chore. Incredibly, in this electronic age, the old-boy/girl network is often the only way to identify people for high-level curriculum chores. It turns up more old political plodders than young (or old) creative talents.

The way curriculum is usually developed is ineffectual. From school to state level, the education establishment loves to talk about changing school curriculum. Committees are struck. Academics do research. Reports are issued. Politicians make pronouncements. Significant changes are bruited, even proclaimed. But rarely are they implemented. Curriculum remains largely obsolete. Some courses (subjects, programs. . .) may be added to accommodate the larger numbers of non-academic students that now inhabit high schools but the main academic thrust continues unchanged. Some more stuff to memorize will certainly be added to an already overloaded school day. *Huckleberry Finn* may be substituted for *Oliver Twist* or vice versa; but otherwise, astute parents would notice little change from the classroom fare they experienced at school a generation earlier.

"The fare experienced at school" is not a bad definition of curriculum. There are plenty of other definitions. One too broad is: everything that happens to a child under the aegis of the school. That would include dating maneuvers in locker corridors and overheard arguments between janitors. Definitions that equate curriculum with courses of study are too narrow. Curriculum is more than the sum of all courses. Unfortunately, the course of study in, say, history, may in fact be the curriculum if the main aim of the teacher is to cover the course rather than uncover it. Any course of study should be just a tool to help achieve larger goals of the curriculum.

There is not a course of study or even a period during the school day for many learning activities that are part of curriculum: debating, student government, clubs, social service, football, etc. So important are untimetabled curriculum activities, or the lack of them, that the character of a school is colored by them. They deliver much of the school's teaching of values and attitudes. If the zenith of life is dressing up in a costume that drags the floor and hanging a bunch of flowers on it, the senior prom conveys the message, not courses of study. If the real spirit of a school is an amalgam of flaunted sex, belligerence, booze and noise, the football pep rally expresses it, not courses of study. If the real climate of a school is racial harmony, friendship patterns in corridors, cafeteria and clubs express it, not courses of study.

Some such activities are formalized as official extra-curricular (co-curricular, co-instructional) activities; others are intermittent or spontaneous; still others are daily customs. Despite the importance of untimetabled curriculum activities, governments and local school authorities virtually ignore them when specifying curriculum.

In many countries, it falls to either state or national government to develop curriculum policy centrally. In Canada it is done by each provincial government. In Japan, the national government does it. In Britain, local school authorities and even individual schools and teachers have much of the responsibility. Typically, the first step is to develop a long list of goals. The idea is to include everything noble and virtuous. Periodic tinkering adds the latest catch words, fads and causes. This list is waved proudly by everyone from principals to cabinet members as proof that the school system must be good since it espouses such exemplary goals. In Western nations, the list of goals is likely to proclaim that schooling enables students to do the following:

BASIC SKILLS:

1. Read, write and compute
2. Acquire information and meaning through observing, listening, reading and experiencing
3. Process information through intellectual and technological means

4. Solve problems by applying basic principles and processes of the sciences, arts and humanities

5. Communicate ideas through written and spoken language, mathematical symbols, and aesthetic expression

LIFE-LONG LEARNING

1. Seek and value learning experiences
2. Act as self-reliant learners
3. Base actions on the knowledge that it is necessary to learn throughout life

UNDERSTANDING AND RELATING TO OTHERS

1. Act on the belief that each individual is worthwhile
2. Base actions on the recognition that people differ in their values, behaviours, and life styles
3. Interact and feel comfortable with others who are different in race, religion, status or personal attributes
4. Develop a sense of responsibility toward others

SELF-CONCEPT DEVELOPMENT

1. Perceive themselves in a positive way
2. Appreciate their own abilities and limitations
3. Set and work toward personal goals
4. Assess praise and criticism realistically
5. Present themselves with confidence

POSITIVE LIFE STYLES

1. Practice appropriate personal hygiene, engage in sufficient physical activity, and maintain a nutritionally balanced diet
2. Avoid harmful use of alcohol and other drugs
3. Cultivate interests that may be the basis for personal development and leisure pursuits
4. Recognize the importance of productive activity
5. Display initiative and pursue tasks diligently
6. Maintain a safe and healthful community

7. Respect and seek to enhance the environment
8. Appreciate beauty in its many natural and constructed forms
9. Express themselves creatively

SPIRITUAL DEVELOPMENT
1. Seek an understanding of the purpose and worth of human existence
2. Develop a knowledge of God
3. Respect family, religion and culture in a pluralistic society

CAREER AND CONSUMER DECISIONS
1. Develop an awareness of career opportunities
2. Develop interests and abilities in relation to vocational expectations
3. Adapt to shifts in employment patterns and technology
4. Make informed consumer decisions

MEMBERSHIP IN SOCIETY
1. Assume responsibility for their own actions
2. Work with others to achieve individual and group goals
3. Participate in the democratic processes of government and perform the duties of citizenship
4. Respect the rights and property of others
5. Act with honesty, integrity, compassion and fairness
6. Develop a sense of national pride and acknowledge the need for international understanding
7. Work toward greater social justice
8. Assume responsibility for dependent persons in a manner consistent with their needs
9. Respect law and authority
10. Exercise the right of dissent responsibly

GROWING WITH CHANGE
1. Work toward immediate and long-term goals
2. Base actions on an understanding that change is a natural process in society

3. Select workable alternatives in response to changing conditions
4. Develop confidence in making decisions that involve risk.

This list happens to be from the province of Saskatchewan, Canada, but give or take a few promises, lists in other jurisdictions and countries are similar. All carry the pretense that schools are organized and operated to work directly at reaching the stated goals when everyone knows most schools are organized and operated to peddle masses of data to masses of students. **Always missing from lists of goals is the actual main goal of nearly all schools: to enable students to pass examinations based on short-term retention.** Also missing is the essential goal of any new-model school: to enable children to take over most of the roles of teachers by carefully teaching children those roles.

The current lists read as though schools offer individualized education. How else could such goals be achieved? So school authorities pretend that schools do indeed provide education tailored to individual needs. In fact, all school systems are funded, structured, programmed and staffed for mass education and that is what they deliver, more or less well.

A fundamental fact of the education mess is that the world has been misled into thinking the benefits of individualized education can be achieved in the present model of schooling with the same amount of funding which yields mass education. That is a lie. It is also a lie that the present model could deliver the goods even if funded like Star Wars. The model is obsolete and no amount of money will turn a Model T truck into a space shuttle.

Even if some exceptional school someplace did manage to individualize education, it would just mean varied routes to a standard result. Turning out a standard product is intrinsic to the present model of schooling. The model and the society that condones it are still far from treasuring or even tolerating the child with individual goals. Any survey of the public, including the young and including various sub-cultures, will show that people are more inclined to conform than to innovate and that imagination and creativity are placed very low on the scale of practiced values. No wonder. Everybody graduated from the present model of schooling. Still, the public is beguiled by the rhetoric of individualization, and accepts official government lists of goals which are phony since they can't be achieved in the current model of schooling.

In many jurisdictions, the list of goals is the basis for one or more **curriculum policy documents** explaining the philosophy and over-all specifications of the total school program. These are important because they set the parameters within which schools must operate. They are also the worst curriculum documents in many jurisdictions because they are developed secretly by governments as political tools. Only when government has already made key decisions are outside organizations consulted. Wrong ideas have already been locked into draft documents and consultation amounts to nothing more than hag-gling about details of a fundamentally flawed plan.

When I worked for a teachers' federation, I was frequently at the Ministry of Education meeting with high officials or serving on Ministry and inter-agency curriculum-related committees. Visiting teachers from other countries were always surprised that the teachers' federation paid me to give so much time to the government. In spite of that close relationship, the government persisted in dropping one bomb after the other. Every time they thought it politically expedient to be seen to be doing something about the education mess, they would hatch another secret scheme and then fly it for me and others to salute or shoot.

There was rarely anything worth saluting. Sometimes I got to shoot before they had actually printed a draft, but usually I was handed a draft copy. Either way, it was too late because the overall concept, always flawed, was already locked in. I sometimes did a clause by clause analysis on behalf of the teachers' federation and usually also went over every new draft document with a committee of teachers. All of this feedback was funneled to the government, but it never deterred them from jumping on one bandwagon after the other, usually hurtling backwards into educational oblivion.

By the time governments release draft documents for vetting, politicians and their bureaucrats already have a stake and feel bound to defend them. The solution is for governments to include expertise from official teachers' organizations and one or two other sources on their original, top-level policy-planning and document-drafting teams. This would give teachers a reason to make new policy concepts work. Instead, governments wait and call in teachers much later to do detail work on follow-up publications.

Once the stink has blown over from the release of ill-conceived policy statements, the responsible branch of government (or other senior authority) usually develops separate **curriculum guidelines** or bulletins for each subject, or in the case of younger children, guidelines for grade levels or clusters of levels. The next step is to turn the guidelines into more specific **courses of study,** programs, or units of work.

Guidelines can be prescriptive or permissive. Generally, in democratic countries, the same guideline document can be turned into scores of different courses, programs or units by exercising options in the guideline. Course-making may be done at the government, school district or school level. In some cases, it is not done at all and individual teachers must work from (or ignore) the general guideline in making up their own courses. Since copies are usually hard to find, many teachers work without reference to the very curriculum policy documents that are supposed to guide their work. They focus on facts from course outlines or textbooks instead of goals from policy statements. They teach course input and forget about desired output. Input becomes output.

Curriculum policy documents and courses of study should be computerized and continuously updated with changes flagged for easy retrieval. Usually they are not. Instead, a printed document is used for years, until long out of date, and then abandoned in favour of a new one. We get massive changes, difficult to implement all at once, instead of minor changes introduced gradually.

There is scandalous duplication of effort. Teachers spend millions of hours in committees at the school and school board level reinventing curriculum that has already been invented elsewhere. They should share. By now, curriculum documents of several nations should be in one data bank available to all. Yet even adjacent school boards are unlikely to do much sharing. It would be helpful for teachers of environmental studies to know how their class work with environmental poisons relates to class work in other courses such as geography, science, health, law, etc. It would be salutary for mathematics teachers in Yonkers, U.S.A. to find that algebra concepts they are about to present to twelve-year-olds are routinely learned by ten-year-olds in Yokahama, Japan.

Curriculum guideline documents for specific programs or subjects are, or should be, concerned with: broad goals, immediate goals, content of courses, teaching methods, process students will experience, standard evaluation conditions and strategies, retraining of teachers, etc. The best curriculum guidelines result when the responsible government authority is wise enough to involve practicing teachers, university professors and other experts and when the authors work as a team rather than as opposing camps trying for a negotiated settlement.

At least half of any curriculum-writing team must be star teachers selected by teacher organizations. Stars are often generalists and from now on generalists must be on all curriculum-writing teams. This is not to say that specialists should be excluded. But specialist teachers and university academics usually write curriculum guidelines narrowly applicable to a few students who want specialization. Such guidelines, and courses of study derived from them, are suitable for only the most academically inclined students. There are few students in any high school who will become biologists so few need a course in biology; however, everybody should know **about** biology, what it is (in a general way), how it relates to other "subjects," how it affects our lives.

There is no justification for boring and frustrating masses of students with memorization of biology data. Or chemistry data. Or history data (beyond cultural literacy). Or mathematics (beyond numeracy). We need first-rate courses for everybody **about** most traditional disciplines — and courses **in** those disciplines for the few who will go on to use the detail in their careers or interests.

All of this creating of general policy documents and specific subject guidelines is the **development** phase of the curriculum process. The next phase is **implementation** and the third phase is **review**. Of the three phases, development is usually done best, implementation worst. A necessary fourth phase, **planning**, based on assessment of future needs, is virtually non-existent.

Implementation sounds easy — like an event. A new curriculum document is sent to all school districts in large numbers (but often not large enough). Usually, it has not been field tested. Usually it does not include a section on how to prepare teachers for its use. Typically, copies are distributed to schools and there may, at best, be an orientation day which can't do more than give teachers an overview of changes called for.

At some point, usually next semester, every teacher is supposed to begin using the new curriculum guideline along with (or sometimes without) a more detailed course of studies based on the guideline. School boards or individual schools set up committees to write specific courses based on the new guideline, but the new course outlines may not be ready by the time the guideline goes into effect. More often than not, textbooks, charts, films, slides, computer programs and other learning materials needed for new courses are non-existent or there is no money to buy them. The same teachers may have to begin using more than one, perhaps several, new course outlines for the different subjects or grades they teach. Work overload is cruel.

The worst disaster though, and the one that prevents most new curriculum from getting into schools, is the failure of government authorities and school systems to retrain teachers for changes they are supposed to put into operation. Experience and research tell us that only five percent of teachers can cope with changed curriculum as typically introduced. The principle that governments, the public and even some school system administrators have not grasped is that curriculum implementation is synonymous with professional development (see chapter 18).

Since curriculum is ultimately the responsibility of some level of government, it is the responsibility of government to implement it. What is the point of developing curriculum if it is left sitting on the shelf?

So **it is the responsibility of government to implement every change in curriculum by first changing (retraining) teachers to make their skills, knowledge, beliefs and practices compatible with changed curriculum.** The reason all governments fail to meet their responsibility to implement curriculum is that it costs money. Naive and penny-pinching publics let governments get away with it.

Every time there is to be a change in curriculum, government agencies must outline in detail the professional development (teacher retraining) that will be required to implement it. Then government must fund and schedule that implementation activity as part of the teacher's working day because it is part of the teacher's job. The actual training should be done through the local school authority which may purchase expertise from universities or private industry using allocated government funds. If that had been done, major curriculum ideas of the twentieth century would have survived and combined to significantly modify the present model. Instead, they all faded away or survived here and there as quaint artifacts.

To see if curriculum developed as phase one was actually implemented as phase two, most jurisdictions have a third phase in the curriculum process called review or evaluation. It is rarely done well. More often than not, some or all of the following problems make reviews suspect:

- The total population is not reviewed and the sample of school boards, schools, teachers, administrators, students, and parents surveyed is not representative.
- Test instruments used for the sample survey of student achievement are invalid or unreliable or otherwise inadequate, or else there is no sample survey of achievement whatsoever.
- Data-collecting instruments used for interviews are not worded and/ or administered so that they will produce valid and reliable results.
- Teachers directly concerned are not meaningfully involved in the entire review process.

- There is not enough money, time or personnel to do an adequate review.
- Some respondents lie or give very subjective or purposely vague responses.
- The summary and written report of the review do not accurately reflect findings.
- Recommendations do not fully reflect findings.
- Recommendations are never implemented.
- Relevance that the fragment of curriculum being reviewed has in the total scheme of things is seldom challenged, and consequently if Voodoo 101 is entrenched, it will almost certainly survive the review and be ritually repeated.

A year or two after a review little or no difference in program will be evident in most schools; however, reviews do sometimes stimulate authorities to rewrite curriculum guidelines and if that happens, a new guideline may be implemented three to six years after the review. It is a slow process. Worse, it is backward-looking. A review of curriculum is by definition a look backwards. That is a necessary and valuable step, but it is not, by itself, an adequate basis for building replacement curriculum. **The major basis for new curriculum should be anticipation of future needs.**

Planning should be added as a fourth step in the curriculum cycle. The order of steps should be: planning, development, implementation, review. All four must be cyclical and continuous rather than intermittent activities of government, school boards and individual schools. Future orientation will not come easily to an education establishment which, worldwide, prepares students for life twenty-five years ago. Most schools don't comprehend the present, let alone the future. Those that do occasionally wrestle with the present, often mistake it for the future.

The perspective of most educators is traditional, and the tradition is respected consciously or subconsciously by much of the population. These are the people who think they are being modern when they ask schools to provide (on top of all the usual stuff) more vocational training, even though we know most jobs for which we train students will not exist soon.

Curriculum today is largely Victorian, a late nineteenth-century expression of the industrial revolution as applied to the education industry. We have tinkered with it but have not changed it. We have learned to do it better, but there is not much joy in doing a marginally better job of the wrong thing. One reason open education failed was that it tried to apply a better teaching method to existing curriculum (with some modification to accommodate children's interests), but it did not include a deliberate, future-oriented curriculum that students were expected to follow.

Open education did, however, appreciate one aspect of future orientation — the need to integrate subjects. Marshall McLuhan put it this way in *Understanding Media* (New York: McGraw-Hill, 1964): "Continued in their present pattern of fragmented unrelation, our school curricula will insure a citizenry unable to understand the cybernated world in which they live." More than a quarter century after McLuhan and open education, subjects are still not integrated.

What we need is curriculum planning based on anticipation of future needs of individuals and society. That will guide us in replacing our linear, sequential, fragmented industrial-age model with a holistic, information-age model. Then, borders between subjects will blur and sometimes disappear. New "subjects" (topics, categories, fields, explorations. . .) will be seen as more important than many old ones. There will be a shift: from content emphasis to pattern recognition; from rote memorization to information exploration; from passive/receptive to active/creative students; from print-on-paper technology to integration of paper and electronic technologies (with emphasis on the latter); from teachers as data peddlers to teachers as resource people, advisers and learning environment managers.

It will take concerted effort by aware citizens and teachers at national and local levels and everywhere in between to exorcise traditions that have a stranglehold on curriculum process. Unfortunately, more citizens and teachers are concerned than are aware. Concern leads them in a backward direction because they are not conscious of more promising alternatives in a forward direction. To provide promising alternatives — curriculum ideas that will turn schools around and reference them to the present and future instead of the past — we need permanent international, national and local **Curriculum Think Tanks** of visionaries. Their first and continuing challenge should be to envision a new model of schooling and curriculum for it.

Without a large representation of creative teachers, think tanks on education are almost useless. The thinkers know too little about schooling to keep their creative strikes on target. In Ontario in 1988, the Premier's Council, a high-powered, thirty-member oracle, *none of them teachers*, took a look at the future of schooling through a rear-view mirror and came up with cliche cure-alls: they would achieve excellence with the game-show gimmick of national and international performance-comparison tests!

The Curriculum Think Tank I am proposing throws creative teachers into the mix to keep others on track. The "others" are: academics from several disciplines; writers, painters and other artists (because their nature is to challenge assumptions and offer alternatives); inventors; electronic communication developers; entrepreneurs; business and industry leaders; futurists; various analysts, etc. Creative elementary and high school students must be included. The job of each Curriculum Think Tank is to scan the horizon annually and come up with school-related ideas that will stimulate another group.

To create and annually update a strategic, long-range curriculum plan is the responsibility of the **Curriculum Council**. It is funded by government to advise but stands at arm's length. It holds annual public hearings at which individuals and groups present curriculum concerns and proposals. The Council is made up almost entirely of educators, particularly creative teachers appointed by teachers' associations. Most university representatives are from colleges of education and all government representatives from the department responsible for education. The Curriculum Council has a permanent secretariat and access to curriculum experts and researchers.

Since the Council is a working group, not an accountability exercise, it must not be bogged down with political appointees ill-equipped to deal with complexities of curriculum planning. The public has the ear of the Curriculum Council at annual hearings, so it should be acceptable to limit seats on the Council to ten percent for non-educators. Consideration must be given to seating student representatives on the Council, but it may prove more feasible to fund student presentations at annual hearings.

The Curriculum Council's annual report to government recommends updating the state's long-range (6 to 10 years) and mid-range (3 to 5 years) strategic plans and proposes modifications in the short-range operational plan (1 to 2 years). The report is released to the public and is a media event. This is important because governments in all countries are notorious for replacing the best long-range educational planning with the worst short-range political plans, and it is time they were held publicly accountable for their commitment to long-range planning.

Government may modify strategic (long-range) plans put forward annually by the Curriculum Council but must endorse and publish its own version, so there is always an official long-range plan before the public.

Management of the official long-range plan and the development from it of the operational plan for the coming two years is the chore of the government branch responsible for education. It should conceive and write such policy using a committee which includes star teachers appointed by official teachers' organizations.

The Curriculum Council will have to include in long-range planning, mandatory phasing-in of all characteristics of information-age curriculum; and it will have to mount a continuing public education program of unprecedented intensity to pry free the sentimental grip of society on outmoded, industrial-age curriculum. The media will have to be won over.

While the Curriculum Council has to be funded by government, it must be free from government pressure. It must also be free of political pressure from teachers' associations that feel they are protecting their turf by protecting the status quo. In fact, teachers protecting the status quo will be protecting their graves because an education system that is a vestigial remain of a bygone age is too costly to maintain as a museum and will be buried unceremoniously by technological revolution sometime in the twenty-first century.

Strategic long and mid-range plans developed by the Curriculum Council encompass every aspect of education from school buildings to teacher education because curriculum subsumes everything else and cannot be planned in isolation from components of the system which could make or break school program. School administrative structure and organization have to be altered in order to break the stranglehold fragmentation (unrelated "subjects," elementary/secondary estrangement) and linear sequence (lock-step grades) have on schools. Otherwise, the Curriculum Council could develop a curriculum plan which integrates subjects and levels only to have it mutilated by school officials trying to stuff it into old machinery. That has been the fate of many innovations in the twentieth century including progressive education, open education, non-grading, open-area education, and team teaching.

In the last decade of the twentieth century and the first decade of the twenty-first, the Curriculum Council, like the Curriculum Think Tank, must be primarily concerned with redefining the model of schooling. Once a new model is in place, they will have to keep renewing it.

The Curriculum Council is a central body coterminous with the senior level of government responsible for education. In countries such as Canada, where provinces rather than the national government have jurisdiction over schooling, there should also be a National Curriculum Council because the national and international implications of curriculum are so great that no national government can afford to abdicate responsibility.

The kind of central planning required is not the kind presently used in many countries. A visitor to a class of fifteen-year-olds having a science lesson in Moscow would have a hard time finding any significant difference if he could instantly transfer to a similar classroom in Vladivostok. That kind of cookie-cutter centralized control is the antithesis of information-age education. The central authority should develop a new model for schooling with broad curriculum guidelines that allow plenty of room for regional and local creativity. It should develop enabling, not limiting, policy. However, essentials must be clearly prescribed: skills to be mastered, process to be experienced by children, and standard criteria for evaluation. And **if strong nationhood is the goal (rather than a weaker federation of states), the highest level of government must specify content of national cultural literacy because without shared national culture and the shared national values that accompany it, successful nationhood is unlikely**.

Government must also produce, commission or stimulate a range of learning equipment and materials, and should constantly have on the drawing boards and in the wind tunnels prototypes of the next generation of schools. Research and development in schooling is a national issue of the highest order and is too expensive to replicate in every sub-jurisdiction. A portion of curriculum should focus on local realities not likely to be adequately addressed by materials developed at the national level. In poor countries, the local portion may be relatively higher because local reality is often survival. Even in developed countries there are regional and ethnic differences that need local expression.

In all countries, national and local matters must share time with curriculum content that is as pertinent in Omaha as in Osaka or Oslo. Children growing up in Grimsby, England will learn about North Sea fishing and oil, but that is not enough because next year or next century some of them may live in Toronto, Tampa or Tasmania. And even if they remain in England, their lives will become increasingly a global village rather than just an English or even a European experience. Curriculum must become increasingly universal, and international literacy as important as national literacy.

This argues powerfully for an **International Curriculum Council** to act as a nerve centre, clearing house of ideas and materials and meeting place for people from national Curriculum Councils. The strategic, long-range plan produced yearly by the International Curriculum Council should comprehend all world issues and include proposals for specific curriculum. **It should be one role of the International Curriculum Council to identify values that must guide curriculum in every country now that allegiance to the world is more important than allegiance to any nation state or sub-group**.

Presently, international meetings of educators are too few and intermittent and, even when they do happen, include the wrong people because governments hold that politicians, bureaucrats and academics know more about schooling than teachers. The Ministers of Education from all Council of Europe countries meet, but there is never a meeting of the most creative thinkers among European classroom teachers. Even international meetings of teachers' associations are attended entirely by teacher politicians or else are narrowly focused on some aspect of schooling. Political strutting and time-wasting is just as rampant at meetings of the World Confederation of Organizations of the Teaching Profession as at meetings of the United Nations. To blast education into the twenty-first century will require a sustained creative explosion from an International Curriculum Council made up, as are national (or state or provincial) Curriculum Councils, of outstanding educational thinkers, primarily creative classroom practitioners.

The International Curriculum Council should be stimulated by an annual report from an **International Think Tank** as diverse in composition as national think tanks. Both the International Curriculum Council and the International Think Tank should be made up of representatives from their national counterparts.

At the other extreme, there should be a **Local Curriculum Council** in every school district because it is locally that classroom action does or doesn't happen. Like its national and international counterparts, the Local Curriculum Council should deal with time frames beyond two years by continuously updating proposed strategic plans for consideration by the local school authority. As at the state level, the local authority will probably modify the strategic plan after public debate. But it will finally adopt a version that will guide development of the short-term (2 year) operational plan written by school district officials using committees made up primarily of teachers selected by official teacher associations.

Education agencies claim they already do strategic planning. In the early eighties, several reports on "environmental scanning" were published by the Ontario Ministry of Education. Even the press was fooled into thinking that a strategic plan would follow and that operational plans would grow from it. In fact, the futuristic publications were dusted off and quoted for effect throughout the late eighties while the jurisdiction that created them was implementing a regressive curriculum policy for high schools that actually pushed the system backwards. Such obfuscation will continue until a concerned public realizes the only way out of the education mess is to endorse a whole new model of schooling and then test all pronouncements of governments against it.

CHAPTER 21

PROGRAM PRINCIPLES

Clearly, there is no more important function for education to fulfill than that of helping us to recognize the world we actually live in and simultaneously, of helping us to master concepts that will increase our ability to cope with it. This is the essential criterion for judging the relevance of all education.

— Neil Postman and Charles Weingartner, *Teaching As A Subversive Activity* (New York: Delacorte, 1969)

Walk into any school in session. Does it have the hum of purposeful activity? Do students seem to be in control of themselves, of each other and of the school? Are teachers generally inconspicuous, though present and busy, in classrooms and all other areas of the school? Probably not. More likely, you will find inert students taking teacher commands or rowdy students ignoring them. Either way, the school is a failure. The first principle of 21st century schooling is **each individual student and group of students is the active initiator not the passive recipient of education.**

Early primary schools come closest, especially in jurisdictions that retain some vestige of open education or are rediscovering it as cooperative learning. Senior elementary and high schools are usually off track: most teachers are still talking books. Teachers should act as very involved consultants: picking up slack in content delivery; feeding in ideas;

making sure nothing and nobody falls through the cracks; sharpening skills; managing and improving process inconspicuously; standing behind or sitting beside every student instead of in front of the group; seeing the whole picture; checking; balancing; listening; counselling; evaluating; facilitating; helping; building self-esteem. And all teachers all the time should carefully teach their students how to perform most of the teaching roles teachers used to perform.

Socrates asked students leading questions. Plato tells us **the students talked more than Socrates**. Most school teachers have not yet got that minimal message at a time when we should be far beyond it in method sophistication. Teachers in late twentieth-century schools speak eighty percent of the time. That is a fact, not a guess. Instead, students should speak eighty percent of the time.

Children teaching themselves and teaching each other are natural, empowering, fulfilling practices that make childhood, including teenhood, relevant and enjoyable. We must turn much of the role of teacher over to students by teaching them how to do it and allowing them to imitate and practice, and by mutual coaching and evaluation among students of their performances. Before junior high school age, nearly all students should be adequate and many should be accomplished seminar leaders, presenters, recorders, researchers, questioners, discussers, summarizers, evaluators, etc.

Some school officials talk as though their systems already do what I suggest. But they are just breaking classes into smaller groups to work on projects. Even that is too great a change for parents who prefer teachers talking in front of passive students. In May 1989, a group called Concerned Parents actually petitioned the school board of Etobicoke (suburban Toronto) to "return to the traditional classroom setup with the teacher instructing from the front of the room." Measured against the first principle of twenty-first century schooling, most schools in all countries fail, partly because of such reactionary parents.

The second principle follows from the first: **schools must see to it that every student is self-propelled.** Children start out that way. They are curious and naturally go about learning, teaching themselves and each other. They learn in three ways: by exploration (touching, tasting, smelling, looking, listening, asking, researching, reading, exploring, discussing, evaluating, doing. . .); by imitation (of parents, teachers, other adults, siblings, peers, heroes. . .); by indoctrination (being told, taught, drilled, ordered, instructed, lectured. . .). Exploration and imitation are active modes while indoctrination makes children passive. The current model of schooling is based largely on indoctrination.

The most complex learning feat children ever accomplish is learning to talk, and they do it, without orders or instruction from teachers, by imitation and exploration because they want to and are encouraged by parents. But schools rarely harness the natural desire of children of all ages to imitate and explore. Instead they kill the desire with lethal doses of rote. **Whatever teachers do — lecture, organize, summarize, plan, initiate, lead discussions, evaluate, find information, explain, question, drill, coach — everything, should be imitated by students and turned over to students at the earliest possible moment**. Instead, teachers keep right on doing it and students sink into feckless passivity. Adults nourish the false notion that only graduate students in universities can be the initiators, the active agents, in their own education. In fact, all children can do it and would do it if we allowed them and helped them. Instead, we expect students to be passive followers, so they become passive. It is a self-fulfilling expectation.

Playwright Edward Albee expressed the usual adult attitude to a New England prep school in 1988. He said, "The real function of a formal education is to teach you how to educate yourself when you're done with your formal education." The notion implicit in his statement is that all the passivity of schooling magically turns to activity on the day of graduation. He should have said, "The real function of formal education is to teach you how to educate yourself **during your school years** so you'll do it throughout childhood and adulthood."

When we do an about-face and expect all children to become self-propelled learners, each will need **high self-esteem** and **an**

array of skills. The two are the fuel of self-propulsion. Virtually all young people could learn to be self-propelled because self-image could be enhanced and skills taught by properly functioning schools. Instead, schools destroy self-image and fail to teach skills. Good self-image is nourished by regular meals of **achievement, praise and affection**. Every child must be considered individually and challenges encouraged that are within abilities but which require exertion and stretching. Increasingly, each student must be held responsible for choosing as well as doing work well; and there must be frequent supportive feedback from a **forever-present** teacher who is consultant, coach, mentor, confidant, helper, hugger, prodder, trainer, listener and ultimately, friend.

Teacher and student must be compatible. There is nothing shameful about admitting incompatibility; what is shameful is allowing it to continue. As vice principal in charge of discipline, I dealt with teachers' problems often enough to know that **too many teachers and students suffer poisonous incompatibility without there ever being official admission of its existence much less honorable, routine redress. Any new model of schooling must require compatibility of teacher and child**. One of the fatal flaws in the open education concept was that it did not.

In common with some adults, some children have rotten personalities. The difference is that children are still young and it might be possible to sweeten soured psyches. The worst cases are too disruptive to be in regular classrooms and must have sheltered, therapeutic environments. All the rest do best when matched with compatible teachers. It makes sense to match pupils and teachers using something more sophisticated than random chance, alphabetical order or examination results. Yet those three remain the norm worldwide.

Even where there is compatibility, sophisticated matching needs to be done in order to guarantee every student a balanced exposure to teaching talents. I know a teacher who is manly, athletic, strong, caring, sensitive, hard-working, sincere, principled, virtuous, handsome and altogether likeable. He is also incapable of writing a decent paragraph, his reading speed is dismally slow and his reading interests limited to sports pages. No attempt is made in the present model of schooling to assure counterbalancing strengths in other teachers. The luck of the draw is supposed to balance things out. But it doesn't. It is not unusual to find children who have reached puberty having never experienced a male teacher. The same children may live with a single female parent. In the seventies, the number of female-led households increased by twenty-three percent. The trend continues, but schools make no effort to compensate by balanced placement.

Computers should be used in matchmaking but that will require profiling students and teachers. So far, we profile only a few special education students. The obviously brilliant and the clearly learning disabled are assessed individually. That takes care of perhaps fifteen percent of children. Appropriate placement follows. But eighty-five percent of students don't qualify for detailed, individual assessment because they are not extreme enough in expression of their individuality. Some day parents of the majority thus disadvantaged will wake up and demand equal treatment for all. Then, discrimination in favour of the extremities will cease and all children will be profiled.

Teachers' associations and school boards resist profiling teachers because it is far easier to pretend that a teacher is a teacher is a teacher: one teacher of history coming up. The fears are that common-sense matching by computer or by allowing students to choose teachers will lead to unreasonable demands by parents or students for perfect teachers, or that certificated teachers will find few computer matches among students and will be voted out of the profession by children opting out of their classes. Fears are exaggerated and also protective of the incompetent. People look for compatibility in doctors, dentists, mechanics and merchants. Why not in teachers?

Since **the school system is responsible for developing self-image in every student,** every school must have for every student an up-to-date assessment of self-image and an image-development program. The recorded assessment is the responsibility of the school but the property of the student. The image profile and the remedial and developmental programs to assure growth are reviewed regularly by a **constantly-available** teacher.

Where self-esteem is being diminished inside the school, it is the responsibility of the full-time mentor/teacher to track down, confront and remedy the problem. **Where self-esteem is being diminished by conditions outside the school, it is the obligation of the school to identify and remedy those conditions.** Other agencies may be involved, but ultimately it is the responsibility of schools to see that no child slips through cracks in the social service screen. Only schools deal with all children and hence are in a position to monitor all. Most children whose lives are forever blighted by diminished self-image never enter the social service network (or enter it too late as young adults). Most damage is done at home by families or fragments of families. Schools must wade in where politicians fear to tread, the last bastion of righteous child-as-chattel bigotry, the home. Another reason open education failed was that it never included this committment to tackle and overcome home-caused problems.

Self-esteem motivates students, but self-propulsion needs more than motivation. Self-propelled students have an arsenal of skills which they deploy like conquering generals on a never-ending conquest. Without these skills, even a motivated student gets no place. **The skills essential to self-propulsion which schools are responsible for developing as the first order of obligatory programs include: language literacy — reading, writing, speaking (conversing, discussing, addressing, explaining, describing, persuading, debating, lecturing, evaluating . . .), listening; numeracy including addition, subtraction, division and elements of mathematics essential for everyday life such as measures, fractions and percentage; researching; problem solving; organizing; cultural literacy; computer literacy. . . .**

Lip-service is given to such skills, but schools have failed to deliver and the public has allowed it to happen. Every child must be at or beyond expectancy for age and intelligence in all designated skills at all times, and **it is the responsibility of schools to see that all activities** (save only those bearing upon health and student govern-ment) are put aside each year for each individual until such time as he/she is up to or beyond expectancy in each skill essential to self-propulsion. A child below expectancy is in crisis and subject to intensive care. There are no ifs, ands or buts. It is every child's right to have these tools for they are the means of acquiring and using knowledge.

Open education proponents believed just the opposite: that skills such as reading and ciphering could always be adequately developed as part of child-chosen activities — with a measure of teacher intervention thrown in. They were wrong. Children do not always build essential skills automatically when they pursue their own interests under the direction of teachers. Some do. Others need the definite, direct, per-sonalized, developmental and remedial teaching and testing that were rejected by open education.

Traditional schools (virtually all schools) do just the opposite to what I am proposing. In most classrooms worldwide, students who can't read, write, speak or listen well enough sit through months and years of lessons in subjects for which competent reading, writing, speaking and listening should be prerequisites. The result is a plague of illiteracy, functional illiteracy, broken lives, unrealized potential, delinquency, low productivity and incalculable dollar cost that is the shame of schools and societies that fund such folly.

In 1991 I monitored a huge public reference library frequented in late afternoon by high school students. That they were doing school work suggests they were a cut above their peers who were hanging around shopping malls. Nonetheless, many of them lacked research and prob-lem-solving skills. Some lacked reading, writing and speaking skills. Few seemed able to scan. Some of their written work was so disorganized as to be incomprehensible. Few knew how to talk to me. They should have been at school learning how to read, write, speak, listen, research, solve problems, organize and compute instead of thrashing about at the reference library. They were drowning because they had been thrown into deep water before being taught to swim.

Teacher time is a central issue in developing self-propulsion skills. In my best teaching years, I was the main teacher of gifted eleven, twelve and thirteen-year-olds who attended a junior high school for two years in an open education atmosphere. Most worked diligently at senior high level and most were self-propelled. But twenty percent had needs in self-esteem and skills which I could not meet, partly because I got them too late in their lives but mainly because there was not enough time. I needed a paid assistant and trained volunteer but had neither. So the school system failed to meet the needs of twenty percent of my students. In a less gifted group, the percent with unmet needs or undeveloped skills could be eighty instead of twenty.

As a matter of principle, **programs to develop skills required for self-propulsion (along with all other obligatory programs) must be separate from optional (elective) programs offered for credit. Credits must not be given for any obligatory program.** Obligatory programs are like essential, involuntary functions of the human organism, like respiration — the school organism breathing. Optional programs for credit are the school system voluntarily flexing mind and muscle using oxygen acquired from breathing obligatory air.

In every year of elementary and secondary school, elective **programs for credit must be closed to students until they are at expectancy level in all obligatory programs.** In obligatory programs, students build and maintain their wings. In optional programs, they fly on their own. Without thorough wing development and maintenance, students crash.

Every student must be free to test out of every skill-building program at any time, and having proven proficiency in a given program, be free of any further requirements in that program until the next semester (or term or year) unless ongoing monitoring by a teacher identifies deficiencies.

The second order of obligatory, non-credit programs in which every student must participate every year to expectancy (in addition to skills for self-propulsion) include

personal fitness (exercise, eating, hygiene, grooming, safety, drugs), sex education and student government.

A fit student might test out of personal fitness for the remainder of a semester but must agree to maintain fitness between tests. Nobody can ever test out of student government because it is the obligation of every citizen to participate fully and continuously in the democratic process.

When achievement in level-one and level-two obligatory programs reaches expectancy, every student every year must participate to expectancy in the third order of obligatory, non-credit programs: international understanding, social service, second language, visual and performing arts (painting, sculpting, writing, acting, singing, playing instruments, dancing. . .), children's rights, values (or ethics), current affairs, media literacy.

Unless a second language is begun by age six (and preferably by two) it will be too late for some. There is no point in introducing an obligatory second language requirement at high school because too many children will be incapable of learning the language in the time available. In high school, all languages other than the first must be electives unless they were begun much earlier.

Arts must be obligatory at all ages because they are essential in the preservation and enhancement of natural creativity. But in most jurisdictions in English-speaking countries arts are undervalued in schools. In 1989, only a third of six hundred elementary schools in New York City had arts programs! Only thirty American states required some kind of arts course for high school graduation and many of those allowed substitution of an inappropriate alternative — a foreign language, a vocational course, driver training, etc. There **is** no substitute for arts.

Fourth-order obligatory, non-credit programs are equal in status to third order but are studied to expectancy level at selected, appropriate ages rather than every year: parenting (ages thirteen through eighteen); labour-management (ages six, eleven and sixteen); law (ages four, six, nine, thirteen and sixteen); driving (age fifteen); science literacy (all ages to

fourteen); world religions (ages seven, ten, thirteen and six-teen); money and finance (ages six, eleven and fifteen); national history (ages five, eight, eleven, and fourteen); national geography (ages six, nine, twelve and fifteen); job search and career planning skills (ages thirteen, fifteen and seventeen). Another reason open education failed was because it did not include these obligatory programs.

Most order-three and four obligatory programs must be decidedly process oriented; hence all students must remain involved to benefit from living the process. Nonetheless, wherever mastering skills or memorizing data are concerned, every student should be able to test out any time. There is never any excuse for holding a student back. Progress is continuous.

Some order-three and -four programs may be short units lasting a few hours, days or weeks. Others may continue all semester, term or year but take only a short time each week. Still others, particularly international understanding and current affairs, will generate major daily activities at all ages. John Dewey was wrong when he wrote, "Existing society is both too complex and too close to the child to be studied." The whole world must be pulled into the classroom every day and laid bare.

It should be evident from the emphasis on process that **a principle of any new model for schooling must be constant attention to development of interpersonal skills and group learning skills. Children of all ages must be <u>taught</u> how to contribute to groups of all sizes.** Obligatory developmental experiences must be thoroughly planned, implemented, and evaluated. Remedial pro-grams must be provided for children below expectancy level in group process skills. Even in the heyday of open education it was common to walk into classrooms and find children had not been systematically trained in group process skills. Today, it is rare to see an elementary or high school discussion group or seminar where students know how to prepare, chair, contribute, listen, agree, disagree, question, analyze, synthesize, build upon ideas, achieve a higher plateau, summarize, evaluate process, etc. They have not been taught because teachers don't know how to identify and teach the skills involved.

When (and only when) a student is performing to expectation in all obligatory, non-credit programs, he or she is eligible at any age to pursue optional programs for credit. Many optional credit programs are traditional subjects required for university admission: chemistry, physics, biology, calculus, algebra, geometry, English Literature, English Composition, modern and classical languages, history, geography, etc. Others may include psychology, journalism, economics, astronomy, technology, entrepreneuring, etc. The possibilities are many; schools should offer what the local situation demands.

There should be no vocational electives. **School is not for job training.** Credits for generic job skill programs (see chapter 10) must not be confused with specific vocational training. Separate job-training centres should be operated by school boards, community colleges or other agencies. In general, **job training should follow high school graduation but should also be available to everyone who leaves high school before graduation by choice or because of being unable to benefit from further schooling.**

Some schools may decide to emphasize electives that encourage selected interests or talents: performing arts, visual arts, science, technology, languages, etc. The special focus in electives and consequent special faculty and equipment may act as a magnet to attract students: hence the name magnet schools. But they must be schools not job-training centres. Pseudo-schools that were conceived for vocational training (such as the New York School of Performing Arts) should be reconceived as magnet schools. And schools that were conceived as magnet schools (such as the North Carolina School for Science and Mathematics) must make sure they remain schools and don't succumb to temptations of job training.

In the unusual case of specific job training that demonstrably requires an early beginning, ballet for example, a conscious decision may be made to go beyond mere encouragement of talent to actual vocational training. A training centre should be established to operate concurrently in conjunction and in cooperation with a school. But the two should be separate even if under one roof. School is school and job training is job training.

Current issues are the stuff of all obligatory non-credit programs but also provide opportunities for focused studies taken as electives for credit. Rock Poetry could be an intensive study of poetry, current cultures, and freedom of information and expression; Baja Whale Watch could be an in-depth study of threatened species and related ecological issues. Surely, threats to the environment and to freedom of speech are critical concerns. Yet both Rock Poetry and Baja Whale Watch were described by William Bennett, U.S. Secretary of Education under Reagan, as academic clutter. Mr. Bennett is representative of a residual army of reactionaries who seem forever stalled at the primitive notion that subject disciplines are the only or best way to organize rigorous content.

In France in the mid-eighties there was a reaction against problem and theme-centred study, particularly of history. Critics thought children pursuing themes might know outlines of major changes in society without knowing details of dates, people and places; students using the theme approach might end up unable to put Napoleon in the right century. Those critics were confusing two separate matters. One matter, problem and theme-centred study, is deep involvement for every child in deciding the future of the planet. The other matter is cultural literacy for every child. All children need both.

If the French think the dates of Napoleon are essential information for every citizen, the dates should be part of a computerized cultural literacy bank of information that every child is required to master. Cultural literacy should always be an obligatory, non-credit program and so should **basic** national history. But many additional history programs should be available as options for credit and they could be well done by examining problems or themes.

Future Studies is an elective for credit. The only reason it need not be an obligatory program every year is that most obligatory programs have within them a futures component or else the entire program has a future orientation. Schools owe it to students to promote anticipatory instead of adaptive learning so children will develop confidence in dealing with uncertainties of constant change.

Credits are also given for electives developed by individual students or groups and supervised or monitored by teachers: part-time jobs, community service, research, experiment, invention, field study, creative projects, etc. And all students who are members of student government, school administration (Adcom), school board, or Curriculum Think Tanks receive credits.

Provided all obligatory skills are up to standard and performance in all obligatory programs is satisfactory, all students of all ages are eligible to take any elective for credit provided they meet honest and necessary prerequisite requirements. If a ten-year-old girl can do calculus and wants to, she is allowed to take credit programs in calculus. People good in language must have Literature and language performance options available at all ages. Many younger children and most by age ten will take some electives for credit; the number will increase as students get older. Pteropaedics must be allowed to fly when ready.

Most students will graduate from this changed model of schooling at seventeen or sooner but may remain voluntarily to do more electives. Much or all of the final year of school at age seventeen or eighteen is a post-graduate year to pursue additional electives for university entrance, as preparation for subsequent career training, or for personal growth. Students earn credits to suit their own needs and abilities.

Theoretically, **no credits and hence no electives are required for graduation.** A student may graduate without electives, having completed all obligatory programs. In practice, nearly all students take many electives. But they are in every sense "elective" — truly "optional." Students know which electives are required by universities or colleges, which are prerequisites for other electives, which please or displease parents, which are compatible with particular career goals, which are of personal interest, which are of no interest, which have outstanding teachers, which suit their individual learning styles. It is not necessary to devise elaborate divisions based on level of difficulty. Students choose electives suited to their needs. They stream themselves.

Every student's record for every term, semester or year, includes a verbal description of every obligatory and elective program and the student's achievements in each program. Where there are skills or content to be mastered in either obligatory or elective programs, the level of mastery achieved is reported. And just as important, the student's participation in and mastery of the daily **process** of schooling is analyzed and described. In a fully-operating new model of schooling, these reports are written by a new kind of home room teacher called a hi (see chapter 22) after consultation with elective teachers and discussions with individual students.

It is up to individual students how transcripts of personal records are used and up to parents, universities, employers, prospective spouses, biographers, obituary writers and others how much value they put on each credit and on obligatory programs. Most children show their records to parents, universities and prospective employers, but if some choose not to, that is their right. Conflicts in this regard are resolved using due process with the interests of the child represented by the school ombudsman.

As a matter of principle, schools are non-graded. Children within about a three-year age span are grouped in ungraded home rooms (living rooms) for most obligatory programs and are free at any age, any time of any year, to take elective programs for credit provided their obligatory programs are well in hand and they meet really necessary prerequisite requirements.

Streaming / Tracking

When some children experience programs at one intensity while others experience higher or lower intensity, they are said to be streamed or tracked. **As a matter of principle, new-model schools are streamed in the sense that all children have the right and**

responsibility to choose among home rooms (living rooms) and options that suit their needs. And all must participate in obligatory and remedial programs according to individual abilities.

Streaming has always existed. In current schools, when children of widely different abilities take the same program, they stream themselves into those who understand what is going on and those who don't, those who pass and those who fail. And in the same classroom are a few who find the whole thing so easy they tune out. If, instead, the school offers three separate classes at different intensities, the same children stream themselves into the most suitable class — high, medium or low.

The perception of some critics is that schools drop poor, working-class and ethnic-minority children through a trapdoor into lowly streams of dross, while anointed white, middle-class-majority children are borne on high to lofty streams of gold. The perception is wrong. Schools, and especially teachers, make heroic efforts (within limits of the present model) to steer all children toward high streams that flow into universities. But **the present model of schooling is not suited to "schooling" children out of lower streams into higher ones.** It is the model of schooling that is wrong, not the concept of streaming.

Critics are much closer to the truth when they say schools do a disservice to many poor, working-class and ethnic-minority children (and to many middle-class children) by trying to steer them into academic, pre-university programs for which they are not suited.

Two significant factors determine whether children stream themselves high, low or somewhere in between: heredity and environment. It is now taboo to talk about either, but that does not alter the truth. My guess is that genetic disposition and home background are at least ninety percent accountable for which stream a child fits and, in the total population, home background is at least twice as significant as heredity.

Neither factor has anything to do with race. Genetic determinants for either quick or slow learning occur in every race. So do negative home conditions. Functional illiteracy of parents is one home condition that predisposes many children away from schooling. Parents failing to read to children frequently is another. So is inability of immigrant parents to speak the first language of their new country. Others are: disorganization or instability in the home; parental lack of respect for schooling; parental abusiveness, lovelessness, disinterest, unavailability, ignorance, laziness, etc.

Lack of respect for schooling and failure to provide an education-centred home atmosphere may be most important. When the home exudes respect for schooling, children do well. In London, sixteen-year-old immigrant children from India are about twice as likely as white British children to pass five or more state examinations even if born into non-English speaking homes. But those Indian homes tend to be middle-class or upward-aspiring working-class, with parents who value schooling highly and provide a home atmosphere compatible with it. In Toronto, the same thing applies to immigrant children from Nigeria and other West African countries, about three-quarters of whom go right through high school and on to university.

The general culture or "great tradition" of an immigrant group may be exceptionally supportive of education. That was true of Asian and Jewish immigrants in Toronto in the twenties. A 1988 study by University of Michigan psychologist, Harold M. Stevenson, for the William T. Grant Foundation found that American parents of Chinese ancestry maintained much higher than average aspirations and expectations for their children even in difficult economic circumstances. Throughout North America, dropout rates are lower than average for students of oriental ancestry.

The "little tradition" or particular culture of the individual home is even more important than the general culture of an ethnic group. No matter what their great tradition, children whose homes are stable, happy, literate and/or practice great respect for schooling and mental discipline, will usually live up to their ability in school. This tends to hold true even in poverty. Nonetheless, poverty is a powerful negative factor in that it adversely modifies the key factors of heredity and environment. Poor children are often smaller, weaker and sicker due to paternal, maternal, pre-natal and ongoing malnutrition; and their home lives are frequently devastated by intellectual, emotional, psychological, physical and social deprivation that is substantially poverty-driven.

All other factors are minor: shortage of teachers from minority groups; lack of emphasis on minority-group history; middle-class reading materials for working-class children; lack of participation by parents in the present model of schooling; lack of upgrading opportunities in parenting skills for the present generation of parents. All of these minor factors deserve some attention, but improvements will have no immediate or major effect. **The only way to move children of any current generation from low to higher streams is to make schools responsible for optimum nurture that parents fail to supply.**

And the only way to do that is to teach all teens how to be good parents, monitor and assist all pregnancies and early infancies, and provide full-time schooling for all children on a voluntary basis starting no later than age two. Even then, many will have missed two years and nine months of optimum nurture. Age four or five is much too late; it is impossible to undo damage done by inadequate nurture at home. One reason open education never fulfilled its promises was that the concept did not include schooling from age two or earlier.

Early, superior nurture and training will improve performance in an artist, athlete or student, but it will not make a champion or even a high-level performer if genetic potential was not there in the first place. People are equal in rights and dignity, not aptitudes. Some people can jump a lot higher than others, or sing more sweetly, or do more complex gymnastics (physical or mental). **There will always be high, low and middle tracks of children, but when environmental determinants have been eliminated, they will have been streamed by nature not neglect, and there will be fewer children in low streams and more in higher streams.**

Putting everyone in the same stream is not sensible because children then stream themselves into winners, losers, mental dropouts, time monopolizers, time wasters, coasters, drowners, etc. **People who think brighter children help slower children without being**

held back are naive and unintentionally cruel. The more homogeneous a group is, the better people in it are served. Even in a streamed group, there will always be a wide range of abilities, and children will help each other, but they will be close enough in ability to understand and respond to each other.

In the same school, I taught English to a low-stream grade nine (most age fifteen or sixteen), a high-stream grade nine (most fourteen) and a gifted grade seven (most eleven). All used the same grammar book. The low-stream grade nine found it incomprehensible, so I had to make up special lessons, and they were able to master only a bit of the program. The high-stream grade nine was comfortable with the text and the program as long as it was dished up in sequence and spoon fed a little at a time. The gifted grade seven already knew most of the grammar but to make sure of it, students took turns running occasional grammar review seminars using the text but in no particular sequence and covering a wide range in every seminar; the class spent only about an eighth of the time taken by the grade nine classes.

Differences in the three classes were just as pronounced in literature, history and geography. The gifted grade seven was evaluated on criteria usually used only at senior high or college. It would have been inconceivable to teach even the high-stream grade nine with the gifted grade seven. Imagine the carnage if middle- and low-stream grade seven students had been mixed with the gifted grade seven. Open education insisted upon that kind of carnage, and that is another reason it failed.

Some activities should be mixed all the time: meals, bussing, relaxing, student government, etc. Many activities should be mixed some of the time: assemblies, games, recreation, clubs, field trips, charity drives, community activities, special events, some arts programs, peer coaching, etc. But in general, mainstreaming or single streaming of school programs is a hoax. It is professionally irresponsible for teachers to participate in such a lie.

In current-model schools, sensible, intentional streaming should be based on important criteria: intelligence, creativity, performance, potential, interest, etc. It should not be based on cultural criteria: ethnicity, manners, obedience, conformity, cleanliness, etc. Presently, too much intentional streaming is done on trivial, harmful or divisive criteria: race, religion, wealth, class, athletic ability, etc. The elite private and religious-school industry is based on them, and so are state school systems in some countries.

Though children always arrive at school pre-streamed by nature and upbringing, it takes time to assess differences. Intentional streaming is a slow and considered process. Increasingly, during and after infancy, the new-model school must provide for, facilitate, and recommend streaming, but children must be the prime movers. They (or in the case of very young children, their advocates) must always choose their own home rooms (living rooms); since home rooms vary in intensity, children stream themselves by choosing.

A child may choose too high a stream for home room, for an elective or for a project. If reach exceeds grasp and unreasonable stress develops, teachers and advocates must help to right matters with a minimum of fuss (see chapter 23). Pushy parents are likely to be the cause of pressure problems and the biggest roadblock to adjusting streams. Children usually self-correct placement if given a chance. The least likely to self-correct are occasional, lazy underachievers who have grown used to lounging along effortlessly in low streams disguising their ability to do high-level work. But even they respond to careful mentoring.

Much is made of the false issue of dead-ending students. The worry is that students who stream themselves out of algebra may be ineligible should they develop latent interest in a career such as architecture which requires mathematics. High schools and colleges should routinely offer make-up courses for every academic pursuit with prerequisites. Since all those who enrol are motivated, the success rate is high and teachers can easily serve more than the usual number of students. Because make-up courses are different from regular schooling, the usual emphasis on process gives way to acquiring skill or knowledge. It can be done quickly using computer programs and other packaged units.

The usual three streams in current high schools may be called: basic, general and advanced; or vocational, ordinary and academic; or terminal, graduation and college entrance; or vocational, technical and academic. Some countries offer only two streams, some five. **Even though all children are different, there are enough similarities that they can best be served in five streams provided the rule applies that individual needs prevail over stream limitations.**

Along with the usual three steams, there should be two special steams, one for children with significant physical and mental learning handicaps and one for very gifted children. Some in the handicapped category may be intellectually very capable and will cross back and forth among streams according to need. It is possible to excel at a high-level program from a stretcher or wheelchair, or without hearing or sight or limbs.

But many of the handicapped have learning disabilities (neurological dysfunctions that interfere with the brain's ability to process information). They require specialized teaching all or some of the time. In the U.S. about eleven percent of children are identified as handicapped and provided with special education, usually within regular schools. The percentage in any country could go much higher depending on criteria used to define handicaps. Probably, at least fifteen percent of children should be so identified and served (see special education in chapter 18).

Four to five percent of children are so intellectually gifted that for most purposes, in the present model of schooling, they can only be properly served individually or in groups separately streamed. Many schools are too inflexible to make those provisions, so the most gifted are often among the worst served. When the model of schooling is sensibly changed, the exceptionally gifted will spend some classroom time with people near their own age in home rooms (living rooms) but will also take optional credit programs with much older students and also do high-level individual or group-planned projects for credit.

Schools use I.Q. and aptitude tests to identify gifted students, but such tests are not perfect; they may be culturally biased and so fail to serve females or children from some cultural or socio-economic backgrounds. Tests are only a tool and only useful if testers are skillful. Equally important in identifying the gifted is daily observation of characteristics, many evident from infancy: long attention span, exceptional curiosity, early and extensive vocabulary, superior generation and manipulation of ideas, non-conformity, adaptability, insight, organizational ability, wide general knowledge, etc. They are good at solving problems, redefining old concepts and identifying new and critical questions. They tend to be opinionated, articulate, imaginative, aware of social issues, etc. And they usually have exceptional abilities in reading, writing and mathematics.

Many jurisdictions have neither the array of curriculum nor the range of teaching styles necessary to serve the five streams. Best served in Western countries are the handicapped and the high (but not gifted) academic streams. The best teaching in a school is likely to be in special education classes for the learning disabled. The reason for this remarkable development is that there was no entrenched tradition to overcome. The handicapped used to be largely dismissed as ineducable. When a more humane society welcomed them into schools, traditional curriculum and teaching methods didn't work, so new and effective ones were invented.

The high (but not gifted) stream is fairly well served because students in it are the ones for whom the present model of schooling was developed. Most are docile, conformist and motivated. They are "academic." If the measure of success is data accumulation for short-term retention, they are successful. Most learn literacy and other skills without much difficulty. Abstractions and rote memorization come fairly easily. They are quick studies. Teachers talk; they listen. There is mutual understanding. And why not? As children, most teachers were themselves members of the high (but not gifted) stream.

Gifted, middle and low streams are usually poorly served. Many people, teachers included, delude themselves that the gifted can be served by piling on more of the same things the high stream does. In fact, they need less of those things. What they need is flights into realms of intellectual inquiry and creativity that most teachers never enter.

People are also wrong to think that middle and low streams can be served by diluting high stream curriculum and methods, or that specific job training disguised in the rhetoric of vocational education or co-op education is a suitable substitute for school curriculum (see job training in Chapter 10).

Aside from a few hands-on programs, there is not much recognition of different learning styles in any of the streams. Teachers, especially in high schools, are likely to be out of their element dealing with middle and low streams. Few schools have developed curriculum or teaching styles for run-of-the-mill children who are not very academic, who are often slow to learn literacy and other skills, who are just-plain-folks. Even attempted modifications such as open education, which worked fairly well for brighter children, failed ordinary children because separate, direct and rigorous skill-building was not part of the philosophy.

A large part of the reason high schools have few adequate programs for just-plain-folks is that the general public wants it that way. Whenever schools try to develop appropriate programs other than those leading to university, the public calls them Mickey Mouse or complains that they are not specific job-training programs. **The public has yet to accept two facts: that most children will not go to university but can still be well educated at high school; and that high schools are not for job training.** The public would quickly accept those two facts if high schools would stop turning out functional illiterates.

Because the high, university-bound stream can read, write, speak, listen and cipher better than the middle and low streams, the public assumes they get that way because they take physics, calculus and especially Shakespeare. And that all children would get that way if they too took lots of physics, calculus and Shakespeare. The truth is that most children learn literacy and other skills by being directly and specifically taught those skills. It has nothing to do with Shakespeare or any traditional "subject." What we have to do is teach all of the just-plain-folks in middle and low streams to read, write, speak, listen and cipher and the public will get off our backs about force-feeding physics and Shakespeare to everyone. They will let us develop curriculum and teaching styles suited to middle and low streams.

The present model of schooling is resistant to changes that would eliminate illiteracy. Most children in low and middle streams of all high schools are in some degree illiterate and will remain that way throughout school, thus foiling occasional efforts of teachers, administrators and teacher trainers to improve curriculum and teaching styles. Computers hold the only great promise that is cost effective for meeting the needs of children with widely differing learning styles in the middle and lower ability groups. But only if schools are fully computerized. The present model of schooling is incompatible with the student-driven nature of computers; it recoils protectively from the electronic interloper.

The current model is so inflexible that it locks children into streams. Many children need to work in two or more streams concurrently because they have abilities or inabilities that cross stream boundaries. Some children need to change streams totally. Immigrant children need to spend a lot of time initially in basic-level study of the new language but may quickly leap into high level mathematics, and some may eventually belong in the gifted stream completely. Instead, they are likely to be locked into the lowest stream because their language needs are never met and especially because of administrative inflexibility.

Schools are so conditioned to the lockstep grade mentality that they can't be fluid when it comes to streaming. Administrators know how to manage frozen grades and frozen streams but have not learned to manage free flow. Administrative paralysis killed continuous progress and is strangling sensible streaming. Teachers are so used to rigidity in the present model that they make academic tracks into ruts by expecting children to keep on matching their present tracks even when mismatch is evident.

Most research and criticism on streaming/tracking are of limited value because researchers and commentators usually assume the present model of schooling is permanent. When they attack streaming as a trap they are really attacking the present model of schooling. **Sensible streaming facilitates movement from stream to stream and never inhibits it.** There is no reason why anybody should be locked into a stream, no reason why anyone should be forced to make irrevocable career choices while still a child. That form of child abuse has nothing to do with streaming and everything to do with administrative rigor mortis. And even if the present model of schooling could magically activate its rigid administrators, it accepts children too late and gives teachers only a fraction of the time it would take to overcome deficits brought from home.

It is the current model of schooling and the parody of sensible streaming spawned by that morbid model that contributes to high dropout rates, not streaming per se. Sensible streaming into fairly homogeneous classes is nothing more or less than a group expression of individualized education, and that would never contribute to the complex of conditions that causes dropouts.

CHAPTER 22

NEW-MODEL SCHOOLS

Running through much of the advice being offered to Mr. Bush is the theme that if the United States is to compete successfully in the emerging global economy, its educational system must not only be improved but altered in fundamental ways.

— Edward B. Fiske, *New York Times*, Feb. 1, 1989.

Schools shortchanging youth of Canada (Prime Minister) Mulroney says.

— Main front page headline, *Toronto Star*, Aug. 26, 1989.

Nothing worth doing is completed in our lifetime; therefore, we must be saved by hope.

— Reinhold Niebuhr

Classroom and related specific aspects of a new model of schooling are outlined in these closing chapters. They remain substantially as redrafted in 1971 following reaction to the first published version, "Kids Deserve a Natural Hi" in the December 1970 edition of *Orbit*, a publication of The Ontario Institute for Studies in Education. Before that, an early version of the school administration aspect (chapter 19) was published in the *Phi Delta Kappan* in November 1959 under the title, "Are Principals Obsolete?" Several aspects of the model were drafted while I was in teacher training.

In September 1952, I arrived back at the last moment from hard labour building an oil pipe line through the Rocky Mountains. The year of teacher training I entered proved tougher than the summer job. Not that the work was hard. Courses were so boring that I wrote a novel, read still more of the literature of education and began this book. I also spent more than required time in schools observing and teaching everything from the start of elementary school to the end of high school.

Going from an elementary school one day to a high school the next, I felt like a peddler bringing news across the wilderness. Schools might be a block apart, but the gulf between was and is vast. John Dewey published *The School And Society* in 1899; he wrote, "they (the different parts of the school system) have never yet been welded into one complete whole." A century later, the rift still makes separate solitudes of elementary and secondary teachers, isolates ages and generations, makes caring practices of interdependence impossible, fragments the learning continuum, reinforces a model of childhood that locks children into preconceived slots, and prescribes the artificial separation of school and society by sanctifying a similar separation within schooling.

The power of separation dogma is evident in North America as high priests of various factions further dismember the corpus of schooling to make early childhood education (daycare) a third consecrated bleeding stump. An important thing my model of schooling does is meld the butchered parts into a healthy whole. Any model that is to resolve the education mess must do that. Open education didn't so it failed.

Another rift that must be healed is that between student and teacher. Some of us recall one teacher with whom we had close rapport. A few people recall two or three. Many recall none because there were none. When the chasm is conquered, the bridge is golden and the passage is to paradise. For a child, it is to be one of a million faceless troops marching past Alexander the Great, when, inexplicably, the general halts the parade, descends from the reviewing throne, sweeps through the parting masses, stops directly in front of you and whispers, "You are special. We are friends. Take my hand."

On the school battlefield, more often than not, it is the soldier who seeks out the general. Usually it is an unconscious advance born of a lucky child's outgoing personality and secure self-image. Sometimes it is calculated. Either way it is beautiful. When it is the teacher who makes the move, it may be done consciously or unconsciously. Either way, it is beautiful. Bonding is always beautiful. Two people cross a barrier onto a higher plateau. If there were time, good teachers could eventually cross that barrier with every student, one by one. But there is no time, so teachers cross with the fortunate few.

The model of schooling is to blame. It pretends that a teacher dispensing data to 30, 60 or 160 students, while constantly hacking at a jungle of administrivia and mired in meetings, can establish and maintain a close relationship with all those students while on the run in an artificially short working day, week and year. That monumental lie is at the heart of the education mess. Unlike open education and all other partial concepts, the model of schooling I am proposing guarantees a close relationship between student and teacher throughout schooling.

The new model could be stuffed into existing schools. But current school architecture is an insult to children no matter what model it houses. There was a time when school buildings shared with churches, town halls and a few other civic structures, the status of community monuments. Some artistry was lavished upon exteriors. But a monument was a monument was a monument. And the imperatives of taste were apt to yield up fortresses differentiated only by accouterments such as spires, columns or cupolas. Inside, everything from train stations to museums had a mausoleum aura. Schools were no more geared to the needs of children than were customs houses or Carnegie libraries.

That era ended with the great depression, and since the Second World War, school architecture has worsened. Many of the old monuments have deteriorated to the point of dereliction though still in use. Those torn down have usually been replaced with undistinguished factories marginally modified to process children instead of widgets. There are, in wealthy countries, permanent schools of unadorned corrugated metal and guy wires or plywood or cinder block. To North American architects, concrete block is the ubiquitous amino acid of pedagogic protein.

Then there are portables. Some are minimally moveable metal monstrosities resembling giant sardine cans or discarded railway cars. Others look like Mechano set mutations grown out of control and seemingly in possession of their own cranes so they can invade schoolyards at will under cover of night. There are wooden shacks, said to be temporary, which never move once dumped behind a school. All are instant pedagogic slums that would not be tolerated for adult occupancy except perhaps by prisoners of war.

Toward the upper end of the school scale are cookie-cutter blockhouses with stock arrangements of interior boxes disguised with primary colors and carpet. This later-day trompe-l'oeil fools even architecture critics. The pen, like the eye, is grateful for any morsel of architectural relief and thrills unabashedly at a simple course of different colored brick running bravely through the wasteland wall of yet another nouveau warehouse.

In every office building and shopping mall we tend the air. In art galleries we are meticulous about it. But fetid air is good enough for galleries in which we stow our most beautiful creations, our children. They are required by law to inhabit premises that are rarely air-conditioned, never humidified, routinely overheated or underheated, poorly ventilated and often polluted. Germs and fungi thrive. Children wilt.

Little in school program and nothing in school architecture acknowledges school as the social centre for student life. Instead, program and architecture conspire to force children into furtive and frenzied social interaction in corridors. Before, between and after classes they mingle madly around lockers, under time constraints and restrictive regulations that would ulcerate seasoned business executives. The other social-interaction possibility is a bolted lunch (thirty minutes is considered adequate, forty ample and fifty excessive) in a cafeteria that owes much of its ambience to prison prototypes. Open education and all its later-day variants failed to deal with architecture but better buildings are essential to any new model of schooling.

In the classroom aspect of my proposed model, a kind of teacher that has never before existed is essential. **Hi** (hies) stands for **human interactor**. I invented a name to describe the role and another name to describe the room in which it is played out. It is not a classroom since "classes" are rarely "taught" there except in early elementary years. It is a **living room**.

A school living room, like a home living room, is the magnet that draws everyone back constantly and just as readily releases them again to experience the outside world. All other rooms in a house, as in the new model school, facilitate, supplement and enhance individual and group activities of the living room. For each hi and his/her assistants and up to thirty students, their living room is the centre of existence. All other rooms and personnel are supportive.

Millennium seems a suitable name for a new-model school: it bespeaks a happier educational era and is due as we begin the third millennium. Millennium has 1500 day students (2000 counting five hundred full and part-time adults). But much smaller or larger would be possible. In his book, *A Place Called School* (New York: McGraw-Hill, 1983), John Goodlad says the maximum number of children in a primary school should be four hundred, in the rest of elementary school another four hundred, and in high school eight hundred: a total of sixteen hundred. But Goodlad would prefer a total of twelve hundred. He has the numbers about right, though he is wrong in cleaving to fragmentation conventions of the present model.

About five hundred Millennium children are **juniors (infants)** six and under; those up to and including age three are **junior A's**; those four, five and six are **junior B's**. About five hundred are **intermediates (pre-teens)** seven through twelve; those seven, eight and nine are **intermediate A's**; those ten, eleven and twelve are **intermediate B's**. Another five hundred are **seniors (teens)** thirteen through eighteen; those thirteen, fourteen and fifteen are **senior A's**; those sixteen, seventeen and eighteen are **senior B's**.

These are natural divisions of childhood, and all schools should recognize them for organizational purposes always providing that **chronological age must never be a trap for individuals who for any reason or in any way need to be free of arbitrary limitations**. A beginning junior A child ordinarily remains with the same hi through age three and then goes to another hi through age six and so on. By high school graduation, a child has usually experienced six hies; however, students may move from one living room to another more or less often for several reasons.

Moving sideways or upward happens as need arises. One at a time, any day of the year, the ten or so oldest students in a living room move upward. They are replaced just as intermittently, by ten or so moving up from a lower level. It is no big deal because **individual students continue with their own obligatory skills programs** (reading, writing, speaking, listening, ciphering, etc. — see chapter 21) **and optional programs** (electives for credit) **no matter which living room they are in**; and the different treatment of other basic, obligatory programs (current affairs, international understanding, children's rights, student government, etc. — see chapter 21) in different living rooms is significant only in terms of process, not sacred content or academic consequence. In such living room activities, full participation in the process is what counts — serious exploration instead of mindless memorization.

If a student wants to stay an extra year with a particular hi, that is possible. It is discussed. If a younger student seems suited to be with a hi whose other students are older, that is possible. It is discussed. No matter which living rooms they are in, all students experience the same basic obligatory programs and have the same options for credit available, so each one may as well be in a milieu which will provide the richest possible process. Being in the most compatible living room definitely enriches process.

Some gifted students prefer to be in living rooms with older students while others equally gifted prefer to stay in living rooms with their own age group but work at their own ability level in some obligatory programs and all options for credit. In either setting, gifted students are free at any age to accumulate all the credits needed for university and can enter whenever they and the university of their choice decide the time is right.

Even though most teenage students at Millennium spend a lot of time on options for credit, most graduate at seventeen. Those who remain at eighteen do so voluntarily to acquire additional optional credits or to pursue in-depth learning interests. The optional final year has high status and is seen by school, universities and public as one of the best choices open to graduates. Very few who remain at eighteen are there because they are still deficient in basic skills or have not yet fulfilled obligations for graduation.

Students with learning disabilities, like all students, work on fully-individualized basic skills programs no matter which living room they are in. They have the same access to optional programs for credit as do all other students. Most such students spend more time than usual with specialized skills tutors on the Millennium faculty. All hies have training in special education for learning disabilities and other handicaps. A few hies at each level have a special interest in learning disabilities and may attract learning disabled students because their living rooms are attuned to learning disabilities. But some learning-disabled or physically-handicapped students choose their hies on other criteria.

Students too young to choose hies are assigned to living rooms by placement committees in consultation with appropriate hies. Willing parents are always temporary members of placement committees dealing with their children; each child participates fully in all meetings dealing with his/her own placement. The committee places students of any age who express no particular preference, and it resolves placement problems.

While much attention is paid to making sure students and hies with similar talents and interests are brought together, the most important consideration is more fundamental: do they like each other? **If either hi or student is doubtful about compatibility, either can honorably decline sharing a living room or can opt for a trial**

period of up to two months. The trial also tells both student and hi whether the style and character of a living room is suited to the student's style and character. Trials usually satisfy student and hi whether the outcome is that the student stays or moves.

Very young children spend most of the day in the living room but, increasingly as they grow older, all students also use other rooms. The living room is home base and every student keeps returning to it (or checking in by phone or computer when on learning missions outside the school). Hies know when and why students leave the living room — usually to attend compulsory or optional programs in other rooms. Most such courses are planned and scheduled months and years in advance, so students and hies always know times and prerequisites. Students enrol by computer.

Lectures may be given to three hundred students where that is desirable. Some teachers, in love with a subject and gifted as performers make superlative **lecturers**. They may be no good at working with small groups or individuals, but on stage, they shine. Millennium shares several lecturers with other schools. The history lecturer supplements the history department in five schools. Some lecturers work for several school boards, sometimes in different states and countries, and make presentations by satellite.

Teachers in charge of non-living room programs such as history or English literature, are called **consultants**. There are many more con-sultants than lecturers. Instead of working with a hundred or three hundred students at a time as lecturers do, consultants work with smaller groups of twenty to forty students. Many Millennium consul-tants were formerly subject specialists in old-model schools and have been retrained to use different teaching methods. They still make occasional presentations (teach lessons), but students book into their programs to be active rather than passive. Most often, students conduct their own seminars and make group or individual presentations or else use computer learning materials while consultants act as managers.

Most courses managed by consultants are available on videotape or laser disks, and for most subjects, computer data bases are available along with computer programs to guide students through various uses of them. Individual students can simulate The Congress of Vienna and then routinely test themselves on whatever facts, concepts or conclusions the curriculum consecrates. Computer materials are consistent with curriculum guidelines issued by the government and the school board. Guidelines are available to students and teachers via computer. Students refer to them to prove their proposed projects fulfill requirements.

Still other subject- and skill-centred teachers deal with very small groups or, more likely, individuals, in lab settings doing skill-development and remedial work. They are expert **tutors** who identify and treat specific learning problems. Students book individual time with tutors or may be scheduled at the same time as a few other people sharing a particular need.

Lecturers and tutors (sometimes consultants) may be invited to living rooms. If a number of students from the same living room are working at the same program at the same time, it makes sense to bring a specialist to them rather than take them to a specialist. An itinerant story teller (lecturer) serving several schools may visit a junior A or junior B living room, but usually some children from several living rooms would go to a large room to hear the story.

The names lecturer, consultant and tutor all bring with them connotations from other levels of education and other industries. It might be better to clean the slate by inventing new names. I have used known names precisely because most of the connotations they bring with them are applicable to the new job descriptions. Whatever names are chosen must be standard worldwide in the interest of good communication. Naming should be done by an international commission.

All hies must be full-time staff members, but lecturers, consultants and tutors may work part-time; however, all part-time faculty maintain the same schedules for long periods so students know exactly when and where each will be available.

When students book by computer into compulsory and optional programs outside the living room, their hies enter approval. And hies use computers to monitor progress of students in every outside activity.

Since students work on word processors, every essay, speech, research report, memo, exercise and note from every program in the school is readily available to hies. So are test results and comments by consultants, tutors and others including staff at the health, library/resource, and fitness/recreation centres. If information is privileged, access is limited to the hi, the student and the person who entered it.

While consultants and tutors monitor progress of students in their own programs, it is hies who are responsible for monitoring **whole** students. A hi constantly evaluates **all** of a student's learning activities in consultation with that student and with appropriate consultants and tutors. Nearly everything students do involves some consultation with their hies. But the intention is to encourage self-propulsion. Students usually come and go on their own but always note their destinations and progress on the computer. Even without that backup mechanism, hies **know** what is going on with each of their students. To **know** their students is the essence of their activity. Contrast that with the essence of teacher activity in old-fashioned schools (circa 1992): to know the content of courses; to tell the content (peddle data); to cover courses; to test for transfer of content from teacher to student for short-term retention; to be concerned with the performance of students only in one's own subjects and classroom.

At junior and intermediate levels, hies build skills necessary for self-propulsion, and to that end they lead and direct groups and individuals as required. In this limited aspect, they resemble open education teachers with the important difference that hies are much more concerned with direct teaching and testing of skills. But they have the equally essential responsibility of protecting and enhancing natural curiosity and initiative. **Hies encourage and *train* children to practice and assume all classroom roles** including teaching roles in a way and to an extent that open education teachers never did.

Children must be taught to chair groups, participate in disciplined and purposeful discussions, evaluate group process, make oral presentations of many kinds, teach groups by asking questions, coach each other, make decisions, read curriculum requirements and plan activities to meet those requirements, schedule classroom activities, etc. These skills and many more are just as necessary as other required skills: reading, writing, speaking, listening, researching, using computers, ciphering, problem solving, etc. Hies-in-training for junior and inter-mediate levels are specifically taught how to develop all these skills.

By the intermediate B level (ages ten, eleven and twelve), rarely does a hi take over leadership of a group. Students lead their own large and small groups and make most presentations (teach most "lessons") whether to the entire class or to sub-groups. In typical schools, teachers talk eighty percent of the time. At Millennium, students talk eighty percent of the time. Hies or their assistants sit-in on group activities and participate inconspicuously to improve performance, process and group evaluation.

Oral evaluation by groups (of presentations by individuals or groups) is always done, always rigorous, always sophisticated; and individuals regularly evaluate their own work in progress in consultation with hies or their assistants. A lot of the time, hies are in consultation with individual students.

Though overall organization of living room activities is their respon-sibility, hies endeavour to transfer even the most complex organization to students. Hies step in only but always when needed. Organization is complex because each student has an individual program and there are about twenty in junior, twenty-five in intermediate and thirty in senior living rooms. Every student is involved in several individual as well as group activities all in some stage of progress within and beyond the living room. Individual learning and initiative are as important as cooperative learning and initiative; they are interwoven. All of this activity is constantly updated on the computer and on various timetables and charts on the walls. Since every modification in scheduling affects everybody, the frequent need for rescheduling is an ever-unfolding experience in organization for every student. Everyone is learning to live with change.

A team made up of the hi, his paid assistant and three students is in charge of scheduling. By the senior A level (ages thirteen, fourteen and fifteen), the three students pretty well run the show with occasional consultation to find out from staff about changes or additions they have identified. Students serve three weeks on the scheduling team. Each week one student cycles onto the team and one off. The middle-week student chairs. The scheduling team is really the curriculum team because it has to constantly check curriculum guidelines and course outlines on the computer for all required programs done in the living room and keep before the whole group the curriculum goals, topics, themes and concepts that lie ahead so they can be worked into future projects and presentations through group planning.

Nearly all group and individual activities within the living room are student-generated to fulfill obligatory requirements as well as personal interests. **Programs that must be handled in every living room (along with basic skills and literacies) are international understanding, student government, social service, children's rights, values (or ethics), and current affairs. Hies are also responsible for most other obligatory activities — almost all in the case of hies with junior living rooms — but some are assigned to consultants in other rooms. Nothing is left to chance.**

Hies may handle optional credits that individual students seek through contracting for personal-interest projects such as major research, creative activity or part-time jobs, though any of these could be supervised by an appropriate consultant. A music consultant would probably supervise a student whose project for credit is to write a sonata; however, a hi with an interest in music could do it.

Hies are trained to be front-line developers and monitors of language skills and literacies. Since living room activities use all skills, much growth is an adjunct of daily life. Because the pursuit of excellence is everybody's business, performance in basic skills tends to be at a high level. If a hi notices a student is weak in reading, organizing, or any other skill or literacy, or if frequent, checkup testing reveals a weakness, the hi or an assistant immediately does specific individual teaching. If the weakness persists, the student is booked into a remedial program with a tutor, which takes precedence over all other activities (except health and student government) until performance is adequate. At all levels, failsafe remedial work in all skills is done outside the living room, in labs, by tutors.

A child who is, for a short or long period, devoting nearly all time to getting up to standard in one or more skills or literacies, can still participate in some living room activities: group contributions of that child are geared specifically to improving weaknesses.

Hies routinely administer tests (reading, writing, listening, ciphering, cultural literacy, etc.), and even more often, individual students test themselves using computerized tests. Content from any source (subject, program) considered essential for any literacy will show up on such tests. So will content or skills considered cumulative and necessary for further obligatory programs. There are no examinations in living rooms. Tutors also use tests but not examinations. However, consultants in charge of options for credit may use examinations and are required to do so where an examination is part of the secs (standard evaluation criteria and strategies) specified by government for a particular program.

Talents and interests of a hi give individuality to a living room. A hi who is an amateur ornithologist might attract some students with a passion for birds: birds of a feather flock together. Occasionally, ornithology might influence individual or group activities; however, it would probably be a low-key presence. Aerospace, on the other hand, could be sufficiently appealing that a hi who is an enthusiast might attract enough mavens to keep aerospace permanently a part of life in the living room. Certainly, students pursuing optional credits through individual initiatives in aerospace would find it a congenial place. But not every student in such a living room would need to have a passion for aerospace.

A hi famous for a specialty can never allow it to monopolize; rather, it must enhance required curriculum. Millennium has a hi who played major-league football and semi-pro hockey and is widely known as an occasional commentator on locally televised games. His living room attracts athletes and the room vibrates with athletic excitement, but that is just a special aura in which the usual work happens.

Hies are trained to understand learning styles and living room activities reflect all styles. That is a requirement. Nonetheless, a hi may become known for exceptional talent in one or two learning styles and may attract children with a leaning to those styles. A hi whose living room constantly generates outstanding hands-on activities will be noticed by hands-on learners. Students with a gift for abstract thinking will hear of living rooms and hies that thrive on intellectual ideas.

All **hies must be outstanding generalists**. The best hies blend a number of disciplines within their obligatory programs and special interests. Borders between traditional subjects are blurring and will eventually disappear. **Instead of being sacred packages of content, programs are focal points for explorations that include aspects of many traditional subject disciplines.** Except for basic skills and literacy programs and some options, most program names are being used for a few years as a transitional comfort device to indicate bases to be touched. Eventually, at Millennium, most living room activity will be characterized simply as **exploration** because the bases to be touched will be universally understood elements of daily process in schools.

Most hies are bilingual. If not, at least one paid assistant and usually one volunteer are fluent in the main second language. Junior living rooms are conducted in two languages so students are bilingual by the time they reach intermediate. Thereafter, living room activities may occur in either language and care is taken to make sure both are used. Any student not fluent in the second language when entering intermediate (age seven) begins a remedial and developmental program, but this is seldom necessary since very young children become bilingual easily and naturally.

A living room at Millennium has a hi, one paid assistant (two in junior rooms), two trained volunteers and, sometimes, a student teacher serving an apprenticeship of six months. Millennium trains its own volunteers.

A typical hi is Steve Harris, a forty-two-year-old widower with two children, Angela sixteen and Mike thirteen. Both children attend Millennium, but neither has chosen their father's living room. Angela prefers hies with a scientific bent. Mike recently moved from an intermediate B to a senior A living room. He chose a hi who shares his interest in art.

Before his wife died of cancer three years ago, Harris lived in a smartly renovated old house a few blocks from school in the middle-class part of the mixed Millennium community. Marie ran a dress shop. When she died, the part-time housekeeper came more often, but after a year of grieving, Steve and the children agreed they would rather live in residence. For two years, Steve has been a staff resident. He likes it and is good at it.

Twenty years ago, when Harris graduated, Millennium didn't exist and he was trained for old-type schools, the kind he attended on the Niagara frontier where his father was an alcoholic car salesman and his mother an efficient housekeeper and tireless church worker. Steve took a degree in political science with arts minors. As an undergraduate he wrote for student publications — profiles and essays, generally conservative but a bit humorous — on political personalities and topics. Later he ventured into short fiction, plays and scripts for student films and TV.

Steve considered journalism, advertising, marketing, television and law but felt drawn to teaching and decided to try combining it with writing. He taught English and history several years at Featherstone Memorial High, a school that tried open education and failed, in part because it did not retrain teachers. When he heard Millennium was opening, he knew he was meant to be a hi and was accepted into the special one-year/two-summer hi-training course for experienced teachers. Teaching turned out to be so consuming that he seldom writes other than school-related material: articles for teacher journals; occasional scripts for school/community television; book reviews for the school literary magazine — and he serves as consultant to the magazine's editorial board. Since Marie died, he has been working on a novel when grieving grips him, especially late at night.

When a hi is male, his paid assistant is usually female and vice versa. Steve Harris is not fluent in French, the second language at Millennium, so his assistant, Anne Dubois was hired partly for her French. She is a qualified assistant, having completed a two-year, post-high school training course at a community college. Anne grew up in Quebec where her father worked on a factory assembly line and her mother was a kindergarten teacher. She is twenty-six and married to a young man who imports pottery from Mexico. With six years experience as a living room assistant, Anne is taking university courses at night, largely for her own growth, but she might decide to qualify as a hi by completing a degree and taking a hi training course abbreviated in recognition of her experience.

Anne writes poems and sometimes sets them to music which she plays on a guitar. Her poems ring with the joy of life. She likes colorful blouses with slacks accompanied one day by spike heels and the next by walking shoes. It depends on her mood and agenda. Steve Harris chose Anne over others for her outgoing nature and flair. He feels it balances his own shyness and tailored suits. He also likes and shares her sense of humour. Anne's bubbling laugh is a characteristic of Steve's living room.

One full-time volunteer is Major Afleck who is seventy-eight. The Major is very British, a long sojourn in the colonies notwithstanding. As a young man, he served with General Montgomery at El Alamein and has total recall, possibly embellished, of that and other battles of the Second World War. But he also likes to talk about world affairs and gardening. He wears a Montgomery beret and polished boots. He calls boys chaps and girls young ladies. They call him the Major and everybody adores him. Last winter when he sprained his ankle, students took turns cleaning his "digs" and preparing his meals, and they pushed him to school in a wheelchair till he could walk. Since then, the Major has moved into residence as a resident volunteer.

The other full-time volunteer is Mrs. Chin. Nobody knows her first name because she always introduces herself as Mrs. Chin. And nobody knows her age because she always says, "Oh, too old. So much old, I forget." In fact, her name is Kam-Ping and she is forty-eight. Mrs. Chin was born in Hong Kong. Her children are working or in university and her husband is a busy restaurant manager, having worked his way up from dishwasher. Three years ago, Mrs. Chin got tired of playing mah jong and enrolled in the training course for volunteers. Steve was impressed with her quick mind and skillful attention to detail as secretary of her class of trainees. At Steve's suggestion, Mrs. Chin also took computer courses at Millennium and now does all of the administrative computer work in Steve's living room and most of his secretarial work. Mrs. Chin speaks Cantonese and Mandarin which is useful since Steve has five students of Chinese descent, and the community is twelve percent Chinese. Mrs. Chin sometimes leaves the living room to help with translation at the health centre or the library/resource centre when people from the Chinese community need her.

There are over two hundred community adults in the part-time volunteer pool. Five are well known to Harris and he calls one or more as needed. He checks the computer listing for special expertise. There is also a pool of volunteer students, particularly senior B students, who may be called upon for duties anywhere in Millennium. Usually, they serve in junior living rooms or in the health, library/resource or fitness/recreation centres. All intermediate and senior students are trained as study coaches for their own age group and for younger students and are expected to spend some time coaching. They also take turns reading aloud to junior children at school, after school, evenings and weekends.

Steve's apprenticing hi is Carla Contini who is twenty-five and has a degree in English Literature and a doctorate in teaching. Had she chosen to be a consultant in English Literature, she would have taken a consultant training course instead of a hi training course (both two years and three summers long). Because her greatest interest is in writing skills (and English Literature deals instead with appreciation and criticism), Carla could have chosen to be a creative writing consultant or tutor and taken consultant or tutor training. Or she could have chosen to train as a lecturer. But she feels her interest in creative writing should be used as a distinctive feature for her own living room in a career as a hi.

Carla was matched by computer with Steve Harris for her apprenticeship. Had either one disagreed, whether initially or after the first month, either could have asked for a change; however, both are pleased. All apprentice hies must take responsibility for one or more immigrant families in the community. Carla has three families, all of whom have one child in Steve's living room. Carla has taken all their problems on her own shoulders. Some mornings her eyes are circled beneath from lack of sleep. Steve is helping her turn some of the work over to volunteers under her supervision. Delegation is an important part of a hi's expertise.

Though students are required to spend only seven hours a day in school, many stay longer. They also attend more than the required five-day week and 220-day year; most spend some evening and weekend time at school and often continue into vacation periods. Millennium is always open. Intermediate and senior living rooms are available evenings, weekends and vacations with volunteers monitoring. Students may be working on group projects but are just as likely to be at school individually to use equipment.

Junior living rooms are also available evenings, weekends and holidays but are supervised by paid assistants supplemented by volunteers. Paid junior-level assistants are graduates of two or three-year courses in early childhood education at community colleges. Hies for the junior level are university graduates whose hi training is specific to early childhood. While it is unlikely that a hi at the junior, or any level, would be routinely on duty evenings or weekends, it is possible if special circumstances exist. And it is even more likely that intermediate and senior hies, like their students, will sometimes be in their living rooms voluntarily weekends and evenings. Half a dozen students in a living room on a Saturday is not unusual and sometimes there are a dozen. It is a nice place to be. And people have things to do there.

Hies, other full-time faculty and paid assistants, as well as students, are required to be on the job seven hours a day, five days a week, 220 days a year. Hies are in their living rooms from 8:30 a.m. till 4:30 p.m. with an hour off for lunch. Paid assistants have the same hours but take lunch at a different time. Full-time volunteers usually work the same hours while part-time volunteers usually supervise earlier and later hours; however, hies and their full-time volunteers may vary arrangements. In Steve Harris' living room, Major Afleck opens up at 6 a.m. because he likes to. Since he lives in residence, he can easily go for a nap during the day and then return, so he usually spends more than seven hours on the job.

The size, layout and furnishings of a living room depend upon age. Junior A living rooms have the amenities of a nursery for infants-in-arms and toddlers. Junior B children of four, five and six, have furniture scaled to their needs and all equipment traditional to kindergarten/primary, but they also have most of the tools of learning found in living rooms for older students: computers, printer, telephone, television, film projector, photocopier, etc.

Steve Harris' senior A living room is slightly larger than a traditional classroom. It has individual study carrels along two sides. Each accommodates a student's own notebook computer that stands alone or links to the hi's computer and to the school board computer (which links with similar computers throughout the country and abroad). In one corner is the hi's office. Glass walls provide enough privacy for personal conversations while allowing visual contact with the room. In another corner is a counter for project work, but it also includes a refrigerator, sink and small cooking unit which anyone may use any time. **Millennium takes responsibility for nutrition**.

One wall has a large television screen, small monitors, movie screen, other electronic visual equipment and a variety of writing and charting surfaces. To one side are TV cameras. In front of this media wall, is a low platform (made up of several moveable smaller units) with chairs gathered around. Sometimes students stand on the platform to address a group; other times, they sit around it to hold seminars or assemble materials. Discussion groups may also be formed anywhere in the room because small tables on casters and light chairs are the main furniture.

All perimeter space is designed to accommodate equipment and storage. The computer printer, photocopier, fax and phones slide under a counter and the movie projector is wall-mounted on a swing-out crane. The floor is carpeted and the seating, including a sofa, is upholstered in earthy colors. Books, periodicals and newspapers are everywhere. Upper walls and ceiling are covered with electronic world maps that can be changed, highlighted and manipulated remotely.

Every living room has a solarium full of greenery, flowers and hydroponic vegetables raised by the children. When it gets too full, students take plants home, transplant them outside, or give them to old people. All living rooms are at ground level and each has a small walled garden directly accessible. It is full of plants grown by students as well as bird and squirrel feeders and seating that can be rearranged. Even senior students make good use of solariums and gardens. The window wall is cut low so students can see out when seated indoors. It is considered essential that they have continuous caring contact with plants and animals.

Every living room has one tiny adjoining room with toilet and sink for use by anyone any time. Using it as needed is so much a normal part of life in Steve Harris' living room that nobody pays the slightest attention, even to frequent users such as Major Afleck who has a prostate problem. There are public toilets elsewhere in the building.

Other rooms vary in size from large lecture or audio-visual theatres accommodating three hundred persons to small lab or tutoring rooms serving half a dozen. Some of the latter are cubicled so several tutors can work with students one-to-one at the same time. Rooms for consultants are about the size of old-fashioned classrooms or slightly larger, with easily moveable seating for thirty to fifty learners and electronic equipment similar to living rooms; some have specialized equipment to suit particular programs such as chemistry.

Most rooms are multi-purpose, even those with specialized equipment, because careful design allows equipment to be closed off when the room is in use for unrelated purposes. Most spaces *except living rooms* are used for night school as well as daytime programs.

One staff under one administration serves everyone in the community from infants-in-arms to centenarians. Some adult daytime learners attend full-time, most part-time. They go mainly to consultants and lecturers and are not organized into living rooms, but they visit living rooms for particular events. There is a proposal before Adcom to organize living rooms for interested full-time adult day students. Many adults use Millennium night school rather than the day school. **All courses and all exercise, recreation and cultural programs at night are also open to children and adults who are day students. Nobody who is capable is restricted from pursuing an interest because of age or time of day.**

The school also provides outreach programs in retirement homes, hospitals, jails, and factories and in small satellite facilities such as those for infants in parents' work places. Distance programs for handicapped, house-bound and isolated individuals are provided using school-based computer, radio, television and other technologies. Millennium's flea-powered radio and television stations reach every home and the library/ resource centre lends computers, programs, cassettes, videodiscs, books, etc.

The school makes use of existing learning opportunities off campus and creates new ones. Millennium has an electronics **project centre** at Luna Systems, a nearby telecommunications corporation, and a theatre project centre at Limelight, a local repertory theatre. There are several such centres all using space and expertise provided by industries, businesses, hospitals, associations, services and cultural institutions. Some project centres offer students paid part-time jobs as well as short courses, seminars and tutorials.

Where several students are employed part-time, a project centre is the meeting place for teachers, employers and students arranging and monitoring learning opportunities in generic job skills. The project centre at Bing Burgers provides training in public relations, corporate ethics, advertising, purchasing, costing, accounting, product develop-ment, quality control, franchising, marketing, personnel development and other aspects of business. The project team of students, teachers and Bing representatives that runs the centre also manages a skill-growth profile for every student employed part-time in a Bing outlet.

Regular review of profiles by the project team makes sure each employed student is having an authentic and varied learning experience and that each is being considered for promotions. While meetings of the project team and learning seminars may happen during the school day, actual paid employment of students is largely limited to weekends and vacation periods with occasional late afternoon and evening work a possibility but always under close monitoring by the project team to make sure it doesn't interfere with the working student's school rights and responsibilities.

Some project centres operate continuously, others cyclically, some temporarily. Millennium is negotiating with an association of farmers for a five-year project using paired fields to compare yield and other variables in a study of identical plants grown in the usual chemical manner and by organic methods. The project is an outgrowth of earlier experiments in living-room gardens. In addition to being on the planning and monitoring team, students will work in the fields during vacations and on weekends as part-time employees of farmers. This is a temporary project, but it could become cyclical or continuous if evaluation indicates need.

Millennium also has a liaison person at museums, art galleries, reference libraries, universities, law courts, newspapers, publishers, broadcasters, industries, etc. Individual students work through liaison people to gain access, assistance and involvement. Three exceptional science students, one of them fourteen-years-old, have security clearance to participate weekends in a nuclear research study at the university. The arrangement was made by one student working through the university liaison officer. Initially, she alone was involved, but she introduced the other two and now all three work at the university on individual study projects in nuclear energy which will earn them Millennium optional credits.

Most arrangements made by individual students through liaison people are for more limited missions: to see how the museum finds and restores artifacts (for a project on preserving ethnic heritage in the program on national history); to observe video news editing methods at a television station (for a media literacy report on manipulation of news); to survey estimating and billing procedures at a car body repair shop (for a consumer studies report); to assess outcomes in the court-room when clients are represented by legal aid lawyers as compared with paid lawyers (for a group presentation in the compulsory law program); to interview men and women in a hospital abortion clinic and protesters demonstrating outside (for a report on children's rights).

Also part of the campus complex are a health/social service clinic, a fitness/recreation centre, and a library/resource centre, all adminis-tered by the school but open day and night to serve the community and to help eliminate separation of school from the outside world. The administration area has general offices and offices for Adcom (adminis-trative committee), consultants, tutors, teacher counsellors, the ombudsman and student government. Studios for school/community radio and television stations, and offices for the school daily newspaper and other publications are in the adjacent communications centre. The school cafeteria and cafe are near the health/recreation centre and are open from early morning till late at night and on weekends.

Any hi or other staff member may apply to live in residence. There are always some who are twenty-four-hour teachers and others who are not. There is room for both, in job assignments and on salary scales. Also resident are volunteer adults, usually retired individuals or couples committed for two or more years. Millennium always has a waiting list of exceptional older people ready to take up residence. They appreciate the opportunity to live in a vertically integrated social group. Most take courses while in residence and most act as trained volunteer assistants in school as well as in residences.

Residences are designed with at least one volunteer's and one teacher's apartment, usually small, but some big enough for couples with dependent children. Residences for junior students (under seven) have rooms for additional live-in, volunteer or paid staff and for one or two live-in, intermediate students and two or three senior students. Inter-mediate residences always have two or three live-in senior students.

Major maintenance and cleaning are done by the school (using several students paid the same wage as adult janitors, but employed a maximum of twelve hours per week), but residents do their own routine house-keeping. Main foods are cooked by the school's central kitchen and delivered, but otherwise residents do their own meal preparation and clean-up. Organization and management of all matters (meals, budget, rules, recreation, fitness, projects, excursions, etc.) is done at house meetings conducted by student residents with participation, support and encouragement from adult residents.

When resident students are infants, adult residents or older students advocate on their behalf at house meetings, but even the very young are involved in decision-making. This important requirement is facilitated by having at least two age groups of children (usually three) live in every junior and intermediate residence. Older children serve as models and helpers for younger children. Three hundred students live in twenty-five residences, but there is a waiting list and one new residence is nearing completion — a new concept which continues the Millennium tradition of house-form residences on cul-de-sac streets but accommodates equal numbers of juniors, intermediates and seniors.

Most resident students go home at will for weekends and vacations. But some live in all year, every year. Some are orphans, many are from broken or dysfunctional families, and others are teenagers unable to get along with parents or unhappy at home. A few have parents on overseas assignments. Some are in residence because they consider it an import-ant learning experience. All are there by choice. All appreciate the community prestige that goes with residence.

Most Millennium students, particularly teens, would like to live in residence for at least a term, but space is so limited that those opting to live in just for the rich experience must depend on luck: a few discretionary spaces, usually one in each residence, are reserved for lottery winners. To enter the lottery, one must have achieved a reputation and record as a substantial contributor to the school community.

Millennium was designed and landscaped by architects who studied childhood and schooling as well as architecture. They consulted contin-uously with creative teachers and children. But nearly everything done at Millennium could be approximated using existing buildings sensibly modified: a high school and some feeder schools could be put under one administration; neighborhood houses could be used as residences; part of a hospital could be given to the school as a health clinic; a community recreation facility could be turned over to the school; within existing schools, some rooms could be refurbished as living rooms; schools built as community schools to serve some adult as well as child needs could be turned into new-model schools. In such make-do arrangements, the school would be decentralized throughout the community instead of being advantageously centralized on one campus. Isolation of parts could institutionalize and replicate a fatal flaw of the old model. But that need not happen.

A group of infants could be the start-up population using the first stage of a newly-built, expandable facility. A new group of infants and additional rooms could be added each year until, in fifteen years or so, the first group would be at the senior level. The just-finished campus complex would then be full of children accustomed from infancy to the new model.

There are many roads to Millennium, but they all have one thing in common: they must be fully pre-planned to include **all** ingredients identified in every chapter of this book, not just particulars described in this chapter and classroom practices described in the next. All previous innovations, including open education and mastery learning, faded without significantly improving education because each concept in turn failed to include necessary changes in **all** aspects of schooling. Current innovations such as cooperative learning and promising concepts like "walkabout/challenge education" (Maurice Gibbons in the *Kappan* magazine, May 1984) will fail for the same reason.

CHAPTER 23

MORNING IN MILLENNIUM

The artists of our era are not so much describing the world as creating a new one.

— William Irwin Thompson, *The Time Falling Bodies Take To Light* (New York, St. Martin's Press, 1981)

Daybreak. Millennium health centre has been open all night for emergencies and crisis counselling. The pace picks up after six with adults coming off night shifts and others going to work. Day students find early morning a good time to visit the health centre and the recreation/fitness centre. The library/resource centre may soon stay open all night for shift workers.

The administration centre has been open with skeleton staff since six, but now, at 7:30, activity is increasing and one member of Adcom is on duty. A few full and part-time tutors and consultants are in their offices meeting with parents, students and others. Some teachers are meeting with their counsellors. Student council offices are busy and the school/community radio station has been on air live since six. The television studio has played learning tapes all night but is now live and students are broadcasting to community and school.

The cafe has been serving breakfast since six; and today's food has already been delivered to living rooms: skim milk; granola; oatmeal porridge; thick vegetable soup with unsalted whole-wheat crackers;

tuna sandwiches on whole wheat; unsweetened pineapple juice; apples, tangerines and bananas. Students help themselves any time without charge or can bring their own food provided it isn't junk. Or they can go to the cafeteria or cafe and pay for a wider variety.

Both volunteer aids, Mrs. Chin and Major Afleck, keep a close eye on the diet of students. The Major has been on duty since six and greets each arriving student with, "I say, spot of porridge? Good stuff, oatmeal." He reminds students new to Millennium to check in on the computer; otherwise, Mrs. Chin will be after him as well as the negligent student. Nearly everyone in Steve Harris' Senior A living room is thirteen through fifteen-years-old and most have been at Millennium for years, so they check in automatically. Mrs. Chin can usually locate anyone in minutes.

The morning papers have arrived. Major Afleck and four students — two having breakfast — discuss the news seated around the big coffee table that doubles as a platform. The Major is relating today's events in the Middle East to the past century. Two early arrivals are there because they are responsible today for news analysis. They have already checked TV and radio news and taped part of it. Both wear earphones. One student at the coffee table swims every morning at 6:15 and is at the living room by 7:30. Another is always there because her mother drops her off at seven on the way to work.

At study carrels, two other students are on computers, one doing algebra, the other physics. The latter is doing a bi-monthly test which she could have done day or night but chose to do this morning. Neither science nor math (beyond literacy level), is a living room program, but students often use living rooms to do work for programs they take elsewhere with consultants or tutors. A third student is doing remedial math that he must complete before he is again fully involved in living room programs. Sometimes he works on it at home using his personal notebook computer, but home is noisy and nobody else there ever studies.

One person has been asleep on the sofa since 6 a.m. when he arrived from the crisis clinic at the health centre. Another is at the project counter preparing visual aids for his solo presentation a few days hence on fundamentalism in major religions.

At 7:40 two girls arrive and set to work on the laser printer making hard copy to be distributed the following day when they make a presentation and lead a discussion on investment finance in the light of North American free trade. They will propose a controversial strategy for diversification of the investment portfolio owned by Steve Harris' living room. As they work, they talk about the bolsa, the Mexico City stock exchange, and about two girls in Guadalajara and two in Dallas who are helping with the project by satellite.

At 7:45 three students on the scheduling team arrive for a meeting. Moments later, two students enter accompanied by a senior student who is coaching them in science and a woman from the government agriculture department whom they have contacted about a grafting experiment in the solarium.

By 8:00, there are nineteen in the living room, all busy individually or in twos or groups. The room is starting to rev up for the day. Two students are waiting by Steve Harris' glass cubicle. Both have documents in hand and are studying them. One is highlighting hers with a yellow marker. Major Afleck is circulating, having a word here and there while looking for signs of strain, fatigue, abuse, depression or ill health. He has been trained to do that. Today, he notes three students that he will mention to Harris.

At 8:05, the Major is joined by apprentice hi Carla Contini and they confer briefly before touring the room inconspicuously. Carla is not exactly inconspicuous this morning; she is wearing a stylish new dress and nearly everyone notices. Some compliment her and two girls have a momentary fashion chat. Paid assistant, Anne Dubois, arrives and is approached by three students. She sits down at a table and meets with them one at a time.

One is having trouble scheduling himself into driver training because of a clash with obligatory remedial writing and with a new part-time job guiding tour groups from abroad, which he hopes to use as an optional credit. Another has menstrual cramps but is scheduled to make a presentation and is wondering if she should postpone. The third has just discovered Margaret Atwood and thinks she can make a presentation about two months hence on Atwood's writing as regards the status of women — but only if some changes in her other commitments are made.

Anne and the student with cramps agree that a dash to the health clinic is in order. She and the boy with the driver-training problem leave a computer message for the consultant who teaches driving and the remedial writing tutor: they will "meet" by phone later in the day. Anne and the Atwood fan go to discuss the matter with the scheduling team.

When Harris arrives at 8:15, he confers briefly with each staff member and then is drawn to the solarium by a student to meet the agriculture specialist. Two minutes later, he meets one at a time with students waiting to see him. Twenty-four are in the room. The other seven are elsewhere in the school or on assignments outside. When scheduled programs begin at 8:30, there is no change in living room activity; some students have already quietly departed to attend programs elsewhere. Another day is rolling.

Three elderly people arrive and are greeted by Amy Sung, the first student who notices them.

"Hello, and welcome to our living room," she says. "Can I help you? I should say "may I" but it sounds funny, doesn't it?"

The visitors have heard on school radio about the 8:45 presentation on social services. Amy shows them to seats. Another student who happens to be at the fridge offers them fruit juice and introduces Major Afleck who offers tea. Guests are frequent in every living room, so everyone knows how to make them welcome without interrupting activity. Some guests are parents or adult day students, but everyone is welcome.

At 8:45, the first scheduled activity is announced by Becky Gage, the girl who had menstrual cramps. She is feeling better, having made a quick trip to the health centre for medication and a later appointment to discuss prevention of cramps. She stands on the platform and says, "Could I have your attention please. Roger and I have finished our survey of local social services and we hope a lot of you can join our presentation."

Thirteen students gather. Pre-planning makes sure at least ten students and one adult attend the whole of every presentation. Others come and go as individual schedules dictate. Nobody pays the least attention when people arrive or depart during a presentation or discussion. It is the rhythm of life. Even the click of computer keys at study carrels continues during presentations and sometimes the phone "rings" by blinking a red light and is quietly answered by the closest person.

Students take turns videotaping every presentation for later viewing by interested students unable to attend. Tapes are also used by hies and students for evaluation and for exchange with other living rooms, other schools and other countries. Some become part of the collection in the library/resource centre. Students may take home copies of tapes in which they appear and most have home libraries of all their tapes. Hies discuss videotapes of their children's work with interested parents.

As Becky flashes graphics on the largest screen, the boy asleep on the sofa stirs and sits up. He gets a bowl of soup and is about to eat and listen when he notices Steve Harris leave his cubicle to join the presentation. Harris is intercepted.

The boy says, "The health centre asked me to give you this slip. There's more information on the computer."

"Let's talk about it," Harris says as he reads the slip. "Can we do it now or is later better for you? What's your day like?"

"Full. I've got three scheduled programs outside the living room. First is chemistry at 9:30, but I'll only be there half an hour. I've tested out of what comes after. English Lit at 11:30. Calculus at 2:30. I'm in one group here as a presenter. That's the second half of the one on responsibilities of different levels of government — at 12:30. And another as chair for the discussion and evaluation — the one on labour/management relations at 3:30. Sakowski's supposed to chair but I'm subbing. He's still tied up with that organic farming negotiation. An hour on the computer. Short appointment with Miss Carry in the library about the new data base on political systems. Student council here at 10:30. I'm interviewing the mayor at 4:45 in the TV studio. I missed my fitness group at 8:00 and the make-up times for my level are 5:30 or

6:00. I guess between now and 9:00 is best. I need to talk to you."

"You're overloaded again so we've got to have a close look at your schedule. Let's make a time this week. But right now let's deal with last night. Come on in and sit down, Cy. But eat while we talk. Your soup's getting cold."

The boy's name is Sai-Yiu Li, but he prefers Cy so at Millennium he is Cy. At home he is Sai-Yiu. The family is ethnically Chinese but lived in Vietnam before emigrating eight years ago when Cy was seven and his sisters five, three and two. They were boat people and the escape was traumatic for everyone. Since then both parents have worked hard to take the family from poverty to home ownership.

Cy speaks Vietnamese, Cantonese, French and fluent English. He chose Steve Harris' living room because he is politically active and loves to write and debate. He is an editorial writer on the school/community daily, *Free Speech*. And he is a celebrity in the community as well as the school because of his radio and TV broadcasts, especially his controversial interviews with public figures. He has already announced his intention to run for Adcom next term and is garnering support.

After two-and-a-half years, Harris knows Cy better than his parents do. There is little communication at home even though Cy is verbal and articulate. He is new-world and his parents are adamantly old-world. They don't like his restless energy and frenetic pace or his white girlfriend, black pal, ever-changing hair styles, late hours, overnight absences, loud stereo, insistence on privacy, angry responses. . . . Last night he stormed out of the house after still another fight when his mother found condoms in his drawer. Cy walked the streets for hours before going to the all-night crisis worker at Millennium's health centre.

After ten minutes, Cy smiles and leaves the glass cubicle to work on a computer simulation problem for his 9:30 credit program in chemistry. Harris dictates a letter to Cy's parents, a memo to the crisis worker, another to the Dean of Residence, and a note for the computer record, all of which Mrs. Chin will type when she arrives. A meeting is being set up. Harris and Cy have decided it is time to consider with all concerned Cy's longstanding wish to move into residence.

While he is at it, Harris dictates two other memos about students and brief minutes in point form from last night's meeting of the volunteer-aid training committee which he attended as representative of resident faculty members. By 9:15, he is talking quietly with a girl who has beckoned him to the phone. She is speaking to a biochemist at the university who can come for her presentation on vitamin deficiency, but it will require a schedule shuffle. Done. Harris notes the change and will confer with the scheduling team about it. He keeps right on writing as he tunes in to the presentation on social services and quietly sits with the group. Nobody pays any attention to his arrival.

Harris has been told that Becky is not feeling well, which may affect her presentation but not her preparation, so he notes a flaw in the organization of her graphics and what seems to be lopsided hearsay evidence about inadequate social services. The presentation comes across as a subjective critique but interesting. He also notes that Roger is still weak in eye contact when speaking to an audience and decides he needs remedial work.

Near 9:30, some leave the room for scheduled commitments and others return. The presentation has moved into the discussion phase and Major Afleck and the elderly guests are being questioned about services for the aged. Mrs. Chin, who has just arrived, is asked about services for immigrants. All think the community buddy system is working — it links every old person and every new arrival with a longtime resident — but they think too many old people and immigrants ignore educational opportunities that would help them integrate. This stimulates a values discussion: what rights do people have to social services and what responsibilities do recipients have in return? Becky offers to work up positions and present them within a month.

During evaluation, Harris' points about the presentation are made by students so he says nothing. As the group disperses, he speaks to Roger privately about help with eye contact. They book remedial time with a tutor. Roger also enters, for the computer record, details of his presentation. Becky will do the same and she will also see the scheduling committee about a date for her follow-up talk. Their preparation materials are already recorded. Anne Dubois, who has been at the entire presentation, will monitor their further entries and will tell Harris that shy Mary Popiel, who chaired the discussion and evaluation, handled the Major tactfully when he got long-winded and that Stan Loftus had two brilliant ideas that need to be passed along to Adcom. Harris will compliment Mary and suggest Stan send a memo to Adcom.

Becky and Roger are conferring with the three elderly guests who have invited them to repeat the presentation for their seniors' club. They also want the videotape for study sessions and permission to copy handouts. Agreement is reached and the guests leave inconspicuously.

Carla Contini is speaking with the two students in charge of today's news. They are sorting out implications for international understanding and children's rights in breaking and continuing stories. That has to be done every day. News is scheduled for 10:30, right after a student council presentation and vote on whether or not Millennium will use part of its fitness budget for inter-school team sports. But the student council session requires a quorum of eighteen students, and if there aren't enough at 10:00, news will be moved up to that slot.

A guest arrives. It is the poet-in-residence being shared by several schools. She has been asked by four students to discuss choral poems they are writing for performing arts. This is to be a short planning meeting for a poetry workshop a week from Saturday. The four introduce their guest to a few people, including Harris, then gather at the coffee table and get to work. Among them is Andrea Hess who is barely twelve but is in this Senior A living room because of her intelligence and maturity and talent for poetry which was identified and nourished by the efficient talent-support system at Millennium.

Another group assembles to work on a future, six-part presentation on third-world poverty.

Two students are busy at the project counter working individually. George Fraser is sorting pictures and clippings for his media literacy presentation concerning children's rights. He is choosing between the effect of media advertising on children and the ageist image of children perpetuated by the media and is explaining his options to Anne Dubois.

George is working alone because a recent discussion with Steve Harris revealed that he has been overemphasizing work in various-sized groups so is weaker in individual presentation experience.

Melina Rallis is preparing graphics for a group presentation in her obligatory national geography program. Her topic deals with regional differences that are cultural and discretionary rather than inevitable and immutable. She is explaining these to Major Afleck who is helping with the graphics.

There are sixteen students in the room, six at computers. Mrs. Chin is at her keyboard. Carla is with the poetry group. Harris is with the third-world poverty group. He makes notes about group process and later will have a word with the chair, Tony Bancroft, about his tendency to bypass slow starters. Tony is summarizing ideas on format for their presentations. This is their second meeting and all members have brought ideas and research on main issues identified in the first meeting. Harris contributes thoughts about organization and production, and occasionally asks a question: Will anyone be dealing with the effect of wealth redistribution on rich countries? What will be the moral implications of universal birth control? Will there be immigration implications for rich countries?

The fifteen students presently out of the living room include student council representative, Olivia Itabashi, who is at her optional credit program in French Literature. But before that session is over, she leaves quietly for the student council office to pick up statistics just compiled: participation levels in inter-school sports; a cost/benefit analysis for money spent on teams; and a list of sports injuries over the last ten years. If there is a quorum in the living room at 10:00, she will make the presentation in French. Olivia is a French aficionado. If there is not a quorum, and the presentation is postponed till 10:30, Cy Li, who is vice president of the student council, will sub for her because she has a play rehearsal then. The reason they have chosen today, the first day the newly-collected statistics are available, is that both are politically active and want their living room to be first with a policy position so they can promote that position in the rest of the school.

Just before 10:00, Olivia confers with Steve Harris on handling the three sets of statistics. They are in English. The decision is to project them, but Olivia (or Cy) will cross reference and analyze them, ad lib, in French.

The poetry and third-world poverty groups break up and most join the student council group. There is a quorum. Olivia is on. The news presenters can relax till 10:30.

At 10:15, while the heated student council discussion continues, Steve Harris and Linda Lukaks move to Harris' cubicle for a meeting scheduled two days ago. Linda is below level in fitness and has passed the two percent limit for absences from fitness sessions. She is overweight and Harris knows she is sensitive about it. Otherwise, she is outspoken and outgoing almost to the point of being loud. She uses a lot of makeup and sometimes wears her mother's clothes which look too tight and too old.

They talk about living where everyone eats meals standing at the fridge door or else orders in fast food if there is any money. "Everyone" includes whatever man Linda's mother has brought home, and three younger siblings. Harris is so familiar with the situation he hardly needs look at Linda's file. They discuss options and decide either the school dietitian or Harris or both should meet with Linda and her mother. Linda prefers Harris alone but is sure her mother won't come to the school. For one thing, she works mornings in the Luna Systems warehouse and drinks afternoons. For another, she doesn't like schools, having been expelled from two by age fifteen. Harris will write her a note suggesting he stop by to discuss Linda's progress. A few days later he will visit in the evening.

Hies make house calls. Harris visits every student at home about twice in three years, more often if necessary. Usually, the purpose is to discuss with students and significant others, their progress and future, a context that covers everything. Often students invite him but sometimes he suggests it. This will be Harris' second visit to Linda's home. The first was just over a year ago when Linda turned fourteen and her mother wanted her to try for a permit to drop out of school so she could babysit at home and bring in some money with a part-time job.

This kind of visiting by hies is not a substitute for counselling by social workers. Most community social workers are based at Millennium, and one has been working with Linda's family for years. It is the frequent help of this social worker along with Mrs. Lukaks' fierce possessiveness and obvious affection for her children that keeps the family together. Harris knows his continuing assessment will be important in deciding whether any or all of the Lukaks children should move into residence. Linda admits to a new, under-age evening job in a restaurant kitchen where she nibbles a lot. She agrees to investigate a support group for overweight students at the health/fitness centre and let Harris know the outcome. And she agrees to meet with Harris and the head of physical education to talk about exercise.

"We'll work this out," he says as they prepare to leave the cubicle. "I've had some experience. I was overweight as a kid. And I was also shy. And gawky. And my father was an alcoholic. And maybe my mother compensated by stuffing me. Anyway I ate too much, but that didn't make me a bad person or a loser. Once I got it all figured out, I got control of myself. And it turned out alright. You'll do even better because you're not shy and you're a lot prettier than I was. Such a great face. You're lucky. You'll be a beautiful woman. And well-educated too. You'll see."

The living room votes against inter-school team sports. Olivia and Cy are pleased because that is what they proposed. They confer with Harris about how to promote their position throughout the school before the student council votes on budget. Cy will write a news report of the debate in their living room for *Free Speech*; he will lobby the editorial board for support and permission to write an editorial. Olivia agrees to write an in-depth analysis of her data in French for the school magazine and will make two appointments with Dubois to confer on progress. Harris agrees to meet on Saturday with the two and their supporters, to plan a program for the school television station. He would also help a student group supporting the other side of the issue if asked.

News is in progress with both presenters using a variety of media and sharing announcing. One is waggish Norman Howe. He shows a short, sharp montage he shot on videotape last night at a raucous city government meeting. Norman's jump-cut editing emphasizes the posturing, petulance and silliness but retains the modicum of meaning in exchanges on low-income housing. His only introductory comment is delivered in a deliberate drawl that mocks the visuals but is clear and correct and faithful to his black Jamaican roots, "Last night city council failed once again to come to grips with the housing crisis. They did however demonstrate effectively certain weaknesses in the democratic process." The item garners applause, an accolade not easily won from this demanding audience.

Major Afleck has alerted Harris that Greg Spellman seems upset. During news he stares out the window. No participation. Now, he drums on his knee with his knuckles. He looks tired. Usually, Greg participates even if his contributions are less organized and less complete than would be expected of most fourteen-year-olds. He has only been at Millennium a few months. Before that, he attended several traditional schools at military bases where his father was stationed. Though he was an honour student at previous schools, he lacks the skills and experience to be fully self-propelled in the Millennium sense. He is learning but still has to be helped by staff and students and will sometimes relapse from the new (to him) active stance to the old passive stance. Greg should be coming to Harris for help, but Harris goes to him and says quietly, "Wanta talk?"

"Yes. . . please."

"Long or short? Now or later?"

"Long, I guess. . . Is now okay?"

"How about short now and long at 4:30 today here or tonight at the fitness centre right after the squash tournament? I should be eliminated by 7:30. Eight at the latest."

"Four-thirty's good."

"You're on." Harris pats his shoulder and the two go to the glass cubicle. It takes five minutes of preliminary talk before Greg is able to say, "I think there's something wrong with me. About girls I mean. About guys. . . . If I'm queer my father'll kill me. He's a sergeant. And we're Catholic."

Harris says, "Everything I see in this file and everything I've seen since you came to Millennium tells me there's nothing "wrong with you." I see a bright person with character and promise. And heart. Last week I saw you — at the bus stop in front of Sears — get off the bus and help the woman who dropped groceries. And it made you miss the bus. In the rain. No big deal but two dozen other people didn't do it. You did. That means a lot more to me than if you're gay or not. If it turns out you happen to be, that has nothing to do with right or wrong. It's just part of you and your own business and you'll figure out how to deal with it positively. We'll talk it through. Okay?"

"You won't tell anyone will you?"

"Not a word to anyone. Never. Nothing in the files. Unless you want me to. You're speaking to the Sphinx. Okay? Can you make it the rest of the day?"

"I'm okay now. I'm fine. See you at 4:30."

Harris heads back to the news discussion but stops beside Sonia Siig who has turned from her keyboard and caught his attention. The news continues while Harris speaks softly with Sonia about her essay on the monitor. Both Harris and Carla Contini have inserted bracketed comments by calling it up on their own screens sometime the previous day or two. Sonia is not quite clear about the intent of Harris' comment and not in agreement with Carla's. They confer. Sonia wins her point of disagreement with Carla on the use of dashes: if Timothy Findley can use twelve dashes on the first page of *The Telling Of Lies*, she should be able to use five on one page.

Harris goes into detail about his inserted comment which has to do with a questionable inference based on inconclusive evidence. The insertion says only "non sequitur S.H." Most students would understand his meaning but Sonia is fairly new. He is happy to explain, but Sonia knows it is her responsibility to ask.

Near 11:00, as news discussion is ending, Mrs. Chin shows Harris several computer printouts. They include routine graphics of attendance for the year, term, month, week and day up to this morning for every student in every required and optional program and all other activities including such occasional events as school dances and regular checkups at the health clinic. She has highlighted two matters of concern and Harris notes them. One is that Melina Rallis has just passed the two percent limit for absences. Harris will meet with her.

Another printout summarizes and charts, for each student, all test scores on routine computer tests of required skills and literacies and tests and examinations used by consultants and tutors outside the living room. Again, Mrs. Chin has highlighted items and Harris notes them. One is that Olivia Itabashi had the highest marks in a term examination in French Literature. Harris will compliment her.

A third printout analyses for every student the nature of participation in all group and individual activities in the living room, elsewhere in the school and in the community. It totals hours on various activities and identifies patterns, strengths, and weaknesses. Mrs. Chin has circled four items. One is a pattern emerging on Brian Burton's record of too much part-time job and too little school participation. Another shows that Greg Spellman failed to make a presentation as scheduled the previous day in his sex education program at the health centre. Cy Li shows as an "overload alert."

The printouts are handed to Anne Dubois for careful checking to see if they reveal matters of concern or interest that Mrs. Chin missed. At least once a month, Harris does this close analysis personally, but usually Dubois does it.

Mrs. Chin questions Harris about detailed profiles she is working up from computer data on behalf of two students who are applying to move on to senior B living rooms. She knows how to do it, but Harris likes to treat each case individually and contribute a personal touch. He has three applications from intermediate B students applying to enter his senior A living room and he feels one lacks the personal touch of the hi concerned, perhaps because he is Millennium's newest hi, having been brought in to replace one elected to Adcom.

Arlix Leung comes to see Mrs. Chin. He is a visa student from Hong Kong who lives in Steve Harris' residence and is in his living room. Arlix is sixteen but looks younger and doesn't feel out of place. Usually a hi in residence doesn't have students from his living room in the same residence, but there are exceptions where a student needs a lot of support. Arlix is shy and speaks ungrammatical English with a heavy accent, though his understanding is good. He has been at Millennium only a few months and before that attended school in Hong Kong where he was a passive memorizer of facts.

This morning at 11:45, Arlix will give his first solo presentation and he is nervous. It will be much tougher for him than the top-level physics, chemistry and mathematics options at which he excels elsewhere in the school. This is to be an overview of governance and inter-relations among Hong Kong, Macao, Taiwan and China. With his previous group presentations, other students and staff have helped him a lot, but this time Arlix has tried to do it on his own. Right now he wants to check with Mrs. Chin on the translation of several Chinese expressions.

Last night at the residence, Arlix conferred with Steve Harris about the reams of data he had accumulated. Steve cautioned him that he had enough for a series of lectures and must cut it to a twenty minute capsule to fit his time slot. Something in more depth might follow at a later date. They worked together at editing and organizing. Now Arlix is almost ready. His graphics are carefully thought out. His notes are on three-by-five-inch cards. He hopes he will be able to look his audience in the eyes. Not get tongue tied. Be able to pronounce the words. Not faint. With half an hour to go, beads of perspiration stand on his forehead. Mrs. Chin wipes them with her handkerchief and says, "You do just fine. You see."

Harris gives him a shoulder hug and says, "If you have difficulties, I'll just ask questions to help you along. We'll do it together. But I'll bet you won't need me."

Ordinarily Major Afleck might slip out for a rest at this hour, but having served in the British garrison at Hong Kong, he wants to hear Arlix. He notices the map in Arlix's hand and says, "Oh, I say, well done old chap," as he draws Harris aside to look at a supply order he has prepared which anticipates materials needed for student presentations now in planning. After a glance, Harris signs the requisitions and the Major takes them to Mrs. Chin for processing.

Four students around the coffee table are preparing a presentation on child-abuse legislation as part of the required program on parenting. Two are having soup. One is talking about his experience last week while serving his parenting practicum in a junior B living room: he discovered whip welts on the back and legs of a four-year-old.

Another group is evaluating outline proposals for travel-study programs in Mexico, Cuba, Haiti, Grenada, Belize, Guyana and Honduras that have been circulated to all senior A living rooms by the student council. The group must narrow the choice to two and then make a presentation to the entire living room. The choice approved by the living room will then be elaborated and defended at student council where the final choice for next year's program will be made. All Millennium students experience one travel-study program abroad and one across their own country.

A third group is meeting with Carla about final editing of the presentation they will make this afternoon on labour/management relations — the first of three. As usual, the problem is how to hone an excess of information to a sharp edge. They can present for forty-five minutes and have only fifteen for discussion, or they can present for half an hour and have the same for discussion. Or they can run overtime and risk criticism from the group for inadequate planning and organization. They wish they had asked for ninety minutes. They decide to tell the audience their topic proved too broad and they would like a follow-up date for a further presentation. This will inconvenience two other groups making subsequent presentations in what was to be a three-part series and now will be four-part.

They also decide that three essays they have prepared will not be used in the presentation, except for quotes, but will be published for living room and community distribution. With desk top publishing, nearly all important work generated in living rooms is printed in professional-looking format for wide, community distribution. This, in addition to school newsletters, newspaper, magazine and yearbook.

Two students wearing earphones are previewing three videos on drugs. Both are making notes. They are preparing a presentation for obligatory health education. One is from another living room and has come to work with one of Harris' students. While they work, a third student, also from another living room, looks in briefly to drop off a third film that might be good for the presentation.

"Better than the others at putting drugs into social context," he says. "But no good if you're looking for specific prevention tactics. Depends on your purpose. But it's well made."

He moves on to pick up an apple, aware that his muscles have attracted admiring glances from a few girls including Sandra Fine with whom he has had an on-and-off relationship, now off. His visit is timed so he can hand Sandra a note of reconciliation. She excuses herself from a brief exchange with Harris about scheduling to accept and read the note.

"I'll think about it and call you," she says.

"How about lunch?"

"Not today. I'm chairing the scheduling team and having lunch with Mr.Harris. I'll call you. But thanks for the note. The P.S. is the nicest thing you ever said."

The visitor exits smiling, chest out, stomach in.

Anne Dubois' bubbling laugh is heard. It has nothing to do with Sandra's suitor. Nobody pays much attention to such ordinary events of life. After all, it is a living room. Anne is laughing about an essay she is reading on a computer screen. It is by Norman Howe on the status of Quebec in North America. He has written it with alternating French and English paragraphs. The final paragraph alternates French and English sentences. The last sentence alternates French and English words. The last word is half French half English: tete/ ache. Anne inserts a few suggestions, then comments in appropriately mixed language using capital letters, C'EST TRES GOOD! JE LIKE IT. She will suggest it for the school literary annual and mention it to Harris. But not right now.

Harris is in his cubicle for the second of two appointments to discuss

Andy Aitken's trial period. Andy is speaking.

"Yes, I'm sure. It'll be two months on Monday and I'm sure. This just isn't for me. Nothing personal. Well, nothing personal about you. Personal for me."

"Personal how?"

"I mean your living room just attracts smart people and I'm not that smart. I'd have to stay up all night to run with this pack. They were easy on me at first but they're starting to pin me down in every evaluation and pretty soon they'll cut me up. You heard them yesterday saying I regurgitated information. No inferences. Didn't analyze. Didn't have a thesis or a hypothesis. No conclusion. I can't do that stuff."

"Can't or don't?"

"Can't. I don't because I can't."

"Not everyone in this room is brilliant. Some are."

"I didn't say brilliant. Smart. Sort of bright and keen. Smart."

"The group gets a feel of what an individual is capable of and that's all they expect. But they do expect that."

"That's it. They expect I'm going to work my butt off but that's not me. I spend a lot of time on other things. I'm thirteen and I'm interested in girls, dancing, rock music, sports, TV. And fun. The gang. I like to hang out. Party. Work in my dad's store. Sure I like to write stuff and that's why I tried this living room. And because I'm a talker. I'm not lazy. I don't think I'm lazy. But I can't operate at this level. Your room's not my style. I'm more laid back."

"There are half a dozen learning styles accommodated in this room."

"But not mine."

"What's yours.?"

"I like to listen and learn. You tell me and I'll memorize it. I'm old-fashioned."

"Also too lazy to dig up your share of information and then share it."

"That too. Don't have time. I got too many other things."

"Too many is right. One of the leisure skills is being selective. Another is balance. Your choices are short on the intellectual dimension, the kind that last a lifetime and give greatest satisfaction. Even your part-time job doesn't qualify for credit because you can't be bothered setting up a generic job skills program with your father and the school. I've asked you several times and your father agreed."

"I'm thinking about it but I don't think my father can teach me job skills. He won't let me do anything important."

"Whichever living room you settle on, I want you to see Mrs. Martinez in the guidance office about her self-help group on leisure skills. She'll also help your father with his part of a generic job skills contract. Look. There are lots of people in this living room who like to do all those things you mentioned — dancing, rock music, sports . . . but not to the exclusion of mental exercise. You're right about style though. Every living room has its own. But you won't find one that lets you just sit and soak up information dished out by others. Have you studied those living room profiles?"

Andy takes two items from the file in his hand.

"I think either John Logue's or Ouida Wilkins' living room might be best for me. I guess I lean to Mrs. Wilkins. Seems like she's brought Jamaica with her. Reggae and all that. But I don't know . . . Mr. Logue's an athlete."

"So's Ouida Wilkins. She beats me at squash."

"So do I."

"Once."

"We only played once."

"So who's counting?"

Andy Aitken smiles. "In this living room, everybody counts everything."

Harris smiles. "Okay, Andy, I've got two suggestions. Let's set up a meeting with John Logue, Ouida Wilkins and the ombudsman. This will be your third change of living room this year so the chairman of the Placement Committee has to be involved too. And let's play squash tomorrow morning at 7:00. I've already got a court reserved for my daughter and me but she'll be helping set up the student council job fair. Gives me a chance to trounce you."

Arlix Leung is on. Harris is pleased that twenty are attending. That kind of support for a maiden flight is typical. Arlix is flying. He is talking so fast it is almost impossible to understand his accent. Harris is about to slow him down by asking a question when Mary Popiel, herself no stranger to shyness and nervousness, says, "Excuse me for interrupting, Arlix, but I wonder if I could ask a couple of background things. You mentioned relations between Taiwan and the mainland but how about Taiwan and Hong Kong?"

Once Arlix is talking to Mary, he slows down. Everybody relaxes including Arlix. Mrs. Chin clears her throat and says, "Almost same for Macao I think. Is that right?" She just wants to remind him to look at other people besides Mary. It works.

Arlix runs five minutes overtime and has a weak, apologetic ending: "I hope you can understand what I saying. . . what I say." But he handles questions and comments well, and everybody can tell he has lots more insights and ideas. The group evaluation acknowledges that and some thirteen other positive attributes, but it also documents in detail almost as many weaknesses. Arlix is uncertain where he stands until Sonia Siig suggests he give a follow-up talk next month. The suggestion gets instant and loud applause. Arlix Leung has landed in the right living room.

It is lunchtime for Steve Harris, and he nods to Anne Dubois as he departs with Sandra Fine to rendezvous with the other two on the scheduling team. Once a week, he lunches with the team. It gives them a chance to talk shop: pacing, production values, balance, timing, curriculum guideline requirements, changes, new ideas. . . . It also allows him, over time, to have business lunches with all his students since all cycle in and out of scheduling duty.

Millennium has no staff dining room. Instead it has a big cafeteria, a cafe and a lunch/meeting room for everyone called the Caucus. People in the cafeteria and cafe are chatty, social and rather noisy. People in the Caucus are all carrying on some kind of business, and the place is always quieter. Some bring food from home; others buy it from the cafeteria. There are meetings all day long.

Today, a table beside Harris' is occupied by three junior B students and a volunteer aid whom Harris recognizes — his former student

Frank Simmons, now in a senior B living room. Usually, junior students eat in their living rooms but sometimes use the cafeteria or the Caucus. Frank Simmons says to Harris, "We're planning a special story-telling game with costumes and a visiting mime as a surprise for their hi. It's his birthday a week from now."

"Only six days," says a five-year-old girl chewing celery. She is turning on a tiny tape recorder on which she has brought a story idea.

At tables pushed together, two faculty members from Millennium and four from other schools are meeting with two teacher counsellors from the teachers' centre. They are evaluating, with a resource person from the university, a seminar they have just finished on new electronic technology for schools. Another table is occupied by a hi meeting with one of her students and his father. In a corner, the Attendance Committee made up of teachers, parents and students is reviewing cases of teachers and students who have exceeded the two percent limit for absences.

Four staff members who are organizing elections to Adcom take advantage of Harris' proximity to remind him of the deadline for declaring candidacy. He has served one three-year term on Adcom and has wide support for a second. If he runs again and wins and serves successfully, it will almost certainly mean a promotion to superintendent if he wants it. He does. Supers have pay equity with brain surgeons, hies with general practitioners; with two children nearing university, he could use extra money. But mainly, he would like the challenge of overseeing operations. But he also likes being a hi. And he wants to serve on the Curriculum Council or the Curriculum Think Tank. And he would like to write more. Life is too short. Harris sighs. His students pick up on it. They know him almost as well as he knows them.

"Decisions. Decisions," Sandra Fine says. "Personally, I hope you remain a hi. But you'd be good on Adcom too. My mother says you were good last time. When she was on too. But we better get on with all this stuff. Six changes that I know about. And we've got to talk about longer time slots. Everybody's asking. Well, quite a few. Four. My mother sent whole wheat bagels. She made them and stuffed them with chick peas and — stuff. Really yummy. And we have to scan curriculum guidelines to block the next set of topics. We should start that today. Please, everybody eat a bagel. My mother'll ask. Anyone who doesn't, she'll kneecap at the P.T.A. and I'll be disinherited. I'm only fifteen. Anything else we have to do today? Okay, first — the six changes."

Steve Harris returns to his living room as the presentation on levels of government is ending. The evaluation is on. Two adult guests make superficial, complimentary remarks probably in reaction to what they think were unappreciative comments by students. That often happens. Adult guests, educated in old-fashioned schools, have lower performance standards than Millennium students. They don't know what to look for. Anne Dubois does, and having waited in vain to see if a student would make the point, she says, "It strikes me that an underlying theme of inconsistency in legislation at different levels of government ran through this presentation without ever being clearly identified and confronted. I thought Jugnu was going to zero in on it toward the end there when he used the chart to compare areas of responsibility. But he didn't. That's another example of what Christine mentioned: that this presentation was perceptive and descriptive but not very analytical."

Harris listens briefly and passes on into his cubicle. In five minutes he has an appointment with Karen Shipley for a look at her progress. He checks the file Mrs. Chin has prepared. Every day, Harris meets with one student for a detailed examination of all records. Five students a week. Twenty a month. It has been six weeks since his last long discussion with Karen though they have had lots of short conversations.

Anne Dubois leaves for lunch as Arlix Leung is returning from his and he says, "Please to come back soon. I have much excitement to say." Arlix has just found out that the irrepressible Cy Li has already phoned the Chinese Business Association and had a positive response to his suggestion that they sponsor a repeat of Arlix's presentation — on school/community television.

As Karen arrives, so does Joe Starr. His stretcher is pushed by Alfred Aimes, a burly, retired loading-platform foreman, now a volunteer attendant at Children's Hospital. Joe is thirteen, paralysed from the neck down and shriveled by a degenerative nerve disorder stabilized for now. He speaks but is incomprehensible to most. Alfred Aimes understands every word and interprets. One minute Alfred is himself, speaking in the blunt bursts of a loading platform. The next moment, he is transformed and from his lips issue the colorful phrases and elegant observations of Joe Starr, aspiring writer.

Together they have applied for admission to Steve Harris' living room and three previous meetings have taken place — more than usual because Joe has previously "gone to school" only in the sense of having visiting teachers at the hospital. It was his latest visiting teacher who suggested he might manage Millennium, and since that moment Joe has been in a state of excitement he describes as "rocketing." Steve Harris already has a full quota, but hies' living rooms are like their hearts: always room for one more child. In the past, Harris has had as many as thirty-three. This afternoon, Joe and Alfred begin their two-month trial.

Steve Harris reaches over and presses Joe's cheek with his palm. Joe responds by pressing his tongue against the inside of his cheek. Harris feels the slight pressure. It is a little greeting they have fallen into at earlier meetings. Spontaneously, Karen does the same thing as Harris introduces her.

Joe speaks and Alfred repeats, "Karen. Nice name. Sounds like caring. It's a beautiful day isn't it?"

And afternoon begins in Millennium.

INDEX